Modern Real Esta

Fillmore W. Galaty
Wellington J. Allaway
Robert C. Kyle

Eleventh Edition

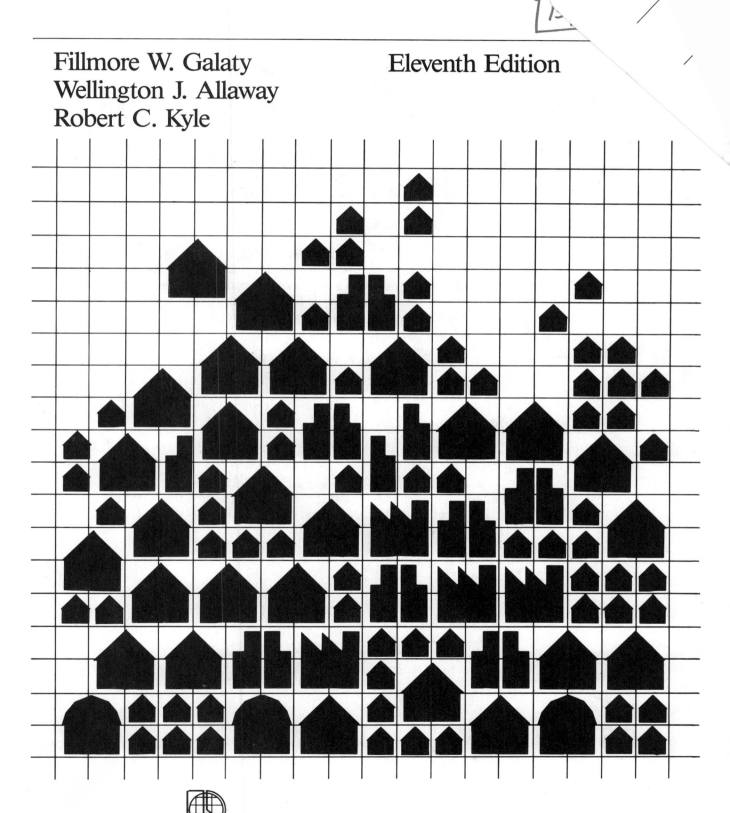

REAL ESTATE EDUCATION COMPANY
a division of Longman Financial Services Institute, Inc.

Published by Real Estate Education Company/Chicago
a division of Longman Financial Services Institute, Inc.

88 89 90 10 9 8 7 6 5 4 3

While a great deal of care has been taken to provide accurate and current information, the ideas, suggestions, general principles and conclusions presented in this text are subject to local, state and federal laws and regulations, court cases and any revisions of same. The reader is thus urged to consult legal counsel regarding any points of law—this publication should not be used as a substitute for competent legal advice.

Library of Congress Cataloging-in-Publication Data

Galaty, Fillmore W.
    Modern real estate practice/Fillmore W. Galaty, Wellington J. Allaway, Robert C. Kyle.—11th ed.
        p.   cm.
    Includes Index.
    ISBN 0-88462-691-1
    1. Real estate business—Law and legislation—United States.
2. Vendors and purchasers—United States.   3. Real property—United States.   4. Real estate business—United States.   I. Allaway, Wellington J.   II. Kyle, Robert C.   III. Title
KF2042.R4G34   1988
346.73004'37—dc19
[347.306437]   87-26519
                                                                                CIP

Executive Editor: Richard Hagle
Sponsoring Editor: Jeny Sejdinaj
Project Editor: Marguerite Duffy
Cover and Internal Design: James A. Buddenbaum

Contents

15 **Real Estate Financing 204**

Preface

Hundreds of thousands of professional men and women have studied *Modern Real Estate Practice* since its first printing in 1959. Although its primary use as a text has been to prepare candidates for state broker and salesperson licensing examinations, many others have studied the book as part of college and university degree programs in real estate and related fields. Still others have read it because of an interest in personal investment or because they hold positions close to the real estate profession in banks, savings and loan associations, mortgage firms, insurance companies, property management firms or corporate real estate departments.

Through the years, the real estate industry has placed a growing emphasis on education and professionalism. State licensing examinations and educational requirements for prospective brokers and salespeople have become more sophisticated since the first edition of this book, requiring the student to demonstrate knowledge and understanding of increasingly technical information. In preparing the Eleventh Edition of *Modern Real Estate Practice,* the authors have revised and updated the text to meet these requirements and to keep pace with recent trends and developments, particularly in the areas of *real estate finance and taxation.*

The Eleventh Edition has been divided into three parts: Essentials, Principles and Practices. *Essentials* consists of Chapters 1 through 4 and provides the student with an introduction to the real estate business as well as to the concepts of real property and home ownership. *Principles* encompasses Chapters 5 through 16 and represents the basic core of knowledge the real estate student must master in the topics of brokerage, ownership, legal descriptions and real estate financing, among others. *Practices* is composed of Chapters 17 through 23 and is devoted to more practical aspects of the profession such as property management, appraisal, investment and closing the transaction. These chapters may be taught or studied in the order suggested by the authors, or they may be adapted to any class outline or lesson plan. The review questions in each chapter have been written to apply to ETS-, ACT- and ASI-administered real estate examinations. Also included are a Mathematics Review, designed to help math-shy students with basic real estate computations; a Residential Construction Appendix, containing many illustrations that will assist the student in identifying important building-component terminology; and an expanded Glossary of Real Estate Terms, providing definitions of hundreds of real estate terms for easy review.

Supplements for *Modern Real Estate Practice* have been developed for more than 30 states, detailing laws, principles and practices specific to the real estate business in those particular states. A *Study Guide for Modern Real Estate Practice* contains additional review questions and study problems to further assist the student in his or her real estate education. In addition, a comprehensive Instructor's Manual and many helpful in-class transparencies are available to instructors as companions to this text. Contact Real Estate Education Company for further details about these materials.

Any comments on this text should be directed to Anita Constant, Senior Vice President, Real Estate Education Company, a division of Longman Financial Services Institute, Inc., 520 N. Dearborn, Chicago, IL 60610.

Acknowledgments

The authors would like to thank Martha R. Williams, J.D., of Lafayette, California, who served as development writer for the Eleventh Edition of *Modern Real Estate Practice*. The authors also thank the following reviewers for their valuable assistance:

Floyd M. Baird, RPA/SMA, First National Bank & Trust Company of Tulsa
John D. Ballou, Attorney-at-Law; Moraine Valley Community College
Robert L. Blount, College of the Ozarks
James H. Boykin, Virginia Commonwealth University
Gerald R. Cortesi, Triton College
Edith Entwistle, Foster & Foster Real Estate School
Nita Everton, Century-21 Real Estate of the Mid-Atlantic States, Inc.
Charles Floyd, University of Georgia
Jerald Frandsen, Frandsen & Frandsen, Ltd.
William R. Gray, Arizona School of Real Estate
Irene M. Hall, Foster Institute of Real Estate
Helen Marie Hartmann, Hartmann Realty, Inc.
Edith Lank, St. John Fisher College
G. Rudi Laub, Jr., Columbia School of Real Estate
James K. Londay, Londay School of Real Estate
Clarke R. Marquis, Attorney
Thomas V. Novak, The Real Estate Tax Education League, Inc.
Margaret Offenberger, Northeast Career Institute
Raye N. Parks, CRB, The Real Estate Academy, Inc.
Wayne Parrish, Arizona School of Real Estate
John Reilly, J.D., Ezra O'Connor Moon & Tam
Lawrence Sager, Madison Area Technical College
David Sirota, Real Estate Consultant
Joan m. Sobeck, Joan m. Sobeck, Inc., Realtors
Margaret Sprencz, Lorain Business College and Dyke College
Paul C. Sprencz, Lorain Business College and John Carroll University
Henry Stockbridge, Stockbridge & Partners
Albert M. Suguitan, Cherry Hill Realty
Peter J. Terhoeve, American School of Real Estate
Arlene Urban, Coldwell Banker Real Estate
John M. Ware, Goodman Segar Hogan Residential Real Estate Corporation
Nancy White, Mississippi County Community College

Thanks are also extended to the many real estate professionals who have contributed to earlier editions of the book. Each new edition builds upon the foundation they have helped us develop.

Furthermore, special credit is extended to the following people or groups for permission to use materials or forms: George E. Cole and Co., DuPage County Bar Association, DuPage Board of REALTORS®, Institute of Real Estate Management, National Association of REALTORS® and Rand McNally and Co. Note that the George E. Cole legal forms are used through the courtesy of the Boise Cascade Corporation. The sample forms may not be applicable to all jurisdictions and are subject to pertinent changes in the law.

Finally, the authors would like to extend their appreciation to the entire staff of Real Estate Education Company for their execution of this Eleventh Edition. Special assistance has been provided by Jeny Sejdinaj, Sponsoring Editor; Marguerite Duffy, Project Editor; Cheryl Wilson, Development Editor; and Margaret Maloney, Editorial Assistant.

Fillmore W. Galaty
Wellington J. Allaway
Robert C. Kyle

Part One

Essentials

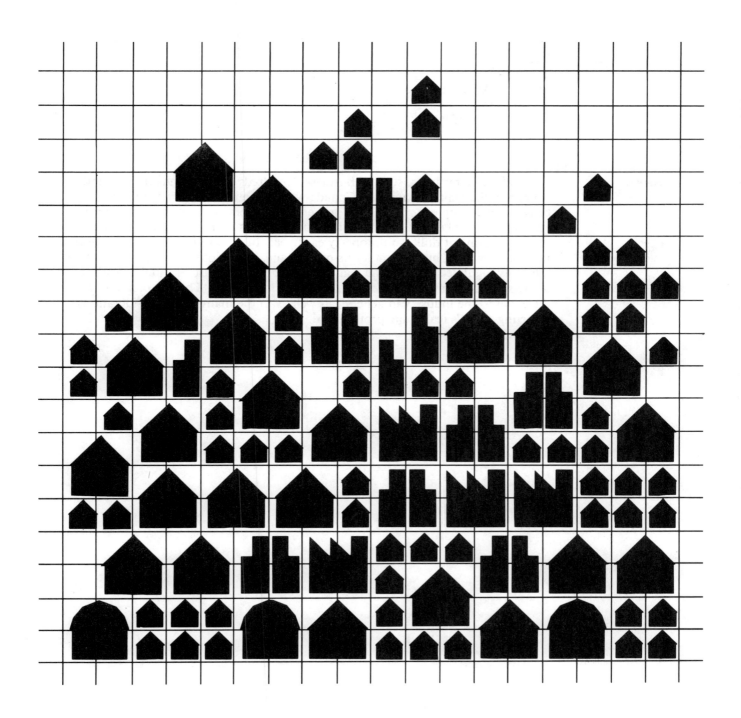

1

Introduction to Modern Real Estate Practice

Key Terms

Attorney
Broker
Bundle of legal rights
Common law
Judicial precedent
Real estate license law
Realtist
REALTOR®
REALTOR-Associate®
Salesperson
Seven sources of law

Overview

The real estate business is "big" business. Hundreds of thousands of men and women in the United States and Canada work in some aspect of the industry as brokers, salespeople, appraisers or property managers, as well as in other areas of specialization. They aid buyers, sellers and investors in making decisions that involve billions of dollars in property each year. In addition to people and money, real estate is a big business in terms of laws and regulations. Because real estate is a heavily regulated market, the real estate practitioner must be familiar with the many sources of law on the federal, state and local levels. This chapter will introduce you to the industry in general, as well as to the many legal considerations affecting today's real estate professional.

Real Estate Transactions

The purchase of real estate—whether vacant land or land that includes a house or other structure—is a special type of transaction. That transaction is very different from the purchase of personal property, such as groceries, clothing, fuel, automobiles or television sets. Although every type of sales transaction creates a change of ownership involving certain legal requirements, *even the simplest of real estate transactions brings into play a body of complex laws.*

Real property (which we commonly refer to as real estate) often has been described as a **bundle of legal rights**. In other words, a purchaser of real estate is actually buying the *rights of ownership* held by the seller. The rights of ownership (see figure 1.1) include the right of *possession*, the right to *control the property* within the framework of the law, the right of *enjoyment* (to use the property in any legal manner), the right of *exclusion* (to keep others from entering or occupying the property) and the right of *disposition* (to be able to sell or otherwise convey the property). Within these ownership rights are included further rights to will, devise, mortgage, encumber, cultivate, explore, lease, license, dedicate, give away, share, trade or exchange the property.

**Figure 1.1
Bundle of Legal Rights**

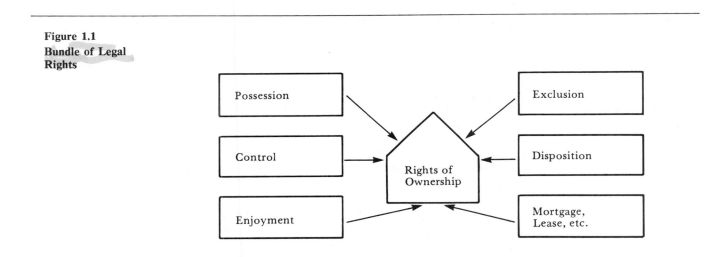

When a person acquires ownership of real estate, that ownership will be subject to any rights that the seller may retain and also to any rights in the property that persons other than the seller may have or acquire. For example, a person may sell real estate while retaining the rights to certain minerals or natural resources located on or beneath the surface of the land. Likewise, a lending institution that holds a mortgage on real estate has the right to force a sale of the property if the loan is not repaid. The various rights in real estate will be discussed in detail later in the text.

Buying real estate is usually the biggest financial transaction of a person's life. The buyer typically pays out more cash, undertakes more debt and has a deeper personal interest in this transaction than in any other purchase made during his or her lifetime.

When a person sells real estate, the situation is similar. The real estate is likely to have been that person's biggest single investment, not only in terms of money, but also of work. Of course, there are people to whom the sale or purchase of real estate is a routine matter, but for most people, it is a very important, emotional and complicated affair, whether the real estate is urban (city) property or rural (country) property.

At the center of this important and sensitive transaction there is generally a middleman—the real estate **broker**. There may be a real estate **salesperson** working on behalf of the broker. The broker and salesperson generally represent a seller and seek a buyer for the seller's property, but both seller and buyer may be represented by their own real estate agents. Each real estate agent will attempt to obtain an offer and acceptance on terms favorable to his or her respective client. Once they achieve this goal they will do their utmost to guide and facilitate the transfer of the real property from one party to the other. The seller and buyer also may retain attorneys to advise them on legal matters involved in the transfer of the real property.

Real Estate Law

The average citizen has very little notion of the nature of law. People generally think of laws as rules laid down by the state to govern their conduct. *Real estate brokers and salespeople must have a broader and better understanding of the sources of law and how various laws affect real estate.*

Sources of Real Estate Law

There are generally **seven sources of law** in the United States, all of which affect the ownership and transfer of real estate (see figure 1.2). These are: the *Constitution of the United States; laws passed by Congress; federal regulations adopted by the various agencies and commissions created by Congress; state constitutions; laws passed by state legislatures; ordinances passed by cities, towns and other local governments; and court decisions.*

The primary purpose of the *U.S. Constitution* and the individual *state constitutions* is to establish the rights of citizens and delineate the limits of governmental authority. In a few areas of the country, municipalities also are empowered to set up local constitutions or charters with similar effects. Even though their provisions are typically set down in the broadest terms, such constitutions may have a direct influence on the real estate business. In California, for instance, a voter-approved amendment to the state constitution has established the upper limit of the real property tax rate.

Laws passed by Congress and by *state and local legislative bodies* may establish specific provisions on any issue, change existing laws or simply set broad standards of conduct and establish administrative and enforcement agencies. Generally, those agencies have the authority to adopt legally enforceable regulations and procedures to expand on the law and to carry out the established standards.

Governmental agencies that enact rules and regulations range from the Federal Housing Administration through state real estate commissions to local zoning boards. The rules and regulations are a means of implementing and enforcing legislative acts. They provide detailed information on legal and illegal actions and practices, and designate penalties and violations.

Court decisions of federal, state and municipal courts serve to clarify and interpret laws, regulations and constitutional provisions by applying the laws to the facts of specific cases. For example, an attorney draws up what appears to be a valid contract under the provisions of state law. The parties signing the contract may later disagree on its provisions, resulting in a lawsuit. If the court disallows the contract, it will render an opinion as to why the contract does not fulfill the legal requirements for such a document. Future contracts in that state will then be based on the **judicial precedent** of the requirements established by such prior court decisions, called *case law*, as well as on the statutes governing contracts.

Figure 1.2
Sources of Real
Estate Law

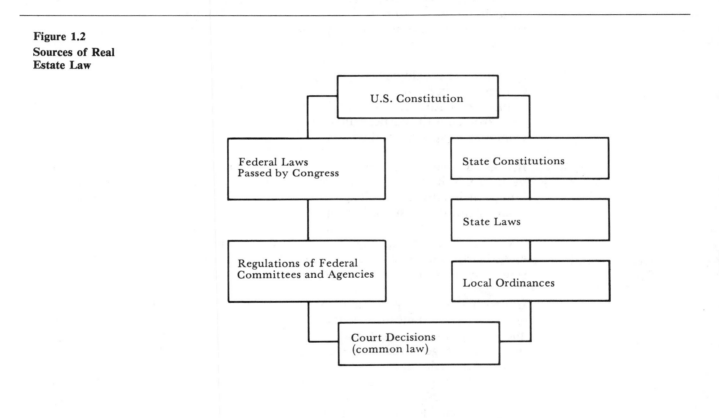

The courts are not always bound by the established precedent. Courts in one jurisdiction (area of authority) may not be bound by the decisions of courts in other jurisdictions. In addition, a court with superior authority in its jurisdiction may, at its discretion, reverse the ruling of a lower court.

Court decisions also reflect our common law heritage. The **common law** is an evolving body of rules and principles founded on custom and usage and manifested in the decisions and opinions of the courts. It is derived mainly from practices developed in England and, as it applies to the United States, dates back to the practices that were in effect at the time of the American Revolution. Real estate ownership and transfer may be directly affected by a court's application of common law principles.

Laws Affecting Real Estate Practice

The general sources of law encompass a number of specific areas that are important to the real estate practitioner. These include the *law of contracts,* the *general property law,* the *law of agency* (which covers the obligations of brokers to the persons who engage their services) and the *real estate license law,* all of which will be discussed in this text.

A person engaged in the real estate business need not be an expert on all areas of real estate law, but should have a knowledge and understanding of the basic principles of the law under which he or she operates. A real estate professional must be able to recognize the technical legal problems involved in transactions that he or she will negotiate and should appreciate the necessity of referring such problems to a competent attorney. An **attorney** is a person trained and licensed to represent another person in court, to prepare documents defining or transferring rights in property and to give advice or counsel on matters of law. *Under no circumstances may a broker or salesperson act as an attorney unless separately licensed and representing a client in that capacity.*

Extreme care should be taken in handling all phases of a real estate transaction. Carelessness in handling the documents connected with a real estate sale can result in expensive legal actions. In many cases, costly court actions could have been avoided if the parties handling negotiations had exercised greater care and employed competent legal counsel.

Real estate license laws. Since real estate brokers and salespeople are engaged in a business that involves other people's real estate and money, the need for regulation of their activities has long been recognized. In an effort to protect the public from fraud, dishonesty or incompetence in the buying and selling of real estate, all fifty states, the District of Columbia and all Canadian provinces have passed laws that require real estate brokers and salespeople to be licensed. The first **real estate license law** was passed in California in 1917. The license laws of the various states are similar in many respects but differ in the details of their requirements.

Under these laws, a person must obtain a license in order to engage in the real estate business. In most cases, the applicant must possess certain stated personal and educational qualifications and must pass an examination to prove an adequate knowledge of the business. In addition, to qualify for license renewal and continue in business, the licensee must follow certain prescribed standards of conduct in the operation of his or her business. Some states also require licensees to complete continuing education courses. Chapter 14 describes more fully the state license laws and the required standards.

In Practice...

If you do not already have a copy of the real estate broker's and salesperson's license law for your state, you should send for it now. Table 1.1 lists the addresses of the real estate commissions or departments for all states and Canadian provinces. When you write to your real estate commission or department, ask for the application for licensure (either the broker's or salesperson's application, depending on which license you plan to secure now), a copy of the real estate license law, a list of examination dates and any other material normally sent to applicants. For a nominal charge, some states furnish certain study material with the application. If your state has such material, the commission will notify you.

The Real Estate Business Is "Big" Business

Billions of dollars' worth of real estate is sold each year in the United States. In addition to this great volume of annual sales, there are rental collections by real estate management firms, appraisals of properties ranging from vacant land to

**Table 1.1
Real Estate License
Law Officials and
Commissions**

Alabama—Executive Director, Alabama Real Estate Commission, State Capitol, Montgomery, 36130.

Alaska—Executive Director, Real Estate Commission, 3601 "C" St. #798, Anchorage, 99503.

Arizona—Commissioner, Arizona Department of Real Estate, 1645 West Jefferson, Phoenix, 85007.

Arkansas—Executive Secretary, Arkansas Real Estate Commission, Number 1 Riverfront Pl., Suite 660, North Little Rock, 72114.

California—Commissioner, Department of Real Estate, 1719 24th St., Sacramento, 95816.

Colorado—Director, Colorado Real Estate Commission, 4th Floor, 1776 Logan St., Denver, 80203.

Connecticut—Real Estate Division, 165 Capitol Ave., Hartford, 06106.

Delaware—Administrative Assistant, Delaware Real Estate Commission, P.O. Box 1401, Dover, 19901.

District of Columbia—Contact Representative, Real Estate Commission, Room 923, 614 H St. N.W., Washington, 20001.

Florida—Director, Division of Real Estate, P.O. Box 1900, 400 West Robinson St., Orlando, 32802.

Georgia—Commissioner, Real Estate Commission, 40 Pryor St., S.W., Atlanta, 30303.

Hawaii—Executive Secretary, Real Estate Commission, P.O. Box 3469, Honolulu, 96801.

Idaho—Executive Director, Idaho Real Estate Commission, Statehouse Mail, Boise, 83720.

Illinois—Commissioner, Dept. of Registration and Education, 320 W. Washington St., 3rd Floor, Springfield, 62786.

Indiana—Deputy Director, Real Estate Commission, 1021 State Office Building, 100 North Senate Ave., Indianapolis, 46204.

Iowa—Director, Iowa Real Estate Commission, Executive Hills, Suite 205, Des Moines, 50319.

Kansas—Director, Kansas Real Estate Commission, 217 E. Fourth, Topeka, 66603.

Kentucky—Executive Director, Kentucky Real Estate Commission, 222 S. First St., Suite 300, Louisville, 40202.

Louisiana—Executive Director, Real Estate Commission, P.O. Box 14785, Baton Rouge, 70898.

Maine—Director, Real Estate Commission, State House Station 35, Augusta, 04333.

Maryland—Maryland Real Estate Commission, 501 St. Paul Pl., Baltimore, 21202.

Massachusetts—Executive Secretary, Board of Registration on Real Estate, Brokers and Salesmen, 100 Cambridge St., Room 1525, Boston, 02202.

Michigan—Board of Real Estate Brokers and Salespersons, P.O. Box 30018, Lansing, 48909.

Minnesota—Director of Licensing, Department of Commerce, 500 Metro Square Building, St. Paul, 55101.

Mississippi—Administrator, Real Estate Commission, 1920 Dunbarton, Jackson, 39216.

Missouri—Missouri Real Estate Commission, 3523 N. Ten Mile Dr., P.O. Box 1339, Jefferson City, 65102.

Montana—Board of Realty Regulation, 1424 9th Ave., Helena, 59601.

Nebraska—Director, Real Estate Commission, 301 Centennial Mall S., Lincoln, 68509.

Nevada—Administrator, Real Estate Division, 201 South Fall St., Carson City, 89710.

New Hampshire—Executive Director, New Hampshire Real Estate Commission, 3 Capitol St., Concord, 03301.

New Jersey—Director, New Jersey Real Estate Commission, 201 E. State St., Trenton, 08625.

New Mexico—Executive Secretary, Real Estate Commission, 4000 San Pedro N.E., Suite A, Albuquerque, 87110.

New York—New York Department of State, Division of Licensing, 162 Washington Ave., Albany, 12231.

North Carolina—Executive Director, Real Estate Commission, P.O. Box 17100, Raleigh, 27619.

North Dakota—Secretary, Real Estate Commission, 314 E. Thayer Ave., Box 727, Bismarck, 58502.

Ohio—Superintendent, Department of Commerce, Division of Real Estate, Two Nationwide Plaza, Columbus, 43215.

Oklahoma—Oklahoma Real Estate Commission, 4040 N. Lincoln Blvd., Suite 100, Oklahoma City, 73105.

Oregon—Commissioner, Oregon Real Estate Commission, 158 12th St., N.E., Salem, 97310.

Pennsylvania—Administrative Officer, Real Estate Commission, P.O. Box 2649, Room 611, Transportation and Safety Building, Commonwealth Ave. and Forester St., Harrisburg, 17105-2649.

Table 1.1
Real Estate License
Law Officials and
Commissions (cont.)

Rhode Island—Deputy Administrator, Real Estate Division, 100 North Main St., Providence, 02903.

South Carolina—Commissioner, Real Estate Commission, P.O. Box 210189, Columbia, 29221.

South Dakota—Secretary, Real Estate Commission, P.O. Box 490, Pierre, 57501.

Tennessee—Executive Director, Real Estate Commission, 706 Church St., Nashville, 37219-5322.

Texas—Administrator, Real Estate Commission, Box 12188, Austin, 78711.

Utah—Dept. of Business Regulation, Real Estate Division, 160 E. 300 South, P.O. Box 45802, Salt Lake City, 84110.

Vermont—Executive Secretary, Vermont Real Estate Commission, 7 E. State St., Montpelier, 05602.

Virginia—Assistant Director of Real Estate, Department of Commerce, 3600 W. Broad St., Richmond, 23230.

Washington—Administrator, Real Estate Division, P.O. Box 247, Olympia, 98405.

West Virginia—Executive Secretary, Real Estate Commission, 1033 Quarrier Street, Suite 400, Charleston, 25301.

Wisconsin—Director, Real Estate Bureau, 1400 E. Washington Ave., P.O. Box 8936, Madison, 53708.

Wyoming—Director of Real Estate, Herschler Building, Cheyenne, 82002.

Canada

Alberta—Superintendent of Real Estate, Consumer and Corporate Affairs, 10065 Jasper Ave., Edmonton, T5J 3B1.

British Columbia—Real Estate Council, 500-626 West Pender St., Vancouver, V6B 1V9.

Manitoba—Registrar, Real Estate Brokers Act, Room 118, 405 Broadway, Winnipeg, R3C 3L6.

New Brunswick—Department of Justice, Consumer Affairs Branch, P.O. Box 6000, Fredericton, E3B 5H1.

Newfoundland—Real Estate Division, Department of Justice, P.O. Box 999, Elizabeth Towers, St. John's, A1C 5T7.

Nova Scotia—Consumer Services Bureau, Real Estate Licensing Division, P.O. Box 998, Halifax, B3J 2X3.

Ontario—Registrar, Ministry of Consumer and Commercial Relations, Business Practices Division, 555 Yonge St., Toronto, M7A 2H6.

Prince Edward Island—Secretary, Prince Edward Island Real Estate Association and MLS, 202 Queen St., Charlottetown, C1A 4B6.

Quebec—Superintendent, 1045 de la Chevrotiere, 7e etage, Quebec, G1R 5E9.

Saskatchewan—Superintendent of Insurance, Department of Consumer and Commercial Affairs, 1871 Smith St., Regina, S4P 3V7.

modern office and apartment buildings, and the lending of money through mortgage loans on real estate.

Millions of people depend on some aspect of the real estate business for their livelihood. Full-time real estate professionals include not only brokers, salespeople, appraisers, managers and mortgage lenders, but also building managers and superintendents who handle real estate belonging to industrial firms, banks, trust companies, insurance firms and other businesses, as well as state, local and federal governments.

The need for trained real estate specialists is increasing. As the technical aspects of real estate activities become more complex, real estate offices require an increasing number of people properly trained to handle such transactions. Many professional and business people and organizations, such as attorneys, banks, trust companies, abstract and title insurance companies, architects, surveyors, accountants and tax specialists, also depend on the real estate specialist.

Professional
Organizations

The real estate business has many active, well-organized trade organizations, the largest being the NATIONAL ASSOCIATION OF REALTORS® (NAR), with over three-quarters of a million members. Founded in 1908 as the National Association of Real Estate Boards, NAR sponsors many specialized institutes offering professional designations upon completion of required courses for brokers, salespeople, appraisers, managers and other real estate professionals. (Such institutes and designations are listed in table 1.2.) The majority of local real estate associations throughout the U.S. and Canada are affiliated with NAR. Active members of state associations and such affiliated local boards subscribe to the Association's strict Code of Ethics and are entitled to be known as **REALTORS®**. Some boards offer a separate category of membership, Realtor-Associate®, to salespeople affiliated with an active REALTOR®and actively engaged in the real estate business as employees or independent contractors. The term REALTOR® is a registered mark. Through its many specialized institutes, the NAR serves the interests of its members by keeping them informed of developments in their field, publicizing the services of members, improving standards and practices and recommending or taking positions on public legislation or regulations affecting the operations of members and member firms.

Table 1.2 NATIONAL ASSOCIATION OF REALTORS® Institutes and Professional Designations	**Institute**	**Designation(s)**
	NAR—NATIONAL ASSOCIATION OF REALTORS®	GRI—Graduate, REALTORS® Institute
	AIREA—American Institute of Real Estate Appraisers	MAI—Member, Appraisal Institute RM—Residential Member
	ASREC—American Society of Real Estate Counselors	CRE—Counselor in Real Estate
	IREF—International Real Estate Federation	CIPS—Certified International Property Specialist
	IREM—Institute of Real Estate Management	CPM®—Certified Property Manager
	RESSI—Real Estate Securities and Syndication Institute	AMO®—Accredited Management Organization ARM®—Accredited Resident Manager
	RLI—REALTORS® Land Institute	SRS—Specialist in Real Estate Securities
	RNMI—REALTORS National Marketing Institute.®	
	SIOR—Society of Industrial and Office REALTORS®	ALC—Accredited Land Consultant CCIM—Certified Commercial-Investment Member
	WCR—Women's Council of REALTORS®	CRB—Certified Residential Broker CRS—Certified Residential Specialist
		SIR—full member
		LTG—Leadership Training Graduate

National Association of Real Estate Brokers. In addition to the NAR, there are also many independent real estate boards and other professional associations that were organized to set high standards for their members, promote their members' best interests and educate the public about the real estate profession. Among them is the National Association of Real Estate Brokers, which was founded in 1947. Its membership includes individual members, as well as brokers who belong to state and local real estate boards that are affiliated with the organization. The members are known as **Realtists**, and subscribe to a Code of Ethics that sets professional standards for all Realtists.

Summary   Even the simplest real estate transactions reflect a complex body of laws. A purchaser of real estate actually purchases from the seller the *legal rights* to use the land in certain ways.

The *seven sources of law* in the United States are the U.S. Constitution, laws passed by Congress, federal regulations, state constitutions, laws passed by state legislatures, local ordinances and court decisions.

The *common law* in the United States has evolved from that of England, and includes the precedent of prior court decisions as well as custom and usage. Much of real property law is founded in common law.

The real estate business is a dynamic industry employing hundreds of thousands of professional men and women. Every state and Canadian province has some type of *licensing requirement* for real estate brokers and salespeople. Students should become familiar with the licensing requirements of their states.

Questions

1. Rules and regulations adopted by government agencies:
   I. are used to administer and enforce legislative acts.
   II. usually outline specific illegal acts and set down penalties for violations.
   a. I only   c. both I and II
   b. II only   d. neither I nor II

2. Professional associations of specialists in various fields of real estate activity were organized to serve the interests of their members. Which of the following is generally a service expected of such organizations?
   a. keeping members informed of developments in their field
   b. improving standards and practices
   c. providing a clearinghouse of information
   d. all of the above

3. There are seven sources of law, including:
   a. court decisions
   b. local ordinances
   c. both a and b
   d. neither a nor b

4. Laws passed by Congress and various state legislatures may:
   a. establish specific provisions on an issue.
   b. change existing laws.
   c. empower administrative agencies to carry out the provisions of the law.
   d. all of the above

5. Court decisions:
   a. clarify and interpret laws.
   b. apply the law to the facts of a specific case.
   c. establish judicial precedents.
   d. all of the above

6. Areas of law that are of particular importance to the real estate broker include:
   a. the law of contracts.
   b. the law of agency.
   c. the general property law.
   d. all of the above

7. The legal concept of judicial precedent:
   I. provides continuity in court decisions.
   II. means that all judges are bound by all earlier decisions.
   a. I only   c. both I and II
   b. II only   d. neither I nor II

8. Constitutional provisions:
   I. establish the rights of citizens and delineate government authority.
   II. may have a direct influence on real estate activities.
   a. I only   c. both I and II
   b. II only   d. neither I nor II

9. Real property is often referred to as a *bundle of legal rights*. Which of the following is *not* among these rights?
   a. right of exclusion
   b. right to use the property for illegal purposes
   c. right of enjoyment
   d. right to sell or otherwise convey the property

10. When a person purchases real estate from a seller:
    I. that person is actually buying from the seller the legal rights to the property.
    II. the seller may retain one or more of the rights of ownership.
    a. I only   c. both I and II
    b. II only   d. neither I nor II

11. The purchase of real estate:
    a. is too complicated for individuals to carry out without assistance.
    b. reflects a complex body of laws.
    c. always requires a real estate broker.
    d. all of the above

12. Real estate license laws:
    I. are in effect in all states.
    II. were passed to protect the public from the possible fraud, dishonesty and incompetence of unscrupulous brokers and salespeople.
    a. I only   c. both I and II
    b. II only   d. neither I nor II

13. Common law:
    I. is derived from practices developed in the Spanish Empire.
    II. includes both customs and court decisions.
    >   a. I only   c. both I and II
    >   b. II only   d. neither I nor II

14. The designation REALTOR® refers to:
    a. any person whose business involves real estate.
    b. any licensed real estate broker.
    c. an active member of a state association or local board affiliated with the NATIONAL ASSOCIATION OF REALTORS®.
    d. an active member of the National Association of Real Estate Brokers.

15. The designation Realtist refers to:
    a. any person whose business involves real estate.
    b. any licensed real estate broker.
    c. an active member of a state association or local board affiliated with the NATIONAL ASSOCIATION OF REALTORS®.
    d. an active member of the National Association of Real Estate Brokers.

16. Government agencies issue rules and regulations in order to:
    a. enlarge the agency's authority.
    b. implement legislative acts.
    c. guarantee adherence to the laws.
    d. confuse the public action.

17. As a real estate professional, a real estate licensee should:
    I. be able to recognize the technical legal problems involved in transactions.
    II. appreciate the necessity of referring such problems to a competent attorney.
    >   a. I only   c. both I and II
    >   b. II only   d. neither I nor II

2

Real Property

Key Terms

Accession
Air rights
Chattel
Fixture
Improvement
Land
Parcel
Personal property
Real estate
Real property
Severance
Subsurface rights
Surface rights
Trade fixture

Overview

Will Rogers is often quoted as saying, "Buy land—they ain't making any more of the stuff!" The preamble to the NATIONAL ASSOCIATION OF REALTORS® Code of Ethics begins with the words, "Under all is the land...." We may see it, touch it and refer to it every day, but what exactly is land? When we own it, do we own just the ground beneath our feet, and if so, how deep does this ownership go? What about the trees we sit under and the air we breathe—are these part of the land also? This chapter will discuss the nature and characteristics of real estate, and define land, real estate and real property. In addition, this chapter will illustrate the distinctions between real property and personal property, and will show how an item of personal property can be converted into real property and vice versa.

Land, Real Estate and Real Property

You have probably heard the words *land, real estate* and *real property* used synonymously to describe the same commodity. While the terms are often used interchangeably, there are subtle but important differences in their technical meanings.

Land

Land is defined as *the earth's surface extending downward to the center of the earth and upward to infinity, including things permanently attached by nature, such as trees and water* (see figure 2.1).

The term *land* thus refers to more than just the surface of the earth. It includes the underlying soil and things that are naturally attached to the land, such as boulders and growing things. Land also includes the minerals and substances below the earth's surface together with the airspace above the land up to infinity. The surface, subsurface and airspace can be owned by different individuals as surface rights, subsurface rights and air rights.

A specific tract of land is commonly referred to as a **parcel**.

Figure 2.1
Land/Real Estate

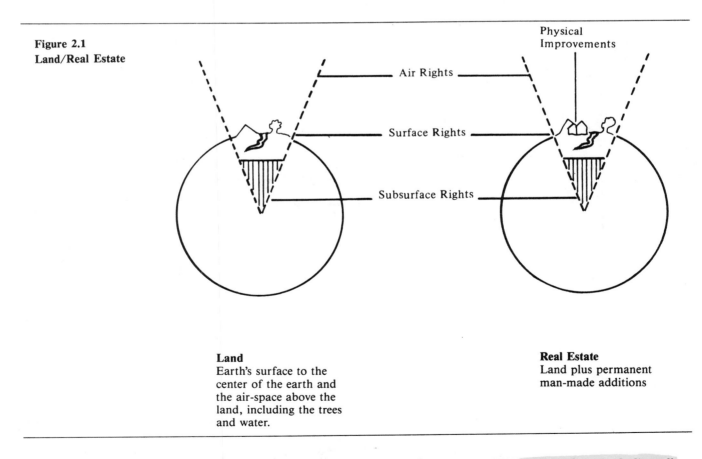

Air Rights

Physical Improvements

Surface Rights

Subsurface Rights

Land
Earth's surface to the center of the earth and the air-space above the land, including the trees and water.

Real Estate
Land plus permanent man-made additions

Real Estate

Real estate is defined as *land at, above and below the earth's surface, including all things permanently attached to it, whether natural or artificial* (see figure 2.1).

The term *real estate* is thus somewhat broader than the term *land*, and includes not only the physical components of the land provided by nature, but also all permanent improvements on and to the land. An **improvement** is any artificial thing attached to land, such as a building or fence. Land is also referred to as *improved* when streets, utilities, sewers and other additions make it suitable for building.

Real Property

Real property is defined as *the interests, benefits and rights inherent in the ownership of real estate* (see figure 2.2).

The term *real property* is thus broader still. It includes the physical surface of the land, what lies below it, what lies above it and what is permanently attached to it, as well as the *legal rights of real estate ownership*. As discussed in Chapter 1, this *bundle of legal rights* includes the rights of possession, control, enjoyment, exclusion and disposition, among others.

In Practice...

When people talk about buying or selling houses, office buildings, land and the like, they usually call all of these things real estate. *For all practical purposes, the term is synonymous with* real property, *as defined here. Thus, in everyday usage,* real estate *includes the legal rights of ownership specified in the definition of real property. Sometimes the term* realty *is used instead.*

Figure 2.2
Real Property

Possession		Exclusion
Control		Disposition
Enjoyment	Oil	Mortgage, Lease, etc.

Real Property. Real estate plus "bundle of legal rights."

Subsurface and air rights. As you have seen, the concept of real property ownership involves more than **surface rights**—the rights to use the surface of the earth—it also includes subsurface rights and air rights.

Subsurface rights are the rights to the natural resources lying below the earth's surface. A transfer of surface rights may be accomplished without transfer of subsurface rights.

For example, a landowner could sell to an oil company the rights to any oil and gas found in the land. The landowner could then sell his or her remaining interest, reserving the rights to all coal found in the land. After the sales, three parties would have ownership interests in the real estate: (1) the oil company would own all oil and gas, (2) the seller would own all coal and (3) the new landowner would own the rights to all the rest of the real estate.

As with the rights to minerals that lie below the surface of the land, the rights to use the air above the land may be sold or leased independently of the land itself. Such **air rights** are an increasingly important part of real estate, particularly in large cities, where air rights over railroads have been purchased to construct huge office buildings like the Pan-Am Building in New York City and the Merchandise Mart in Chicago. For the construction of such a building, the developer must purchase not only the air rights above the land but also numerous small portions of the land's surface in order to construct the building's foundation supports, called *caissons*. The caisson locations are regularly spaced, and the caisson portions usually are planned to meet the lower limit of the airspace about 30 feet or so above the land so that the finished foundation supports do not interfere with the operation of trains over the surface of the railroad's remaining land ownership (see figure 2.3).

Until the development of airplanes, a property's air rights were considered to be unlimited. Today, however, the courts permit reasonable interference with these rights, such as is necessary for aircraft, as long as the owner's right to use and occupy the land is not unduly lessened. Governments and airport authorities often purchase air rights adjacent to an airport to provide glide patterns for air traffic.

With the continuing development of solar power, air rights—more specifically, *sun rights*—may be redefined by the courts. They may consider tall buildings that block sunlight from smaller solar-powered buildings to be interfering with the smaller buildings' sun rights.

In summary, one parcel of real property may be owned by many people, each holding a separate right to a different part of the real estate. There may be: (1) an owner of the surface rights; (2) an owner of the subsurface mineral rights; (3) an owner of the subsurface gas and oil rights; and (4) an owner of the air rights.

Real Property Versus Personal Property

Property may be classified as either real property or personal property. As you know, real property is defined as the interests, benefits and rights inherent in the ownership of the earth, including the permanent additions or growing things attached to the earth, the air space above it and the minerals below it.

Personal property, on the other hand, sometimes referred to as "personalty," is considered to be *all property that does not fit the definition of real property.* Thus, personal property has the characteristic of being *movable*. Items of personal property, also referred to as **chattels**, include such tangibles as chairs, tables, clothing, money, bonds and bank accounts (see figure 2.4).

**Figure 2.3
Air Rights**

Building held
by owner of
air rights

Constructed over . . .

Railroad tracks
held by owner of
surface rights

30 feet

Caissons

It is possible to change an item of real property to personal property by **severance**. For example, a growing tree is real estate. If the owner cuts down the tree and thereby severs it from its attachment to the earth, it becomes personal property. Similarly, an owner can pick an apple from a tree or harvest a crop of wheat.

Trees and crops are generally considered in one of two classes. Trees, perennial bushes and grasses that do not require annual cultivation (*fructus naturales—* fruits of nature) are considered real property. Annual crops of wheat, corn, vegetables and fruit, known as *emblements* (*fructus industriales*—fruits of industry), are generally considered personal property. As long as an annual crop is growing, it will be transferred as part of the real property if no special provision is made in the sales contract. A tenant may re-enter land, if necessary, to harvest crops that result from the tenant's labor.

As previously noted, ownership of real property usually includes not only rights to the surface of the ground but also rights to the minerals and substances below the surface of the ground. When a landowner drills into the land, discovers oil and stores the oil in tanks ready for transport, the oil is converted from real property to personal property.

The reverse situation—changing personal property into real property—is also possible. If a landowner buys cement, stones and sand, and constructs a concrete walk on the land, the component parts of the concrete, which were originally personal property, are converted into real property. They have become a permanent improvement on the land.

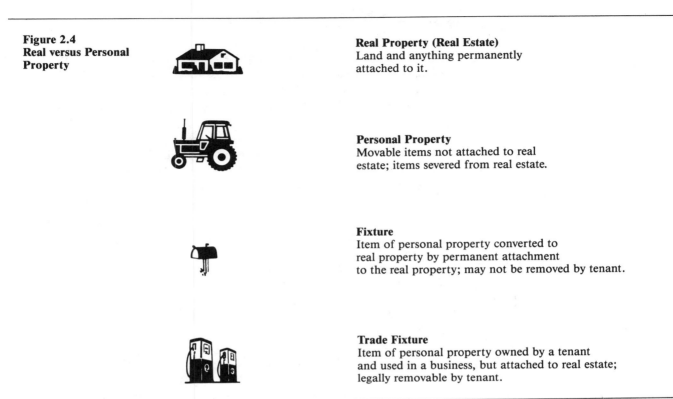

**Figure 2.4
Real versus Personal
Property**

Real Property (Real Estate)
Land and anything permanently
attached to it.

Personal Property
Movable items not attached to real
estate; items severed from real estate.

Fixture
Item of personal property converted to
real property by permanent attachment
to the real property; may not be removed by tenant.

Trade Fixture
Item of personal property owned by a tenant
and used in a business, but attached to real estate;
legally removable by tenant.

A mobile home is generally considered to be personal property, even though its mobility may be limited to a single trip to a mobile-home park. A mobile home may, however, be considered real property if it is permanently affixed to land, as prescribed by state law. Real estate licensees should be familiar with local laws before attempting to market mobile homes. In some states, new mobile homes may be sold only by mobile home dealers.

**Classification of
Fixtures**

In considering the differences between real property and personal property, it is important to be able to distinguish between a *fixture* and personal property.

Fixtures. *An article that was once personal property but has been so affixed to land or to a building that the law construes it to be a part of the real estate is a* **fixture.** Examples of fixtures are heating plants, elevator equipment in high-rise buildings, radiators, kitchen cabinets, light fixtures and plumbing fixtures. As a matter of fact, almost any item that has been added as a *permanent part* of a building is considered a fixture.

An article owned by a tenant and attached to a rented space or building for use in conducting a business is a **trade fixture**, also called a **chattel fixture**. Examples of trade fixtures are bowling alleys, store shelves, bars and restaurant equipment. Agricultural fixtures, such as chicken coops and tool sheds, are also included in this definition (see figure 2.4). Trade fixtures must be removed on or before the last day the property is rented. The tenant is responsible for any damage caused by removal of a fixture. Trade fixtures that are not removed become the real property of the landlord. Acquiring the property in this way is known as **accession**.

Trade fixtures, or chattel fixtures, differ from fixtures generally in the following three ways:

1. Fixtures are part of the real property and belong to the owner of that property. Trade fixtures are usually owned and installed by a tenant for his or her use and are the tenant's personal property.

2. Fixtures are considered a permanent part of a building, but trade fixtures are removable. Trade fixtures may be attached to a building as are other fixtures. Due to the relationship of the parties (landlord and tenant), however, the law gives a tenant the right to remove trade fixtures provided the removal is completed before the term of the lease expires and the rented space restored to approximately its original condition.

3. Since fixtures are legally construed to be real property, they are included in any sale or mortgage of the real property. Trade fixtures are not included in the sale or mortgage of real property except by special agreement.

Legal tests of a fixture. Courts apply four basic tests to determine whether an article is a fixture, and therefore a part of the real property, or personal property. These tests are based on: (1) the intention and relationship of the parties; (2) the adaptation of the article to the real estate; (3) the method of annexation of the item; and (4) the existence of an agreement.

The *intent of the parties* at the time an article was attached is generally considered the most important factor in deciding whether or not an article is a fixture. For example, a tenant may be allowed to bolt bookshelves to a wall, being careful to cause no permanent damage to the wall. If he or she wishes to remove them later, he or she may do so.

The *adaptation of an article* to use in a particular building is another test of the nature of the article. For example, an air conditioner installed in a wall slot specifically constructed for that purpose would be considered a fixture even if it could be readily removed.

The *permanence of the manner of annexation*, or attachment, often provides a third basis for court decisions relating to fixtures. For instance, a furnace, although it is removable, is usually attached in such a way that it cannot be taken out without causing extensive damage to the property. Moreover, the furnace is considered an essential part of the complete property and, as such, is a fixture.

Although these three tests seem simple, there is no uniformity in court decisions regarding what constitutes a fixture. Articles that appear to be permanently affixed have sometimes been held by the courts to be personal property, while items that do not appear to be permanently attached have been held to be fixtures.

In the sale of property, the one certain way to avoid confusion over the nature of an article is to make *a written agreement between the parties* establishing which items are considered part of the real property. The real estate broker or salesperson should ensure that a sales contract includes a list of all articles that are being included in the sale, particularly if there is any doubt as to whether they are permanently attached fixtures. Articles that might cause confusion include television antennas, built-in appliances, built-in bookcases and wall-to-wall carpeting.

Characteristics of Real Estate

Real estate possesses seven basic characteristics that affect its use both directly and indirectly. These characteristics fall into two broad categories—economic characteristics and physical characteristics (see figure 2.5).

Economic Characteristics

The basic economic characteristics of land are the factors that influence its value as an investment. They are: (1) scarcity, (2) improvements, (3) permanence of investment and (4) area preferences.

Scarcity. Although we don't usually think of land as a rare commodity, the total supply of land is fixed. While a considerable amount of land is still not used or inhabited, the supply of land in a given location or of a particular quality can be limited. *Creates higher price.*

Improvements. The building of an improvement on one parcel of land has an effect on the value and utilization of other neighboring tracts. Not only does an improvement affect adjoining tracts, it can often have a direct bearing on whole communities. For example, the improvement of a parcel of real estate by the construction of an industrial plant or the selection of a site for the building of an atomic reactor can directly influence a large area. Such land improvements can influence other parcels and other communities favorably or unfavorably and may affect not only the land use itself but also the value and price of land.

**Figure 2.5
Characteristics of
Real Estate**

```
                        ┌──────────────┐
                        │ Real Estate  │
                        └──────┬───────┘
                 ┌─────────────┴─────────────┐
        ┌────────────────────┐      ┌──────────────────────┐
        │ Economic           │      │ Physical             │
        │ Characteristics    │      │ Characteristics      │
        └────────────────────┘      └──────────────────────┘

   ┌──────────────────┐                    ┌──────────────────────┐
   │ Scarcity         │                    │ Immobility  Land     │
   └──────────────────┘                    │ Deed of transfer     │
                                           │ describes the land.  │
   ┌──────────────────┐                    └──────────────────────┘
   │ Improvements     │
   └──────────────────┘                    ┌──────────────────────┐
                                           │ Indestructibility    │
   ┌──────────────────┐                    └──────────────────────┘
   │ Permanence       │
   │ of investment    │                    ┌──────────────────────┐
   └──────────────────┘                    │ Nonhomogeneity       │
                                           └──────────────────────┘
   ┌──────────────────┐
   │ Area preferences │
   └──────────────────┘
```

Permanence of investment. Once land has been improved, the capital and labor used to build the improvement represent a large fixed investment. Although even a well-built structure can be razed to make way for a newer building or other use of the land, improvements such as drainage, electricity, water, and sewerage remain, because they generally cannot be dismantled or removed economically. The return on such investments will tend to be long-term and relatively stable. This permanence generally makes improved real estate unsuitable for short, rapid turnover investing.

Area preferences. This economic characteristic, sometimes called *situs,* does not refer to a geographical location per se but rather to people's choices and preferences for a given area. It is the unique quality of people's preferences that results in different valuations being attributed to similar units.

Examples of likes and dislikes are numerous. Social preferences influenced the rapid movement of people to suburban areas. Some are now returning to the urban areas, however, preferring the environments and amenities offered by city living to those offered by suburbia. *Area preference is the most important economic characteristic of land*.

Physical Characteristics

Land has certain basic physical characteristics. It is: (1) immobile, (2) indestructible, and (3) unique.

Land Is Immobile. It is true that some of the substances of land are removable and that topography can be changed, but *the geographic location of any given parcel of land can never be changed*. It is rigid; it is fixed.

Because land is immobile, the rights to use land are more easily regulated than are other forms of property. For example, local governments are supported largely by property taxes on real estate. The taxes become a lien on the land. If the owner does not pay the tax due, the land is readily available to be sold to satisfy the lien. The fixed amount of land in a given area enables the local government to rely on a certain amount of annual revenue from property taxes, which in turn allows the government to make long-range plans based on the projected income.

Land Is Indestructible. Just as land is immobile, it is *durable* and *indestructible*. This permanence of land, coupled with the long-term nature of the improvements (including the buildings) that are placed on it, has tended to stabilize investments in land.

The fact that land is indestructible does not, of course, change the fact that the improvements on land do depreciate and can become obsolete, thereby reducing values—perhaps drastically. This gradual depreciation should not be confused with the fact that the *economic desirability* of a given location can change, thus creating "ghost towns."

Land Is Unique. No two parcels of land are ever exactly the same. Although there may be substantial similarity, *all parcels differ geographically*, as each parcel has its own location. The uniqueness of land is also referred to as its *heterogeneity* or *nonhomogeneity*.

Characteristics Define Land Use

The various characteristics of a parcel of real estate affect its desirability for a specific use. Some specific physical and economic factors that would affect land use include: (1) contour and elevation of the parcel, (2) prevailing winds, (3) transportation, (4) public improvements and (5) availability of natural resources, such as water. For example, hilly, heavily wooded land would need considerable work before it could be used for industrial purposes, but could be ideally suited for residential use. Likewise, flat land located along a major highway network could be desirable for residential use, but even better-located for industry.

Summary

Although most people think of *land* as the surface of the earth, land is the *earth's surface* and also the *mineral deposits under the earth* and the *air above it*. The term *real estate* further expands this definition to include *all natural and man-made improvements attached to the land*. *Real property* is the term used to describe the "bundle of legal rights" associated with ownership of real estate.

The different rights to the same parcel of real estate may be owned and controlled by different parties, one owning the *surface rights*, one owning the *air rights* and another owning the *subsurface rights*.

All property that does not fit the definition of real estate is classified as *personal property,* or *chattels*. When articles of personal property are permanently affixed to land, they may become *fixtures*, and as such are considered a part of the real estate. Personal property attached to real estate by a tenant for the purpose of his or her business is classified as a *trade*, or *chattel, fixture* and remains personal property.

The special nature of land as an investment is apparent in both its economic and physical characteristics. The economic characteristics are controlled by such factors as *scarcity, improvements, permanence of investment* and *area preferences*. Physically, land is immobile, indestructible and unique.

Questions

1. Which of the following is not a physical characteristic of land?

   a. indestructibleness
   b. scarcity
   c. immobility
   d. uniqueness

2. A construction firm builds an office center over a railroad right-of-way. This means:

   I. trains can no longer operate on the tracks under the building during business hours if the noise disturbs the occupants of the office center.
   II. the construction firm has built the office center using the subsurface rights to the property.

      a. I only
      b. II only
      c. both I and II
      d. neither I nor II

3. The term nonhomogeneity refers to which of the following?

   a. scarcity
   b. uniqueness
   c. immobility
   d. b and c

4. John Sexton purchases a parcel of land and sells the rights to any minerals located in the ground to an exploration company. This means that Sexton now owns all but which of the following with regard to this property?

   a. air rights
   b. surface rights
   c. subsurface rights
   d. a and b

5. A store tenant firmly attaches appropriate appliances for his restaurant business on the leased premises. These appliances are:

   I. trade fixtures.
   II. part of the real estate once they are installed.

      a. I only
      b. II only
      c. both I and II
      d. neither I nor II

6. The definition of real estate includes many elements. Which of the following items would *not* be a part of real estate?

   a. fences
   b. permanent buildings
   c. farm equipment
   d. growing trees

7. Emblements are:

   a. fructus naturales.
   b. fructus industriales.
   c. fixtures.
   d. improvements.

8. Which of the following best defines real estate?

   a. land and the air above it
   b. land, including all things permanently attached to it
   c. land and the buildings permanently affixed to it
   d. land and the mineral rights in the land

9. A fixture:

   I. is considered to be real estate.
   II. is an item that at one time was personal property.

      a. I only
      b. II only
      c. both I and II
      d. neither I nor II

10. The definition of *land* includes all but which of the following?

    a. minerals in the earth
    b. the air above the ground up to infinity
    c. trees
    d. buildings

11. Fred and Celia Evers are building a new enclosed front porch to their home. The lumber dealer with whom they are contracting has just unloaded in front of their house a truckload of lumber that will be used to build the porch. At this point, the lumber is considered to be:

    I. personal property.
    II. real estate.

       a. I only
       b. II only
       c. both I and II
       d. neither I nor II

12. When the Evers' new front porch, as described in question 11, is completed, the lumber that the dealer originally delivered will be considered to be:

   I. personal property.
   II. real estate.
   - a. I only
   - b. II only
   - c. both I and II
   - d. neither I nor II

13. The "bundle of legal rights" is included in the definition of:
   - a. land.
   - b. real estate.
   - c. real property.
   - d. trade fixtures.

14. The definition of the term *real property* includes all but which of the following?
   - a. items of personal property permanently affixed to the real estate
   - b. legal ownership rights
   - c. air and subsurface rights
   - d. chattels

15. Man-made, permanent additions to real property are called:
   - a. chattels.
   - b. parcels.
   - c. improvements.
   - d. trade fixtures.

16. Real estate may be converted into personal property:

   I. by severance.
   II. by accession.
   - a. I only
   - b. II only
   - c. both I and II
   - d. neither I nor II

17. Steve Jackson rents a detached, single-family home under a one-year lease. Two months into the rental period, Jackson installs awnings over the building's front windows to keep the sun away from some delicate hanging plants. Which of the following is true?
   - a. Jackson must remove the awnings before the rental period is over.
   - b. Because of their permanent nature, the awnings are considered to be personal property.
   - c. The awnings are considered to be fixtures.
   - d. a and b

18. *Area preference* refers to:

   I. relative scarcity.
   II. a physical characteristic of land.
   - a. I only
   - b. II only
   - c. both I and II
   - d. neither I nor II

19. Which of the following physical and economic factors would a land developer take into consideration when determining the optimum use for a parcel of land?
   - a. transportation
   - b. natural resources available
   - c. contour and elevation
   - d. all of the above

20. Personal property may be converted to real property by:
   - a. conversion.
   - b. severance.
   - c. accession.
   - d. interference.

3

The Real Estate Business

Key Terms

Agricultural real estate
Business cycle
Commercial real estate
Demand
Industrial real estate
Market
Point of equilibrium
Residential real estate
Special-purpose real estate
Supply

Overview

The business of real estate is much more than just the neighborhood storefront with the sign "Realty" hanging in the window, and it employs many more persons than just brokers and salespeople. The real estate marketplace supports an industry composed of a variety of professional people specializing in many different fields and dealing with many different types of real estate. Whether sales, management or appraisal, this industry deals primarily with the real estate market. This chapter will discuss the many facets of the real estate industry, and in particular how it is shaped by the influences of supply and demand in the real estate market.

Real Estate—A Business of Many Specializations

Some people think of the real estate business as being made up of only brokers and salespeople. Today's real estate industry, however, employs scores of well-trained, knowledgeable individuals in areas other than real estate brokerage. Modern real estate practice provides many specializations for people who want to serve the community while earning their livelihoods.

Real Estate Professions

The specializations that make up the real estate business include brokerage, appraisal, property management, real estate financing, property development, counseling and education. Each of these is a business unto itself. To be truly competent, however, a person working in any phase of the real estate business must possess at least basic knowledge of all these specializations.

Brokerage. The bringing together of people interested in making a real estate transaction is *brokerage.* Typically, the broker acts as an *agent;* that is, he or she negotiates the sale, purchase or rental of property on behalf of others for a fee or commission. The agent's commission is generally a percentage of the amount involved in the transaction. It is usually paid by the seller or, in a rental transaction, by the owner of the property. Brokerage is discussed further in Chapter 5.

Appraisal. The process of estimating the value of a parcel of real estate is *appraisal.* Although brokers must have some understanding of valuation as part of their training, qualified appraisers are generally employed when property is financed or sold by court order. The appraiser must have sound judgment, experience and a detailed knowledge of the methods of valuation. Appraisal is covered in Chapter 18.

Property management. Someone who operates a property for its owner is involved in *property management.* The property manager may be responsible for soliciting tenants, collecting rents, altering or constructing new space for tenants, ordering repairs and generally maintaining the property. The manager's basic responsibility is to protect the owner's investment and maximize the owner's return on the investment. Property management is discussed in Chapter 17.

Financing. The business of providing the funds necessary to complete real estate transactions is *financing.* Most transactions are financed by means of a loan secured by a mortgage or trust deed by which the property is pledged as security for the eventual payment of the loan. This and other methods of real estate financing are examined in Chapter 15.

Property development. The profession of *property development* includes the work of subdividers who purchase raw land, divide it into lots, build roads and install sewers. Property development also includes the skills of land developers who improve the building lots with houses and other buildings and who sell the improved real estate, either themselves or through brokerage firms. Finally, there is the work of builders and architects who plan and construct the houses and other buildings. Property development is discussed in Chapter 20.

Counseling. Providing competent independent advice, sound guidance and informed judgment on a variety of real estate problems, including the purchase, use

fee for consulting services

and investment of property, is *counseling*. A counselor attempts to furnish his or her client with direction in choosing among alternative courses of action. Increasing the client's knowledge is every counselor's function in rendering services.

Education. Both the real estate practitioner and the consumer can learn more about the complexities of the real estate business through *education*. Colleges, schools, real estate organizations and continuing education programs conduct courses and seminars in all areas of the business. These courses are often taught by experienced real estate professionals.

Uses of Real Property

Just as there are many areas of specialization within the real estate industry, so too are there many different types of property in which to specialize (see figure 3.1). Real estate can generally be classified into one of the following categories according to its use.

Figure 3.1
Uses of Real Property

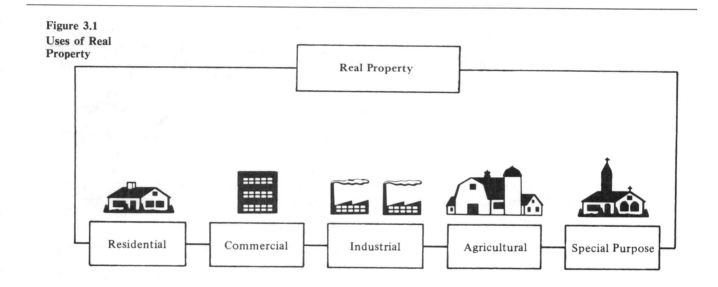

1. **Residential**—all property used for housing, from acreage to small city lots, both single- and multifamily, in urban, suburban and rural areas.
2. **Commercial**—business property, including offices, shopping centers, stores, theaters, hotels and parking facilities.
3. **Industrial**—warehouses, factories, land in industrial districts and power plants.
4. **Agricultural**—farms, timberland, ranches and orchards.
5. **Special purpose**—churches, schools, cemeteries and government-held lands.

The market for each of these types of properties can be further subdivided into: (1) the sale market, which involves the transfer of title, and (2) the rental market, which involves the transfer of space on a rental basis.

In Practice...

Although a real estate person or firm can, in theory, perform all the services listed above and handle all five classes of property, this is rarely done except in small towns. Most real estate firms tend to specialize to some degree, especially in urban areas. In some cases, a real estate person may perform only one service for one type of property. Residential property brokers and industrial property appraisers are two examples of such specialization.

Since the greatest number of individuals in the real estate field are involved in residential brokerage, most people tend to think of the marketing of real estate as the primary activity in the field. But many other people are also a part of the real estate business. For example, people associated with mortgage banking firms and those who negotiate mortgages for banks and savings and loan associations, people in property management firms and real estate departments of corporations, and officials and employees of such government agencies as zoning boards and assessing offices all are involved in the real estate business.

The Real Estate Market	In literal terms a **market** is a place where goods can be bought and sold, where value for those goods can be established and where it is advantageous for buyers and sellers to trade. The function of the market is to facilitate this exchange by providing a setting in which the **supply and demand forces** of the economy can establish market value.
Supply and Demand	The economic forces of **supply** and **demand** continually interact in the market to establish and maintain price levels. Essentially, *when supply goes up, prices will drop as more producers compete for buyers; when demand increases, prices will rise as more buyers compete for the product.*

Production will slow or stop during a period of over-supply, since market prices must at least equal the cost of production. When there is more demand than the market can meet, production will increase to take advantage of demand. Supply and demand are balanced at what is called the **point of equilibrium**.

Supply and demand in the real estate market. The characteristics of the goods in the marketplace determine how quickly the forces of supply and demand will be able to achieve equilibrium. Such characteristics are:

1. the degree of standardization of the product.
2. the mobility of the product.
3. the mobility of the parties (buyer and seller).

Real estate is not a standardized product; no two parcels can ever be exactly alike. The apparent exceptions to this are in some developments where a number of units may be built to the same specifications. But even where this condition exists, each parcel of real estate is unique because it has its own geographic location.

Since real estate is fixed in nature (immobile), it cannot be moved from area to area to satisfy the pressures of supply and demand. Property buyers are also generally limited in their mobility—retirees are a major exception in regard to residences. For these reasons the real estate business has tended toward local markets where offices can maintain detailed familiarity with market conditions and available units. The increasing mobility of the population, however, and the growing impact of new technologies in communication and data handling have resulted in growing interest in geographic expansion of real estate firms. Computer-based market data networks have led to joint undertakings by widely dispersed real estate organizations.

Where standardization and mobility are relatively great, the supply and demand forces will balance relatively quickly. But because of real estate's characteristics of uniqueness and immobility, the real estate market is generally relatively slow to adjust. To a certain extent the product can be removed from the market (as when a home offered for resale is withdrawn), yet an oversupply usually results in a lowering of price levels. Since development and construction of real estate take a considerable period of time from conception to completion, increases in demand may not be met immediately. Building and housing construction may occur in uneven spurts of activity due to such factors.

Factors Affecting Supply

Factors that tend to affect supply in the real estate market include the labor force, construction costs, government controls and financial policies (see figure 3.3).

Labor force and construction costs. A shortage of labor in the skilled building trades, an increase in the cost of building materials or a scarcity of materials will tend to decrease the amount of housing that will be built. The impact of the labor force on price levels depends on the extent to which higher costs can be passed on to the buyer or renter in the form of higher purchase prices or rents. Technological advances that result in cheaper materials and more efficient means of construction may tend to counteract some price increases.

Government controls and financial policies. Government monetary policy can have a substantial impact on the real estate market. The Federal Reserve Board, as well as such government agencies as the Federal Housing Administration

**Figure 3.2
Factors Affecting
Supply and Demand**

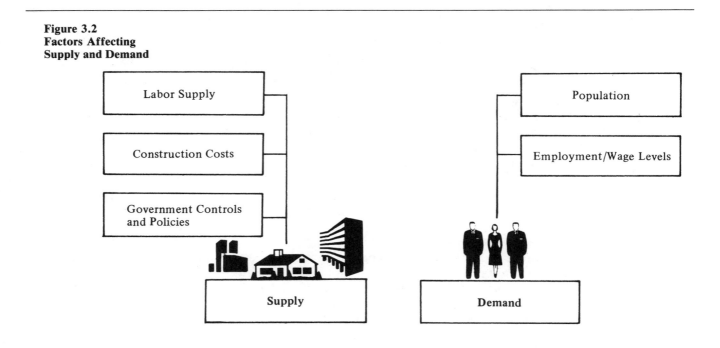

(FHA), the Government National Mortgage Association (GNMA) and the Federal Home Loan Mortgage Corporation (FHLMC), can affect the amount of money available to lenders for mortgage loans (see Chapter 15).

In addition to acting through these agencies, the government can influence the amount of money available for real estate investment through its fiscal and/or monetary policies. Such policies include the amount of money taken out of circulation through taxation and other methods and the amount of money the government puts into circulation through spending programs ranging from welfare to farm subsidies.

At the local level, real estate taxation is one of the primary sources of revenue for government. Policies on taxation of real estate can have either positive or negative effects. Tax incentives have been one way for communities to attract new businesses and industries to their areas. And, of course, along with these enterprises come increased employment and expanded residential real estate markets.

Local governments can also affect market operations and the development and construction of real estate by applying land-use controls. Building codes and zoning ordinances are used by communities to control and stimulate the highest potential use of land. Real estate values and markets are thereby stabilized. Community amenities such as churches, schools and parks, and efficient governmental policies are influential factors affecting the real estate market.

Factors Affecting Demand

Factors that tend to affect demand in the real estate market include population and employment and wage levels (see figure 3.2).

Population. Since shelter (whether in the form of owned or rented property) is a basic human and family need, the general need for housing will grow as the population grows. Even though the total population of the country may continue to increase, growth is not uniform. Some areas are growing faster than others. The "sun belt" still attracts businesses, retirees and others, but effective local controls can make northern areas attractive for newcomers as well. Some areas are not growing at all. We even have modern-day ghost towns, where the exhaustion of natural resources or the termination of an industrial operation has resulted in a mass exodus of population.

In a consideration of the impact of population on the real estate market, the makeup of the population, or demographics, must also be taken into account. Family size and the ratio of adults to children are important in estimating housing needs. Doubling up—two or more families using one housing unit—is generally on the increase. Many young people who would prefer apartments or houses of their own will have one or more roommates or remain in their parents' homes. These trends are indications of an increasing shortage of affordable housing.

Employment and wage levels. Decisions on home ownership or rental are closely related to ability to pay. Employment opportunities and wage levels in a small community can be drastically affected by decisions made by major employers in the area. Individuals involved in the real estate market in such communities must keep themselves well informed about the business plans of local employers.

In order to estimate how changes in wage levels will affect people's decisions concerning real estate, it is also important to look for trends in how individual income is likely to be used. General trends in the economy (availability of mortgage money, interest rates, rate of inflation and the like) will influence an individual's decision as to how income will be spent. Americans are notoriously poor savers, yet personal savings are still a main source of mortgage loan money.

Business Cycles

Over the years, business has had its ups and downs. These upward and downward fluctuations in business activity are called **business cycles**. Although business cycles often seem to recur within a certain number of years, they are actually caused primarily by internal forces (such as population growth) and external forces (such as wars and oil embargoes) rather than by the passage of time.

The business cycle can generally be characterized by four stages: *expansion, recession, depression,* and *revival*. The movements of the cycle are gradual and not clearly defined.

In analyzing the patterns of business cycles, it is possible to consider a number of trends simultaneously. The long-term trend (referred to as the *secular trend*) tends to be smooth and continuous. It is most affected by such basic influences as population growth, technological advances, capital accumulation and so on. Within this overall pattern are business cycles of varying lengths. Various segments or industries within the economy (including real estate) may have shorter cycles with different timing and different characteristics. Seasonal cycles also reflect characteristics in particular industries. Some relate to climatic conditions, consumer buying habits, vacation patterns and the like. Some industries (such as real estate) are much more subject to seasonal fluctuations than others.

The real estate cycle. As stated earlier, the real estate market is slow in adjusting to variations in supply and demand. Because one factor of the real estate cycle is building activity, the time lag between the demand for units and the completion of those units causes real estate cycles to peak after the rest of the economy does and to take longer to recover from depressed periods than other economic sectors. It is also important to remember that the local character of the real estate market creates many local conditions that may not correspond to the general movement of the real estate cycle.

Governmental anticyclical efforts. Since the Great Depression of the 1930s, the federal government has attempted to establish fiscal and monetary policies to prevent extreme fluctuations in the business cycle. By increasing government spending during times of recession and taking money out of circulation through taxation and control of lending institutions during times of inflation/expansion, the government attempts to promote steady, gradual economic growth. The goal of a completely stable economy often seems elusive, nonetheless.

Summary

Although selling is the most widely recognized activity of the real estate business, the industry also involves many other services, such as *appraisal, property management, property development, counseling, property financing,* and *education*. Most real estate firms specialize in only one or two of these areas. However, the highly complex and competitive nature of our society requires that a real estate person be an expert in a number of fields.

Real property can be classified according to its general use as either *residential, commercial, industrial, agricultural* or *special purpose.* Although many brokers deal with more than one type of real property, they usually specialize to some degree.

A *market* is a place where goods and services can be bought and sold and price levels established. The ideal market allows for a continual balancing of the forces of supply and demand. Because of its unique characteristics, real estate is relatively slow to adjust to the forces of supply and demand.

The supply of and demand for real estate are affected by many factors, including *population changes, wage and employment levels, construction costs and availability of labor* and *governmental monetary policy and controls.*

Fluctuations of business activity in this country are observed in *cycles.* Business cycles occur in four stages: *expansion, recession, depression* and *revival.* The real estate cycle involves similar stages, but it tends to peak after the rest of the economy does, and it takes longer to recover than other sectors of the business community do.

Questions

1. A theater or hotel is an example of:
   a. residential real estate.
   b. commercial real estate.
   c. industrial real estate.
   d. special-purpose real estate.

2. The factors that influence the demand for real estate include:
   I. wage levels and employment opportunities.
   II. the number of real estate brokers.
      a. I only   c. both I and II
      b. II only   d. neither I nor II

3. Property that is part of the commercial market includes:
   a. office buildings for lease.
   b. single-family homes.
   c. churches.
   d. factories.

4. Business cycles:
   I. involve periods of expansion, recession, depression and revival.
   II. can be regulated somewhat by government fiscal and monetary policy.
      a. I only   c. both I and II
      b. II only   d. neither I nor II

5. The forces that affect supply in the real estate market include:
   a. construction costs.
   b. labor force.
   c. government controls.
   d. all of the above

6. The real estate market is considered local in character because:
   a. land is fixed, or immobile.
   b. most people are not generally mobile enough to take advantage of available real estate in distant areas.
   c. local controls can have a significant impact on the market.
   d. all of the above

7. In general, when the supply of a certain commodity increases:
   a. prices tend to rise.
   b. prices tend to remain level.
   c. prices tend to drop.
   d. prices can no longer be established.

8. In an average market, certain characteristics of the goods sold will determine how quickly the forces of supply and demand will establish the goods' prices. Which of the following is *not* one of these characteristics?
   a. the product's mobility
   b. the product's cost
   c. the mobility of buyer and seller
   d. whether or not the product is standardized

9. Compared to typical markets, the real estate market:
   I. is relatively quick to adapt to the forces of supply and demand.
   II. is national in scope.
      a. I only   c. both I and II
      b. II only   d. neither I nor II

10. In general terms, a *market* refers to which of the following?
    a. a place where buyers and sellers come together
    b. the amount of goods available at a given price
    c. a forum where price levels are established
    d. both a and c

11. The demand for real estate in a particular community is affected by:
    a. population.
    b. wage levels.
    c. employment.
    d. all of the above

4

Concepts of Home Ownership

Key Terms
Actual cash value
Apportionment clause
Capital gain
Coinsurance clause
Equity
Homeowner's insurance policy
Investment
Liability coverage
Replacement cost
Subrogation clause

Overview
While the term *home ownership* once referred mainly to detached single-family dwellings, today's homebuyer must choose among many different types of housing designed to satisfy individual needs, tastes and financial capabilities. This chapter will discuss the various types of housing available as well as the factors a potential homeowner must consider in deciding the what, where, and how much of buying real estate. The chapter will also cover the many tax benefits available to all homeowners and the forms of property insurance designed to protect one of the biggest investments of a person's life. Note that this chapter is devoted to the ownership of a *personal residence;* the ownership of income-producing property will be discussed in Chapter 22, "Real Estate Investment."

Home Ownership

The desire to own one's home is a deep-rooted characteristic of American culture. To many people, home ownership represents financial stability, a psychological and emotional pride in ownership and a sense of belonging to the community. It can also represent a form of investment. Some of the expenses of home ownership, including mortgage interest and property tax payments, are partially compensated by a reduction in federal income tax.

Traditionally, the residential real estate market was composed predominantly of single-family dwellings. The typical buyer was a married couple, usually with small children. Today, however, a variety of social changes, population shifts and economic considerations have altered the real estate market considerably. For example, many real estate buyers today are *singles,* unmarried men and women; many are *empty nesters,* married couples whose housing needs change after their children move away from home; and many are *never nesters,* married couples who choose not to have children or unmarried couples living together.

Types of Housing

As the residential market evolves, the needs of its buyers become more specialized. Thus, aside from single-family dwellings, the real estate market in any given area may include apartment complexes, condominiums, cooperatives, planned unit developments, converted-use properties, retirement communities, singles' developments, high-rise developments, mobile homes, modular homes and time-shared occupancy.

Apartment complexes continue to be popular. A complex consists of a group of apartment buildings with any number of units in each building. The buildings may be low-rise or high-rise, and the amenities may include parking as well as clubhouses, swimming pools and in some instances, golf courses.

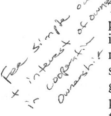

The *condominium* is a popular form of residential ownership, particularly for people who want the security of owning property but do not want the responsibilities of caring for and maintaining a house. Ownership of a condominium apartment or townhouse—which will share party walls with other units—involves shared ownership of common facilities, such as halls, elevators and surrounding grounds. Management and maintenance of building exteriors and grounds are provided by agreement, with expenses paid out of monthly assessments charged to owners. Office buildings and shopping centers may also be established as condominiums, allowing businesses to build equity in the space they occupy while avoiding unpredictable rent increases. The condominium form of ownership will be discussed in detail in Chapter 8.

A *cooperative* is very similar to a condominium in that it involves units within a larger building with common walls and facilities. An owner of a cooperative unit, however, owns not the unit itself but rather shares of stock in the corporation that holds title to the building. In return for stock in the corporation, the owner receives what is called a proprietary lease, which entitles him or her to occupancy of a particular unit in the building. Each unit owner must pay his or her share of the building's expenses in the same way that a condominium unit owner does. Cooperatives will be further discussed in Chapter 8.

Planned unit developments (PUDs) are zoned under special cluster zoning requirements that compute roads and park areas as a percentage of the square feet of land required for homes or living units. A PUD can thus make maximum use of open space by reducing lot sizes and street areas. A community association formed as a corporation maintains common areas through fees paid by homeowners. Unlike condominium owners, PUD owners have no direct ownership interest in common areas.

Converted-use properties are existing structures, such as factories, office buildings, hotels, schools and churches, that have been converted to residential use as either rental or condominium units. For economic, structural and/or locational reasons, such buildings have been abandoned by their original owners or tenants. Rather than demolish them to make way for new structures, developers often find it both aesthetically and economically appealing to renovate the existing buildings into affordable housing. In this manner, an abandoned warehouse may be transformed into luxury loft condominium units, a closed hotel may become an apartment building and an old factory may become a shopping complex.

Retirement communities lend themselves particularly well to those areas of the country with temperate weather conditions. Retirement communities, often structured as PUDs, may provide shopping, recreational opportunities and health-care facilities, in addition to residential units.

Single-person developments are a relatively recent concept that has been implemented throughout the country. They cater to unmarried people and often provide recreational facilities and planned social activities as well as living units. Such a development may be one apartment building, a PUD or an apartment complex.

High-rise developments, sometimes called mixed unit developments (MUDs), combine office space, stores, theaters and apartment units, and are popular across the country. The most successful high-rise developments effectively use such natural assets as rivers, lakes and forest preserves. MUDs usually are self-contained and include laundry facilities, restaurants, food stores, valet shops, beauty parlors, barber shops, swimming pools and other attractive and convenient features.

Mobile homes are one of the housing industry's fastest-growing areas of development in times of high-priced housing. Mobile homes were once considered to be useful only as temporary residences or for traveling. Now many people live in them as principal residences or use them as stationary vacation homes. The lower cost of mobile homes as compared to other types of residences, coupled with the increased living space available in the newer, double-wide and triple-wide models, has made mobile homes an attractive alternative to the conventionally constructed residence. The increase in mobile-home sales has resulted in growing numbers of mobile-home parks. These parks offer complete residential environments with permanent community facilities as well as semipermanent foundations and hookups for gas, water and electricity.

Modular homes are also gaining popularity as the base price of newly constructed homes rises. Modular homes are prefabricated structures that arrive on-site in units preassembled at the factory. As the name implies, they are modular in construction. Each preassembled room is lowered into place on the building site by a crane; workers later finish the structure and connect plumbing and wiring. In this manner, entire developments can be built at a fraction of the time and cost of conventional types of construction.

Time-shared occupancy enables many buyers to purchase ownership shares in one vacation home. These shares, usually available in one-week increments, entitle each owner to occupy the property for a definite fixed period of time each year. In addition to the purchase price, time-share owners pay annual fees. Time-share resale prices in some areas are significantly lower than purchase prices due to high initial marketing costs.

Factors Influencing Home Ownership

After 35 years of steady advances, the percentage of housing units occupied by their owners declined from an all-time high of 65.6 percent in 1980 to 63.8 percent in the third quarter of 1986. The high inflation of the 1970s caused housing prices to rise rapidly, but individual incomes failed to keep pace. The result is that the average home is now beyond the means of most single wage earners and even some two-income households.

The decline in home ownership is most severe among the young. First-time buyers may have difficulty saving the 10 to 20 percent down payment required for a conventional mortgage. The government-sponsored programs that provided a boost up the housing ladder for many now have more stringent requirements, and proposals for higher down payments and fees may take effect in the future.

Certainly not all individuals or families should own homes. Home ownership involves substantial commitment and responsibility, and the flexibility of renting suits some individuals' needs better than ownership does. People whose work requires frequent moves from one location to another or whose financial position or future is uncertain will particularly benefit from renting. Renting also provides more leisure time by freeing tenants from management and maintenance responsibilities.

Those who choose to take on the responsibilities of home ownership must evaluate and make important decisions based on a variety of factors, including mortgage terms, ownership expenses, ability to pay, property features and investment considerations.

Mortgage Terms

Liberalization of mortgage terms and payment plans over the last six decades has helped to make the dream of home ownership a reality for many. The amount of a conventional mortgage loan in relation to the value of a home (called *loan-to-value ratio*) has increased from 40 percent in 1920 to, typically, 80 percent today. Payment periods of conventional mortgages have also been extended, from five years in the 1920s to 15 to 30 years in the '80s. Adjustable rate mortgages have gained popularity among lenders in today's unsettled financial market.

Low-down-payment mortgage loans are still available through the federal programs of the Federal Housing Administration (FHA) and the Veterans Administration (VA). In addition, private mortgage insurance companies offer programs to assist loan applicants in receiving higher loan-to-value ratios from private lenders than they could otherwise obtain. Mortgages and mortgage lending will be discussed in detail in Chapter 15.

Ownership Expenses

A portion of each of a homeowner's monthly mortgage payments may be used to build up a reserve fund for taxes and property insurance. (The lender may even require such a fund.) That portion of the loan payment that is applied to interest also represents an expense to the owner. There are many other obvious and not-so-obvious expenses connected with home ownership, including real estate taxes, depreciation (wearing out of the building through use), insurance, maintenance and repairs, utilities and such necessary services as garbage pickup and water supply. The owner also loses the investment return that could be realized if the money invested in a home were available for another use. The median total home ownership expenses in 1985 was 30.2 percent of income, about three times the average of the 1970s.

Traditionally, lenders used as a rule of thumb the formula that the monthly cost of buying and maintaining a home (mortgage payments plus taxes and insurance) should not exceed 25 percent of a borrower's pre-tax monthly income. Some lenders have modified this percentage upward depending on such factors as the borrower's age, potential future earnings, number of dependents and so forth. Lenders generally allow payments on *all* debts to be no more than 36 percent of monthly income.

Property Features

Location is the single most important influence on a homebuyer's decision. The choice of community from the variety available in every area must be followed by the choice of a neighborhood within the community. The elements that contribute to the desirability of a community and neighborhood encompass far more than the geographic area and include such major factors as:

1. *Employment opportunities:* Industrial and commercial development offering vocational opportunities.
2. *Cultural advantages:* Schools, colleges, churches, libraries, theaters, museums, zoos, sports attractions and parks.
3. *Governmental structure:* Police and fire protection, sanitation, water and public utilities (gas, power and telephone service) add to the desirability of an area, as do various quasi-municipal authorities, such as ports, public transportation, anti-pollution practices, forest preserves and the like.
4. *Social services:* The availability and quality of hospitals, clinics, community centers and similar facilities.
5. *Transportation:* A community's accessibility to people and goods depends on available air, rail, and highway systems and navigable waterways.

Buyers of single-family homes must consider the relative benefits of buying (1) a used home, (2) a ready-built new home or (3) a new home built to specification. A custom-built home may satisfy strong desires to plan for and create one's own lifestyle but may ultimately be too expensive for most buyers. In addition, the buyer may not be able to recoup the added costs for special features when the property is resold.

The feelings and preferences of buyers always influence the marketability of a particular property. No buyer can estimate exactly what specific characteristics will influence his or her ability to sell a parcel of real estate in the future. However, the more standard features with demonstrated general appeal a well-located property has, the more likely it is to retain its value and marketability.

Investment Considerations

The purchase of a home offers financial advantages to a buyer. The monthly mortgage payments a homeowner makes represent an **investment**; that is, the purchase of an asset that has the potential for profit. The profit may be in the form of present income received, or it may be a long-term gain due to increased value (**appreciation**) when the asset is sold. In the case of a residence, as mortgage debt is reduced, the owner's equity in the property increases. **Equity** represents the financial interest an owner has in real estate in excess of the amount outstanding on any mortgage loan. At any time, equity is equal to market value less debt balance. The owner hopes to establish financial security for the future by investing and building up equity in a residence that should also appreciate. In addition, as you will see in the following section, homeowners enjoy substantial tax advantages not available to renters.

Tax Benefits for Homeowners

To encourage home ownership, the federal government allows homeowners certain income-tax advantages. Even though the Tax Reform Act of 1986 (TRA) greatly restricted or eliminated tax deductions in other areas, benefits for homeowners were kept largely intact. For example, a homeowner may deduct from income—for tax purposes—the cost of mortgage interest (with a limitation we will discuss), real estate taxes and certain other expenses. A homeowner may even defer or eliminate tax liability on the profit received from the sale of a home. (See the illustration of these benefits in table 4.1.)

Tax-Deductible Interest Payments

Homeowners may deduct from their taxable income:

1. mortgage interest payments on first and second homes, subject to the limitation described below;
2. real property taxes (but *not* interest paid on overdue taxes);
3. certain loan origination fees; and
4. mortgage prepayment penalties.

Interest is deductible only on a loan secured by a first or second home in an amount no greater than the original purchase price of the property plus any improvements made to it, *unless* the funds borrowed against the real property are used for property improvements or for qualified medical or educational purposes. The funds borrowed may never exceed the fair market value of the home. This provision is effective for loans funded as of August 17, 1986.

Capital Gains

Capital gains are the profits realized from the sale or exchange of property. Before TRA, when property was held for a minimum of six months before a sale or exchange, profits were treated as long-term capital gains and only 40 percent of the gain was taxed. Short-term capital gains on property held less than six months were taxed at the regular rates.

The Tax Reform Act eliminated the favorable treatment for long-term capital gains. Such profits are now taxed as ordinary income; that is, the entire profit is included in the taxpayer's ordinary income to be taxed at the regular rate. Since the tax rates were decreased by TRA, however, the taxpayer reporting short-term capital gains has benefited.

Table 4.1 Homeowners' Tax Benefits	**Income Tax Deductions**	**Age 55 or Older**
	Mortgage interest on first and second homes, subject to limitation Mortgage origination fees Mortgage prepayment penalties Real estate taxes	Once in lifetime, homeowner may exclude up to $125,000 of profit on sale of home owned and used as principal residence for at least three years during last five year before sale
	Deferment of Tax on Profit	
	Tax on some or all of profit on sale postponed if another residence is purchased within 24 months before or after sale	

Deferment of tax on capital gain. All or part of the gain (profit) on the sale of a personal residence is exempt from immediate taxation if a new residence is bought and occupied within 24 months before or 24 months after the sale of the old residence. In this situation, the capital gains tax is not avoided but rather is *deferred* until the property is later sold in a taxable transaction (such as when another home is not purchased).

If the new home is of value equal to or greater than that of the house sold, the entire gain may be deferred.

55 or older exclusion. Taxpayers aged 55 or older are entitled to a one-time exclusion from taxation of up to $125,000 of profit from the sale or exchange of property used as the taxpayer's principal residence for at least three of the last five years preceding the sale or exchange.

Each homeowner may elect to exclude gains from taxation under the "over 55" provision *only once in a lifetime*, even if the total gain excluded is less than the $125,000 limit. When this exclusion is taken by a married couple selling a home, the tax laws hold that *both parties* have given up their once-in-a-lifetime exemption. Thus, if the over-55 exclusion is taken by a married couple and they subsequently divorce, neither one would be able to claim the exclusion in the future. Similarly, if the exclusion is taken by a married couple and one spouse dies, the survivor would not be able to claim the exclusion, even if he or she were to marry a person who has not claimed the exclusion.

In Practice...

You should consult the Internal Revenue Service, a certified public accountant or a tax lawyer for further information on and precise applications of these and other income-tax issues. IRS regulations are subject to frequent revision and official interpretation. Never attempt to counsel clients and customers on tax issues, except in broad, general terms. *Always refer such parties to the aforementioned authorities for specific, accurate information and advice.*

Homeowners' Insurance

Because home ownership represents a large financial investment for most purchasers, homeowners usually protect their investment by taking out insurance on the property. Although it is possible for a homeowner to obtain individual policies for each type of risk, most residential property owners take out insurance in the form of a packaged **homeowner's insurance policy**. These policies insure holders against the destruction of their property by fire or windstorm, injury to others if it occurs on the property and theft from the premises of any personal property that is owned by the insured or members of the insured's family.

The package homeowner's policy also includes **liability coverage** for: (1) personal injuries to others resulting from the insured's acts or negligence, (2) voluntary medical payments and funeral expenses for accidents sustained by guests or resident employees on the property of the owner and (3) physical damage to the property of others caused by the insured. Voluntary medical payments will cover injuries to a resident employee but will not cover benefits due under any workers' compensation or occupational disease law.

Characteristics of Homeowners' Packages

Although coverage provided may vary among policies, all homeowners' policies have three common characteristics: fixed ratios of coverage, an indivisible premium, and first- and third-party insurance. With *fixed ratios of coverage*, each type of coverage in a homeowner's policy must be maintained at a certain level. The amount of coverage on household contents and other items must be a fixed percentage of the amount of insurance on the building itself. While the amount of contents coverage may be increased, it cannot be reduced below the standard percentage. In addition, theft coverage may be contingent on the full amount of the contents coverage.

An *indivisible premium* combines the rates for covering each peril into a single amount. For the single rate, the insured receives coverage for all the perils included in the policy (see the lists that follow). The insured may not pick and choose the perils to be included.

First- and third-party insurance is the liability coverage previously discussed. It not only provides coverage for damage or loss to the insured's property or its contents, but also covers the insured's legal liability for losses or damages to another's property as well as injuries suffered by another party while on the owner's property.

There are four major forms of homeowners' policies. The basic form provides property coverage against the following perils:

1. fire or lightning
2. glass breakage
3. windstorm or hail
4. explosion
5. riot or civil commotion
6. damage by aircraft
7. damage from vehicles
8. damage from smoke
9. vandalism and malicious mischief
10. theft
11. loss of property removed from the premises when endangered by fire or other perils

Increased coverage is provided under a broad-form policy which covers the following additional perils:

12. falling objects
13. weight of ice, snow or sleet
14. collapse of the building or any part of it
15. bursting, cracking, burning or bulging of a steam or hot water heating system, or of appliances used to heat water
16. accidental discharge, leakage or overflow of water or steam from within a plumbing, heating or air-conditioning system
17. freezing of plumbing, heating and air-conditioning systems and domestic appliances
18. injury to electrical appliances, devices, fixtures, and wiring from short circuits or other accidentally generated currents

Further coverage is made possible by use of policies that cover almost all possible perils.

Other policies include a broad-form policy designed specifically for apartment renters and a broad-form policy for condominium owners. Apartment and condominium policies generally provide fire and windstorm, theft and public liability coverage for injuries or losses sustained within the unit, but do not usually extend to cover losses or damages to the structure. The structure is insured by either the landlord or the condominium owners' association (except, in condominium ownership, for additions or alterations made by the unit owner, and not covered by the association's master policy).

Claims

Most homeowners' insurance policies contain a **coinsurance clause**. This provision usually requires the insured to maintain insurance on the property in an amount equal to at least 80 percent of the **replacement cost** of the dwelling (not including the price of the land). If the owner carries such a policy, a claim may be made for the cost of the repair or replacement of the damaged property without deduction for depreciation.

For example, a homeowner's dwelling has a replacement cost of $100,000 and is damaged by fire. The estimated cost to repair the damaged portion of the dwelling is $71,000.

Replacement cost of dwelling	$100,000
	$\times$ 80%
Minimum coverage required on the dwelling	$ 80,000

Thus, if the homeowner carries at least $80,000 insurance on his or her dwelling, then the claim against the insurance company can be for the full $71,000.

If the homeowner carries coverage of less than 80 percent of the full replacement cost of the dwelling, the loss will be either settled for the **actual cash value** (replacement cost less depreciation) or prorated by dividing the percentage of replacement cost actually covered by the policy by the minimum coverage requirement (usually 80 percent). For example, if the building is insured for only 60 percent of its value and there is a $71,000 loss, the insurance company will pay only $53,250 (60% ÷ 80%, or 75%, of $71,000 = $53,250).

In any event, *the total settlement cannot exceed the face value of the policy.* Because of coinsurance clauses, it is important for homeowners to periodically review all policies to be certain that the coverage is equal to at least 80 percent of the current replacement cost of their homes.

Most insurance policies will have an **apportionment clause**. Such a clause provides that, if the insured is covered by more than one policy, the total amount paid will be apportioned according to the amounts of coverage provided. The insured thus will not collect more than the value of the loss. For example, suppose that a building insured by Company A for $320,000 and Company B for $400,000 is damaged by fire and a $160,000 loss is incurred. Company A will be liable for $70,400 (44 percent of the loss) and Company B will be liable for $89,600 (56 percent of the loss).

Most policies will also have a **subrogation clause** providing that if the insured collects for damage from the insurance company, any rights the insured may have to sue the person who caused the damage will be assigned to the insurance company. A subrogation clause allows the insurer to pursue legal action to collect the amount paid out from the party at fault and prevents the insured from collecting twice for the same damage.

Federal Flood Insurance Program

The National Flood Insurance Act of 1968 was authorized by Congress to help owners of property located in flood-prone areas by subsidizing flood insurance. As of 1975, such property owners must obtain flood damage insurance on properties financed by mortgages or other loans, grants or guarantees obtained from federal agencies and federally insured or regulated lending institutions. The program also seeks to improve future management for flood-plain areas through land-use and control measures.

The Department of Housing and Urban Development (HUD), which administers the flood program, has maps prepared by the Army Corps of Engineers that identify specific flood-prone areas throughout the country. Property owners in the designated areas who do not obtain flood insurance (either because they don't want it or because they don't qualify as a result of their communities' not having properly entered the program) are unable to obtain federal and federally related financial assistance.

In designated areas, flood insurance coverage is required on all types of buildings—residential, commercial, industrial and agricultural—for either the value of the property or the amount of the mortgage loan, subject to the maximum limits available. Policies are written annually and can be purchased from any licensed property insurance broker, the National Flood Insurance Program or the designated servicing companies in each state.

For other, less dangerous areas, flood insurance may or may not be required, at the lender's option.

Summary

One of the main goals of most Americans is the ownership of a home.

In addition to single-family homes, current trends in *home ownership* include apartment complexes, condominiums, cooperatives, planned unit developments, retirement communities, single-person developments, high-rise developments, converted-use properties, modular homes, mobile homes and time-shared occupancy of vacation homes.

In considering the purchase of a home, a prospective buyer should be aware of both the advantages and disadvantages of home ownership. While a homeowner gains financial security and pride of ownership, the costs of ownership—both the initial price and the continuing expenses—must be considered. When purchasing a home, a prospective buyer should note its specific characteristics and evaluate the desirability of the community (and neighborhood) based on the standards of its cultural activities, employment opportunities, recreational and social facilities and transportation.

One of the *income-tax benefits* available to homeowners allows them to deduct mortgage interest payments (with certain limitations) and property taxes from their federal income tax returns. Income tax on the gain from a sale may be deferred if the homeowner purchases and occupies another residence within 24 months before or after the sale. Homeowners aged 55 or older are given additional benefits.

To protect their investment in real estate, most homeowners purchase insurance. A standard *homeowner's insurance policy* covers fire, theft and liability and can be extended to cover many types of less common risks. Another type of insurance, which covers personal property only, is available to people who live in apartments and condominiums.

If a homeowner carries insurance issued by more than one company, any benefits paid out will be prorated according to the insured amount under each policy.

A subrogation clause enables an insurer to sue the party responsible for damage to the insured's property.

In addition to homeowner's insurance, the federal government makes flood insurance mandatory for people who, living in flood-prone areas, wish to obtain federally regulated or federally insured mortgage loans.

Many homeowners' policies contain a *coinsurance clause* that requires the policyholder to maintain insurance in an amount equal to 80 percent of the replacement cost of the home. If this percentage is not met, the policyholder may not be reimbursed for the full repair costs if a loss occurs.

Questions

1. The real cost of owning a home includes certain costs or expenses that many people tend to overlook. Which one of the following is *not* a cost or expense of owning a home?
   a. interest paid on borrowed capital
   b. homeowner's insurance
   c. maintenance and repairs
   d. taxes on personal property

2. Federal income tax laws allow for:
   I. a tax on one-half of the capital gains realized from the sale of a residence.
   II. the deduction from a homeowner's taxable income of all home mortgage interest paid.
   a. I only
   b. II only
   c. both I and II
   d. neither I nor II

3. When a person buys a house using a mortgage loan, the difference between the amount owed on the property and its market value represents the homeowner's:
   a. tax basis.
   b. equity.
   c. replacement cost.
   d. capital gain.

4. When a homebuyer chooses a location in which to live, he or she is likely to be influenced by the area's:
   a. transportation facilities.
   b. employment opportunities.
   c. social services.
   d. all of the above

5. A typical homeowner's insurance policy covers:
   a. the cost of medical expenses for a person injured in the policyholder's home.
   b. theft.
   c. vandalism.
   d. all of the above

6. A building that is remodeled into residential units and is no longer used for the purpose for which it was originally built would be a(n):
   a. converted-use property.
   b. example of urban homesteading.
   c. planned unit development.
   d. modular home.

7. Which of the following would be likely to affect a person's decision to purchase a home?
   I. current interest rates
   II. investment considerations
   a. I only
   b. II only
   c. both I and II
   d. neither I nor II

8. Which of the following factors should a person consider when purchasing a home as a long-term investment?
   I. affordability
   II. the future marketability of the real estate
   a. I only
   b. II only
   c. both I and II
   d. neither I nor II

9. In a homeowner's insurance policy, *coinsurance* refers to:
   a. the specific form of policy purchased by the owner.
   b. the stipulation that the homeowner must purchase insurance coverage equal to at least 80 percent of the replacement cost of the structure in order to be able to collect the full insured amount in the event of a loss.
   c. the stipulation that the homeowner must purchase fire insurance coverage equal to at least 70 percent of the replacement cost of the structure in order to be able to collect the full insured amount in the event of a loss.
   d. a and b

10. Federal flood insurance:
    I. is required in certain areas to insure
       properties financed by federally related
       mortgage loans against flood damage.
    II. is a common part of a homeowner's
        insurance policy.

    a. I only   c. both I and II
    b. II only   d. neither I nor II

11. Federal income tax laws do *not* allow a
    homeowner to deduct which of the following
    expenses from his or her taxable income?

    a. mortgage origination fees
    b. real estate taxes
    c. all home improvements
    d. mortgage prepayment penalties

12. Under the provisions for liability coverage in
    a homeowner's insurance policy, the
    insurance company may settle a claim for:

    a. physical damage to the insured's
       property.
    b. funeral expenses for the insured's child.
    c. personal injury to a delivery person who
       is injured on the insured's property.
    d. a and c

13. A townhouse may be associated with which
    of the following types of housing?

    a. high-rise development
    b. condominium
    c. mobile home
    d. ranch house

14. Traditionally, mortgage lenders will not
    make a loan if the monthly payment will
    exceed what percentage of a borrower's
    monthly pre-tax income?

    a. 25 percent
    b. 20 percent
    c. 15 percent
    d. none of the above

15. A homeowner's equity in the home is:

    a. market price less purchase price.
    b. market value less debt balance.
    c. both a and b
    d. neither a nor b

16. The profit a homeowner receives from the
    sale of the homeowner's principal residence:

    I. is the homeowner's tax basis.
    II. is not subject to federal income taxes.

    a. I only   c. both I and II
    b. II only   d. neither I nor II

17. A residence is sold for $127,500. Selling
    expenses were $750; the house had been
    purchased new three years earlier for
    $75,000. What is the seller's profit on this
    transaction?

    a. $53,250   c. $51,750
    b. $52,500   d. $75,000

18. In question 17, how much of the profit will
    ordinarily be subject to income tax?

    a. all of it   c. $21,300
    b. $20,700   d. $21,000

19. Brendon Wilson, age 38, sells his home of
    eight years and realizes a $25,000 gain from
    the sale. Income tax on the profit from the
    sale of his home may be:

    a. eliminated by claiming a
       once-in-a-lifetime exclusion.
    b. deferred by purchasing another home of
       equal or greater value.
    c. reduced by the amount of mortgage
       interest paid over the life of the
       property's ownership.
    d. a or b

20. Frieda Wilson, age 62, sells the home she
    has occupied for the last 15 years and
    realizes a $52,000 gain from the sale.
    Income tax on the profit from the sale of
    her home may be:

    a. eliminated by claiming a
       once-in-a-lifetime exclusion.
    b. deferred by purchasing another home of
       equal or greater value.
    c. reduced by the amount of mortgage
       interest paid over the life of the
       property's ownership.
    d. a or b

Part Two

Principles

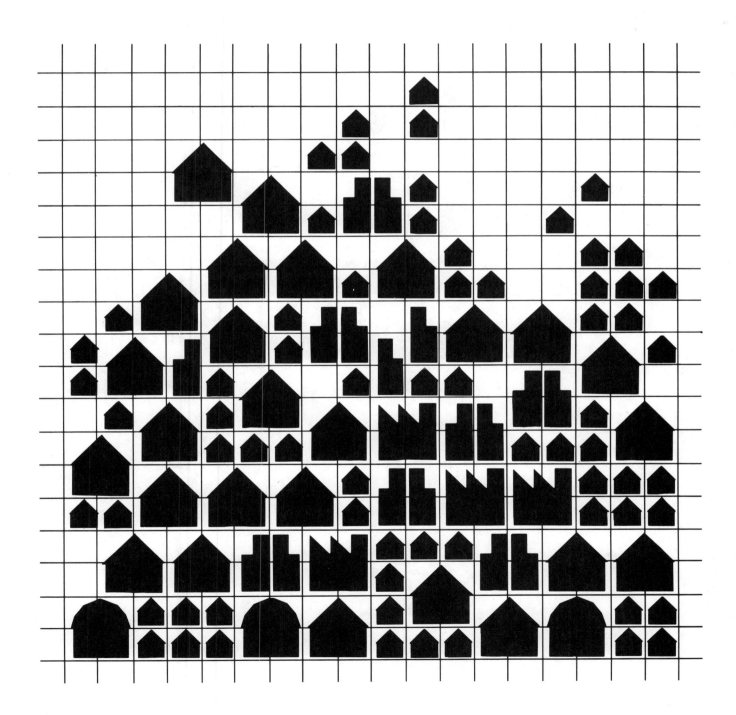

5

Real Estate Brokerage

Key Terms

Agency coupled with an interest
Agent
Antitrust laws
Broker
COALD
Commission
Dual agency
Employee
Estoppel
Express agreement
Fiduciary
Finder's agreement
Fraud

General agent
Implied agreement
Independent contractor
Law of agency
Listing agreement
Principal
Procuring cause of sale
Puffing
Ratification
Ready, willing and able buyer
Salesperson
Special agent

Overview

The term *broker* can be traced back several centuries to the Norman French word *brocour*, literally meaning "wine dealer." At that time the local pub was a village's central meeting place, and it was common practice for a customer to tell the wine dealer if there was something that person wanted to buy or sell. The wine dealer would then pass the word on to other customers; if a sale was made, the *brocour* would receive a fee for his or her services. Although this is the essence of brokerage, *real estate brokerage* today is a much more complex operation involving strictly defined legal relationships with buyers and sellers. This chapter will discuss these legal relationships and will also examine the nature of the real estate brokerage business itself.

Agency Defined	An **agent** is a person who represents the interests of someone called a **principal** in dealings with third persons. The relationship of agent and principal is called an **agency**. An agent may be authorized by the principal to use the assistance of others in carrying out the purpose of the agency. Those persons would act as **subagents** of the principal.
Brokerage Defined	The business of bringing buyers and sellers together in the marketplace is *brokerage*. Buyers and sellers in many fields employ the services of brokers to facilitate complex business transactions. In the real estate business, a **broker** is defined as a person who is licensed to buy, sell, exchange or lease real property for others and to charge a fee for his or her services. A brokerage—the broker's business—may be established as a sole proprietorship, a corporation or a partnership with another broker. Working on behalf of and licensed to represent the broker is the real estate **salesperson.** The principal who employs the broker may be a seller, a prospective buyer, an owner who wishes to lease his or her property or a person seeking property to rent. The real estate broker acts as the agent of the principal, and the salesperson as the subagent of the principal. The principal usually compensates the broker with a commission. This commission is contingent upon the broker's successfully performing the service for which he or she was employed, which generally is negotiating a transaction with a prospective purchaser, seller, lessor or lessee who is ready, willing and able to complete the contract. A typical real estate listing contract will authorize the broker to use the assistance of salespeople employed by the broker, as well as the assistance of other **cooperating brokers.** Cooperating brokers act as subagents of the principal and they may, in turn, employ their own salespeople. As you will learn, the relationship of a salesperson to an employing broker is also an agency. The salesperson is thus the agent of the broker in addition to being the subagent of the person utilizing the broker's services. (In some states, a licensed broker may choose to work only for another broker, as an associate broker, and would have the same agency status to the client as a salesperson.)
Law of Agency	In the typical real estate transaction, the broker is hired by a seller to market his or her real estate. In this situation, the broker is an *agent* of the seller; the seller is the broker's *client*. Unless there has been another agreement, a buyer who contacts the broker in order to review properties listed with his or her firm is merely the broker's *customer*. Though obligated to deal fairly with all parties to a transaction, the broker is strictly accountable *only to the principal*—in this case, the seller. The role of a broker as the agent of the principal is a fiduciary relationship. A **fiduciary** is one who is placed in a position of trust and confidence and normally is responsible for the money and/or property of another. The body of law that governs the rights and duties of principal, agent and third persons is the **law of agency**.

Types of Agent   An agent is someone who is authorized by another to perform some activity for that person. The authorized activity will be as simple or complex as the principal allows. An agent may be classified as a general agent or special agent, based upon his or her authority.

A **general agent** is empowered to represent the principal in a *range of matters*. The general agent may bind the principal to any contracts within the scope of his or her authority. This type of agency is also created by a *general power of attorney*. A power of attorney makes the agent an *attorney-in-fact*, as opposed to someone licensed to practice as an *attorney-at-law*.

A **special agent** is authorized to represent his or her principal in *one specific transaction or business activity only*. A real estate broker is generally a special agent, hired by a seller to find a ready, willing and able buyer for the seller's property. A *special power of attorney* is another means of authorizing an agent to carry out only a specified act or acts.

Creation of Agency   An agency relationship is created by an oral or written agreement of the parties. The real estate broker-seller relationship normally is created by an employment contract, commonly referred to as a **listing agreement.**

Principal and agent may make an **express agreement**. Although a written listing agreement is usually preferred, it is not necessary in all states. Some states construe an oral agreement as binding.

An agency may also be created by **implied agreement**. This occurs when principal and agent, without formally agreeing to the agency, act as if one existed.

If there is no agreement, but someone claims to be an agent, the "principal" can establish an agency by **ratification** of the conduct of the "agent." The ratification can be by any act that accepts the conduct of the agent acting in that capacity.

An agency relationship may be created by **estoppel** if someone states incorrectly that another person is his or her agent. If a third person relies on that representation in dealing with the "agent," the "principal" cannot later deny the existence of an agency.

By use of a *multiple listing agreement*, a principal can authorize the use, by the broker, of the members of the broker's multiple listing service. This and other provisions of listing agreements will be discussed in greater detail in Chapter 6.

Termination of Agency   An agency between a principal and an agent may be terminated at any time, except in the case of an agency coupled with an interest. An agency may be terminated for any of the following reasons:

1. Death or incapacity of either party (notice of death is not necessary).
2. Destruction or condemnation of the property by eminent domain.
3. Expiration of the terms of the agency.
4. Mutual agreement to terminate the agency.
5. Breach by one of the parties, such as abandonment by the agent or revocation by the principal. (The breaching party might be liable for damages.)

6. By operation of law, as in a bankruptcy of the principal (since title to the property would be transferred to a court-appointed receiver).
7. Completion or fulfillment of the purpose for which the agency was created.

An **agency coupled with an interest** is an agency relationship in which the agent is given an interest in the subject of the agency (such as the property being sold). Such an agency *cannot be revoked by the principal, nor can it be terminated upon the principal's death*. For example, a broker might supply the financing for a condominium development, provided the developer agrees to give the broker the exclusive right to sell the completed condo units. Since this is an agency coupled with an interest, the developer would not be able to revoke the listing agreement after the broker provided the financing.

Buyer as Principal

Generally, a real estate broker is hired by a seller to locate a buyer for the seller's real property. In some cases, however, a broker may be hired by a potential buyer to find that person a parcel of real estate that possesses certain characteristics or is usable for specific purposes. A prospective purchaser seeking commercial or industrial property is particularly likely to hire a broker for this reason. In this situation, the broker and the buyer will usually draw up an agreement commonly referred to as a **finder's agreement**, or *buyer agency agreement*. This document sets forth in detail the nature of the property desired and the amount of the broker's compensation. Note that regardless of whether an employment agreement between the broker and principal is a contract to sell or a contract to acquire property, it usually authorizes the broker to act for the principal but does not carry with it a guarantee that the broker will be able to perform. As an agent of the principal, however, the broker is obligated to make a reasonable effort to carry out the assumed agency duties successfully.

Agent's Responsibilities to Principal

The broker, as an agent, owes the principal certain duties. These duties are clear and specific. They are not simply moral or ethical; they are the law—the *law of agency*. An agent has a *fiduciary relationship* to the principal; a relationship of trust and confidence. This confidential relationship carries with it certain duties that the broker must perform—the duties of **care, obedience, accounting, loyalty** and **disclosure**, easily remembered by the acronym **COALD** (see figure 5.1).

**Figure 5.1
Agent's
Responsibilities**

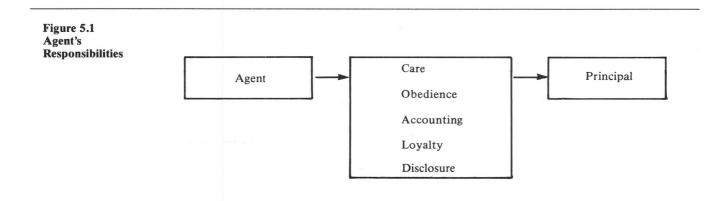

| Agent | → | Care

Obedience

Accounting

Loyalty

Disclosure | → | Principal |

Care. The broker, as an agent, must exercise a reasonable degree of care and skill while transacting the business entrusted of the principal. Remember, the broker is liable to the principal for any loss resulting from negligence or carelessness.

Obedience. The broker is at all times obligated to act in good faith and in conformity with the principal's instructions and authority. Again, a broker is liable for any losses incurred by the principal due to any acts the broker performs that are not within the broker's authority. The broker is not, however, required to obey unlawful or unethical instructions. The broker may disobey a principal or perform unauthorized acts in an emergency, as long as the broker's actions are in the principal's best interests.

Accounting. The broker must be able to report the status of all funds received from, or on behalf of, the principal. Most state real estate license laws require brokers to give accurate copies of all documents to all parties affected by them and to keep copies of such documents on file for a specified period of time. In addition, the license laws generally require the broker to deposit immediately, or within 24 to 48 hours, all funds entrusted to him or her in a special trust, or escrow, account. It is illegal for the broker to *commingle* such monies with personal funds.

Loyalty. Loyalty is a must—the broker owes the principal 100 percent, the utmost in loyalty. An agent must always place the principal's interests above those of the other persons with whom the agent deals. Thus, an agent cannot disclose such information as the principal's financial condition, the fact that the principal (if the seller) will accept a price lower than the listing price for the offered real estate or any similar confidential facts that might harm the principal's bargaining position.

The duty of loyalty also requires the agent to act without self-interest, unless with the principal's knowledge and consent. All states forbid brokers or salespeople to buy property listed with them for their own accounts, or for accounts in which they have a personal interest, without first notifying the principal of such interest and receiving the principal's consent. Likewise, by law neither brokers nor salespeople may sell property in which they have a personal interest without informing the purchaser of that interest.

Disclosure. Along with these four responsibilities goes the duty of disclosure. It is the broker's duty to keep the principal fully informed at all times of all facts or information the broker obtains that could affect the transaction. In certain instances, the broker may be held liable for damages for failure to disclose such information.

The duty of disclosure goes further than information that is brought to the broker's attention. The real estate agent may also be liable for facts he or she *should have known and revealed to the principal*, but did not. This *duty of discovery* includes facts favorable or unfavorable to the principal's position, even if the disclosure of those facts would "kill the deal." For instance, when a potential buyer offers other property as part of the purchase price, it is the broker's responsibility to verify the appraised value of that property to protect the seller's interests during negotiations.

Agent's Responsibilities to Third Parties

Even though an agent's primary responsibility is to the principal, the agent also has duties to the third parties with whom he or she deals. The duties of agent to buyer include:

1. reasonable care and skill in performance of the agent's duties;
2. honest and fair dealing;
3. disclosure of all facts known to the agent that materially affects the value or desirability of the property and that are not known to the buyer.

The old doctrine of *caveat emptor* ("let the buyer beware") has no place in the modern real estate transaction. The duty of disclosure has been expanded by the courts and legislature of at least one state (California) to include not only facts of which the broker is aware, but facts of which the broker, by a reasonably diligent property inspection, *should* have been aware. In other words, the broker could be liable for damages to a buyer if there is a property defect that the broker could have discovered and revealed to the buyer, but did not.

In dealing with a buyer, a broker, as an agent of the seller, must exercise extreme caution and be aware of the laws and ethical considerations that affect this relationship. For example, brokers must be careful about the statements they or their staff members make about a parcel of real estate. Statements of opinion are permissible as long as they are offered as opinions and without any intention to deceive.

Statements of fact, however, must be accurate. Statements that exaggerate a property's benefits are called **puffing.** Brokers and salespeople must be alert to ensure that none of their statements can in any way be interpreted as involving **fraud.** Fraud is the *intentional* misrepresentation of a material fact in such a way as to harm or take advantage of another person. In addition to false statements about a property, the concept of fraud covers intentional concealment or nondisclosure of important facts. If a contract to purchase real estate is obtained as a result of fraudulent misstatements made by a broker or by that broker's salespeople, the contract may be disaffirmed or renounced by the purchaser. In such a case, the broker will lose a commission. If either party suffers loss because of a broker's misrepresentations, the broker can be held liable for damages. If the broker's misstatements are based upon the owner's own inaccurate statements to the broker, however, and the broker had no independent duty to investigate their accuracy, the broker may be entitled to a commission even if the buyer rescinds the sales contract.

A seller is also responsible for revealing to a buyer any hidden, or latent, defects in a building. *A latent defect is one that is known to the seller but not to the buyer and that is not discoverable by ordinary inspection.* Buyers have been able to either rescind the sales contract or receive damages when such defects had not been revealed. Examples of such circumstances are cases in which a house was built over a ditch that was covered with decaying timber, a buried drain tile caused water to accumulate or a driveway was built partly on adjoining property. Cases in which the seller neglected to reveal violations of zoning or building codes have also been decided in favor of the buyer.

In Practice...

Because real estate licensees have, under the law, enormous exposure to liability, some brokers purchase what is known as errors and omissions insurance *policies for their firms. Operating similarly to malpractice insurance in the medical field, such policies generally cover liabilities for errors, mistakes and negligence in the usual listing and selling activities of a real estate office or escrow company.*

Dual Agency

In dealing with buyers, the broker must be careful of any situation that might be considered a **dual agency.** Sometimes a broker may have the opportunity to receive compensation from both the buyer and seller in a transaction. Theoretically, however, an agent cannot be loyal to two or more distinct principals in the same transaction. Thus, state real estate license laws generally prohibit a broker from representing and collecting compensation from both parties to a transaction without their prior mutual knowledge and consent. Note, however, that although the courts tend to accept this *informed consent exception,* many indicate a reluctance to permit brokers to act as dual agents. In fact, some courts reject the consent exception altogether because of public policy considerations. Many brokers today believe in what is known as the *single agency* concept, which strictly holds that a broker can effectively be a principal to only one party at a time in a given transaction.

In Practice. . .

Before entering into a listing agreement, a licensee should fully explain to a seller/ principal the nature of the agency relationship and the provisions of the document that creates it. Also, to avoid potential problems arising from misunderstanding under the usual agency arrangement, in which the seller is principal, a licensee should inform each buyer/customer that he or she represents the seller and owes the seller 100-percent loyalty. However, giving this information does not relieve the licensee from dealing fairly and honestly with the buyer/customer.

Broker's Compensation

The broker's compensation is specified in the listing agreement, management agreement or other contract with the principal. Compensation is usually in the form of a **commission** or brokerage fee computed as a *percentage of the total amount of money involved.* Such commission is usually considered to be earned when the broker has accomplished the work for which he or she was hired; it is due at the closing of the sale or other transaction. Most sales commissions are payable when the sale is consummated by *delivery of the seller's deed,* and this provision is customarily included in the listing agreement or in the real estate sales contract.

In order to be entitled to a sales commission, a selling agent must be a licensed real estate broker, employed by the seller to make the sale, and the procuring cause of the sale. In order to be considered the **procuring cause of sale,** the broker must have taken action to start or cause a chain of events that resulted in the sale. A broker who causes or completes such action without a contract or promise to be paid is termed a *volunteer* and has no legal claim for compensation. The state license law may require a written listing agreement in order for the broker to have a legally enforceable claim for a commission.

Once a seller accepts an offer from a ready, willing and able buyer, the seller is technically liable for the broker's commission. A **ready, willing and able buyer** is one who is *prepared to buy on the seller's terms and ready to take positive steps toward consummation of the transaction.*

A broker who has produced a buyer who is ready, willing and able to meet the listing terms may still be entitled to a commission even if the transaction is *not* consummated. Some reasons why a transaction might not be completed are:

- The owner has a change of mind and refuses to sell.
- The owner's spouse refuses to sign the deed.
- There are defects in the owner's title that are not corrected.
- The owner commits fraud with respect to the transaction.
- The owner is unable to deliver possession within a reasonable time.
- The owner insists on terms not in the listing (for example, the right to restrict the use of the property).
- The owner and the buyer mutually agree to cancel the transaction.

In other words, *a broker is generally due a commission if a sale is not consummated because of the principal's default.*

The rate of a broker's commission is *negotiable in every case.* For members of the profession to attempt, however subtly, to impose uniform commission rates would be a clear violation of state and federal antitrust laws (which will be discussed later in this chapter). Yet, a broker is free to set the minimum rate that is acceptable. The important point is for broker and client to agree on a rate before the agency relationship is established. If no amount or percentage rate of commission is stated in the listing contract, and a legal action results, the court may determine a reasonable amount of commission by evidence of the custom in a particular community.

Most (but not all) license laws make it illegal for a broker to share a commission with someone who is not licensed as a salesperson or broker. This has been construed to include the giving of certain items of personal property (for instance, a broker giving a new TV to "a friend" for providing a valuable lead) and other premiums (vacations and the like) as well as finder's fees and portions of the commission.

Salesperson's Compensation

The compensation of a salesperson is set by mutual agreement between the broker and the salesperson. The broker may agree to pay the salesperson a salary or a share of the commissions from transactions originated by the salesperson. A salesperson may have a drawing account against his or her earned share of commissions. Some brokers require salespeople to pay all or part of the expenses of advertising listed properties.

A recent innovation in salespeople's compensation is the *100-percent commission plan.* In a brokerage firm where this system has been adopted, all salespeople who achieve a predetermined sales quota pay a monthly service charge to the broker (to cover the costs of office space, telephones and supervision) and receive 100 percent of the commissions from the sales they negotiate.

However the salesperson's compensation is structured, it may come only from the employing broker. The salesperson cannot receive any fee or other compensation initiating from a seller, a buyer or outside broker unless the employing broker first agrees in writing to the payment.

Legal Rights and Obligations

Every real estate transaction involves legal rights. As each contract is prepared for signature, the broker should advise the parties of the desirability of securing legal counsel to protect their interests.

During the last several years, discussions (and, in some cases, court suits) have arisen between bar associations and real estate boards. These discussions are concerned with the protection of the legal rights and obligations of the parties to a real estate transaction.

While real estate brokers and salespeople do bring buyers and sellers together, they cannot offer legal advice—only an attorney may do this. This matter has been brought before the supreme courts of some states. These courts uniformly recognize that a real estate broker must have the authority to secure some form of agreement between a buyer and seller, evidencing the transaction and providing for payment of the broker's commission.

In many states a special form of sales contract that must be used by real estate brokers has been approved by the bar associations and real estate boards. A broker has no authority in these states to use any other form of contract, and in some instances, if a broker were to use another form his or her license could be revoked. Other states have not adopted a specific form of contract. It is your responsibility to ascertain the rules in effect in your state by checking with your local real estate commission or board of REALTORS®.

Antitrust Laws

The real estate industry is subject to federal and state **antitrust laws.** Generally, these laws prohibit monopolies and contracts, combinations and conspiracies that unreasonably restrain trade. The most common antitrust violations that can occur in the real estate business are price fixing and allocation of customers or markets.

Illegal *price fixing* occurs when brokers conspire to set prices (sales commissions, management rates) for the services they perform rather than let those prices be established through competition in the open market.

Allocation of customers or markets involves an agreement between brokers to divide their markets and refrain from competing for each other's business. Allocations may take place on a geographic basis, with brokers agreeing to specific territories within which they will operate exclusively. The division may also take place along other lines; for example, two brokers may agree that one will handle only residential properties under $100,000 in value, while another will handle residential properties over $100,000 in value.

The penalties for such acts are severe. For example, under the Sherman Antitrust Act people who fix prices or allocate markets may be found guilty of a felony punishable by a maximum $100,000 fine and three years in prison. For corporations, the penalty may be as high as $1 million. In a civil suit, a person who has suffered a loss because of the antitrust activities of a guilty party may recover triple the value of the actual damages plus attorney's fees and costs.

Nature of the Brokerage Business

Whether affiliated with any national franchise or marketing organization or not, a real estate broker is an independent businessperson who sets the policies of his or her own office. A broker engages employees and salespeople, determines their compensation and directs their activities. A broker is free to accept or reject agency relationships with principals. This is an important characteristic of the brokerage business: *A broker has the right to reject agency contracts that in the broker's judgment violate the ethics or high standards of the office.* However, once a brokerage relationship has been established, the broker represents a principal. The broker owes that person the duty to exercise care, skill and integrity in carrying out instructions.

Real Estate License Laws

Every state and Canadian province requires real estate brokers and salespeople to be licensed. Knowledge of your state's real estate broker's and salesperson's license law is essential to the understanding of brokers' and salespeople's legal authority and responsibilities. Basically, the license laws of the various states differ only in degree, but many contain unique provisions. License laws are discussed in Chapter 14. In that chapter, the terms *broker* and *salesperson* are covered in greater depth. General and educational requirements and the nature of the state license examinations are explained.

The state real estate license laws generally regulate many of the day-to-day business operations of a real estate brokerage. Such matters often include location of a definite, regular place of business for the firm, minimum size and exact placement of business signs, requirements for establishing and maintaining branch brokerage offices, proper accounting procedures, correct handling of client trust fund accounts and specified manner of execution and retention of documents involved in real estate transactions. Check your state law for specific regulations. The license law analysis form in Chapter 14 will help you organize your research.

Broker-Salesperson Relationship

A person licensed to perform real estate activities on behalf of a licensed real estate broker is known as a real estate salesperson. *A salesperson licensed under a broker is responsible only to that broker* and can carry out only those responsibilities assigned by that broker. The salesperson is the agent of the broker and the sub-agent of the seller.

A broker is licensed to act as the principal's agent and can thus collect a commission for performing the assigned duties. A salesperson, on the other hand, has no authority to make contracts or receive compensation directly from a principal. The broker who employs salespeople is fully responsible for their actions. *All of a salesperson's activities must be performed in the name of the supervising broker.*

Independent contractor vs. employee. The agreement between a broker and a salesperson should be set down in a written contract that defines the obligations and responsibilities of the relationship. State license laws generally treat the salesperson as the employee of the broker in defining legal responsibilities. The broker is thus liable for all acts performed by the salesperson within the "scope" of the salesperson's employment; that is, the real estate business. This is despite the fact that a salesperson may be hired and considered by a broker for tax purposes as either an employee or an independent contractor. Whether a salesperson is treated as an employee or an independent contractor will affect the structure of the salesperson's work responsibilities and the broker's liability to pay and withhold taxes from the salesperson's earnings (see figure 5.2).

Figure 5.2
Independent Contractor
VS. Employee

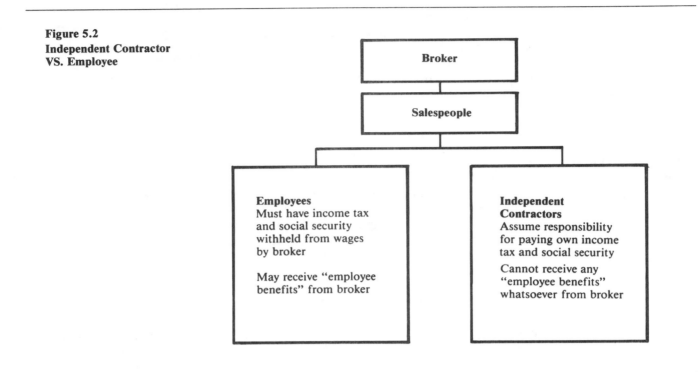

The nature of the employer-employee relationship allows a broker to exercise certain *controls* over salespeople who are employees. The broker may require an **employee** to adhere more strictly to regulations concerning such matters as working hours and office routine. As an employer, a broker is required by the federal government to withhold social security tax and income tax from wages paid to employees. The broker is also required to pay unemployment compensation tax on wages paid to one or more employees, as defined by state and federal laws. In addition, a broker may provide employees with such benefits as health insurance and profit-sharing plans.

A broker's relationship with an independent contractor is very different. As an **independent contractor** a salesperson operates more independently than an employee, and the broker may not control the salesperson's activities in the same way. Basically, the broker may control *what* the independent contractor will do but not *how* it will be done. An independent contractor assumes responsibility for paying his or her own income and social security taxes. An independent contractor receives from the broker nothing that could be construed as an employee benefit (such as health insurance).

In Practice...

The Internal Revenue Service often investigates the independent contractor/ employee situation in many brokers' offices. The best way to ensure either status officially is for a broker to have a clearly drawn employee or independent contractor agreement with each salesperson on the staff. The broker should have an attorney verify that such agreements are in effect and are being followed explicitly. Brokers' difficulties in this area seem to stem primarily from an overreliance on signed agreements; a signed agreement would mean little to an IRS auditor if the actions of the parties were contrary to the document's provisions.

Summary

Real estate brokerage is the bringing together, for a fee or commission, of people who wish to buy, sell, exchange or lease real estate. All states and Canadian provinces require that real estate brokers and salespeople be licensed.

An important part of real estate brokerage is the *law of agency*. A real estate broker is the *agent*, usually hired by the seller, but occasionally by a buyer, to sell or find a particular parcel of real estate. The person who hires the broker is the *principal*. The principal and the agent have a *fiduciary relationship*, under which the agent owes the principal the duties of care, obedience, accounting, loyalty and disclosure.

The broker's compensation in a real estate sale ordinarily takes the form of a *commission*, which usually is a percentage of the real estate's selling price. The broker is considered to have earned a commission when he or she procures a *ready, willing and able buyer* for a seller.

A broker may hire salespeople to assist in this work. The salesperson works on the broker's behalf as either an *employee* or an *independent contractor*.

Many of the general operations of a real estate brokerage are regulated by the real estate license laws. In addition, state and federal *antitrust laws* prohibit brokers from conspiring to fix prices or allocate customers or markets.

Questions

1. Under the law of agency, a real estate broker owes his or her principal the duty of:

    a. care.
    b. obedience.
    c. disclosure.
    d. all of the above

2. A real estate broker acting as the agent of the seller:

    a. is obligated to render faithful service to the seller.
    b. can make a profit if possible in addition to the commission.
    c. can agree to a change in price without the seller's approval.
    d. can accept a commission from the buyer without the seller's approval.

3. To establish a firm legal contract between a broker and seller, the broker should:

    I. get an oral listing agreement from the seller.
    II. file a suit in court.
       a. I only   c. both I and II
       b. II only   d. neither I nor II

4. A real estate broker may lose the right to a commission in a real estate transaction if he or she:

    a. did not advertise the property.
    b. was not licensed when hired as an agent.
    c. did not have a written agreement.
    d. b and c

5. The statement "in order to recover a commission for brokerage services, a broker must be employed" means that:

    a. the broker must work in a real estate office.
    b. the seller must have made an agreement to pay a commission to the broker for selling the property.
    c. the broker must have asked the seller the price of the property and then found a ready, willing and able buyer.
    d. the broker must have a salesperson employed in the office.

6. A real estate broker hired by an owner to sell a parcel of real estate must comply with:

    a. any instructions of the owner.
    b. the law of agency.
    c. the principle of *caveat emptor*.
    d. all of the above

7. As an employee of a real estate broker, a real estate salesperson has the authority to:

    a. act as an agent for a seller.
    b. assume responsibilities assigned by the broker.
    c. accept a commission from another broker.
    d. a and b

8. A broker is entitled to collect a commission from both the seller and the buyer:

    a. when the broker holds a state license.
    b. when the buyer and the seller are related.
    c. when both parties agree to such a transaction.
    d. when both parties have attorneys.

9. Mickie Michaels, a licensed broker, learns that his neighbor, Paul Cella, wishes to sell his house. Michaels knows the property well, and is able to persuade Barney Schultz to make an offer. Michaels then asks Cella if he can present an offer to him and Cella agrees. At this point:

    a. Cella is not obligated to pay Michaels a commission.
    b. Schultz is obligated to pay Michaels a commission for locating the property.
    c. Cella must pay Michaels a commission.
    d. b and c

10. In the fact situation described in question 9, Cella agreed to accept Schultz's offer and signed a contract that included a provision for a sales commission of 6 percent to be paid to Michaels from the sale proceeds at the time of closing. Which of the following is (are) true?

    a. Cella must pay Michaels a 6 percent commission.
    b. Schultz must pay Michaels a 6 percent commission.
    c. Cella is not obligated to pay Michaels a commission.
    d. a and b

11. A person who has the authority to enter into contracts concerning all business affairs of another is called a(n):

    a. general agent.
    b. secret agent.
    c. special agent.
    d. attorney.

12. The term *fiduciary* refers to:

    a. the sale of real property.
    b. principles by which a real estate seller must conduct his or her business.
    c. one who has legal power to act on behalf of another.
    d. the principal in a principal-agent relationship.

13. The legal relationship between broker and seller is generally a:

    a. special agency.
    b. general agency.
    c. secret agency.
    d. universal agency.

14. Broker Duncan Rivera lists Sam and Adele Kaufmann's house for $87,000. Adele has been transferred to another state and the couple must sell their house quickly. To expedite the sale, Rivera tells a prospective buyer that the couple will accept at least $5,000 less for the house. In this situation:

    I. Rivera has violated his agency responsibilities to the Kaufmanns.
    II. Rivera should not have disclosed this information to the prospective buyer, since it is not in the seller's best financial interests.

    a. I only   c. both I and II
    b. II only   d. neither I nor II

15. An agency relationship may be terminated by all but which of the following means?

    a. the owner decides not to sell the house
    b. the broker discovers that the market value of the property is such that he or she will not make an adequate commission
    c. the owner dies
    d. the broker secures a ready, willing and able buyer for the seller's property

16. A real estate broker who engages salespeople as independent contractors must:

    I. withhold income tax and social security from all commissions earned by them.
    II. require them to participate in office insurance plans if he or she requires other salespeople hired as employees to do so.

    a. I only   c. both I and II
    b. II only   d. neither I nor II

17. A broker may be hired as agent by which of the following?

    a. an owner of a large apartment building, to find suitable tenants and collect rents
    b. a seller of real estate, to find a buyer who is ready, willing and able to purchase the property
    c. a person looking for a three-flat apartment building at a certain price
    d. all of the above

18. Which of the following would be considered a violation of antitrust laws?

    a. Brokers representing the Tri-City, ABC and All-American Property Management Companies decide to de-escalate their current price war by charging more uniform rates.

    b. Salespeople Joe Jones and Emma Smith, working for two local firms, agree that Jones should accept listings only from the east side of town and Smith should accept listings only from the west side of town.

    c. a and b

    d. none of the above

19. A real estate broker:

    a. who makes deliberate misstatements about real property he or she is selling is committing fraud.

    b. generally enters into a finder's agreement with a seller to find a buyer.

    c. is usually the seller's general agent.

    d. a and c

20. Which of the following types of agencies may be created by a power of attorney?

    a. general agency

    b. special agency

    c. ostensible agency

    d. a and b

6

Listing Agreements

Key Terms
Automatic extension
Competitive market analysis
Exclusive-agency listing
Exclusive-right-to-sell listing
Listing agreement
Market value
Multiple listing service
Net listing
Open listing
Option listing
Special agency

Overview
A retailer may employ the best salespeople in the business, maintain the most attractive shop in town and spend thousands of dollars on public relations and advertising to further the company's image only to go out of business because he or she does not have an adequate supply of goods on hand to sell. Such is the case in the real estate business. Without a well-stocked inventory of listed property to sell, a broker or salesperson is no more than an office clerk without an income. The listing agreement that secures the broker's inventory can take many forms, each with its own rights and responsibilities for principal and agent. This chapter will examine these forms of listing agreements as well as some of the factors a broker or salesperson must consider when "taking a listing."

Listing Property	Every real estate sale involves two parties. The first is the seller. The second, of course, is the buyer. It is the seller who furnishes the real estate broker and salesperson with the necessary inventory—that is, the *listing*. How complete and accurately priced the inventory is will determine the broker's ultimate success.

To acquire their inventories, brokers and salespeople must obtain listings. As discussed in Chapter 5, a listing agreement creates a **special agency** relationship between a broker (agent) and a seller (principal), whereby the agent is authorized to represent the principal's property for sale, solicit offers and submit the offers to the principal. Listing agreements normally are written contracts of employment, although in many states oral agreements may be used under certain circumstances. Other states, however, provide that a broker cannot institute a court action to collect a commission unless he or she had a written listing agreement with the seller.

Under the provisions of the state real estate license laws, only a broker can act as agent to list, sell or rent another person's real estate. Throughout this chapter, unless otherwise stated, the terms *broker, agent* and *firm* are intended to include both the broker and a salesperson working under the broker. While both have the authority to list, lease and sell property and provide other services to a principal, state real estate license laws stipulate that these acts must be done in the name and under the supervision of the broker.

Listing Agreements

The forms of **listing agreements,** or employment contracts, generally used are: (1) open listing, (2) exclusive-agency listing and (3) exclusive-right-to-sell listing. Their similarities and differences are discussed below.

Open listing. In an **open listing** (also known in some areas as a *general listing*), the seller retains the right to employ any number of brokers as agents. The brokers can act simultaneously, and the seller is obligated to pay a commission only to that broker who successfully produces a ready, willing and able buyer. If the seller personally sells the property *without the aid of any of the brokers,* the seller is not obligated to pay any broker a commission. If a broker was in any way a procuring cause of the transaction, however, he or she may be entitled to a commission. A listing contract ordinarily creates an open listing unless wording that specifically provides otherwise is included. An advertisement of property "for sale by owner" may indicate "brokers protected" or in some other way invite offers brought by brokers. Such an invitation does not by itself create any form of listing agreement. The terms of even an open listing would still need to be negotiated.

Exclusive-agency listing. In an **exclusive-agency listing,** *only one broker* is specifically authorized to act as the exclusive agent of the principal. The *seller* under this form of agreement *retains the right to sell the property by himself or herself* without obligation to the broker. The seller is obligated to pay a commission to the broker if the broker has been the procuring cause of a sale *or* if any other broker sells the property.

Exclusive-right-to-sell listing. In an **exclusive-right-to-sell listing**, one broker is appointed as sole agent of the seller and is given the exclusive right, or *authorization,* to represent the property in question. Under this form of contract, the seller must pay the broker a commission *regardless of who sells the property* if it is sold while the listing is in effect. In other words, if the seller gives a broker an exclusive-right-to-sell listing but finds a buyer without the broker's assistance, the seller must still pay the broker a commission. This is usually the most popular form of listing agreement among brokers. (An example of this form of agreement is reproduced in figure 6.1, near the end of this chapter.)

Special Listing Provisions

Multiple listing. A *multiple listing clause* may be included in an exclusive listing. Brokers who are members of a **multiple listing service (MLS)** agree to pool their listings.

The multiple-listing provision gives additional authority to the listing broker to *distribute the listing to other brokers who belong to the multiple listing service.* The contractual obligations among the member brokers of a multiple listing organization vary widely. Most provide that upon sale of the property *the commission is divided between the listing broker and the selling broker.* Terms for division of the commission are agreed upon by the brokers.

Under most MLS contracts, the broker who secures a listing is not only authorized but *obligated* to turn the listing over to the multiple listing service within a definite period of time so that it can be distributed to the other member brokers. The length of time during which the listing broker can offer the property exclusively without notifying the other member brokers varies, but usually is less than 72 hours.

A multiple listing provision offers advantages to both the broker and the seller. Brokers develop a sizable inventory of properties to be sold and are assured a portion of the commission if they list a property or participate in its sale. Sellers also gain under this form of listing agreement because all members of the multiple listing organization are eligible to sell their property and are made aware of its availability.

A broker who chooses to represent a buyer may reject the subagency offered by the multiple listing, but must so inform the listing agent in writing before any other communication regarding the transaction.

Net listing. A **net listing** provision refers to the amount of money the seller will receive if the property is sold. The seller's property is listed for this net amount, and the broker is free to offer the property for sale at any price higher than the listing price. If the property is sold, the broker receives from the seller any proceeds over the stipulated net amount to be retained by the seller. *This type of listing is illegal in some states* and is not recommended in most of the other states. The question of fraud is frequently raised because of uncertainty over the sale price set or received by the broker.

Option listing. An **option listing** provision gives the broker the right to purchase the listed property. Use of an option listing may open the broker to charges of fraud unless the broker is scrupulous in fulfilling all obligations to the property owner. In some states, a broker who chooses to exercise such an option must first inform the property owner of the broker's profit in the transaction and secure *in writing* the owner's agreement to it.

Termination of Listings

A listing agreement may be terminated for any of the following reasons: (1) fulfillment of the purpose of the listing; (2) expiration of the time period stated in the agreement; (3) breach or cancellation by one of the parties, although that party may be liable to the other for damages; (4) transfer of title to the property by operation of law, as in a bankruptcy; (5) mutual consent; (6) death or incapacity of either party; (7) destruction of the property or a change in property use by outside forces (such as a change in zoning or condemnation by eminent domain).

Remember that a listing agreement is a *personal service contract*. As such, its success depends on the personal efforts of the broker who is a party to the agreement. The broker cannot turn the listing over to another broker. If the broker abandons the listing by failing to perform any work toward its fulfillment, or revokes the agreement, the property owner cannot force the broker to comply with it. The property owner can, however, sue the broker for damages.

The property owner could fail to fulfill the terms of the agreement by refusing to cooperate with reasonable requests of the broker (such as allowing tours of the property by prospective buyers) or refusing to proceed with a sales contract. The property owner could also simply cancel the listing agreement. In either case, the property owner could be liable for damages to the broker.

Expiration of listing period. All listings should specify a definite period of time during which the broker is to be employed. *In most states, failure to specify a definite termination date in an exclusive listing under which a licensee claims, demands or receives any compensation is grounds for suspension or revocation of the agent's real estate license.*

The use of automatic extensions of time in exclusive listings has been discouraged by the courts and outlawed in some states. Many listing contract forms specifically provide that there can be no automatic extensions of the agreement. An example of an **automatic extension** is a listing that provides for a base period of 90 days and "continues thereafter until terminated by either party hereto by 30 days' notice in writing." Some court decisions have held that such an extended period is to be considered an open listing rather than part of the original exclusive-agency listing.

Obtaining Listings

All legal owners of the listed property or their authorized agents, as well as the listing salesperson and/or broker, should sign the listing agreement. A listing salesperson signs the contract in the broker's name if authorized by the broker.

Information needed for listing agreements. It is important to obtain as much information as possible concerning a parcel of real estate when taking a listing. This ensures that all possible contingencies can be anticipated and provided for, particularly when the listing will be shared with other brokers and salespeople in a multiple-listing arrangement. This information generally includes the following (where appropriate):

1. names and addresses of owners.
2. legal (or other sufficient) description of the property.
3. size of lot (frontage and depth) and improvements (square footage).
4. number and sizes of rooms.
5. construction and age of the building.

6. information relative to the neighborhood (schools, churches, transportation and so forth).

7. current taxes.

8. existing financing (including interest payments, other costs and whether the loan is assumable or if the buyer can purchase subject to the existing loan) and financing acceptable to the seller.

9. utilities and average payments.

10. appliances to be included in the transaction.

11. date of occupancy or possession.

12. possibility of seller financing.

13. zoning classification (especially important for vacant land).

14. a detailed list of exactly what will and what will not be included in the sales price.

Never forget that a real estate broker, as an agent of the seller, is responsible for the disclosure of any material information regarding the property. Getting as much initial information from the seller as possible—even if it becomes necessary to ask penetrating and possibly embarrassing questions—will pay off in the long run by saving both principal and agent from potential legal difficulties. The agent should also assume the responsibility of searching the public records for such pertinent information as legal description, lot size and yearly taxes.

In Practice...

Some brokers use a separate information sheet (also known as a profile or data sheet) for recording many of the foregoing property features, including room sizes, lot sizes and taxes. In these firms, listing agreements contain mainly the specific contract terms—listing price, duration of the agreement, signatures of the parties and so forth.

Pricing the Property

Once a listing is secured and all necessary information obtained, the pricing of the real estate is of primary importance. While it is the responsibility of the broker or salesperson to advise and assist, it is ultimately the *seller* who must determine the listing price for the property. Since the average seller does not usually have the background to make an informed decision about a fair market price, however, real estate agents must be prepared to offer their knowledge, information and expertise in this area.

A broker or salesperson can help the seller determine a listing price for the property by means of a **competitive** (or **comparative**) **market analysis (CMA)**. Essentially, this is a comparison of the prices of recently sold properties that are similar in location, style and amenities to that of the listing seller. If no such comparisons can be made, or if the seller feels his or her property is unique in some way, a full-scale real estate appraisal—a detailed estimate of a property's value by a professional appraiser—may be warranted.

Whether a CMA or formal appraisal, the figure sought is the property's market value. **Market value,** as you will learn in Chapter 18, is the most probable price property would bring in an arm's-length transaction under normal conditions on the open market. A broker performing a CMA will estimate market value as likely to fall within a range of figures (for example, $135,000-$140,000).

While it is the property owner's privilege to set whatever asking price he or she chooses, a broker should reject any listing in which the price is substantially exaggerated.

Seller's return. One of the main concerns of every seller is how much money will be made from the sale. To find the price at which a property must be sold in order for the seller to receive a given amount from the sale when, for example, the seller is considering a counteroffer, the following computations can be made:

Assume that a seller wants to receive $100,000 after paying the broker's commission, closing costs and necessary repair costs (such as those indicated by a termite inspection). The selling price, therefore, should be $100,000 *plus* estimated closing costs, repair costs and the broker's commission (7 percent in this hypothetical situation).

1. The unknown selling price is: 100%
   Subtract the broker's commission that will be
   included in the selling price: −7%
   The seller's portion of the selling price
   will therefore be: **93%**

2. The seller wants to net $100,000, to which are added estimated
   closing costs of $2,000 and repairs of $1,500 for a total of $103,500. This is
   93 percent of the full sales price, so:

$$93\% = .93 \qquad .93)\overline{\$103,500}^{\,\$111,290.32 \text{ selling price}}$$

3. The broker's commission will be: $111,290.32
                                         $\times$ .07
                                         ――――――――――
                                         $ 7,790.32

4. The seller receives: $111,290.32
                                         —7,790.32
                                         ――――――――――
                                         $103,500.00
                                         —3,500.00
                                         ――――――――――
                                         $100,000.00

The example assumes that the seller owns the property free and clear. In most cases, the seller must also account for any outstanding loan balance(s). With a remaining mortgage loan balance of, for example, $57,000 as of the date of closing, the seller in the example would receive $43,000 ($100,000—$57,000), less any prepayment penalty charged by the lender.

The selling price reached in this way—by considering the seller's expected return—should still fall within the acceptable range determined for the property's market value by the competitive market analysis.

Sample Listing Agreement

Figure 6.1 is a typical listing agreement. Note that the individual specifics of a listing may vary from area to area and that state law may require that additional provisions be added to such contracts. Following is a section-by-section analysis of the sample agreement; numerical references are to the specific provisions of the contract.

**Figure 6.1
Sample Listing
Agreement**

SAMPLE FORM

EXCLUSIVE RIGHT TO SELL LISTING CONTRACT (1)

This agreement is made and entered into this _____ day of _____, 19__(2)_, by and between
_____(3)_____ as owner or owners (referred to herein as
"owner"), of the real estate described herein and _____ of _____(4)_____,
Indiana, as licensed real estate broker (referred to herein as "broker"). The parties, by signing this contract,
agree as follows:

    1.   The broker hereby agrees to list for sale the property described herein and to use his best efforts
to find a purchaser for the property upon the terms and conditions set out in this agreement or
upon such other terms as are acceptable to the owner. Owner agrees that broker shall have the
exclusive right to sell said property for the period of this listing contract upon the terms specified
herein or any other terms accepted by owner. (5)

    2.   In return for the broker's acceptance of this exclusive right to sell listing contract the owner
hereby agrees:

    (a)   that, in the event the broker, owner or other person finds a purchaser who is ready, willing
and able to purchase the property described herein upon the terms specified herein or any
other terms accepted by the owner, the broker shall have completed his performance under
this contract and the owner shall pay the broker a commission for his services in an amount
equal to (6)_____.

    (b)   that, in the event negotiations with a potential purchaser are begun by the broker, owner or
any other person during the period of this listing contract or if negotiations are begun after
its expiration date with a purchaser who was first contacted during the period of this listing
contract and the property is sold to such purchaser within _____ days after the
expiration date of this contract on the terms hereof or on any other terms accepted by the
owner, owner shall pay the broker a commission on the same basis as set out herein unless the
property at the time of sale is listed with another licensed broker. Owner hereby represents
that there is not now any other listing contract in force with another licensed broker. (7)

In order to promote the purposes for which this contract is entered into and to further define the rights and
duties of the owner and the broker, it is further agreed:

    1.   The broker is authorized to retain on behalf of the owner any earnest money deposit which may
be made by the potential purchaser and to retain it until the sale is completed. In the event that a
contract of sale is entered into and the purchaser defaults, the earnest money deposit shall be
applied first to the broker's advertising expenses and other expenses incurred by the broker under
this listing contract and the balance shall be divided between the owner and the broker. Both parties agree, however, to do whatever is necessary to enforce the contract made with such purchaser
to collect any sums which may be due under such contract. (8)

    2.   The broker or his representatives (including other brokers or salesmen under any multiple listing
arrangement to which the broker may be a party) shall have access to the property described below
at all reasonable times for the purposes of showing to prospective purchasers. The broker is authorized to place a "For Sale" sign on this property, to reveal any and all information which appears in
this listing contract and to advertise the property for the purpose of promoting its sale. (9)

    3.   The listing price includes the balances due on all mortgages, liens, assessments for municipal
improvements, current real estate taxes and balances due on personal property or fixtures

which are a part of the property described herein and that such balances shall be paid by the owner prior to or at the time of sale of the property unless the contract of sale provides otherwise. Seller recognizes his responsibility for and agrees to advise the broker of any municipal improvements contracted for. (10)

4. The owner represents and warrants that the property is free and clear of all encumbrances except those noted above and except easements and restrictions of record and current taxes and that the present use of the property does not violate any restriction or zoning ordinance; (11) that the owner is the sole owner of the property and that he will execute a general warranty deed or land contract (if applicable) in the event of sale and will furnish an abstract of title showing a merchantable title or a title insurance policy showing an insurable title for the amount of the sales price; (12) that all information appearing anywhere in this contract including that on the reverse side is true and correct to the best of owner's knowledge; (13) and that all operating equipment which is included in the sale of the property will be in good operating order at the time of closing of the sale except _____ (14) _____.

5. The property is offered for sale without regard to race, color, religion, national origin, sex or physical disability in accordance with applicable State and Federal laws. (15)

The period of this listing is from _____ A.M./P.M. of _____, 19_____, up to and including 11:00 P.M. of _____(16)_____, 19_____. The agreed upon listing price is $ _____, in cash or upon any other price, term, or exchange to which owner agrees. Both parties agree that this contract: is freely entered into; this writing constitutes the entire agreement; is binding upon their heirs, administrators, executors and assigns; is without relief from valuation and appraisement laws; includes the obligation to pay necessary attorney's fees of the other for its enforcement. Owner by signing below, hereby acknowledges receipt of a copy of this contract. The address and location of the listed property are: _____

the legal description of which is: _____

Other Conditions: _____

_____   _____
(Owner)   (Owner)

                                     _____
                                     (Real Estate Broker or Firm)

                            by_____

                            Title:_____

1. *Exclusive Right to Sell.* The title specifies that this document is an "exclusive right to sell" real property.

2. *Date.* The date of the listing contract is the date it is executed; however, this may not necessarily be the date that the contract becomes effective.

3. *Names.* The names of all persons having an interest in the property should be specified and all such persons should enter into the agreement. If the property is owned under one of the forms of co-ownership discussed in Chapter 8, that fact should be clearly established. If one or more of the owners is married, it is wise to obtain the spouse's signature to release marital rights, which will also be discussed in Chapter 8.

4. *Broker or Firm.* The name of the broker or firm entering into the listing must be clearly stated in the agreement.

5. *Contract.* This section establishes the document as a legal contract and states the promises by both parties that create and bind the agreement.

6. *Commission Rate.* This paragraph establishes the broker's rate of commission. Price fixing is illegal, and a broker's commission is open to negotiation between owner and broker.

7. *Extension Clause (also called Safety Clause, Protection Clause or Carryover Clause).* This section, permitted in most states, will protect the broker if the owner or another person sells the property after the listing expires to a person with whom the original broker negotiated. In other words, the broker is guaranteed a commission for a set period of time after the agreement expires (generally a matter of months) if the broker was the procuring cause of the sale, although did not actually consummate the transaction. This extension clause does not apply, however, if the owner signs a new listing agreement with another broker after the original agreement expires.

8. *Broker's Responsibilities.* This paragraph defines the rights and duties of the broker.

9. *Broker's Authority.* Here the broker is expressly given the authority to place a sign on the property and show it to buyers, as well as the permission to supply the buyers with any and all information that may appear on the listing form.

10. *Listing Price.* The listing price is a gross sales price, and the owner should understand that any obligations such as taxes, mortgages and assessments remain the owner's responsibility and must be paid out of the proceeds of the sale.

11. *Encumbrances.* This paragraph points out responsibilities of the seller regarding encumbrances, which are especially important to the broker because they may determine whether or not the property is in fact salable.

12. *Evidence of Ownership and Deed.* The type of deed to be executed and proof of ownership in the form of a title are stated here.

13. *Liabilities.* The owner protects both buyer and broker with this statement.

14. *Warranty of Fitness.* Although the buyer has the duty to inspect the property, exhaustive tests of all equipment are not necessary. This warranty of fitness protects the buyer against misrepresentation.

15. *Civil Rights Legislation.* This clause serves to alert the owner that both federal and state legislation exist to protect against discrimination.

16. *Termination of Agreement.* Both the exact time and the date serve to remove any ambiguity in regard to termination of the contract. A particular termination date does not necessarily include that day itself unless the phrase "up to and including" is used.

Summary

To acquire an inventory of property to sell, brokers and salespeople must obtain listings. The various kinds of listing agreements include open listings, exclusive-agency listings and exclusive-right-to-sell listings.

An *open listing* is one in which, to obtain a commission, the broker must find a buyer before the property is sold by the seller or another broker. Under an *exclusive-agency listing,* the broker is given the exclusive right to represent the seller, but the seller can avoid paying the broker a commission by selling the property without the broker's help. With an *exclusive-right-to-sell listing,* the seller employs only one broker and must pay that broker a commission regardless of whether it is the broker or the seller who finds a buyer—provided the buyer is found within the listing period.

A *multiple listing* provision may appear in an exclusive listing and gives the broker the additional authority and obligation to distribute the listing to other members of the broker's multiple listing organization. A *net listing,* which is outlawed in some states and considered unethical in most areas, is based on the net price the seller will receive if the property is sold. The broker under a net listing is free to offer the property for sale at the highest available price and will receive as his or her commission any amount over and above the seller's stipulated net. An *option listing,* which must also be handled with caution, gives the broker the option to purchase the listed property.

A listing agreement may be terminated for the same reasons as any other agency relationship.

Questions

1. A listing agreement is:
   a. a broker's employment contract with salespeople.
   b. a broker's employment contract with a principal.
   c. generally an oral agreement.
   d. none of the above

2. Which of the following is a similarity between an exclusive-agency and an exclusive-right-to-sell listing?
   a. under both types of listing the seller retains the right to sell his or her real estate without the broker's help and without paying the broker a commission
   b. both are open listings
   c. both give the responsibility of representing the seller to one broker only
   d. under both the seller authorizes only one particular salesperson to show his or her property

3. The asking price of a listed property should be based on:
   a. net value.
   b. market value.
   c. whatever the seller chooses.
   d. the maximum of a range of values.

4. Which of the following is a similarity between an open listing and an exclusive-agency listing?
   a. under both the seller avoids paying the broker a commission if the seller sells the property unassisted
   b. both listings grant a commission to any licensed broker who finds a buyer for the seller's property
   c. both are net listings
   d. under both the broker earns a commission regardless of who sells the property so long as it is sold within the listing period

5. A multiple listing clause:
   a. involves more than one parcel of real estate.
   b. is the same as an open listing agreement.
   c. benefits only the seller.
   d. benefits both broker and seller.

6. A listing may be terminated by:
   I. the broker's failure to spend time on it.
   II. expiration of the time period stated in the listing.
   a. I only   c. both I and II
   b. II only   d. neither I nor II

7. A broker sold a residence for $88,000 and received $6,160 as her commission in accordance with the terms of the listing agreement. What percentage of the sales price was the broker's commission.
   a. 6 percent   c. 7 percent
   b. 6½ percent   d. 7½ percent

8. A listing agreement that runs for a set period of time and renews itself for another listing period after the initial period ends:
   I. contains an automatic extension provision.
   II. is illegal in some states.
   a. I only   c. both I and II
   b. II only   d. neither I nor II

9. When a broker or salesperson takes a listing, who should sign the agreement?
   a. the seller
   b. the listing broker or salesperson
   c. all brokers in a multiple listing situation
   d. a and b

10. The selling price of a parcel of real estate is determined by:
    I. the seller alone.
    II. the broker or salesperson.
    a. I only   c. both I and II
    b. II only   d. neither I nor II

11. Which of the following provisions is (are) usually included in listing agreements?

    a. the rate of commission
    b. the minimum price the seller will accept
    c. the date the agreement commences and the date it terminates
    d. a and c

12. Salesperson Joseph Franks has just secured a listing to sell Joyce Randolph's home. When completing the listing agreement, Franks should:

    a. submit the completed form to his broker.
    b. obtain as much information about the property from Randolph as possible.
    c. refuse the listing if he thinks Randolph wants to price it far higher than the fair market value.
    d. all of the above

13. A competitive market analysis:

    I. can help the seller set a fair price.
    II. is a comparison of recently sold properties similar to the seller's.

        a. I only   c. both I and II
        b. II only   d. neither I nor II

14. A seller's residence is listed with a broker and the seller stipulates that she wants to receive $85,000 from the sale but that the broker can sell the residence for as much as possible and keep the difference as a commission. The broker agrees. This type of listing:

    I. is called an open listing.
    II. may be illegal.

        a. I only   c. both I and II
        b. II only   d. neither I nor II

15. A property was listed with a broker who belonged to a multiple-listing service and was sold for $53,500 by another broker member. The total commission was 6 percent of the sales price. The selling broker received 60 percent of the commission, and the listing broker received the balance. How much was the listing broker's commission?

    a. $2,142   c. $1,464
    b. $1,926   d. $1,284

7

Interests in Real Estate

Key Terms

Allodial system
Curtesy
Determinable fee
Dower
Easement
Easement appurtenant
Easement by condemnation
Easement by necessity
Easement by prescription
Easement in gross
Eminent domain
Encroachment
Encumbrance
Escheat
Estate in land
Fee simple absolute
Fee Simple Defeasible
Fee simple subject
　　to condition subsequent

Fee simple subject
　　to special limitation
Feudal system
Freehold estate
Future interests
Homestead
Leasehold estate
License
Lien
Life estate
Littoral rights
Police power
Prior appropriation
Remainder interest
Restriction
Reversionary interest
Riparian rights
Taxation

Overview

Ownership of a parcel of real estate is not necessarily absolute; that is, ownership is dependent upon the type of interest a person holds in the property. For example, a person may own all rights to real property and be able to pass those property rights on to heirs, or a person's ownership may exist only as long as he or she lives. Real estate ownership may be restricted so that the owner can use the property only for one specific purpose; likewise, it may be restricted so that the owner must refrain from using it for a specific purpose. In addition, the interest in real estate a person possesses may be reduced by the interests others possess in the property. This chapter will discuss the various interests in real estate and how they affect real estate ownership and use.

Historical Background	According to old English common law, the government or king held title to all lands under what was known as the **feudal system** of ownership. Under this system, the individual was merely a tenant whose rights of use and occupancy of real property were held at the sufferance of an overlord. Through a series of social reforms in the seventeenth century, however, the feudal system evolved into the **allodial system** of ownership. Under the allodial system, the individual was entitled to property rights without proprietary control being held by the king.

Land in the United States is held under the allodial system. The Bill of Rights of the U.S. Constitution firmly establishes the private ownership of land.

Government Powers	Although an individual in the United States has maximum rights to the land he or she owns, these ownership rights are subject to certain powers, or rights, held by federal, state and local governments. Because they are for the general welfare of the community, these limitations on the ownership of real estate supersede the rights of the individual. Such government rights include the following:

1. **Police power:** This is the power vested in a state to establish legislation to preserve order, protect the public health and safety and promote the general welfare. There is no federal police power as such—it exists in this manner on a state level only. A state's police power is passed on to municipalities and counties through legislation called *enabling acts*. The use and enjoyment of property is subject to restrictions authorized by such legislation, including both environmental protection laws and zoning and building ordinances regulating the use, occupancy, size, location, construction and rents of real estate. See Chapter 19 for more information on police power.

2. **Eminent domain:** Through what is called a condemnation suit, a government may exercise this right to acquire privately owned real estate for public use. Three conditions must be met: (a) the proposed use must be declared by the court to be a public use, (b) just compensation must be paid to the owner and (c) the rights of the property owner must be protected by due process of law.

   The exercise of decision-making under the right of eminent domain is generally granted by state laws to quasi-public bodies, such as land-clearance commissions and public housing or redevelopment authorities, as well as to publicly held companies such as railroads, public utilities and mining companies.

   Condemnation proceedings are instituted only when the owner's consent cannot be obtained. Otherwise, public agencies acquire real property through direct negotiation and purchase from the owner.

3. **Taxation:** Taxation is a charge on real estate to raise funds to meet the public needs of a government. See Chapter 10 for more information on real estate taxes.

4. **Escheat:** While escheat is not actually a limitation on ownership, state laws provide for ownership of real estate to revert, or escheat, to the state when an owner dies and leaves no heirs and no will disposing of the real estate. In some

states, real property will escheat to the county the land is located in, rather than to the state. Escheat occurs only when a property becomes ownerless.

As a memorization aid, note that combining the first letter of each of the government rights enumerated above spells the word "PETE."

Estates in Land

The degree, quantity, nature and extent of interest that a person has in real property is an **estate in land.**

Estates in land are divided into two major classifications: (1) freehold estates and (2) leasehold estates (those involving tenants). These two classifications exist for basically historical reasons. Under the common law, freehold estates were classified as real estate, while leasehold estates were considered contracts and construed to be personal property. This classification of estates was based primarily on the duration of the estate or interest. Note that there are various lesser interests or rights to real estate that are not estates in land.

Freehold estates are *estates of indeterminable length,* such as those existing for a lifetime or forever. These include (1) fee simple, (2) defeasible fee, (3) conventional life estate and (4) legal life estate.

The first two of these estates continue for an indefinite period and are inheritable by the heirs of the owner. The third and fourth terminate upon the death of the person on whose life they are based.

Leasehold estates are *estates for a fixed term of years.* These are (1) estate for years, (2) estate from period to period, (3) estate at will and (4) estate at sufferance. Leasehold estates will be covered in Chapter 16.

The various estates and interests in real estate are illustrated in figure 7.1.

Fee Simple Estate

An estate in **fee simple** is the *highest type of interest in real estate recognized by law.* A fee simple estate is one in which the holder is entitled to all rights incident to the property. It is complete ownership. Because this estate is of unlimited duration, upon the death of its owner it passes to his or her heirs or as provided in the owner's will. A fee simple estate is thus an *estate of inheritance.* It is, however, subject to the governmental powers previously explained.

Fee simple absolute. If there are no limitations on fee simple ownership (other than the governmental powers), it is a **fee simple absolute.** In common usage, the terms *fee* and *fee simple* are used interchangeably with *fee simple absolute.*

Fee simple defeasible. A **fee simple defeasible** (or *defeasible fee estate*) is qualified and may be lost on the occurrence or nonoccurrence of a specified event.

A fee simple may be qualified by a **condition subsequent,** which dictates some action or activity that the new owner must not perform. The former owner retains a **right of reentry,** so that, if the condition is broken, the former owner can retake possession of the property. A grant of land "on the condition that" there be no consumption of alcohol on the premises is a fee simple on condition subsequent. If alcohol is consumed on the property, the former owner has the right to

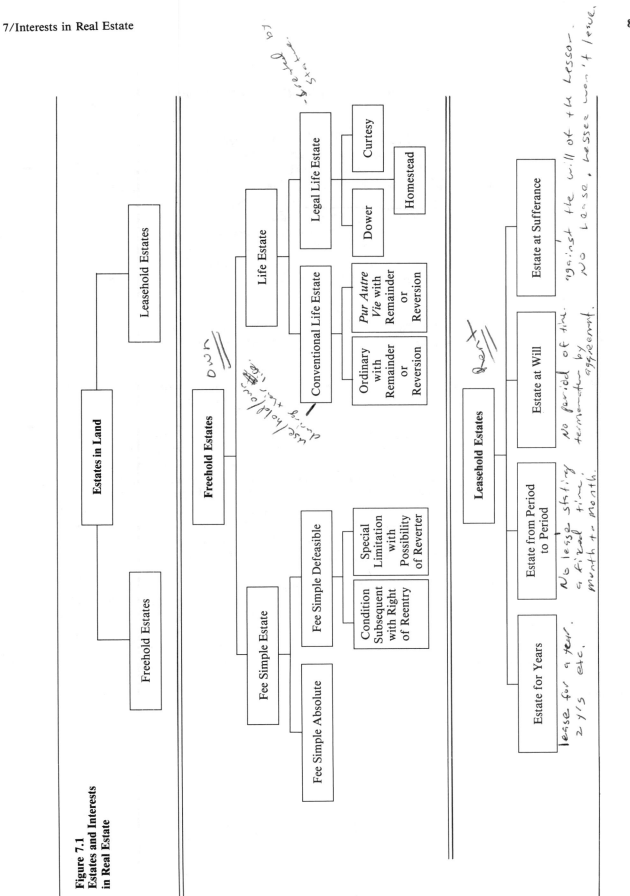

**Figure 7.1
Estates and Interests
in Real Estate**

reacquire full ownership. It will be necessary for the grantor (or the grantor's heirs or successors) to go to court to assert that right.

If a fee simple estate has a **special limitation,** the estate ends automatically upon failure to comply with the limitation. The former owner (or the former owner's heirs or successors) retains a **possibility of reverter** and reacquires full ownership, with no need to reenter the land. A fee simple with a special limitation is also called a **fee simple determinable** since it may end automatically. The language used to distinguish a special limitation—the words "so long as" or "while" or "during"—is the key to the creation of this estate. For example, a grant of land from Aunt Fran to her church "so long as" the land is used only for religious purposes is a fee simple with a special limitation. If the church uses the land for a non-religious purpose, title automatically reverts back to Aunt Fran (or her heirs or successors).

Because they will take effect, if at all, only at some time in the future, the *right of entry* and *possibility of reverter* are termed **future interests.**

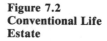

Life Estate

A **life estate** is an estate in land that is *limited in duration to the life of the owner or to the life or lives of some other designated person or persons.*

An *ordinary life estate* is limited to the lifetime of the owner of the life estate (the life tenant); that is, it *ends with the death of the person to whom it was granted* (see figure 7.2). A life estate created for the life of another person is known as an *estate pur autre vie* (for the life of another). For example, A, who owns fee simple title to Blackacre, can convey a life estate in Blackacre to C for the life of D. C is the life tenant, but the measuring life is D's. While a life estate is not considered an estate of inheritance, a life estate pur autre vie provides a qualified right in that it can be inherited by the life tenant's heirs, but only until the death of the person against whose life the estate is measured.

Remainder and reversion. A fee simple owner who creates a life estate must also consider the future ownership of the property after the termination of the life estate. The future interest may take one of two forms:

**Figure 7.2
Conventional Life
Estate**

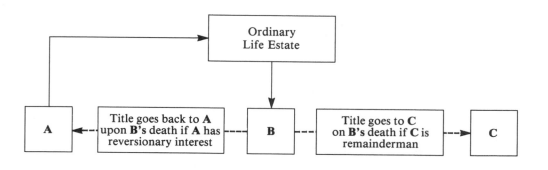

1. **Remainder interest:** If the deed or will that creates a life estate names someone to whom title will pass upon the termination of the life estate, the person named (the *remainderman*) is said to own a remainder interest or estate. The remainder interest is a nonpossessory estate—a *future interest*.

2. **Reversionary interest:** If the creator of a life estate does not convey a remainder interest, then upon the termination of the life estate, full ownership returns to the original fee simple owner (if deceased, to the heirs or devisees set forth in the fee simple owner's will). This interest or estate is called a *reversion,* and is also a *future interest*.

Thus, upon the termination of the life estate, the holder of the future interest, whether remainder or reversion, will be the owner of a fee simple estate.

A life tenant's interest in real property is a true ownership interest. In general, the life tenant is not answerable to the holder of the future interest. A life tenant's rights are not absolute, however. A life tenant can enjoy the rights of the land but cannot encroach upon those of the reversioner or remainderman. In other words, the life tenant cannot perform any acts that would permanently injure the land or property. Such injury to real estate is known in legal terms as *waste*. In such a case, those having a future interest in the property would be able to bring legal action for damages or seek an injunction against the life tenant.

A life tenant is entitled to all income and profits arising from the property during the life tenancy. A life interest may be sold, leased or mortgaged, but such interest will always terminate upon the death of the person against whose life the estate is measured.

Conventional life estate. A *conventional life estate* is created by grant from the owner of the fee simple estate. The owner retains a reversionary interest in the property or names a remainderman.

Legal Life Estate. A *legal life estate* is one created by statute in some states. A legal life estate becomes effective automatically by operation of law upon the occurrence of certain events. Curtesy, dower and homestead are the forms of legal life estate currently used in some states. Check the chart in table 7.1 to see which (if any) of these legal life estates apply in your state.

Most states have abolished the common-law concepts of dower and curtesy. **Dower** is the life estate that a wife has in the real estate of her deceased husband. A husband's life estate in the real estate of his deceased wife is called **curtesy.** Under the common law, a husband's curtesy interest attached, or became effective, only if a child was born of the marriage. In some states, a husband is given dower right in his wife's real estate, and in others, both husband and wife are given a fee simple interest in each others' real property.

In states where it is still used, a dower (or curtesy) interest usually means that upon the death of the owning spouse, the surviving spouse has a right to a one-third interest (one-half interest in some states) in the real property for the rest of his or her life. The purpose of dower is to give the surviving spouse a means of support when the other spouse dies. The surviving spouse has a right to demand and receive a one-third (or one-half) life estate in the real property, or its equivalent, even if the deceased spouse wills the real estate to others.

Table 7.1	State	Curtesy	Dower	Homestead
Legal Life Estates	Alabama			•
	Alaska			•
	Arizona			•
	Arkansas		•	•
	California			•
	Colorado			•
	Connecticut			
	Delaware			
	District of Columbia		•[1]	
	Florida			•
	Georgia			•
	Hawaii			•
	Idaho			•
	Illinois			•
	Indiana			•
	Iowa			•
	Kansas			•
	Kentucky	•	•	•
	Louisiana			•
	Maine			•
	Maryland			
	Massachusetts		•[1]	•
	Michigan		•	•
	Minnesota			•
	Mississippi			•
	Missouri			•
	Montana			•
	Nebraska			•
	Nevada			•
	New Hampshire			•
	New Jersey			
	New Mexico			
	New York			•
	North Carolina			•
	North Dakota			•
	Ohio		•[1]	•
	Oklahoma			•
	Oregon			•
	Pennsylvania			
	Rhode Island			
	South Carolina		•	•
	South Dakota			•
	Tennessee			•
	Texas			•
	Utah			•
	Vermont			•
	Virginia	•	•	•
	Washington			•
	West Virginia		•[1]	•
	Wisconsin			•
	Wyoming			•

[1]Includes husband's rights.

Generally, the right of dower (or curtesy) becomes effective only upon the death of a spouse. During the lifetimes of the parties, the dower right is *inchoate,* or incomplete—merely the possibility of an interest. For this reason, the right of dower cannot be assigned or transferred to another party and the owning spouse cannot cancel the right by selling the property.

Upon the death of the owning spouse, the dower (or curtesy) right becomes *consummate* (complete). In most states, the surviving spouse can choose to take a dower interest in the deceased spouse's estate, the fee simple interest given by the deceased's will, or, if there is no will, the share of an heir as provided by the law of descent. These alternatives will be explained in Chapter 12.

As previously mentioned, many states have abolished the common-law concepts of dower and curtesy. In many cases, such rights have been repealed in favor of community property laws or the provisions of the state's law of descent or probate code. The statutes replacing dower and curtesy frequently allow the surviving spouse to take a specific portion of the estate in fee (rather than as a life estate). In addition, many such statutes limit these rights to land owned by the deceased in fee simple at the time of death rather than allowing an interest in all land owned by the deceased at any time during the marriage. Under a number of these statutes the inheritance right is inchoate, like dower; under other state laws, the inheritance right does not attach until the owning spouse dies.

In Practice...   *The right of dower (or curtesy) can usually be released to a purchaser of property by both spouses signing the deed of conveyance. One spouse can also release his or her interest by executing a separate quitclaim deed to the other spouse. If the dower right is not so released when property is conveyed, it can create a cloud, or imperfection, on the title to the property. It is therefore* essential *that both spouses sign any conveyance of one spouse's real estate. It is also a good idea for the non-owning spouse to sign any sales contract or other document involved in the transaction as well.*

Even in states where dower and curtesy have been abolished in favor of descent or community property laws, it is important that both spouses sign all instruments of conveyance. A nonowning spouse's signature on a conveyance releases any such statutory interests in the real estate being sold.

A **homestead** *is a tract of land that is owned and occupied as the family home.* In those states that have homestead exemption laws, a portion of the area or value of such land is protected, or exempt, from judgments for unsecured debts. A family can have only one homestead at any one time.

Homestead laws vary from state to state and are not uniform in their wording or scope, but generally include the following requirements: (1) In order to create a homestead, one must first *establish a family.* (In some states, a single person may establish a homestead.) (2) The family must *occupy the premises as a home.* (3) The head of the family, or householder, must *own or lease the property.* In some states the homestead interest attaches by operation of law, but in others the family must protect its homestead interest by filing a notice as required by local statute.

The homestead exemption may protect a homeowner from the court-ordered sale of the home to satisfy *unsecured* debts. An unsecured debt is one in which there is no collateral as security for payment of the loan. A charge account or personal loan would be an example of an unsecured debt. The homestead exemption would not apply to real estate taxes levied against the property or to a mortgage for purchase money or the cost of improvements, provided both spouses join in executing the mortgage.

There are a few states where the entire homestead is exempt from being sold. Usually, the homestead right merely reserves a certain amount of money for the family in the event of a court sale. For example, if the state homestead exemption is $15,000 and a court sale brings $25,000 for a property, the homeowner would receive the first $15,000 of the proceeds and the remaining $10,000 would be applied to the homeowner's debts. This basic example assumes that there are no unpaid taxes, mortgage liens or mechanics' liens (all of which are excepted from homestead protection). If such debts were outstanding, they would be satisfied before the family received any share. A sale would not be ordered, if the amount to be realized would cover no more than debts secured by the home (such as a mortgage) and the amount of the exemption. If property is sold, the amount exempted from creditors' claims must usually be reinvested in another homestead.

The rights to occupy the homestead and enjoy the exemption benefits generally continue for the lives of the husband and wife and their survivor(s) and also for children until they reach the age of majority. Homestead rights may be released by husband and wife joining in executing a deed. Homestead rights in property may be lost by abandonment, such as when the home is sold and the householder plans to move to a new home. Intention of the householder is a key factor.

The homestead exemption should not be confused with the frontier practice of homesteading or with the Federal Housing Administration's "Urban Homestead" program. Likewise, this right should not be confused with the homestead tax exemption, a reduction in property taxes granted to homeowners in many states (see Chapter 10).

Encumbrances

A claim, charge or liability that attaches to and is binding on real estate is an **encumbrance.** In plain words, an encumbrance is *anything* that affects title to real estate (see figure 7.3). It is a right or interest held by a party who is not the fee owner of the property. An encumbrance may lessen the value or obstruct the use of the property, but it does not necessarily prevent a transfer of title.

Liens

A charge against property that provides security for a debt or obligation of the property owner is a **lien.** If the obligation is not repaid, the lienholder, or creditor, has the right to have it paid out of the debtor's property, usually from the proceeds of a court sale. Real estate taxes, mortgages and trust deeds, judgments and mechanics' liens (for people who have furnished labor or materials in the construction or repair of real estate) all represent possible liens against an owner's real estate. Liens will be discussed in detail in Chapter 10.

Restrictions

Deed restrictions (also referred to as *conditions, covenants* and *restrictions*) are private agreements placed in the public record that affect the use of land. They are usually imposed by an owner of real estate when property is sold, and are included in the seller's deed to the buyer. Deed restrictions would typically be imposed by a developer or subdivider to maintain specific standards in a sub-

**Figure
7.3
Encumbrances**

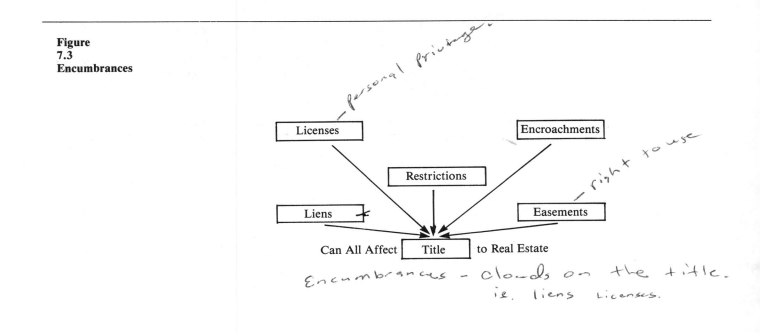

personal privilege

right to use

Licenses

Encroachments

Restrictions

Liens

Easements

Can All Affect | Title | to Real Estate

_Encumbrances - clouds on the title.
ie. liens Licenses._

division, and they would be listed in the original development plans for the sub-division filed in the public record. Deed restrictions are discussed further in Chapter 19.

Easements

A right to use the land of another for a particular purpose is an **easement.** An easement right may be in any portion of land, including the air space above a parcel.

Because _an easement is a right to use land,_ it is classified as an interest in real estate, but it is not an estate in land. The holder of an easement has only a right, not an estate or ownership interest, in the land over which the easement exists. An easement is sometimes referred to as an _incorporeal right_ in land (a nonpossessory interest). An easement may be either appurtenant or in gross (see figure 7.4).

Easement appurtenant. An easement that is _annexed to the ownership and used for the benefit of another's parcel of land_ is an **easement appurtenant.** For an easement appurtenant to exist, there must be two adjacent tracts of land owned by different parties. The tract over which the easement runs is known as the _servient tenement;_ the tract that is to benefit from the easement is known as the _dominant tenement._ For example, if _A_ and _B_ own adjacent properties in a lake resort community and only _A's_ property borders the lake, _A_ may grant _B_ an easement across _A's_ property so that _B_ can have access to the beach. _A's_ property is the servient tenement; _B's_ property is the dominant tenement. An easement appurtenant is considered part of the dominant tenement, and if the dominant tenement is conveyed to another party, the easement passes with the title. In legal terms it is said that the easement _runs with the land._

A **party wall** is an exterior wall of a building that straddles the boundary line between two owners' lots, with half of the wall on each lot. Each lot owner owns the half of the wall on his or her lot and each has an easement appurtenant in the other half of the wall for support of his or her building. A written party-wall agreement should be used to create the easement rights. Expenses to build and maintain the wall are usually shared. A **party driveway** shared by and partly on the land of adjoining owners should also be created by written agreement, specifying responsibility for expenses.

Easement in gross. *A mere personal interest* in or right to use the land of another is an **easement in gross.** The right of use belongs to an individual (whether a person or a corporation) and is not appurtenant to any ownership estate in land. Examples of easements in gross are the easement rights a railroad has in its right-of-way or the right-of-way for a pipeline or high-tension power line. Commercial easements in gross may be assigned or conveyed and may be inherited. However, personal easements in gross usually are not assignable and terminate upon the death of the easement owner. Easements in gross are often confused with the similar personal right of license, which is discussed later in this chapter.

Figure 7.4
Easements

The owner of Lot A has an **easement appurtenant** across Lot B to gain access to his property from the paved road. The owner of Lot B has an **easement appurtenant** across Lot A so that she may reach the lake. Lot A is the servient tenement; Lot B is the dominant tenement. The utility company has an **easement in gross** across both parcels of land for its electric power lines.

▨▨▨▨ Easement appurtenant

▬▬▬▬ Easement in gross

Creating an easement. Today, an easement is commonly created by written agreement between the parties establishing the easement right. Easements may also be created in a number of other ways: (1) by *express grant* in a deed from the owner of the property over which the easement will run; (2) by *express reservation* by the grantor in a deed of conveyance reserving an easement over the sold land; (3) by longtime usage, as in an easement by prescription; (4) by necessity; and (5) by condemnation.

To create an easement there must be *two separate parties,* one of whom is the owner of the land over which the easement runs. It is impossible for the owner of a parcel of property to have an easement over his or her own land. Thus, where a valid easement exists and the dominant tenement is acquired by the owner of the servient tenement, the easement is extinguished.

An **easement by necessity** or **easement by implication of law** arises because all owners must have rights of ingress to and egress from their land—they cannot be landlocked. The easement will be implied over an adjoining parcel of the grantor of the landlocked parcel, or, if the grantor owns no adjoining property, over the property that provides the most efficient road access. When a claimant has made use of another's land for a certain period of time as defined by state law, an **easement by prescription** is acquired. This *prescriptive period* is usually from 10 to 20 years, depending upon state statutes. The claimant's use must have been continuous, exclusive and without the owner's approval. Additionally, the use must be visible, open and notorious, so that the owner could readily learn of it.

Through the concept of *tacking,* a party not in possession of real property for the entire required statutory period may successfully establish a claim of an easement by prescription. Successive periods of continuous, uninterrupted occupation by different parties may be tacked on, or combined, to reach the prescriptive period. In order to tack on one person's possession to that of another, the parties must have been *successors in interest,* such as an ancestor and his or her heir, landlord and tenant, or seller and buyer.

An **easement by condemnation** is acquired for a public purpose, such as a power line, through the power of eminent domain. The owner of the servient tenement must be compensated for any loss in property value.

Terminating an easement. Easements may be terminated:

1. when the purpose for which the easement was created no longer exists.
2. when the owner of either the dominant or the servient tenement becomes the owner of the other (a situation called a *merger*).
3. by release of the right of easement to the owner of the servient tenement.
4. by abandonment of the easement (the intention of the parties is the determining factor).
5. by nonuse of a prescriptive easement.
6. by adverse possession by the owner of the servient tenement.
7. by destruction of the servient tenement, as in the demolition of a party wall.
8. by lawsuit (an *action to quiet title*) against someone claiming an easement.
9. by excessive use, as when a residential use is converted to commercial purposes.

Licenses

A personal privilege to enter the land of another for a specific purpose is a **license.** It is *not* an estate in land; it is a personal right of the party to whom it is given. A license differs from an easement in that *it can be terminated or canceled by the licensor* (the person who granted the license). If a right to use another's property is given orally or informally, it will generally be considered to be a license, rather than a personal easement in gross. A license ceases upon the death of either party and is revoked by the sale of the land by the licensor. Examples of license would include permission to park in a neighbor's driveway and the privileges that are granted by the purchase of a ticket for the theater or a sporting event.

Encroachments   When a building (or some portion of it) or a fence or driveway illegally *extends beyond the land of its owner* and covers some land of an adjoining owner or a street or alley, an **encroachment** arises. Encroachments are usually disclosed by either a physical inspection of the property or a spot survey. A spot survey shows the location of all improvements located on a property and whether any improvements extend over the lot lines. If the building on a lot encroaches on neighboring land, the neighbor may be able either to recover damages or to secure removal of the portion of the building that encroaches. Encroachments of long standing (for the prescriptive period) may give rise to easements by prescription.

In Practice...   *Since an undisclosed encroachment could render a title unmarketable, the existence of an encroachment should be noted in a listing agreement, and the sales contract governing the transaction should be made subject to the existence of the particular encroachment. Encroachments are not disclosed by the usual title evidence provided in a real estate sale unless a survey is submitted while the examination is being made.*

Water Rights   One of the interests that may attach to the ownership of real estate is the right to use adjacent bodies of water. Since water is essential to maintain life, the laws affecting its ownership and use are important to everyone. In the United States, the ownership of water and the land adjacent to it is determined by either the doctrines of riparian and littoral rights or the doctrine of prior appropriation.

Riparian Rights   Many states subscribe to the common-law doctrine of **riparian rights.** These rights are granted to owners of land located along the course of a river, stream or lake. Such an owner has the unrestricted right to use the water, provided such use does not interrupt or alter the flow of the water or contaminate the water. In addition, an owner of land that borders a nonnavigable waterway owns the land under the water to the exact center of the waterway. Land adjoining navigable rivers is usually owned to the water's edge, with the state holding title to the submerged land (see figure 7.5). Navigable waters are considered public highways in which the public has an easement or right to travel. The laws governing and defining riparian rights differ from state to state.

Littoral Rights   Closely related to riparian rights are the **littoral rights** of owners whose land borders on large, navigable lakes and oceans. Owners with littoral rights enjoy unrestricted use of available waters, but own the land adjacent to the water only up to the mean high-water mark (see figure 7.6). All land below this point is owned by the government.

Riparian and littoral rights are appurtenant (attached) to the land and cannot be retained when the property is sold. This means that the right to use the water belongs to whoever owns the bordering land and cannot be retained by a former owner after the land is sold.

Where land adjoins streams or rivers, an owner is entitled to all land created through *accretion*—increases in the land resulting from the deposit of soil by the natural action of the water. (Such deposits are called *alluvion* or *alluvium*.) If water recedes, new land is acquired by *reliction*.

Figure 7.5
Riparian Rights

Figure 7.6
Littoral Rights

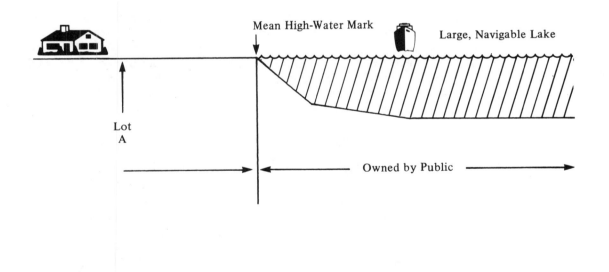

Likewise, an owner may lose land through *erosion,* the gradual and imperceptible wearing away of the land caused by flowing water (or other natural forces). This is in contrast to *avulsion,* the sudden removal of soil by an act of nature.

Doctrine of Prior Appropriation

In states where water is scarce, the ownership and use of water are often determined by the **doctrine of prior appropriation.** Under this doctrine, *the right to use any water, with the exception of limited domestic use, is controlled by the state rather than by the adjacent landowner.* Ownership of the land bordering bodies of water in states recognizing this doctrine is generally determined in the same way as riparian and littoral ownership.

To secure water rights, a person must show a beneficial use for the water, such as crop irrigation, and obtain a permit from the proper state department. Although statutes governing prior appropriation vary from state to state, the priority of the water right is usually determined by the oldest recorded permit date.

Once granted, water rights may be perfected through the legal processes prescribed by the individual state. When the water right is perfected, it generally becomes attached to the land of the person holding the permit. The permit holder may sell such a water right to another party.

Issuance of a water permit does not grant access to the water source. All access rights-of-way over the land of another (easements) must be obtained from the property owner.

Summary

An *estate* is the degree, quantity, nature and extent of interest a person holds in land. *Freehold estates* are estates of indeterminate length. Less than freehold estates are called *leasehold estates,* and they concern tenants.

A freehold estate may be a fee simple estate or a life estate. A fee simple estate can be absolute or defeasible upon the happening of some event. A conventional life estate is created by the owner of a fee estate; a legal life estate is created by law. Legal life estates include *curtesy, dower* and *homestead*.

Encumbrances against real estate may be in the form of liens, deed restrictions, easements, licenses and encroachments.

An *easement* is the right acquired by one person to use another's real estate. Easements are classified as interests in real estate, but are not estates in land. *Easements appurtenant* involve two separately owned tracts. The tract benefited is known as the *dominant tenement;* the tract that is subject to the easement is called the *servient tenement*. An *easement in gross* is a personal right, such as that granted to utility companies to maintain poles, wires and pipelines.

Easements may be created by agreement, express grant or reservation in a deed, necessity, prescription or condemnation. They can be terminated when the purpose of the easement no longer exists, by merger of both interests, by release or by abandonment of the easement, by nonuse of a prescriptive easement, adverse possession, destruction, excessive use or a lawsuit.

A *license* is permission to enter another's property for a specific purpose. A license is usually created orally, is of a temporary nature and can be revoked.

An *encroachment* is an unauthorized use of another's real estate.

Ownership of land encompasses not only the land itself but also the right to use the water on or adjacent to it. Many states subscribe to the common-law doctrine of *riparian rights,* which gives the owner of land adjacent to a nonnavigable stream ownership of the stream to its midpoint. *Littoral rights* are held by owners of land bordering large lakes and oceans and include rights to the water and ownership of the land up to the high-water mark. In states where water is scarce, water use is often decided by the doctrine of prior appropriation. Under prior appropriation, water belongs to the state and it is allocated to users who have obtained permits.

Questions

1. The term *dower* refers to which of the following?
   a. a conventional life estate in real property
   b. ownership of a homestead
   c. a marital right
   d. none of the above

2. The right of a governmental body to take ownership of real estate for public use is called:
   a. escheat.
   b. eminent domain.
   c. condemnation.
   d. police power.

3. Peter Kelly has fenced his property. The fence extends one foot over his lot line onto the property of a neighbor, Alice Manley. The fence is an example of an:
   a. encumbrance.
   b. encroachment.
   c. avulsion.
   d. a and b

4. A homeowner may be allowed certain protection from judgments of creditors as a result of a state's:
   a. homestead exemption.
   b. curtesy rights.
   c. doctrine of prior appropriation.
   d. all of the above

5. A purchaser of real estate learned that his ownership rights will continue forever and that no other person claims to be the owner or has any ownership control over the property. This person owns a:
   a. fee simple interest.
   b. life estate.
   c. determinable fee estate.
   d. fee simple estate subject to a condition subsequent.

6. Ed Roberts has the legal right to pass over the land owned by his neighbor. This is an:
   a. estate in land.
   b. easement.
   c. emblement.
   d. a and b

7. A husband's life estate in property owned by his deceased wife is:
   I. curtesy.
   II. granted by statute in all states.
   a. I only
   b. II only
   c. both I and II
   d. neither I nor II

8. Janet Auden owned the fee simple title to a vacant lot adjacent to a hospital and was persuaded to make a gift of the lot. She wanted to have some control over its use, so her attorney prepared her deed to convey ownership of the lot to the hospital "so long as it is used for hospital purposes." After completion of the gift, the hospital will own:
   a. a fee simple absolute estate.
   b. a license.
   c. a determinable fee estate.
   d. a leasehold estate.

9. After Peter Desmond had purchased his house and moved in, he discovered that his neighbor regularly used Desmond's driveway to reach a garage located on the neighbor's property. Desmond's attorney explained that ownership of the neighbor's real estate includes an easement over the driveway. Desmond's property is properly called:
   a. the dominant tenement.
   b. a tenement.
   c. a leasehold.
   d. the servient tenement.

10. A father conveys ownership of his residence to his son but reserves for himself a life estate in the residence. The interest the son owns during the father's lifetime is:
    a. pur autre vie.
    b. a remainder.
    c. a reversion.
    d. a and b

11. If the owner of real estate does not take action before the prescriptive period has passed, then someone may acquire:

    a. an easement by necessity.
    b. a license.
    c. an easement by implication of law.
    d. none of the above

12. Which one of the following best describes a life estate?

    a. an estate conveyed to *A* for the life of *Z*, and upon *Z's* death to *B*.
    b. an estate held by *A* and *B* in joint tenancy with right of survivorship
    c. an estate without condition
    d. a fee simple estate

13. Encumbrances on real estate:

    I. may include liens, easements and deed restrictions.
    II. make it impossible to sell the encumbered property.

      a. I only   c. both I and II
      b. II only   d. neither I nor II

14. An estate in land that will automatically extinguish upon the occurrence of a specified event is called a:

    a. right of entry.
    b. fee simple subject to a condition subsequent.
    c. fee simple with a special limitation.
    d. a and b

15. A *license* is an example of a(n):

    a. easement.   c. encumbrance.
    b. encroachment.   d. restriction.

16. A tenant in an apartment building holds a:

    I. less-than-freehold estate.
    II. determinable fee estate.

      a. I only   c. both I and II
      b. II only   d. neither I nor II

17. Many states determine water use by allocating water to users who hold recorded beneficial-use permits. This type of water-use privilege is called:

    a. the doctrine of riparian rights.
    b. the doctrine of highest and best use.
    c. the doctrine of prior appropriation.
    d. none of the above

18. When a homeowner who is entitled by state law to a homestead exemption is sued by his or her creditors, then the creditors:

    a. can have the court sell the home and apply the full proceeds of sale to the debts.
    b. have no right to have the debtor's home sold.
    c. can force the debtor to sell the home to pay them.
    d. can request a court sale and apply the sale proceeds, in excess of the statutory exemption and secured debts, to the unsecured debts.

19. Under the allodial system, individual landowners have maximum rights, subject to certain government powers such as:

    I. police power.
    II. eminent domain.

      a. I only   c. both I and II
      b. II only   d. neither I nor II

20. Property deeded to a school "for educational purposes only" conveys:

    a. fee simple absolute.
    b. fee simple on condition precedent.
    c. fee simple on condition subsequent.
    d. fee simple with special limitation.

8

How Ownership Is Held

Key Terms

Beneficiary
Common elements
Community property
Condominium
Cooperative
Co-ownership
Corporation
General partnership
Joint tenancy
Limited partnership
Partition
Partnership

Right of survivorship
Separate property
Severalty
Syndicate
Tenancy by the entirety
Tenancy in common
Time-share ownership
Trust
Trustee
Trustor
Undivided interest

Overview

There are many different forms of ownership that purchasers must consider before taking title to a parcel of real estate. The choice of ownership will affect such matters as the owner's legal right to sell the real estate without the consent of others, the owner's right to choose who will own the property after his or her death and the rights of creditors in the future. The choice will also in many cases have tax implications, both in terms of a possible gift tax resulting from a present transfer and in terms of future income and estate taxes. This chapter will discuss the many basic forms of real estate ownership available to individuals, as well as to business entities, and will also include a discussion of the cooperative and condominium forms of ownership.

Forms of Ownership	A fee simple estate in land may be held (1) in **severalty,** which means that title is held by one owner, (2) in **co-ownership,** where title is held by two or more persons or (3) in **trust,** where title is held by a third person for the benefit of another or others, called the beneficiary or beneficiaries.

The form by which property is owned is important to the real estate broker's work for two reasons: (1) *the form of ownership existing when a property is sold determines who must sign the various documents involved* (listing contract, acceptance of offer to purchase or sales contract, and deed); and (2) *the purchaser must determine in what form to take title.* For example, if there is one purchaser taking title in the purchaser's name alone, tenancy in severalty is created; if there are two or more purchasers, they may take title as tenants in common or as joint tenants. Married purchasers' choices are governed by state laws. Some states provide for married couples to own real estate as tenants by the entireties or under community property laws. Other states allow a married couple to choose the form of ownership they prefer.

The forms of ownership available are controlled by the laws of the state in which the land is located. When questions about these forms are raised by the parties to a transaction, the real estate broker should recommend that the parties seek legal advice. Refer to table 8.1 to determine the forms of ownership applicable to your state. Concentrate on these as you study this chapter.

Ownership in Severalty	When title to real estate is *vested in* (presently owned by) one person or one organization, that person or organization is said to own the property *in severalty.* This person is also referred to as the *sole owner.* Various states have special laws that affect title held in severalty by either a husband or a wife. In some states, when either the husband or wife owns property in severalty, it is still necessary for the spouse to join in signing documents: (1) to release dower or curtesy rights in states that have such rights, (2) to release homestead rights in states that provide a homestead exemption for homeowners or (3) when the wife is a minor. In other states, only the owner's signature is needed.

Co-Ownership	When title to one parcel of real estate is vested in two or more persons or organizations, those parties are said to be *co-owners,* or *concurrent owners,* of the property. There are several forms of co-ownership, each having unique legal characteristics. The forms most commonly recognized by the various states are: (1) tenancy in common, (2) joint tenancy, (3) tenancy by the entirety, (4) community property and (5) partnership property. Each of these forms of co-ownership will be discussed separately.

Tenancy in Common	A parcel of real estate may be owned by two or more people as **tenants in common.** There are two important characteristics of a tenancy in common.

Table 8.1
Chart of Ownership

State	Sole — Individual	Tenancy in Common	Joint Tenancy	Tenancy by the Entirety	Community Property	Trust	Condominium
Alabama	•	•	•			•	•
Alaska	•	•		•		•	•
Arizona	•	•	•		•	•	•
Arkansas	•	•	•	•		•	•
California	•	•	•		•	•	•
Colorado	•	•	•			•	•
Connecticut	•	•	•			•	•
Delaware	•	•	•	•		•	•
District of Columbia	•	•	•	•		•	•
Florida	•	•	•	•		•	•
Georgia	•	•	•			•	•
Hawaii	•	•	•	•		•	•
Idaho	•	•	•		•	•	•
Illinois	•	•	•			•	•
Indiana	•	•	•	•		•	•
Iowa	•	•	•			•	•
Kansas	•	•	•			•	•
Kentucky	•	•	•	•		•	•
Louisiana[1]						•	•
Maine	•	•	•			•	•
Maryland	•	•	•	•		•	•
Massachusetts	•	•	•	•		•	•
Michigan	•	•	•	•		•	•
Minnesota	•	•	•			•	•
Mississippi	•	•	•	•		•	•
Missouri	•	•	•	•		•	•
Montana	•	•	•			•	•
Nebraska	•	•	•			•	•
Nevada	•	•	•		•	•	•
New Hampshire	•	•	•			•	•
New Jersey	•	•	•	•		•	•
New Mexico	•	•	•		•	•	•
New York	•	•	•	•		•	•
North Carolina	•	•	•	•		•	•
North Dakota	•	•	•			•	•
Ohio[2]	•	•		② No longer used any longer		•	•
Oklahoma	•	•	•			•	•
Oregon	•	•		•		•	•
Pennsylvania	•	•		•		•	•
Rhode Island	•	•	•	•		•	•
South Carolina	•	•	•			•	•
South Dakota	•	•	•			•	•
Tennessee	•	•	•	•		•	•
Texas	•	•	•		•	•	•
Utah	•	•	•	•		•	•
Vermont	•	•	•	•		•	•
Virginia	•	•	•	•		•	•
Washington	•	•	•		•	•	•
West Virginia	•	•	•	•		•	•
Wisconsin[3]	•	•	•			•	•
Wyoming	•	•	•	•		•	•

[1]In Louisiana, real estate can be owned by one person and by two or more persons, but these ownership interests are created by Louisiana statute. There are no estates comparable to those of joint tenancy, tenancy by the entirety, or community property, nor is there any statutory estate giving surviving co-owners the right of survivorship. Two or more persons may be co-owners under indivision, or joint, ownership.
[2]Ohio does not recognize joint tenancy, but permits a special form of survivorship by deed through an instrument commonly called a "joint and survivorship deed."
[3]As of 1986, Wisconsin recognizes "marital property" that is similar to community property.

First, the ownership interest of a tenant in common is an **undivided interest;** there is a *unity of possession* between the co-owners. This means that although a tenant in common may hold, say, a one-half or one-third interest in a property, it is impossible to distinguish physically which specific half or third of the property the tenant in common owns. The deed creating a tenancy in common may or may not state the fractional interest held by each co-owner; if no fractions are stated, the tenants are presumed to hold equal shares. For example, if five people hold title, each would own an undivided one-fifth interest.

The second important characteristic of a tenancy in common is that *each owner holds his or her undivided interest in severalty* and can sell, convey, mortgage or transfer that interest without consent of the other co-owners. Upon the death of a co-owner, that tenant's undivided interest passes to his or her heirs. The interest of a deceased tenant in common does not pass to another tenant in common unless the surviving co-owner is an heir or purchaser (see figure 8.1). In many states, the spouse of a married tenant in common must sign a deed to a purchaser in order to release any dower or homestead rights.

When two or more people acquire title to a parcel of real estate and the deed of conveyance does not stipulate the character of the tenancy created, then by operation of law the grantees usually acquire title as tenants in common. If the conveyance is made to a husband and wife with no further explanation, this assumption may not apply. In some states, a conveyance made to a husband and wife creates a tenancy by the entirety, in others, community property, and in at least one state, a joint tenancy. It is therefore important to know the legal interpretation of such a situation under your state law.

Figure 8.1
Tenancy in Common

A and B are tenants in common

A	B
½	½

B dies and will his interest to C and D equally

A	C	D
½	¼	¼

Joint Tenancy

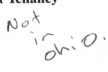

Most states recognize some form of **joint tenancy,** which is an estate, or unit of interest, in land owned by two or more people. While there are many similarities between a tenancy in common and a joint tenancy, the distinguishing feature of joint tenancy is the **right of survivorship.** The death of one of the joint tenants does not destroy the unit; it only reduces by one the number of people who make up the owning unit. The joint tenancy continues until there is only one owner, who then holds title in severalty. The surviving tenant has the same rights to dispose of the property as any sole owner (see figure 8.2).

Note that the right of survivorship refers to the rights of the co-owners of the joint tenancy, not to their heirs. As each successive joint tenant dies, the surviving joint tenant(s) acquire the interest of the deceased joint tenant. The last survivor

Figure 8.2
Joint Tenancy with
Right of Survivorship

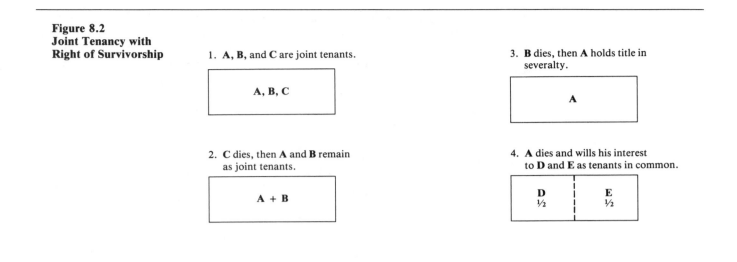

1. **A, B,** and **C** are joint tenants.

A, B, C

2. **C** dies, then **A** and **B** remain as joint tenants.

A + B

3. **B** dies, then **A** holds title in severalty.

A

4. **A** dies and wills his interest to **D** and **E** as tenants in common.

D ½	E ½

takes title in severalty and then has all of the rights of individual ownership, including the right to have the property pass to his or her heirs.

In Practice...   *Married couples often take title to property as joint tenants, so that the surviving spouse automatically becomes sole owner of the property. The surviving spouse can thus enjoy the benefits of ownership without waiting for the conclusion of probate proceedings. This benefit of survivorship also applies to property held in a tenancy by the entirety, discussed later in this chapter.*

In some states, however, special probate consideration is given to a surviving spouse, who may acquire the right to dispose of marital property simply and quickly. There are also important tax considerations, as property passed by right of survivorship will then be subject to taxation in the survivor's estate.

In short, the form under which title is to be taken (particularly by a married couple) should always be discussed with an attorney. Joint tenancy should not be used as a substitute for a will.

Joint tenants own an undivided interest, as do tenants in common. A joint tenant can also convey his or her interest without consent of the other joint tenants, but in doing so will destroy the joint tenancy as to that interest. The new owner would then hold that share as a tenant in common with the remaining joint tenants.

Creating joint tenancies. A joint tenancy can be created only by grant or purchase (through a deed of conveyance) or by devise (by will). It cannot be implied or created by operation of law. The conveyance must specifically state the intention to create a joint tenancy, and the grantees or devisees must be explicitly identified as joint tenants. For example, typical wording in a conveyance creating a joint tenancy would be "to *A* and *B* as joint tenants and not as tenants in common." Some states, however, have abolished the right of survivorship as a distinguishing characteristic of joint tenancy. In these states, the conveyance must also explicitly indicate the intention to create the right of survivorship in order for that right to exist. In such cases, appropriate wording might be "to *A* and *B* and to the survivor of them, his or her heirs and assigns, as joint tenants."

There are four requirements to create a joint tenancy. There must be:

1. unity of *possession*—all joint tenants hold an undivided right to possession.
2. unity of *interest*—all joint tenants hold equal ownership interests.
3. unity of *time*—all joint tenants acquire their interest at the same time.
4. unity of *title*—all joint tenants acquire their interest by the same instrument of conveyance.

The four unities (PITT) are present when title is acquired by *one deed, executed and delivered at one time, and conveying equal interests to all the grantees, who hold undivided possession of the property as joint tenants.*

In many states, if real estate is owned in severalty by a person who wishes to create a joint tenancy between him- or herself and others, the owner will have to convey the property to an intermediary (usually called a *nominee*, or *straw man*), and the nominee must convey it back, naming all the parties as joint tenants in the conveyance.

Some states have eliminated this "legal fiction" by allowing an owner in severalty to execute a deed to him- or herself and others "as joint tenants and not as tenants in common" and thereby create a valid joint tenancy without the actual presence of the four unities. In some states that have tried to accomplish this same result, the courts have held that such a conveyance creates a wholly new estate, usually referred to as an *estate of survivorship.*

Most state laws hold that there is no dower in joint tenancy. Thus, business associates can hold title to a parcel of real estate as joint tenants, and their spouses, if any, are not required to join in a conveyance in order to waive dower rights.

Terminating joint tenancies. A joint tenancy is destroyed when any one of the essential unities of joint tenancy is terminated. Thus, while a joint tenant is free to convey his or her interest in the jointly held property, doing so will destroy the unity of interest and, in turn, the joint tenancy as it applied to the conveying ten-

Figure 8.3
Combination of
Tenancies

A, B, and C are joint tenants.

A, B, C

A sells her interest to D.

D 1/3	B + C 2/3

D becomes a tenant in common with B and C as joint tenants.

ant. Rights of other joint tenants *in their interests* will be unaffected. For example, if *A, B* and *C* hold title as joint tenants and *A* conveys her interest to *D*, then *D* will own an undivided one-third interest in severalty as a tenant in common with *B* and *C*, who will continue to own their undivided two-thirds interest as joint tenants (see figure 8.3).

Joint tenancies may also be terminated by operation of law, such as in bankruptcy or foreclosure sale proceedings. In addition, in states where a mortgage on real property is held to be a conveyance of land, a joint tenant who mortgages his or her property without the other tenants joining in the mortgage will also destroy the joint tenancy.

Termination of Co-Ownership by Partition Suit

Tenants in common or joint tenants who wish to terminate their co-ownership of real estate may file in court a suit to **partition** the land. The right of partition is a legal way to dissolve a co-ownership when the parties do not voluntarily agree to its termination. If the court determines that the land cannot actually be divided into parts, it will order the real estate sold and divide the proceeds of the sale among the co-owners according to their fractional interests.

Tenancy by the Entirety

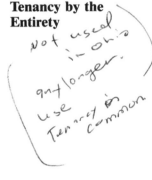

Not used in ohio any longer. use Tenancy in common

Some states allow **tenancy by the entirety,** which is a special form of tenancy in which the owners are husband and wife. Each spouse has an equal, undivided interest in the property; each, in essence, owns the entire estate. Upon the death of one spouse, the tenancy operates like a joint tenancy—full title automatically passes to the surviving spouse.

The distinguishing characteristics of tenancy by the entirety are: (1) the owners must be husband and wife; (2) the owners have rights of survivorship; (3) during the owners' lives, title can be conveyed *only by a deed signed by both parties* (one party cannot convey a one-half interest); and (4) there is generally no right to partition. Under early common law, a husband and wife were held to be one person in the eyes of the law—the wife's legal personality was merged with that of her husband's. As a result, real estate owned by a husband and wife as tenants by the entireties is considered to be held by one indivisible legal unit.

Under the common law, a grant to husband and wife created a tenancy by the entirety, even if no form of ownership was specified. Most states that recognize it now require that the intention to create a tenancy by the entirety be specifically stated. Unless the specific intention to create a tenancy by the entirety is stated in the original document, a tenancy in common usually results.

A tenancy by the entirety may be terminated by:

1. the death of either spouse;
2. divorce (leaving the parties as tenants in common);
3. mutual agreement;
4. execution proceedings in favor of a *joint* creditor of husband and wife.

Community Property Rights

The concept of community property originated in Spanish law rather than English common law and was adopted by eight states (Arizona, California, Idaho, Louisiana, Nevada, New Mexico, Texas and Washington). There are many variations among the community property laws of these states.

Community property laws are based on the concept that a husband and wife, rather than merging into one entity, are equal partners. Thus, any property acquired during a marriage is considered to be obtained by mutual effort. Community property states recognize two kinds of property. **Separate property** is that which is owned solely by either spouse before the marriage or is acquired by gift or inheritance after the marriage. Such separate property also includes any property purchased with separate funds after the marriage. Any income earned from a person's separate property generally remains part of his or her separate property. Property classified as sole and separate can be mortgaged or conveyed by the owning spouse without the signature of the nonowning spouse.

Community property consists of all other property, real and personal, acquired by either spouse during the marriage. Any conveyance or encumbrance of community property requires the signatures of both spouses. Upon the death of one spouse, the survivor automatically owns one-half of the community property. The other half is distributed according to the deceased's will. If the deceased died without a will, the other half is inherited by the surviving spouse or by the deceased's other heirs, depending upon state law.

Examples of Co-Ownership

To clarify the concepts of co-ownership further, note the following four examples of co-ownership arrangements:

1. A deed conveys title to *A* and *B*. The intention of the parties is not stated, so generally ownership as tenants in common is created. If *A* dies, her one-half interest will pass to her heirs.
2. A deed conveying title one-third to *C* and two-thirds to *D* creates a tenancy in common, with each owner having the fractional interest specified.
3. A deed to *H* and *W* as husband and wife creates a tenancy by the entirety, community property or other interests between the husband and wife as provided by state law.
4. A conveyance of real estate to two people (not husband and wife) by such wording as "to *Y* and *Z*, as joint tenants and not as tenants in common" may create a joint tenancy ownership. Upon the death of *Y*, the title to the property usually passes to *Z* by right of survivorship. In those states that do not recognize the right of survivorship, additional provisions are required (such as "and to the survivor and his or her heirs and assigns").

Note also that *a combination of interests can exist in one parcel of real estate.* For example, when *M* and spouse hold title to an undivided one-half as joint tenants and *S* and spouse hold title to the other undivided one-half as joint tenants, the relationship among the owners of the two half interests is that of tenants in common.

Trusts

In most states, title to real estate can be held in a trust. In order for a trust to be created, the title to the real estate involved must be conveyed by the **trustor** (also known as a *settlor*), the person originating the trust, to a **trustee,** who will own the property for one or more people or legal entities, call **beneficiaries.** The trustee is a *fiduciary,* one who acts in confidence or trust, and has a special legal relationship with the beneficiary or beneficiaries. The trustee can be either an individual or a corporation, such as a trust company. The trustee has only as much power and authority as is given by the instrument that creates the trust.

Such an instrument may be a trust agreement, will or deed (see figure 8.4). In many states, the deed *of* trust (or trust deed) is the preferred form of security interest in real estate. Real estate ownership can be held under either: (1) living or testamentary trusts or (2) land trusts. In addition, real estate may be held by a number of people in a *real estate investment trust,* which will be discussed in Chapter 22.

**Figure 8.4
Trust Ownership**

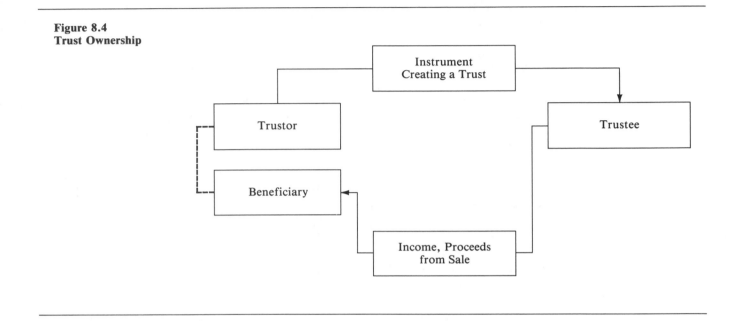

**Living and
Testamentary Trusts**

Property owners may provide for their own financial care and/or that of their families by establishing a trust. Such trusts may be created by agreement during a property owner's lifetime (living) or established by will after his or her death (testamentary).

The individual creating a trust—the trustor—makes an agreement with a trustee (usually a corporate trustee) by which the trustor conveys assets (real and/or personal) to the trustee with the understanding that the trustee will assume certain duties. Those duties may include the care and investment of the trust assets to produce an income. After payment of operating expenses and trustee's fees, the income is paid to or used for the benefit of the beneficiary. The trust may continue for the lifetime of the beneficiary, or the assets can be distributed when the beneficiary reaches a predetermined age.

Land Trusts

A few states permit the establishment of land trusts in which real estate is the only asset. As in all trusts, the legal title to the property is conveyed to a trustee (in this case, by a deed *in* trust), and the beneficial interest is in the beneficiary, who, in the case of land trusts, is usually the trustor. While the beneficial interest in the trust real estate is considered to be *personal property,* the beneficiary retains management and control of the property and has the right of possession as well as the right to any income or proceeds from its sale.

One of the distinguishing characteristics of a land trust is that the *public records do not indicate the beneficiary's identity.* A land trust may thus be used for secrecy when assembling separate parcels, and there are many other benefits to a land trust. A beneficial interest in a land trust can be transferred by assignment, making the formalities of a deed unnecessary. A collateral assignment can be made (the property pledged as security for a loan) without having a mortgage placed on record. Real property is subject to the laws of the state in which it is located, but since the beneficiary's interest is personal property, it will pass, on the beneficiary's death, under the laws of the state in which the beneficiary resided. If the deceased owned property in several states, additional probate costs and inheritance taxes can thus be avoided.

Usually only individuals create land trusts, but corporations as well as individuals can be beneficiaries. A land trust ordinarily continues for a definite term, such as 20 years. If the beneficiary does not extend the trust term when it expires, the trustee is usually obligated to sell the real estate and return the net proceeds to the beneficiary.

Ownership of Real Estate by Business Organizations

A business entity is an organization that exists independently of the people who are members of the organization—for example, a corporation. Ownership by a business organization makes it possible for many people to hold an interest in the same parcel of real estate. There are various ways in which investors may be organized to finance a real estate project. Some provide for the real estate to be owned by the entity itself; others provide for direct ownership of the real estate by the investors.

The purchase or sale of real estate by any business organization involves complex legal questions, and legal counsel is usually required. Business organizations may be categorized as partnerships or corporations. Partnerships and corporations are discussed next; then follows a discussion of business syndicates formed for real estate investment.

Partnerships

An association of two or more people to carry on a business as co-owners and share in the business's profits and losses is a **partnership.** There are two kinds of partnerships, general and limited. In a **general partnership,** all partners participate to some extent in the operation and management of the business and may be held personally liable for business losses and obligations. A **limited partnership** includes one or more general partners as well as limited, or silent, partners. The business is run by the general partner or partners. The limited partners are not legally permitted to participate, and each can be held liable for the business's losses *only* to the extent of his or her investment. The limited partnership is a popular method of organizing investors in a real estate project.

Under common law, a partnership is not a legal entity and cannot own real estate. Title must be vested in the partners as individuals in a tenancy in common or joint tenancy, not in the partnership. Most states, however, have adopted the *Uniform Partnership Act,* under which realty may be held in the partnership name, and the *Uniform Limited Partnership Act,* which establishes the legality of the limited partnership form and also provides that realty may be held in the partnership name.

General partnerships are dissolved and must be reorganized if one partner dies, withdraws or goes bankrupt. In a limited partnership, the agreement creating the partnership may provide for the continuation of the organization upon the death or withdrawal of one of the partners.

Corporations

A **corporation** is an artificial person, or legal entity, created under the authority of the laws of the state from which it receives its charter. A corporation is managed and operated by its *board of directors*. A corporation's charter sets forth the powers of the corporation, including its right to buy and sell real estate after passage of a resolution to that effect by its board of directors. Some charters permit a corporation to purchase real estate for any purpose; others limit such purchases to land that is needed to fulfill the entity's corporate purpose.

As a legal entity, a corporation exists in perpetuity until it is formally dissolved. The death of one of the officers or directors does not affect title to property that is owned by the corporation.

Individuals participate, or invest, in a corporation by purchasing stock. Since stock is *personal property,* stockholders do not have a direct ownership interest in real estate owned by a corporation. Each stockholder's liability for the corporation's losses is usually limited to the amount of his or her investment.

One of the main disadvantages of corporate ownership of income property is that the profits are subject to double taxation. As a legal entity, a corporation must file an income-tax return and pay tax on its profits. In addition, the portions of the remaining profits distributed to stockholders as dividends are taxed again as part of the stockholders' individual incomes.

Syndicates

Generally speaking, a **syndicate** is a *joining together of two or more people or firms in order to make and operate a real estate investment.* A syndicate is not in itself a legal entity; however, it may be organized into a number of ownership forms, including co-ownership (tenancy in common, joint tenancy), partnership, trust or corporation. A *joint venture* is a form of partnership in which two or more people or firms carry out a *single business project.* Joint ventures are characterized by a time limitation resulting from the fact that the joint venturers do not intend to establish a permanent relationship. More will be said about these organizations in Chapter 22.

Cooperative and Condominium Ownership

During the first half of this century, the nation's population grew rapidly and concentrated in the large urban areas. This population concentration led to multiple-unit housing—high-rise apartment buildings in the center city and low-rise apartment complexes in adjoining suburbs. Initially these buildings were occupied by "tenants" under the traditional rental system. But the urge to "own a part of the land," together with certain tax advantages that accrue to such ownership, led to *cooperative* ownership and, more recently, to the *condominium* form of ownership of multiple-unit buildings.

Cooperative Ownership

Under the usual **cooperative** arrangement, title to land and building is held by a *corporation* (or land trust). The building management sets a price for each apartment in the building. Each purchaser of an apartment in the building receives stock in the corporation when he or she pays the agreed-upon price for the apartment. The purchaser then becomes a stockholder of the corporation and, *by virtue of that stock ownership, receives a proprietary lease* to his or her apartment for the life of the corporation.

The cooperative building's real estate taxes are assessed against the corporation as owner. The mortgage is signed by the corporation, creating one lien on the entire parcel of real estate. Taxes, mortgage interest and principal, and operating and maintenance expenses on the property are shared by the tenant-shareholders in the form of monthly assessments.

Thus, while the cooperative tenant-owners do not actually own an interest in real estate (they own stock, which is *personal property*), for all practical purposes they control the property through their stock ownership and their voice in the management of the corporation. For example, the bylaws of the corporation generally provide that each prospective purchaser of an apartment lease must be approved by an administrative board.

One disadvantage of cooperative ownership became particularly evident during the Depression years and must still be considered. This is the possibility that if enough owner-occupants became financially unable to make prompt payment of their monthly assessments, the corporation might be forced to allow mortgage and tax payments to go unpaid. Through such defaults, the entire property could be ordered sold by court order in a foreclosure suit. Such a sale would usually destroy the interests of all occupant-shareholders, even those who have paid their assessments. Another disadvantage is that some cooperatives provide that a tenant-owner can sell his or her interest back to the cooperative only at the original purchase price, so that the cooperative gains any profits made on the resale. These limitations have diminished the appeal of this form of ownership and resulted in greater preference for the condominium form of ownership.

Condominium Ownership

The **condominium** form of occupant ownership of apartment buildings was popular in Europe for many years before gaining wide acceptance in the United States. Condominium laws, often called horizontal property acts, have been enacted in every state. Under these laws, the occupant-owner of each apartment holds a *fee simple title* to the apartment and also a specified share of the indivisible parts of the building and land, known as the **common elements** (see figure 8.5). The individual unit owners in a condominium own these common elements together as *tenants in common*. State law usually limits this relationship among unit owners in that there is *no right to partition*.

The condominium form of ownership is usually used for apartment buildings. These may range from freestanding high-rise buildings to townhouse arrangements. The common elements include such items as the land, exterior structure, hallways, elevators, stairways and roof. In some instances (particularly with townhouse developments) lawns and recreational facilities such as swimming pools, clubhouses, tennis courts and golf courses, may also be considered common elements. In addition, the condominium form of ownership is used for such other types of properties as commercial property, office buildings or multi-use buildings that contain offices and shops as well as residential units.

Creation of a condominium. State laws usually specify that a condominium is created and established when the owners or developers of the property execute and record a *declaration* of its creation in the county where the property is lo-

**Figure 8.5
Condominium
Ownership**

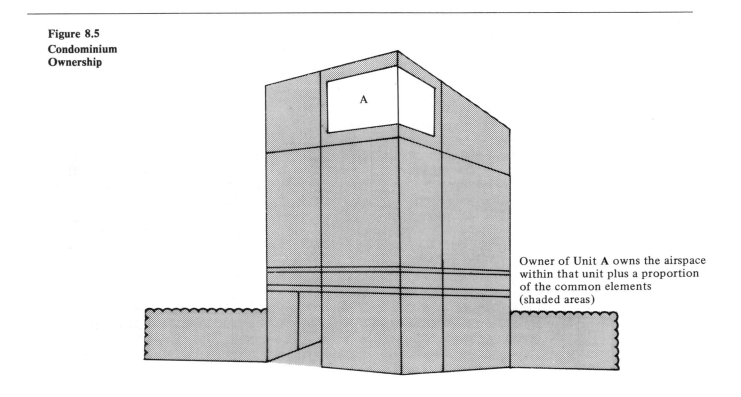

Owner of Unit **A** owns the airspace
within that unit plus a proportion
of the common elements
(shaded areas)

cated. The various state laws require many items to be contained in or attached to
the declaration. Generally these items include: (1) a legal description of the land,
(2) a plat map illustrating and identifying each unit, (3) a list of the value of the
land and of each unit, (4) a list of the percentage of undivided interest in all common areas and facilities assigned to each unit, (5) a copy of the condominium's
bylaws and (6) provisions for the establishment of a condominium owners' association.

Ownership. Once the property is established as a condominium, each unit becomes a separate parcel of real estate that may be dealt with in the same way as
any other parcel of real property. A condominium unit is *owned in fee simple and
may be held by one or more people in any type of ownership or tenancy that is
recognized by state law.*

Real estate taxes are assessed and collected on each unit as an individual property.
Default in the payment of taxes or a mortgage loan by one unit owner may result
in a foreclosure sale of that owner's unit, but does not affect the ownership of the
other unit owners.

Operation and administration. The condominium property generally is administered by an association of unit owners according to the bylaws set forth in the
declaration. The association may be governed by a board of directors or other
official entity, it may manage the property on its own or it may engage a professional property manager to perform this function.

Acting through its board of directors or other officers, the association must enforce any rules it adopts regarding the operation and use of the property. The association is responsible for the maintenance, repair, cleaning and sanitation of the common elements and structural portions of the property. It must also maintain fire and extended-coverage insurance as well as liability insurance for those portions of the property.

Expenses incurred in fulfilling the association's responsibilities are paid by the unit owners in the form of monthly *assessments* collected by the owners' association. Such fees are assessed each unit owner. They are due monthly, quarterly, semiannually or annually, depending on the provisions of the bylaws. If such assessments are not paid, the association usually has the option to seek a court-ordered judgment to have the property sold to cover the outstanding amount.

Unlike a cooperative, owners of condominium units can sell or transfer their property to whomever they choose, without approval of the association.

Termination. State laws usually stipulate that a building can be removed from condominium ownership under certain circumstances. In such cases, most or all of the unit owners must be party to a revocation agreement filed in the public record in the county where the property is located. All unit owners would then become tenants in common, each owning an undivided interest in the entire property that is equal to the percentage of ownership in the common elements he or she previously held.

Time-shared ownership. *Time-sharing* permits multiple purchasers to buy interests in real estate—usually a unit of a resort hotel or development—with each purchaser having a right to use the facility for a fixed or variable time period. A *time-share estate* includes an estate interest in the property, but a *time-share use* does not.

Some time-sharing programs allow for a rotation system in which the tenant in common can occupy the unit at different times of the year in different years. Other programs sell only specific months or weeks of the year. For example, 12 individuals could own equal, undivided interests in one condominium unit, with each owner entitled to use the premises for a specified month in each year. Maintenance and other common expenses are prorated among the unit owners.

The laws regarding the origination and sale of time-shared units are generally complex and vary from state to state. Time-shares may be subject to subdivision requirements, for instance. You should be familiar with the provisions of the relevant statutes before dealing with such properties.

Summary

Sole ownership, or *ownership in severalty,* indicates that title is held by one person or entity. Under the designation *co-ownership,* there are several ways in which title to real estate can be held concurrently by more than one person.

Under *tenancy in common,* each party holds a separate title but shares possession with other tenants. An individual owner may sell his or her interest. Upon death, a tenant in common's interest passes to the tenant's heirs. There are no special requirements to create this interest. When two or more parties hold title to real estate, they will hold title as tenants in common unless there is an expressed intention otherwise. *Joint tenancy* indicates two or more owners with the right of survivorship. The intention of the parties to establish a joint tenancy with right of survivorship must be clearly stated. In some states the four unities of *possession, interest, time* and *title* must be present; other states have by statute eliminated this legal requirement.

Tenancy by the entirety, in those states where it is recognized, is actually a joint tenancy between husband and wife. It gives the husband and wife the right of survivorship in all lands acquired by them *jointly* during marriage. During their lives, both must sign the deed for any title to pass to a purchaser. *Community property* rights exist only in certain states and pertain only to land owned by husband and wife. Usually the property acquired by joint efforts during the marriage is community property and one-half is owned by each spouse. Properties acquired by a spouse before the marriage and through inheritance or gifts after the marriage are termed *separate property*. Community property is a statutory right, and as a result, each state that has established the right of community property has also defined the rights it encompasses.

Real estate ownership may also be held in *trust*. In creating a trust, title to the property involved is conveyed to a *trustee* under a living or testamentary trust, or a land trust.

Various types of business organizations may own real estate. A *corporation* is a legal entity and can hold title to real estate in severalty. While a *partnership* is technically not a legal entity, the *Uniform Partnership Act* and the *Uniform Limited Partnership Act,* adopted by most states, enable a partnership to own property in the partnership's name. A *syndicate* is an association of two or more people or firms to make an investment in real estate. Many syndicates are *joint ventures* and are organized for only a single project. A syndicate may be organized as a co-ownership, trust, corporation or partnership.

Cooperative ownership of apartment buildings indicates title in one entity (corporation or trust) that must pay taxes, mortgage interest and principal, and all operating expenses. Reimbursement comes from shareholders or beneficiaries through monthly assessments. Shareholders have proprietary, long-term leases entitling them to occupy their apartments. Under *condominium ownership,* each occupant-owner holds fee simple title to an apartment unit plus a share of the common elements. Each unit owner receives an individual tax bill and may mortgage the unit as desired. Expenses for operating the building are collected by an owners' association through monthly assessments. A variation of condominium ownership called *time-sharing* enables multiple purchasers to own an estate or use interest in real estate, with the right to use it for a part of each year.

Questions

1. The *unities* necessary to create a joint tenancy include which of the following?

   a. interest   c. possession and title
   b. time   d. all of the above

2. A parcel of real estate was purchased by Howard Evers and Charles Chance. The seller's deed received at the closing conveyed the property "to Howard Evers and Charles Chance," without further explanation. Thus:

   a. Evers and Chance are joint tenants.
   b. Evers and Chance are tenants in common.
   c. Evers and Chance each own an undivided one-half interest in the property.
   d. b and c

3. Martin, Barton and Fargo are joint tenants owning a tract of land. Fargo conveys her interest to Vonder. This means that:

   I. Martin and Barton are still joint tenants.
   II. Vonder is a tenant in common with Martin and Barton.

   a. I only   c. both I and II
   b. II only   d. neither I nor II

4. A tenant in common owns:

   a. an undivided interest.
   b. a fractional interest.
   c. an interest in severalty.
   d. all of the above

5. A purchaser under the cooperative form of ownership receives:

   I. a deed to his or her unit.
   II. a proprietary lease and the right to use the common elements.

   a. I only   c. both I and II
   b. II only   d. neither I nor II

6. Ownership of real property by one person without the ownership participation of others is called:

   a. trust.   c. solety.
   b. severalty.   d. condominium.

7. The *right of survivorship* is closely associated with a:

   a. corporation.   c. trust.
   b. cooperative.   d. joint tenancy.

8. Peterson and Kelley have purchased a block of apartment buildings in a large city and have decided, for business reasons, to take ownership to the real estate under a land trust, as permitted in their state. Under this ownership arrangement:

   a. the beneficiaries' identities will not appear in the public records.
   b. the beneficiaries will be unable to control the property or personally participate in the buildings' management.
   c. both a and b
   d. neither a nor b

9. In a trust, the person in whom title is vested is called the:

   a. trustee.   c. beneficiary.
   b. trustor.   d. straw man.

10. Which of the following forms of ownership may be created by operation of law?

    a. joint tenancy
    b. tenancy by the entirety
    c. joint tenancy with right of survivorship
    d. all of the above

11. If property is held by two or more owners as tenants in common, the interest of a deceased co-tenant will pass:

    a. to the remaining owner or owners.
    b. to the heirs of the deceased.
    c. to the surviving owner or heirs.
    d. to the state by eminent domain.

12. Joan Smith has organized a group of investors to finance the development of a shopping center. This group of investors:

    a. may be called a syndicate.
    b. may be organized as a limited partnership.
    c. may be a joint venture.
    d. all of the above

13. Real estate owned by a corporation:
    a. may be sold upon a stockholder's request.
    b. is held in trust for stockholders.
    c. is held in the corporation's name.
    d. all of the above

14. Alma Johnson bought for her personal use an apartment in a large building and received a deed conveying to her a fee simple estate. Each year Johnson receives a tax bill on her apartment. Her form of apartment ownership is called a:
    a. real estate investment trust.
    b. cooperative.
    c. corporation.
    d. condominium.

15. Gayle Dickins and Sam Swenson are getting married. Under the laws of the state in which they live, any real estate that either owns at the time of their marriage will remain that spouse's property in severalty. Property acquired by either after the wedding, except by gift or inheritance, will belong to both of them equally. This form of ownership is called:
    a. general partnership property.
    b. joint tenancy.
    c. tenancy by the entireties.
    d. community property.

16. Harold Albertson owns a fee simple title to unit 12 and 4½ percent of the common elements. Albertson:
    I. owns a life estate.
    II. may mortgage unit 12 without placing a lien on the title of the other unit owners.
    a. I only   c. both I and II
    b. II only   d. neither I nor II

17. A legal arrangement whereby title to property is held for the benefit of a beneficiary is a:
    I. trust.
    II. limited partnership.
    a. I only   c. both I and II
    b. II only   d. neither I nor II

18. Which of the following statements applies equally to joint tenants and tenants by the entireties?
    a. There is no right to file a partition suit.
    b. The survivor becomes sole owner.
    c. A deed signed by one will convey a fractional interest.
    d. A deed will not convey any interest unless signed by both spouses.

19. A, B and C were co-owners of a parcel of real estate. B died and his interest passed, according to his will, to become part of his estate. B was a:
    a. tenant by the entirety.
    b. joint tenant.
    c. tenant in common.
    d. corporate officer.

20. In a tenancy by the entirety:
    I. the co-owners are husband and wife.
    II. the co-owners have the right to partition.
    a. I only   c. both I and II
    b. II only   d. neither I nor II

21. A condominium is created:
    a. when construction is completed on the structure.
    b. when the owner or developer files a declaration of condominium in the public record.
    c. when a condominium owners' association is established.
    d. when all unit owners file documents in the public records asserting their decision.

22. Generally, a condominium building:
    I. is managed under the supervision of an association of unit owners.
    II. may not be converted back to apartment status once it has been declared a condominium.
    a. I only   c. both I and II
    b. II only   d. neither I nor II

23. Which of the following best describes ownership of a cooperative?
   a. The purchaser is a stockholder.
   b. The purchaser holds a fee simple title.
   c. The purchaser holds a reverter.
   d. a and c

24. Ownership that allows possession for only a specific time each year is a:
   a. cooperative.   c. condominium.
   b. time-share.   d. syndicate.

9

Legal Descriptions

Key Terms

Air lot
Base line
Benchmark
Check
Correction line
Datum
Fractional section
Government lot
Guide meridian
Legal description
Lot and block system
Metes and bounds
Monument
Plat of subdivision
Point of beginning
Principal meridian
Range
Rectangular (government) survey system
Section
Township line
Township square

Overview

In everyday life, we often describe real estate casually, perhaps as "the lot at 1546 East Main Street," or "the big house on the corner of Main and Oak." In real estate practice, however, parcels of land cannot always be referred to in such an imprecise manner. Deeds, sales contracts and other documents must state the exact size and location of real estate according to an established system of land description. This chapter will explain how land is identified and measured and will include discussions of the forms of legal description used in the United States.

Describing Land

One of the essential elements of a valid deed is an accurate description of the land being conveyed. The real estate involved must be identifiable from the wording of the deed and with reference to only the documents named in the deed. The courts have usually held that a description of land is legally sufficient if a competent surveyor can locate the real estate in question.

The courts of most states have accepted a street address as being sufficient to locate or identify a parcel of real estate, but not to serve as a legal description. However, the legal description in a deed or mortgage may be followed by the words "commonly known as" and the street address. A **legal description** is an *exact way of describing real estate in a contract, deed, mortgage or other document that will be accepted by a court of law.*

The average parcel of land has been conveyed and transferred many times in the past. The description of the land in a deed, mortgage or other instrument should be the same as that used in the previous instrument of conveyance. Discrepancies, errors and legal problems can be avoided or reduced if this practice is followed in drawing subsequent conveyances.

Methods of Describing Real Estate

There are three basic methods of describing real estate: (1) metes and bounds, (2) rectangular survey and (3) lot and block. A combination of methods may also be used. Consult figure 9.1 to determine the system of land description historically used in your state.

Metes and Bounds

A **metes-and-bounds description,** the earliest form of legal description used in the United States, makes use of the boundaries and measurements of the land in question. Such a description starts at a definitely designated place called the **point of beginning** (POB) and proceeds around the boundaries of the tract by reference to linear measurements and directions. A metes-and-bounds description always ends at the POB, so that the tract being described is fully enclosed.

In a metes-and-bounds description, the actual distance between monuments takes precedence over linear measurements set forth in the description if the two measurements differ. **Monuments** are fixed objects used to establish real estate boundaries. Natural objects such as stones, large trees, lakes and streams, as well as streets, highways and markers placed by surveyors, are commonly used as monuments. (Under the rectangular survey system, as discussed later, section lines, quarter-section lines, township lines and similar points of reference are used in the same way as are monuments in the description and location of property.) Measurements often include the words "more or less"; the location of the monuments is more important than the distance stated in the wording.

An example of a metes-and-bounds description of a parcel of land (pictured in figure 9.2) follows:

Figure 9.1
Public Land Survey
Systems of the
United States

Principal meridians, baselines, and the areas they describe are illustrated as shown above.

Areas in which metes and bounds descriptions are used are left blank.

The United States Military Tract located in central Ohio is subdivided into five-mile-square townships instead of six.

Although a small section in the southwestern corner of Kentucky (the Jackson Purchase) was subdivided into townships by a special state survey, land in Kentucky is described by metes and bounds, not by reference to the rectangular survey system (government survey method).

Land in New Mexico is not surveyed from the Navajo Meridian even though it is located on the northwestern boundary of that state. However, certain land in Arizona is surveyed from this meridian.

Alaska uses the rectangular survey system. Its principal meridians are Copper River, Fairbanks, Seward, Umiat, and Kateel River.

Land in Hawaii is surveyed through the metes and bounds method.

"A tract of land located in Red Skull, Virginia, described as follows: Beginning at the intersection of the east line of Jones Road and the south line of Skull Drive; thence east along the south line of Skull Drive 200 feet; thence south 15° east 216.5 feet, more or less, to the center thread of Red Skull Creek; thence northwesterly along the center line of said creek to its intersection with the east line of Jones Road; thence north 105 feet, more or less, along the east line of Jones Road to the place of beginning."

**Figure 9.2
Metes-and-Bounds
Tract**

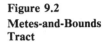

When used to describe property within a town or city, a metes-and-bounds description may begin as follows:

"Beginning at a point on the southerly side of Kent Street, 100 feet easterly from the corner formed by the intersection of the southerly side of Kent Street and the easterly side of Broadway; thence...."

In this description, the POB is given by reference to the corner intersection. *The description must close by returning to the POB.*

Metes-and-bounds descriptions may be very complex and should be handled with extreme care. When they include compass directions of the various lines and concave or convex curved lines, they can be difficult to understand. In such cases, the advice and counsel of a surveyor should be sought.

Rectangular (Government) Survey System

The **rectangular survey system,** sometimes called the *government survey method,* was established by Congress in 1785, soon after the federal government was organized. The system was developed as a standard method of describing all lands conveyed to or acquired by the federal government, including the extensive area of the Northwest Territory.

The rectangular survey system is based on sets of two intersecting lines: principal meridians and base lines. The **principal meridians** run north and south, and the **base lines** run east and west. Both are located exactly by reference to degrees of longitude and latitude. Each principal meridian has a name or number and is crossed by a base line. These lines are pictured in figure 9.1. Each principal meridian and its corresponding base line are used to survey a definite area of land, indicated on the map by boundary lines.

Each principal meridian affects or controls *only* the specific area of land shown by the boundaries on the chart. No parcel of land is described by reference to more than one principal meridian, and the meridian used may not necessarily be the nearest one.

Ranges. The land on either side of a principal meridian is divided into *six-mile-wide strips* by lines that run north and south, parallel to the meridian. These north-south strips of land are called **ranges** (see figure 9.3). They are designated by consecutive numbers east or west of the principal meridian. For example, Range 3 East would be a strip of land between 12 and 18 miles east of its principal meridian.

Townships. Lines running east and west parallel with the base line and six miles apart are referred to as **township lines,** and form *strips* of land (or *tiers*) called *townships* (see figure 9.3). These tiers of townships are designated by consecutive numbers north or south of the base line. For instance, the strip of land between 6 and 12 miles north of a base line is Township 2 North.

The **township squares** formed by the intersecting township and range lines are the basic units of the rectangular survey system. Theoretically, townships are six miles square and contain 36 square miles (23,040 acres). Note that *although a township square is part of a township strip, the two terms do not refer to the same thing.* In this discussion, the word *township* used by itself refers to the township square.

Figure 9.3
Principal Meridian and Base Line

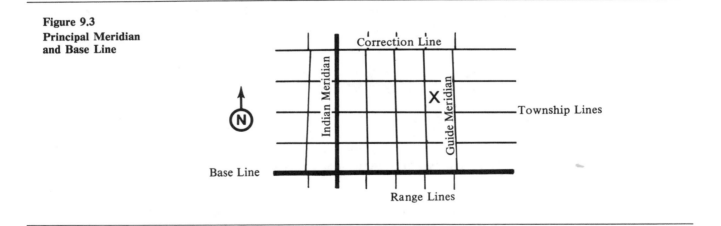

Each township is given a legal description by using: (1) the designation of the township strip in which the township is located, (2) the designation of the range strip and (3) the name or number of the principal meridian for that area. For example, in figure 9.3, the township marked *X* is described as Township 3 North, Range 4 East of the Indian Meridian because the township is the third strip, or tier, north of the base line. This strip (or tier) designates the township number and direction. The township is also located in the fourth range strip (those running north and south) east of the Indian Meridian. Finally, reference is made to the Indian Meridian because the land being described is within the boundary of land surveyed from that meridian. This description is abbreviated as *T3N, R4E Indian Meridian.*

Sections. Each township contains 36 **sections**, each one square mile, or *640 acres.* Sections are numbered 1 through 36, as shown in figure 9.4. Section 1 is always in the northeast, or upper right-hand, corner. By law, each section number 16 has been set aside for school purposes and is referred to as a *school section.* The sale or rental proceeds from this land were originally available for township school use.

Figure 9.4
Sections in a
Township

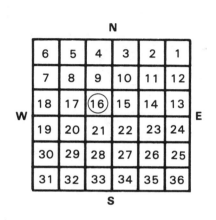

16 = School Section

Sections are divided into *halves* (320 acres), *quarters* (160 acres), and halves and quarters of those divisions. The southeast quarter, which is a 160-acre tract, is abbreviated SE¼. The SE¼ of SE¼ of SE¼ of Section 1 would be a ten-acre square in the lower right-hand corner of Section 1. Sometimes this description is written without the word *of:* SE¼, SE¼, SE¼ Section 1. It is possible to combine portions of a section, as: NE¼ of SW¼ and N½ of NW¼ of SE¼ of Section 1. In computing areas or locating parcels, you begin with the *last* division and work backward. Notice that because of the word *and* in this description, the area is 60 acres.

Correction lines. Due to the curvature of the earth, the convergence of the north and south lines (range lines) must be compensated for. All range lines continually approach each other and, if extended northward, would eventually meet at the North Pole. An accurate survey of a township would show its north line to be about 50 feet shorter than its south line. In the case of the fourth township north of the base line the difference is four times as great, or about 200 feet. The rectangular survey system compensates for the resulting shortages with **correction lines** (see figure 9.3). Every fourth township line is designated a correction line, and on each correction line the range lines are measured to the full distance of six miles apart. **Guide meridians** run north and south at 24-mile intervals from the principal meridian. A **check** is the area bounded by two guide meridians and two correction lines, approximately 24 miles square. Because of the curvature of the earth and the crude instruments used in early days, in practice few townships are exactly six-mile squares or contain exactly 36 square miles.

**Figure 9.5
A Section**

Since most townships contain a smaller area than required, surveyors follow well-established, uniform rules in adjusting such errors. These rules provide that any overage or shortage in the 36-square-mile area of a township be adjusted in those sections adjacent to its north and west boundaries. All other sections are to be one square mile. These correction provisions explain some of the variations of acreage in sections and townships under the rectangular survey system of land descriptions.

Fractional sections and government lots. Undersized or oversized sections are classified as **fractional sections** and may occur for a number of reasons. For example, part of a section may be submerged under water. In some areas, the rectangular survey was made by separate crews and may have resulted in gaps less than a section wide being left when the surveys met. Other errors may have resulted from the difficulties encountered in the actual survey.

Areas smaller than full quarter sections were numbered and designated as **government lots** by government surveyors. An overage or shortage was corrected whenever possible by placing the government lots in the north or west portions of the fractional sections. For example, a government lot might be described as Government Lot 2 in the northwest quarter of fractional section 18, Township 2 North, Range 4 East of the Salt Lake Meridian.

In Practice...

When reading a government survey description of land, read from the end of the description to the beginning to determine the location and size of the property. For example, consider the following description:

"The S¹/₂ of the NW¹/₄ of the SE¹/₄ of Section 11, Township 8 North, Range 6 West of the Fourth Principal Meridian."

To locate this tract of land from this citation alone, first search for the Fourth Principal Meridian on a map of the United States. Then, on a regional map, find the township in which the property is located by counting six range strips west of the Fourth Principal Meridian, and eight townships north of its corresponding base line. After locating Section 11, you would then divide the section into quarters, the SE¼ into quarters and then the NW¼ of that into halves. The S½ of that NW¼ contains the property in question.

In computing the size of this tract of land, first determine that the SE¼ of the section contains 160 acres (640 acres divided by 4). The NW¼ of that quarter section contains 40 acres (160 acres divided by 4), and the S½ of that quarter section—the property in question—contains 20 acres (40 acres divided by 2). In general, if a government survey description does not use the conjunction "and" (indicating various parcels are combined), the longer *the description, the* smaller *the tract of land it describes.*

Metes-and-bounds descriptions with rectangular survey system. Land within states using the rectangular survey system may also require a metes-and-bounds description. This usually occurs in describing an irregular tract, a tract too small to be described by quarter sections, or a tract that does not follow either the lot or block lines of a recorded subdivision or section, quarter section or other fractional section lines. An example of a combined metes-and-bounds and rectangular survey system description is as follows (see figure 9.6):

"That part of the northwest quarter of Section 12, Township 10 North, Range 7 West of the Third Principal Meridian, bounded by a line described as follows: Commencing at the southeast corner of the northwest quarter of said Section 12, thence north 500 feet; thence west parallel with the south line of said section 1,000 feet; thence south parallel with the east line of said section 500 feet to the south line of said northwest quarter; thence east along said south line to the point of beginning."

Figure 9.6
Metes and Bounds
with Rectangular
Survey

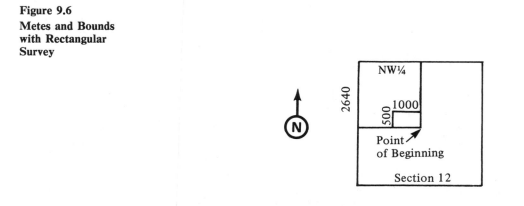

Lot and Block System

The third method of land description is the **lot and block system,** using *lot and block numbers* referred to in a **plat of subdivision** placed in the public records of the county where the land is located.

The first step in subdividing land is the preparation of a *plat of survey*—by a licensed surveyor or engineer—as illustrated in figure 9.7. On this plat the land is divided into numbered or lettered blocks and lots, and streets or access roads for public use are indicated. Lot sizes and street details must be indicated completely and must comply with all local ordinances and requirements. When properly signed and approved, the subdivision plat may be recorded in the county in which the land is located; it thereby becomes part of the legal description. In describing a lot from a recorded subdivision plat, the lot and block number, name or number of the subdivision plat, and name of the county and state are used. For example:

Lots 2, 3 and 4 in Block 5 of L. Robinson's Subdivision of the northwest quarter of Section 9, Township 4 North, Range 3 East of the Seward Principal Meridian in _____ county, _____ (state).

Some subdivided lands are further divided by a later resubdivision. For example, if Alan Roswell bought two full blocks of John Welch's subdivision and resubdivided this land into different-sized lots, then Roswell might convey:

Lot 1 in Block A of Roswell's resubdivision of Blocks 2 and 3 of John Welch's Hometown Subdivision of the west one-half of Section 19, Township 10 North, Range 13 East of the Black Hills Principal Meridian in _____ county, _____ (state).

This most recent method of land description is used at least in part in all states. Some states have passed *plat acts* that specify the smallest tract that may be conveyed without a subdivision plat being prepared, approved and recorded. In some states, for example, the minimum size is five acres.

Preparation and Use of a Survey

Legal descriptions should not be changed, altered or combined without adequate information from a competent authority, such as a surveyor or title attorney. Legal descriptions should *always* include the name of the county and state in which the land is located. Meridians often relate to more than one state and occasionally relate to two base lines, so a description cannot be certain unless the county and state are given. For example, the description "the southwest quarter of Section 10, Township 4 North, Range 1 West of the Fourth Principal Meridian" could refer to land in either Illinois or Wisconsin.

A licensed surveyor is trained and authorized to locate a given parcel of land and to determine its legal description. The surveyor does this by preparing a *survey,* which sets forth the legal description of the property, and a *survey sketch,* which shows the location and dimensions of the parcel. When a survey also shows the location, size and shape of buildings located on the lot, it is referred to as a *spot survey.* Surveys are required in many real estate transactions, such as when: (1) conveying a portion of a given tract of land, (2) conveying real estate as security for a mortgage loan, (3) showing the location of new construction, (4) locating roads and highways and (5) determining the legal description of the land on which a particular building is located.

In Practice...

Because legal descriptions of newly subdivided land, once recorded, affect title to real estate, they should be prepared only *by a surveyor or attorney. Real estate*

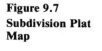

Figure 9.7
Subdivision Plat
Map

licensees who attempt to draft legal descriptions create potential risks for themselves and their clients and customers. Further, when entered on a document of conveyance, legal descriptions should be copied with care. For example, an incorrectly worded legal description in a sales contract may obligate the seller to convey or the buyer to purchase more or less land than intended. Title problems can arise for the buyer who seeks to convey the property at a future date. Even if the contract can be corrected by the parties involved before the sale is closed, the licensee runs the risk of losing a commission. In addition, the licensee may be held liable for damages suffered by an injured party because of an improperly worded legal description.

Measuring Elevations

Measurements

Datum. *A point, line or surface from which elevations are measured or indicated is a datum.* For the purpose of the United States Geological Survey, datum is defined as the mean sea level at New York harbor. It is of special significance to surveyors in determining the height of structures, establishing the grade of streets and similar situations.

Virtually all large cities have established a local official datum that is used in place of the U.S. Geological Survey datum. For instance, the official datum for Chicago is known as the *Chicago City Datum* and is a horizontal plane below the surface of the city. This plane was established in 1847 as corresponding to the low water level of Lake Michigan in that year, and is considered to be zero elevation.

A surveyor's measurement of elevation based on the USGS datum will differ from one computed according to a local datum. A surveyor can always translate an elevation based on a local datum to the elevation based on the USGS.

Benchmarks. To aid surveyors, permanent reference points called **benchmarks** have been established throughout the United States (see figure 9.8). Cities with local datums also have designated local benchmarks, which are given official status when assigned a permanent identifying number. Local benchmarks simplify surveyors' work, for measurements may be based on them rather than on the basic benchmark, which may be miles away.

Certain Hts above a Datum.

Figure 9.8 Benchmark

Air Lots

The owner of a parcel of land may subdivide the air above his or her land into **air lots.** Air lots are composed of airspace within specific boundaries located over a parcel of land. This type of description is found in titles to tall buildings located on air rights, generally over railroad tracks. (See the discussion of air rights in Chapter 2.) Similarly a surveyor, in preparing a subdivision plat for condominium use, describes each condominium unit by reference to the elevation of the floors and ceilings on a vertical plane above the city datum.

The condominium property acts passed in all states (see Chapter 8) require that a registered land surveyor prepare a plat of survey showing the elevations of floor and ceiling surfaces and the boundaries of a condominium apartment with reference to an official datum. Typically, a separate plat will be prepared for each floor in the condominium building.

The following is an example of the legal description of a condominium apartment unit that includes a fractional share of the common elements of the building and land:

"UNIT _____ as delineated on survey of the following described parcel of real estate (hereinafter referred to as Development Parcel): The north 99 feet of the west ½ of Block 4 (except that part, if any, taken and used for street), in Sutton's Division Number 5 in the east ½ of the southeast ¼ of Section 24, Township 3 South, Range 68 West of the Sixth Principal Meridian, in Denver County, Colorado, which survey is attached as Exhibit A to Declaration made by Colorado National Bank as Trustee under Trust No. 1250, recorded in the Recorder's Office of Denver County, Colorado, as Document No. 475637; together with an undivided ____% interest in said Development Parcel (excepting from said Development Parcel all the property and space comprising all the units thereof as defined and set forth in said Declaration and Survey)."

Land Units and Measurements

It is important to know and understand land units and measurements—they are an integral part of legal descriptions. Some commonly used measurements are listed in table 9.1. Remember that a *section* of land is one square mile and contains 640 acres; a *quarter section* contains 160 acres; a *quarter of a quarter section* contains 40 acres. A *circle* contains 360 degrees; a *quarter segment* of a circle contains 90 degrees; a *half segment* of a circle contains 180 degrees. One *degree* (1°) can be subdivided into 60 minutes (60′), each of which contains 60 seconds (60″). One-and-a-half degrees would be written 1°30′0″.

Table 9.1
Units of Land Measurement

Unit	Measurement	Metric Equivalent
mile	5,280 feet; 320 rods; 1,760 yards	1.609 kilometers
rod	5.50 yards; 16.5 feet	5.029 meters
sq. mile	640 acres	2.590 sq. kilometers
acre	4,840 sq. yards; 160 sq. rods; 43,560 sq. feet	4,047 sq. meters
sq. yard	9 sq. feet	0.836 sq. meters
sq. foot	144 sq. inches	0.093 sq. meters
chain	66 feet or 100 links	20.117 meters
kilometer	0.62 mile	1,000 meters
hectare	2.47 acres	10,000 sq. meters

Summary

Documents affecting or conveying interests in real estate must contain accurate descriptions of the property involved. There are three methods of *legal description* of land in the United States: (1) metes and bounds, (2) rectangular (government) survey system and (3) lot and block system. A legal description is a precise method of identifying a parcel of land. A property's description should always be the same as the one used in previous documents.

In a *metes-and-bounds description,* the actual location of monuments takes precedence over the written linear measurement in a document. When property is being described by metes and bounds, the description must always enclose a tract of land; that is, the boundary line must end at the point at which it started.

The *rectangular survey system* is used in 30 states. It involves surveys based on 35 principal meridians. Under this government survey system, each principal meridian and its corresponding base line are specifically located. Any particular parcel of land is surveyed from only one principal meridian and its base line. The area surveyed from each meridian is also outlined by boundaries as shown in figure 9.1.

East and west lines parallel with the base line form six-mile-wide strips called *township tiers.* North and south lines parallel with the principal meridian form *ranges.* The resulting squares are each 36 square miles in area and are called *townships.* Townships are designated by their township tier and range numbers and their principal meridian—for example, Township 3 North, Range 4 East of the _____ Meridian. Townships are divided into 36 *sections* of one square mile each.

When a tract is irregular or its boundaries do not coincide with a section, regular fractions of a section, or a boundary of a lot or block in a subdivision, a surveyor can prepare a combination rectangular survey and metes-and-bounds description.

Land in every state can be subdivided into lots and blocks by means of a *recorded plat of subdivision.* An approved plat of survey showing the division into blocks, giving the size, location and designation of lots, and specifying the location and size of streets to be dedicated for public use is filed for record in the recorder's office of the county in which the land is located. *It is possible to resubdivide portions of a previously recorded subdivision.* A subdivision plat will give the legal description of a building site in a town or city by lot, block and subdivision in a section, township and range of a principal meridian in a county and state.

The services of licensed surveyors are necessary in the conduct of the real estate business. A plat of survey prepared by a surveyor is the usual method of certifying the legal description of a certain parcel of land. When a survey also shows the location, size, and shape of the buildings located on the lot, it is referred to as a *spot survey.* Spot surveys are customarily required in purchases of real estate when a mortgage or new construction is involved.

Air lots, condominium descriptions and other measurements of vertical elevations may be computed from the United States Geological Survey *datum,* which is the mean sea level in New York harbor. Most large cities have established local survey datums for surveying within the area. The elevations from these datums are further supplemented by reference points, called *benchmarks,* placed at fixed intervals from the datums.

Questions

1. A *monument* is used in which of the following types of legal descriptions?
   a. lot and block
   b. metes and bounds
   c. rectangular survey
   d. all of the above

2. What is the proper description of the following shaded area?

   a. SW¼ of the NE¼ and the N½ of the SE¼ of the SW¼
   b. N½ of the NE¼ of the SW¼ and the SE¼ of the NW¼
   c. SW¼ of the SE¼ of the NW¼ and the N½ of the NE¼ of the SW¼
   d. S½ of the SW¼ of the NE¼ and the NE¼ of the NW¼ of the SE¼

3. When surveying land, a surveyor refers to the principal meridian that is:
   a. nearest the land being surveyed.
   b. in the same state as the land being surveyed.
   c. not more than 40 townships or 15 ranges distant from the land being surveyed.
   d. within the area boundary of the land being surveyed.

4. The N½ of the SW¼ of a section contains:
   a. 40 acres.   c. 160 acres.
   b. 20 acres.   d. 80 acres.

5. A street address identifying a parcel of real estate:
   a. may be used in conjunction with a metes-and-bounds legal description.
   b. is generally by itself an adequate legal description.
   c. is never necessary.
   d. all of the above

6. In describing real estate a system that uses feet, degrees and natural markers as monuments is:
   a. rectangular survey.
   b. metes and bounds.
   c. government survey.
   d. lot and block.

7. Government lots:
   I. are generally irregular in size.
   II. are owned by the federal government.

   a. I only   c. both I and II
   b. II only   d. neither I nor II

8. A *school section:*
   a. contains 640 acres.
   b. is section 16 within a township.
   c. both a and b.
   d. neither a nor b.

Questions 9 through 12 refer to the following illustration of a township:

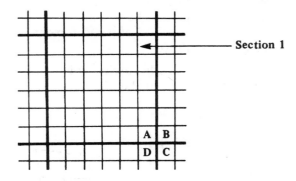

Section 1

9. The section marked *A* is which of the following?
   a. school section   c. section 31
   b. section 36   d. government lot

10. Which of the following is section 6?
    a. D   c. B
    b. C   d. A

11. The section directly below *C* is which of the following?
    a. section 12   c. section 30
    b. section 25   d. section 7

12. Which of the following is lot *D*?

    a. section 36   c. section 1
    b. section 31   d. section 6

13. An acre contains:

    a. 160 square feet
    b. 43,560 square feet.
    c. 640 square feet.
    d. 360 degrees.

14. How many acres are there in the following tract?
    Beginning at the NW corner of the SW¼, thence south along the west line to the SW corner of the section, then east along the south line of the section 2,640 feet, more or less, to the SE corner of the said SW¼, then in a straight line to the POB.

    a. 100 acres   c. 90 acres
    b. 160 acres   d. 80 acres

15. A legal description for a newly subdivided parcel of real estate should be prepared by which of the following persons?

    a. attorney   c. surveyor
    b. real estate broker   d. a or c

16. A *datum* is:

    a. used in the description of an air lot.
    b. measured in New York only.
    c. a calendar method of measurement.
    d. all of the above

17. Which of these shaded areas depicts the NE¼ of the SE¼ of the SW¼?

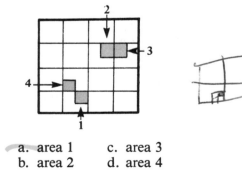

    a. area 1   c. area 3
    b. area 2   d. area 4

18. The proper description of the shaded township area in this illustration is:

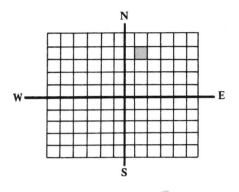

    a. T4N R2W.   c. T4N R2E.
    b. T2W R4N.   d. T2E R4N.

19. If a farm described as "the NW¼ of the SE¼ of Section 10, Township 2 North, Range 3 West of the 6th. P.M." sold for $1,500 an acre, what would the sale price be?

    a. $30,000   c. $45,000
    b. $15,000   d. $60,000

20. A *rod* is:

    a. a point of reference in a metes-and-bounds description.
    b. 16.5 feet.
    c. 0.62 mile.
    d. 2 hectares.

10

Real Estate Taxes and Other Liens

Key Terms

Ad valorem tax
Assessment roll
Attachment
Corporation franchise tax
Equalization factor
Equitable lien
Estate taxes
General lien
Inheritance taxes
Internal Revenue Service tax lien
Involuntary lien
Judgment
Lien
Mechanic's lien
Mill

Mortgage lien
Priority
Redemption
Special assessment
Specific lien
Statutory lien
Subordination agreement
Surety bail bond
Tax foreclosure
Tax lien
Tax sale
Vendee's lien
Vendor's lien
Voluntary lien

Overview

As discussed in previous chapters, the ownership interest a person has in real estate can be diminished by the interest of others. Specifically, taxing bodies, creditors and courts can lessen an ownership interest by placing a claim—called a *lien*—on a person's property to secure payment of taxes, debts and other obligations. This chapter will discuss the nature of liens, specifically focusing on real estate tax liens, which affect every owner of real estate. In addition, the chapter will describe liens other than taxes that involve real and personal property.

Liens

A **lien** is defined as a charge against property that provides security for a debt or obligation of the property owner. A lien allows a creditor (lienor) to force the sale of property that has been given as security by the debtor (lienee) to satisfy the lienee's debt in case of default. A lien does not constitute ownership; it is a type of *encumbrance*—a charge or burden on a property that may diminish its value. Note, however, that while all liens are encumbrances, not all encumbrances are liens. As discussed in Chapter 7, encumbrances that are not liens (such as easements and deed restrictions) are *incorporeal rights* in real estate and give the parties in question certain rights, or interests, in the real estate.

Generally, liens are enforced by court order. A creditor must institute a legal action requesting the court to order the sale of the real estate in question for full or partial satisfaction of the debt.

A lien may be voluntary or involuntary. A **voluntary lien** is created by the lienee's action, such as taking out a mortgage loan. An **involuntary lien** is created by law and can be either statutory or equitable. A **statutory lien** is created by statute. An **equitable lien** arises out of common law and may be created by a court when justice and fairness require it. A real estate tax lien, for example, is an involuntary, statutory lien; that is, it is created by statute without any action by the property owner. A court-ordered judgment requiring payment of the balance on a delinquent charge account would be an involuntary, equitable lien on the debtor's property.

Liens may be further classified into two other categories: general and specific. As illustrated in figure 10.1, **general liens** usually affect all the property of a debtor,

**Figure 10.1
General Liens**

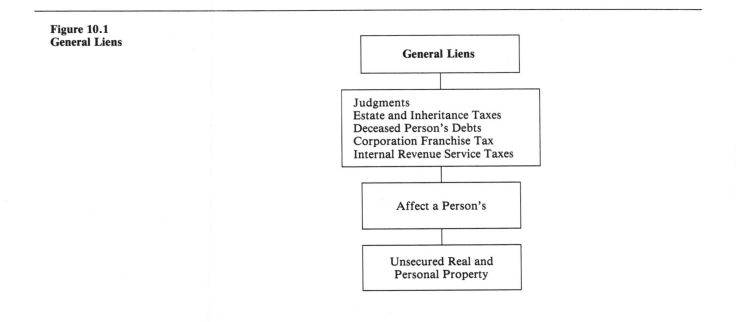

both real and personal, and include judgments, estate and inheritance taxes, debts of a deceased person, corporation franchise taxes and Internal Revenue Service taxes. **Specific liens,** on the other hand, are usually secured by specific property and affect only that particular property. As illustrated in figure 10.2, specific liens on real estate include mechanics' liens, mortgage liens, tax liens and liens for special assessments and utilities. Specific liens can also secure personal property, as when a vendor's lien is placed on a car to secure payment of a loan.

Figure 10.2
Specific Liens

Utility lien

Special Assessment Lien

Ad Valorem Tax Lien

Mortgage Lien

Mechanic's Lien

Vendor's Lien

Effects of Liens on Title

Although the fee simple estate held by a typical real estate owner can be reduced in value by the lien and encumbrance rights of others, the owner is still free to convey his or her title to a willing purchaser. The purchaser will, however, buy the property subject to any liens and encumbrances of the seller. Once properly established, a lien will *run with the land;* that is, it will bind successive owners if steps are not taken to clear the lien.

Remember, liens attach to property, not to the property owner. Thus, although a purchaser who buys real estate under a delinquent lien is not responsible for payment of the debt secured by the lien, he or she faces a possible loss of the property if the creditors take court action to enforce payment of their liens.

Priority of Liens. Real estate taxes and special assessments generally take **priority** over all other liens. This means that if the property goes through a court-ordered sale to satisfy unpaid debts or obligations, outstanding real estate taxes and special assessments will be paid from the proceeds *first.* The remainder of the proceeds will be used to pay other outstanding liens in the order of their priority.

For example, if the courts ordered a parcel of land sold to satisfy a judgment lien entered in the public record on February 7, 1988, subject to a first mortgage lien recorded January 22, 1983, and to this year's as-yet unpaid real estate taxes, the proceeds of the sale would be distributed in the following order:

1. to the taxing bodies for this year's real estate taxes.
2. to the mortgage lender for the entire amount of the mortgage loan outstanding as of the date of the sale.
3. to the creditor named in the judgment lien (if any proceeds remain after paying the first two items).
4. to the foreclosed-upon landowner (if any proceeds remain after paying the first three items).

Liens other than general taxes and special assessments may take priority from the date of recording in the public records of the county where the property is located. Exceptions include mechanics' liens (discussed later in this chapter), which take priority as provided by state law but never take priority over tax and general assessment liens.

Subordination agreements are written agreements between lienholders to change the priority of mortgage, judgment and other liens under certain circumstances. Priority and recording of liens will be discussed in detail in Chapter 13, "Title Records."

Tax Liens

As discussed in Chapter 7, the ownership of real estate is subject to certain government powers. One of these powers is the right of state and local governments to impose **tax liens** for the support of their governmental functions. Because the location of real estate is permanently fixed, the government can levy taxes with a high degree of certainty that the taxes will be collected. Since the annual taxes levied on real estate usually have priority over other previously recorded liens, they may be enforced by the court-ordered sale of the real estate free of such other liens.

Real estate taxes can be divided into two types: (1) *general real estate tax,* or **ad valorem tax,** and (2) **special assessment,** or *improvement tax.* Both of these taxes are levied against specific parcels of property and automatically become liens on those properties.

General Tax (Ad Valorem Tax)

The general real estate tax is made up of the taxes levied on real estate by various governmental agencies and municipalities. These include cities, towns, villages and counties. Other taxing bodies are school districts or boards (including local elementary and high schools, junior colleges and community colleges), drainage districts, water districts and sanitary districts. Municipal authorities operating recreational preserves such as forest preserves and parks are also authorized by the legislatures of the various states to levy real estate taxes.

General real estate taxes are levied for the *general support or operation* of the governmental agency authorized to impose the levy. These taxes are known as *ad valorem* taxes because the amount of the tax varies in accordance with the *value of the property being taxed.*

Exemptions from general taxes. Under most state laws, certain real estate is exempt from real estate taxation. For example, property owned by cities, various municipal organizations (such as schools, parks and playgrounds), the state and federal governments, and religious corporations, hospitals or educational institutions is tax exempt. Usually the property must be used for tax-exempt purposes.

Many state laws also allow special exemptions to reduce real estate tax bills for certain property owners or land uses. *Homeowners* and *senior citizens* are frequently granted set reductions in the assessed value of their homes. Some states offer real estate tax reductions to attract industries, and many states offer tax reductions for agricultural land.

Assessment. Real estate is valued, or assessed, for tax purposes by county or township assessors or appraisers. The land is usually appraised separately from the building. Some states require assessments to be a certain percentage of true, or market, value. State laws may provide for property to be reassessed periodically.

Property owners who claim that errors were made in determining the assessed value of their property may present their objections, usually to a local board of appeal or board of review. Protests or appeals regarding tax assessments may ultimately be taken to court.

Equalization. In some jurisdictions, when it is necessary to correct general inequalities in state-wide tax assessments, uniformity may be achieved by use of an **equalization factor.** Such a factor may be provided for use in counties or districts where the assessments are to be raised or lowered. The assessed value of each property is multiplied by the equalization factor, and the tax rate is then applied to the equalized assessment. For example, the assessments in one county are determined to be 20 percent lower than the average assessments throughout the rest of the state. This underassessment can be corrected by decreeing the application of an equalization factor of 120 percent to each assessment in that county. Thus, a parcel of land assessed for tax purposes at $98,000 would be taxed on an equalized value of $117,600 ($98,000 × 1.20 = $117,600).

Tax rates. The process of arriving at a real estate tax rate begins with the *adoption of a budget* by each county, city, school board or other taxing district (see figure 10.3). Each budget covers the financial requirements of the taxing body for the coming fiscal year, which may be the January to December calendar year or some other 12-month period designated by statute. The budget must include an estimate of all expenditures for the year and indicate the amount of income expected from all fees, revenue sharing and other sources. The net amount remaining to be raised from real estate taxes is then determined from these figures.

The next step is *appropriation,* the action taken by each taxing body that authorizes the expenditure of funds and provides for the sources of such monies. Appropriation generally involves the adoption of an ordinance or the passage of a law setting forth the specifics of the proposed taxation.

The amount to be raised from the general real estate tax is then imposed on property owners through a *tax levy,* the formal action taken to impose the tax, by a vote of the taxing district's governing body.

The *tax rate* for each individual taxing body is computed separately. To arrive at a tax rate, the total monies needed for the coming fiscal year are divided by the total assessments of all real estate located within the jurisdiction of the taxing body. For example, a taxing district's budget indicates that $300,000 must be raised from real estate tax revenues, and the assessment roll (assessor's record) of all taxable real estate within this district equals $10,000,000. The tax rate is computed thus:

Figure 10.3
Ad Valorem Taxation

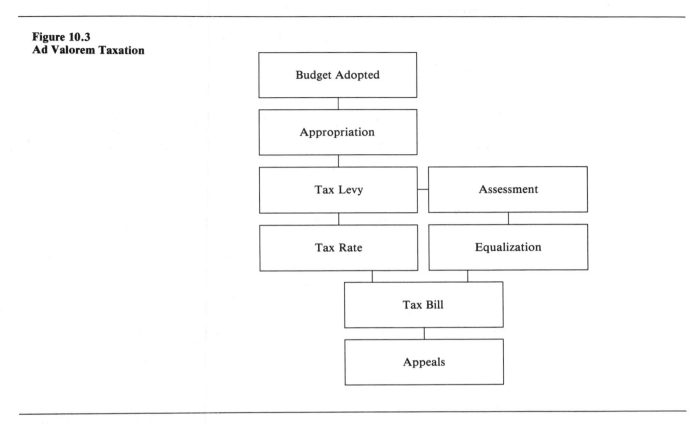

$$\$300{,}000 \div \$10{,}000{,}000 = .03, \text{ or } 3\%$$

The tax rate may be stated in a number of different ways. In many areas it is expressed in mills. A **mill** is *1/1,000 of a dollar, or $.001*. The tax rate may be expressed as a mill ratio, in dollars per hundred or in dollars per thousand. The tax rate computed in the foregoing example could be expressed as:

30 mills
or
$3 per $100 of assessed value
or
$30 per $1,000 of assessed value

Tax bills. A property owner's tax bill is computed by applying the tax rate to the assessed valuation of the property. For example, on property assessed for tax purposes at $90,000, at a tax rate of 3 percent, or 30 mills, the tax will be $2,700 ($90,000 × .030 = $2,700). If an equalization factor is used, the computation on a property with an assessed value of $120,000 and a tax rate of 4 percent with an equalization factor of 120 percent would be as follows:

$$\$120{,}000 \times 1.20 = \$144{,}000$$
$$\$144{,}000 \times .040 = \$5{,}760 \text{ tax}$$

Generally, one tax bill that incorporates all real estate taxes levied by the various taxing districts is prepared for each property. In some areas, however, separate bills are prepared by separate taxing bodies. Sometimes the real estate taxing bodies may operate on different budget years, so that the taxpayer receives separate bills for various taxes at different times during the year.

Due dates for payment of taxes are usually set by statute. In many areas, taxes are payable in two installments. Collection procedures vary: In some areas, taxes become due during the current tax year; in others, they are payable in arrears during the year after the taxes are levied; and in still others, a partial payment is due in the year of the tax, with the balance due the following year. Knowledge of local tax-payment schedules is especially important in computing the proration of current taxes when a property is sold.

Some states offer discounts to encourage prompt payment of real estate taxes. Penalties in the form of monthly interest charges are added to all taxes that are not paid when due. The due date may also be called the *penalty date.*

Enforcement of tax liens. To be enforceable, real estate taxes must be valid, which means they must be: (1) properly levied, (2) used for a legal purpose and (3) applied equitably to all affected property. Tax liens are generally given priority over all other liens against a property. Real estate taxes that have remained delinquent for the period of time specified by state law can be collected by the tax collecting officer through either **tax foreclosure** (similar to mortgage foreclosure) or **tax sale**. While there are substantial differences in the methods and details of the various states' tax-sale procedures, the results are the same.

Tax sales are usually held pursuant to a published notice after a court has rendered a judgment for the tax and penalties and ordered that the property be sold. Since there is a definite amount of delinquent tax and penalty to be collected, the purchaser at a tax sale must pay at least this amount. Since a defaulted owner has the right of **redemption** (the right to buy back the real estate), in many areas bidding takes place on the percentage of interest the bidder may receive from the defaulted owner if and when the property is redeemed. In this type of bidding, *the person bidding the lowest interest rate becomes the successful purchaser.* A *certificate of sale* is usually given to the successful bidder when he or she pays the delinquent tax amount.

Generally, the delinquent taxpayer can redeem the property at any time before the tax sale by paying the delinquent taxes plus interest and charges (any court costs or attorney's fees); this is known as an *equitable right of redemption.* Most state laws also grant a period of redemption *after the tax sale* during which the defaulted owner or lienholders (creditors of the defaulted owner) may redeem the property by paying the amount paid at the tax sale plus interest and charges (including any taxes levied since the sale); this is known as the *statutory right of redemption.* If no redemption is made within this statutory redemption period, the certificate holder can apply for a *tax deed.* The quality of the title conveyed by a tax deed varies from state to state according to statutory provisions.

In some states, titles to tax-delinquent land are sold or conveyed to the state or a taxing authority. At the expiration of the redemption period, titles to these lands are then sold at auction to the highest bidder(s). The tax deeds issued to purchasers in such cases are regarded as conveying good title, since they are considered conveyances by the state of state-owned land. In some jurisdictions, tax-delinquent land that is not sold at a tax sale due to lack of buyers is forfeited to the state. The state may then either use the land for its own purposes or sell it later.

Special Assessments (Improvement Taxes)

Special assessments are *special taxes levied on real estate that require property owners to pay for improvements that benefit the real estate they own.* These taxes are often levied to pay for such improvements as streets, alleys, street lighting, curbs and similar items, and are enforced in the same manner as general real estate taxes. The procedures for making a special assessment vary widely from state to state, but usually include the following steps:

1. The authority to recommend or initiate the *specific improvement* is vested either in the property owners, who may petition for an improvement, or in a proper legislative authority, such as the city council or board of trustees, who may initiate the proposal for an improvement. Hearings are held, and notices are given to the owners of the property affected.

2. After the preliminary legal steps have been taken, the legislative body authorized by statute to act in such cases adopts an *ordinance* that sets out the nature of the improvement, its cost, and a description of the area to be assessed.

3. The proper authority spreads the assessment (called the **assessment roll**) over the various parcels of real estate that will benefit. The amount of the assessment for each parcel is usually determined by one of the following criteria: (1) estimated benefit each tract will receive by reason of the assessment and (2) front footage. Regardless of the basis used, the assessment will usually vary from parcel to parcel, as all will not benefit equally from the improvement.

4. After hearing the benefits and nature of improvements to be made, and after hearing any objections from members of the local community affected by the improvements, the local authority, usually a court of record, will either approve or reject the proposal. This is often referred to as *confirming the assessment roll.*

5. After all of these steps have been taken, the assessment becomes a lien on the land assessed. When the improvement has been completed, a *warrant* is issued by the proper authority, often the clerk of the court that approved the roll. This warrant gives the local collector the authority to issue special assessment bills and begin collection.

In most states, an assessment becomes a *lien* following the confirmation of the roll. Special assessments are usually due and payable in equal annual installments over a period of five to ten years. Interest is also charged each property owner on the total amount of his or her assessment. The first installment usually becomes due during the year following confirmation. The bill will include yearly interest on the entire assessment. As subsequent installments are billed in following years, each bill will include a year's interest on the unpaid balance. Property owners usually have the right to prepay any or all installments and thus avoid further interest charges.

Liens Other Than Taxes

Aside from real estate tax and special assessment liens, the following types of liens may also be charged against real property—either voluntarily or involuntarily: mortgage liens, mechanics' liens, judgments, estate and inheritance tax liens, vendors' liens, vendees' liens, liens for municipal utilities, surety bail bond liens, corporation franchise tax liens and Internal Revenue Service tax liens.

Mortgage Liens

In general, a **mortgage lien** is a voluntary lien on real estate given to a lender by a borrower as security for a mortgage loan. It becomes a lien on real property when the mortgage funds are disbursed and the lender files or records the mortgage in the office of the proper official of the county where the property is located. Mortgage lenders generally require a preferred lien, referred to as a *first mortgage lien;* this means that (aside from real estate taxes), there are no other major liens against the property that would take priority over the mortgage lien.

Mortgages and mortgage liens will be discussed in detail in Chapter 15, "Real Estate Financing."

Mechanics' Liens

A mechanic's lien is a right *granted by statute.* No such lien existed under common law. The purpose of the **mechanic's lien** is to *give security to those who perform labor or furnish material in the improvement of real property.* A mechanic's lien is a specific, involuntary lien and is available to contractors, subcontractors, architects, mechanics, equipment lessors, surveyors, teamsters, laborers and others.

In order for a person to be entitled to a mechanic's lien, the work that was done must have been by contract (express or implied consent) with the owner or owner's authorized representative. Such a lien is relied on to cover situations in which the owner has not fully paid for the work, or when the general contractor has been paid but has not paid the subcontractors or suppliers of materials. Generally, a person claiming a mechanic's lien must file a notice of lien in the public record of the county where the property is located within a certain period of time after the work has been completed.

The time at which a mechanic's lien attaches to the real estate varies according to state law. For example, priority may be established as of the date: (1) the construction began or materials were first furnished; (2) the work was completed; (3) the individual subcontractor's work was either commenced or completed; (4) the contract was signed or work ordered; or (5) a notice of the lien was recorded, filed, posted or served.

In most states, while a mechanic's lien takes priority from the time it attaches, a claimant's notice of lien will not be filed in the public records until some time after that. A purchaser of property that has been recently constructed, altered or repaired should therefore be cautious about possible unrecorded mechanics' liens against the property.

In some states, mechanics' liens may be given priority over previously recorded liens (such as mortgages). Inasmuch as the rights of a claimant are statutory, they are controlled by the requirements of the laws of the state in which the real estate is located. It is usually provided that a claimant must take steps to enforce the lien within a certain time (usually one or two years after the filing of the lien claim) or the lien will expire. Enforcement usually requires a court action to foreclose the lien through the sale of the subject real estate in order to obtain the money to satisfy the lien.

If improvements that were not ordered by the property owner have commenced, the property owner should execute a document called a *notice of nonresponsibility* to relieve him- or herself from possible mechanics' liens. By posting this notice in some conspicuous place on the property and recording a verified copy of it in the public record, the owner gives notice that he or she will not be responsible for the work done.

Judgments

A **judgment** is a *decree issued by a court.* When the decree provides for the awarding of money and sets forth the amount of money owed by the debtor to the creditor, the judgment is referred to as a *money judgment.*

A judgment becomes a *general, involuntary lien on both real and personal property* owned by the debtor. Since a lien usually covers only property located within the county in which the judgment is issued, a notice of the lien must be filed in any county to which a creditor wishes to extend the lien coverage. To enforce a judgment, the creditor must obtain from the court a *writ of execution* directing the sheriff to levy upon and sell as much of the debtor's property as is necessary to pay the debt and the expenses of the sale. A judgment differs from a mortgage in that a *specific* parcel of real estate was not given as security at the time that the debtor-creditor relationship was created.

A judgment takes its priority as a lien on the debtor's property from one or a combination of the following (as provided by the law of the state in which the real estate is located): (1) the date the judgment was entered by the court, (2) the date the judgment was filed for record in the recorder's office or (3) the date a writ of execution or levy was issued. When property is sold to satisfy a debt, the debtor should demand a legal document known as a *satisfaction of judgment,* or *satisfaction piece,* which should be filed with either the clerk of the court or, in some states, the recorder of deeds, so that the record will be cleared of the judgment.

Attachments. To prevent a debtor from conveying title to previously unsecured real estate while a court suit is being decided, a creditor may seek a writ of **attachment.** By this writ, the court retains custody of the property until the suit is concluded. The creditor must first post with the court a surety bond or deposit sufficient to cover any possible loss or damage the debtor may sustain during the period the court has custody of the property, in case the judgment is not awarded to the creditor.

Lis pendens. A judgment or other decree affecting real estate is rendered at the conclusion of a lawsuit. Generally, there is a considerable time lag between the filing of a lawsuit and the rendering of a judgment. When any suit is filed that affects title to a specific parcel of real estate (such as a foreclosure suit), a notice known as a *lis pendens* (Latin for "litigation pending") is recorded, or registered. A lis pendens is not a lien, but rather a *notice of a possible future lien.* Recording of the lis pendens gives notice to all interested parties, such as prospective purchasers and lenders, and establishes a priority for the later lien, which is dated back to the date the lis pendens was recorded.

Estate and Inheritance Tax Liens

Federal **estate taxes** and state **inheritance taxes** (as well as the debts of deceased persons) are *general, statutory, involuntary liens* that encumber a deceased person's real and personal property. These are normally paid or cleared in probate court proceedings. Probate and issues of inheritance will be discussed in Chapter 12, "Transfer of Title."

Vendors' Liens

A **vendor's lien** is a *seller's claim* against the title of property conveyed to a buyer; it occurs in cases where the seller did not receive the full, agreed-upon purchase price. This is a *specific, equitable, involuntary lien* for the amount of the unpaid balance due the seller.

Vendees' Liens

A **vendee's lien** is a *buyer's claim* against a seller's property in cases where the seller failed to deliver title. This usually occurs when property is purchased under an installment contract (contract for deed, agreement of sale), and the seller fails to deliver title after all other terms of the contract have been satisfied. A vendee's lien is a *specific, equitable, involuntary lien* for any money paid plus the value of any improvements made to the property by the buyer.

Liens for Municipal Utilities

Municipalities are generally given the right to a *specific, equitable, involuntary lien* on the property of an owner who refuses to pay bills for water or other municipal utility service.

Surety Bail Bond Lien

A real estate owner charged with a crime for which he or she must face trial may choose to put up real estate instead of cash as surety for bail. The execution and recording of such a **surety bail bond** creates a *specific, voluntary lien* against the owner's real estate. This lien is enforceable by the sheriff or other court officer if the accused person does not appear in court as required.

Corporation Franchise Tax Lien

State governments generally levy a **corporation franchise tax** on corporations as a condition of allowing them to do business in the state. Such a tax is a *general, statutory, involuntary lien* on all property, real and personal, owned by the corporation.

IRS Tax Lien

An **Internal Revenue Service (IRS) tax lien** results from a person's failure to pay any portion of federal IRS taxes, such as income and withholding taxes. A federal tax lien is a *general, statutory, involuntary lien* on all real and personal property held by the delinquent taxpayer.

Summary

Liens are claims, or charges, of creditors or tax officials against the real and personal property of a debtor. A lien is a type of encumbrance. Liens are either *general*, covering all real and personal property of a debtor-owner, or *specific*, covering only the specific property described in the mortgage, tax bill, or building or repair contract or other document.

With the exception of real estate tax liens and mechanics' liens, the priority of liens is generally determined by the order in which they are placed in the public record of the county in which the debtor's property is located.

Real estate taxes are levied annually by local taxing authorities. Tax liens are generally given priority over other liens. Payments are required before stated dates, after which penalties accrue. An owner may lose title to property for nonpayment of taxes, since such tax-delinquent property can be sold at a tax sale. Some states allow a time period during which a defaulted owner can redeem his or her real estate from a tax sale.

Special assessments are levied to allocate the cost of improvements, such as new sidewalks, curbs or paving, to the real estate that benefits from them. Assessments are usually payable annually over a five- or ten-year period, together with interest due on the balance of the assessment.

Mortgage liens are voluntary, specific liens given to lenders to secure payment for mortgage loans.

Mechanics' liens protect general contractors, subcontractors and material suppliers whose work enhances the value of real estate.

A *judgment* is a court decree obtained by a creditor, usually for a monetary award from a debtor. The lien of a judgment can be enforced by court issuance of a *writ of execution* and sale by the sheriff to pay the judgment amount and costs.

Attachment is a means of preventing a defendant from conveying property before completion of a suit in which a judgment is sought.

Lis pendens is a recorded notice of a lawsuit that is awaiting trial in court and may result in a judgment that will affect title to a parcel of real estate.

Federal estate taxes and *state inheritance taxes* are general liens against a deceased owner's property.

Vendors' liens and *vendees' liens* are liens against specific property. A vendor's lien is a seller's claim against a purchaser who has not paid the entire purchase price, and a vendee's lien is a purchaser's claim against a seller under an installment contract who has not conveyed title.

Liens for *water charges or other municipal utilities* and *surety bail bond liens* are specific liens, while *corporation franchise tax liens* are general liens against a corporation's assets.

Internal Revenue Service tax liens are general liens against the property of a person who is delinquent in payment of IRS taxes.

Questions

1. Which of the following best refers to the type of lien that affects all real and personal property of a debtor?
   - a. specific lien
   - b. voluntary lien
   - c. involuntary lien
   - d. general lien

2. General contractor Ralph Hammond was hired to build a room addition to Thom and Harriet Elkin's home. Hammond completed the work several weeks ago, but still has not been paid. Hammond is entitled to a mechanic's lien. Which of the following is correct concerning his lien?
   - a. It is a general lien.
   - b. It is a specific lien.
   - c. Hammond must file a notice of his lien in the public records.
   - d. b and c

3. After real estate has been sold by the state or county to satisfy a delinquent real estate tax lien, the owner usually has a right to:
   - a. buy another parcel of land.
   - b. remain in possession indefinitely.
   - c. redeem the property from sale within the time specified by state law.
   - d. have the sale canceled.

4. *Priority of liens* refers to which of the following?
   - a. the order in which a debtor assumes responsibility for payment of obligations
   - b. the order in which liens will be paid if property is sold by court order to satisfy a debt
   - c. the dates liens are filed for record; the lien with the earliest recording date will always take priority over other liens
   - d. the fact that specific liens have greater priority than general liens

5. A lien on real estate made to secure payment for specific municipal improvements is which of the following?
   - a. mechanic's lien
   - b. special assessment
   - c. ad valorem
   - d. utility lien

6. When real estate is assessed for tax purposes:
   - I. the homeowner may appeal the assessment.
   - II. an equalization factor may be used.
     - a. I only
     - b. II only
     - c. both I and II
     - d. neither I nor II

7. A mechanic's lien is available to:
   - a. a contractor.
   - b. a subcontractor.
   - c. a teamster.
   - d. all of the above

8. A specific parcel of real estate has a market value of $80,000 and is assessed for tax purposes at 25 percent of market value. The tax rate for the county in which the property is located is 30 mills. The tax bill will be:
   - a. $60.
   - b. $550.
   - c. $600.
   - d. $700.

9. Which of the following taxes is (are) used to distribute the cost of public services among real estate owners?
   - a. personal property tax
   - b. sales tax
   - c. real property tax
   - d. all of the above

10. A mechanic's lien claim arises when a general contractor has performed work or provided material to improve a parcel of real estate on the owner's order and the work has not been paid for. Such a contractor has a right to:
    - a. tear out his or her work.
    - b. record a notice of the lien.
    - c. record a notice of the lien and file a court suit within the time required by state law.
    - d. have personal property of the owner sold to satisfy the lien.

11. Which of the following is (are) a lien(s) on real estate?

    a. an easement running with the land
    b. an unpaid mortgage loan
    c. an encroachment
    d. a license

12. A mortgage lien and a judgment lien have which of the following characteristics in common?

    I. Both may involve a debtor-creditor relationship.
    II. Both are general liens.

    a. I only
    b. II only
    c. both I and II
    d. neither I nor II

13. Which of the following is classified as a general lien?

    a. vendor's lien
    b. surety bail bond lien
    c. debts of a deceased person
    d. general real estate taxes

14. Which of the following liens would usually be given higher priority?

    a. a mortgage dated last year
    b. the current real estate tax
    c. a mechanic's lien for work started before the mortgage was made
    d. a judgment rendered yesterday

15. Which of the following steps is usually required *before* a special assessment becomes a lien against a specific parcel of real estate?

    a. An ordinance is passed
    b. The improvement is completed
    c. Work on the improvement is begun
    d. A new tax year begins

16. Special assessment liens:

    a. take priority over mechanics' liens.
    b. are voluntary liens.
    c. are general liens.
    d. a and c

17. What is the annual real estate tax on a property that is valued at $135,000 and assessed for tax purposes at $47,250 with an equalization factor of 125 percent, when the tax rate is 25 mills?

    a. $1,417.50
    b. $1,476.56
    c. $4,050.00
    d. none of the above

18. Which of the following is a voluntary, specific lien?

    a. IRS tax lien
    b. mechanic's lien
    c. mortgage lien
    d. vendor's lien

19. Mary Williams sold Ernest Tully a parcel of real estate. Title has passed, but to date, Tully has not paid the purchase price in full as originally agreed upon. If Williams does not receive payment, which of the following would she be entitled to enforce?

    a. attachment
    b. vendee's lien
    c. lis pendens
    d. vendor's lien

20. General contractor Kim Kelly is suing homeowner Bob Baker for nonpayment for services; suit will be filed in the next few weeks. Recently Kelly learned that Baker has listed the property with a local real estate broker for sale. In this instance, which of the following will probably be used by Kelly and her attorneys to protect her interest?

    a. lis pendens
    b. attachment
    c. vendee's lien
    d. a and b

Real Estate Contracts

Key Terms

Agreement in writing
Assignment
Bilateral contract
Breach of contract
Consideration
Contract
Counteroffer
Earnest money
Equitable title
Escrow instructions
Executed contract
Executory contract
Express contract
Implied contract
Installment contract

Legality of object
Legally competent parties
Novation
Offer and acceptance
Option
Parol evidence rule
Real estate sales contract
Specific performance suit
Statute of frauds
Statute of limitations
Unenforceable contract
Unilateral contract
Valid contract
Void contract
Voidable contract

Overview

"Get it in writing" is a phrase commonly used to warn one party to an agreement to protect his or her interests by entering into a written *contract* with the other party, outlining the rights and obligations of both. The real estate business makes use of many different types of contracts, including listing agreements, leases and sales contracts. Brokers and salespeople must understand the content and uses of such agreements and must be able to explain them to buyers and sellers. This chapter will first deal with the legal principles governing contracts in general, and will then examine the types of contracts used in the real estate business.

Contracts	In the course of their business, brokers and salespeople use many types of contracts and agreements to carry out their responsibilities to sellers, buyers and the general public. Among these are listing agreements, sales contracts, option agreements, installment contracts, leases and escrow instructions.
	Before studying these specific types of contracts, you must first understand the general body of law that governs the operation of such agreements; it is known as *contract law*.

Contract Law	A **contract** is a legally enforceable promise or set of promises that must be performed and for which, if a breach of promise occurs, the law provides a remedy. Depending on the situation and the nature or language of the agreement, a contract may be: (1) express or implied; (2) unilateral or bilateral; (3) executory or executed; and (4) valid, unenforceable, voidable or void. These terms are used to describe the type, status and legal effect of a contract and are discussed in the sections that follow.

Express and Implied Contracts	Depending upon how a contract is created, it may be express or implied. In an **express contract,** the parties state the terms and show their intentions in words to that effect. An express contract may be either oral or written. In an **implied contract,** the agreement of the parties is demonstrated by their conduct.

In Practice. . .	*In the usual agency relationship, a listing agreement is an express contract between the seller and the broker naming the broker as the fiduciary representative of the seller. The courts have held that a broker may, in certain situations, also have an implied contract to represent a buyer. In one case, a broker took a listing for a residence and showed it to several potential purchasers, one of whom requested that a physical inspection of the property be made. The broker complied, but mistakenly hired an unqualified person to make the inspection. The interested party bought the property, discovered a serious physical defect and sued the broker. The court ruled that, although the broker was the agent of the seller, in complying with the buyer's request he had by implication accepted an agency agreement to represent the purchaser. By hiring an inspector who was not competent to do the job, the broker violated his duty to the purchaser under this implied agreement.*

Bilateral and Unilateral Contracts	Contracts may also be classified as either bilateral or unilateral. In a **bilateral contract,** both parties promise to do or refrain from doing something; one promise is given in exchange for another. A real estate sales contract is a bilateral contract because the seller promises to sell a parcel of real estate and deliver title to the property to the buyer, who promises to pay a certain sum of money for the property.
	In a **unilateral contract,** one party makes a promise in order to induce a second party to do something. The second party is not legally obligated to act; however,

if the second party does comply, the first party is obligated to keep the promise. An offer of a reward would be an example of a unilateral contract. For example, if a person runs a newspaper ad offering a reward for the return of a lost pet, that person is promising to pay if the act of returning the pet is fulfilled.

Executed and Executory Contracts

A contract may be classified as either executed or executory, depending on whether or not the agreement is completely performed. An **executed contract** is one in which both parties have fulfilled their promises and thus performed the contract. (Don't be confused by the fact that we also use the word execute to refer to the signing of a contract.) An **executory contract** exists when something remains to be done by one or both parties.

Validity of Contracts

A contract can be described as either valid, void, voidable, or unenforceable (see table 11.1), depending on the circumstances.

Table 11.1
Legal Effects of Contracts

Type of Contract	Legal Effect	Example
Valid	Binding and Enforceable on Both Parties	Agreement Complying with Essentials of a Valid Contract
Void	No Legal Effect	Contract for an Illegal Purpose
Voidable	One or Both Parties May Disaffirm	Contract Between Intoxicated Parties
Unenforceable	Neither Party May Sue to Force Performance	Certain Oral Agreements

A **valid contract** complies with all the essential elements that will be discussed later in this chapter, and is binding and enforceable on both parties.

A **void contract** is one that has no legal force or effect because it does not meet the essential elements of a contract. For example, since one of the essential conditions for a valid contract is a legal purpose, a contract to commit a crime is void.

A **voidable contract** is one that seems on the surface to be valid but may be rescinded, or disaffirmed, by one of the parties, who might be injured if the contract were to be enforced. (In some cases, this may be both parties.) For example, if someone makes a contract while drugged or intoxicated, the contract is voidable by that person. A voidable contract will be considered by the courts to be a valid contract if the party who has the option to disaffirm the agreement does not do so within a prescribed period of time.

An **unenforceable contract** has all the elements of a valid contract; however, neither party can sue the other to force performance. For example, in many states an oral listing agreement is unenforceable. In these states a broker taking an oral listing runs the risk of being unable to sue a seller if the broker sells the seller's property but is not paid a commission as promised. Unenforceable contracts are said to be "valid as between the parties," because once the agreement is fully executed and both parties are satisfied, neither would have reason to initiate a lawsuit to force performance.

Elements Essential to a Valid Contract

In general, the essentials of a valid contract include the following:

1. **Legally competent parties:** Both parties to the contract must be of legal age and have sufficient mental capacity. In most states, 18 is the age of contractual capacity. In some states a contract with a minor is void; in other states, such a contract is voidable by the minor. A party who understands the nature and effect of the contract has sufficient mental capacity. Mental capacity is not the same as medical sanity.

2. **Offer and acceptance:** There must be an offer by one party that is accepted by the other. This requirement, also called *mutual assent,* means that there must be a "meeting of the minds." Courts look to the objective intent of the parties to determine if they intended to enter into a binding agreement. The terms of the agreement must be fairly definite and understood by both parties.

3. **Legality of object:** To be valid, a contract must not contemplate a purpose that is illegal or against public policy.

4. **Consideration:** Courts will not enforce gratuitous (free) promises. Consideration is something of legal value (usually one party suffering a legal detriment), bargained for and given in exchange for a promise or an act. Any return promise to perform that has been bargained for and exchanged is legally sufficient to satisfy the consideration element.

No misrepresentation, fraud, undue influence or duress. To be valid, a contract must be entered into as the free and voluntary act of each party. Misrepresentation, fraud, undue influence or duress would deprive a person of the ability to enter into a contract freely using reasonable judgment and caution. If these detriments are present, the contract is voidable by the injured party. If the uninjured party were to sue for breach, the injured party could use lack of voluntary assent as a defense.

Revocation of an offer. An offer may be **revoked** by the offeror at any time prior to acceptance, if the revocation is communicated directly to the offeree by the offeror. It also is revoked if the offeree learns of the revocation from a reliable source (such as the listing broker) and observes the offeror act in a manner that indicates that the offer no longer exists.

Agreement in writing and signed. Not all contracts need to be in writing to be enforceable; however, every state has adopted the common-law doctrine known as the **statute of frauds,** which requires certain types of contracts to be in writing in order to be enforceable in a court of law.

Contracts for the sale of real estate, or the lease of real estate ending more than one year from the date of agreement, *must* be in writing.

The **parol evidence rule,** another heritage of the common law, is a rule of evidence that dictates that no prior or contemporaneous oral or written negotiations or agreements that vary or contradict the terms of a written contract may be considered in a lawsuit based on the written agreement. The written contract is assumed to be the complete manifestation of the agreement of the parties. The many exceptions to the rule include evidence that a contract was entered into illegally or evidence intended to clarify ambiguous contract terms.

Signatures. A real estate sales contract requires the signatures of the buyer and seller. The seller's spouse may also be required to sign, to release potential marital or homestead rights. An agent may sign for a principal when proper authority, such as a power of attorney, has been granted. When sellers are co-owners, all co-owners must sign if the entire ownership is being transferred.

Accurate description of the property. A real estate sales contract must contain an accurate description of the property being conveyed. The test that most courts use is whether the subject property can be identified with reasonable certainty. This may require a legal description, but in many cases a street address is sufficient.

In Practice...

If there is any ambiguity in a contract, the courts generally will interpret the agreement against the party who prepared it. For example, a broker usually prepares a listing agreement. If there were any doubt whether a listing agreement was an exclusive agency or an exclusive right to sell, a court would probably construe it to be an exclusive agency, thus ruling against the broker who prepared the document.

Performance of Contract

Under any contract, each party has certain rights and duties to fulfill. The question of when a contract must be performed is an important factor. Many contracts call for a specific time at or by which the agreed-upon acts must be completely performed. In addition, many contracts provide that "time is of the essence." This means that the contract should be performed within the time limit specified, and any party who has not performed on time will be liable for breach of contract.

When a contract does not specify a date for performance, the acts it requires should be performed within a reasonable time. The interpretation of what constitutes a reasonable time will depend upon the situation. Generally, if the act can be done immediately—such as a payment of money—it should be performed immediately, unless the parties agree otherwise.

In Practice...

Despite the best efforts of buyer and seller, it may be impossible to close the transaction on the date stipulated. The seller may not be able to have necessary repairs completed before that date. The buyer's lender may be swamped with loan applications and unable to provide funding on the date requested. Buyer and seller can adjust the closing date (or any other contract term) by a modification of the contract—a written addendum signed by all parties. The broker may negotiate the new term(s), but may not sign the modification on behalf of any of the parties.

Assignment and Novation

Often after a contract has been entered into, one party may want to withdraw without actually terminating the agreement. This may be accomplished through either assignment or novation.

Assignment refers to a transfer of rights and/or duties under a contract. Generally speaking, rights may be assigned to a third party unless the agreement forbids such an assignment. Duties may also be assigned (delegated), but the original obligor remains secondarily liable for them (after the new obligor), unless he or she is specifically released from this responsibility. A contract that requires some personal service or unique ability of one of the parties may not be assigned. Most contracts include a clause that either permits or forbids assignment.

A contract may also be terminated by **novation,** or the substitution of a new contract for an existing agreement with the intent of extinguishing the old contract. The new agreement may be between the same parties, or a new party may be substituted for either *(novation of the parties).* The parties' intent must be to discharge the old obligation. The new agreement must be supported by consideration and must conform with all the essential elements of a valid contract. For example, when a real estate purchaser assumes the seller's existing mortgage loan (see Chapter 15), the lender may choose to release the seller and substitute the buyer as the party primarily liable for the mortgage debt.

Discharge of Contract

A contract may be completely performed, with all terms carried out, or it may be breached (broken) if one of the parties defaults. In addition, there are various other methods by which a contract may be discharged (canceled). These include:

1. *Partial performance of the terms along with a written acceptance* by the person for whom acts have not been done or to whom money has not been paid.
2. *Substantial performance,* in which one party has substantially performed the contract but does not complete all the details exactly as the contract requires. Such performance—for example, under construction contracts—may be sufficient to force payment, with certain adjustments for any damages suffered by the other party.
3. *Impossibility of performance,* in which an act required by the contract cannot be legally accomplished.
4. *Mutual agreement* of the parties to cancel.
5. *Operation of law,* as in the voiding of a contract by a minor, or as a result of fraud or the expiration of the statute of limitations (discussed on the next section), or as a result of the alteration of a contract without the written consent of all parties involved.

Default—Breach of Contract

A **breach of contract** is a violation, without legal excuse, of any of the terms or conditions of a contract—such as when a seller breaches a sales contract by not delivering title to the buyer under the conditions stated in the agreement. The breaching, or defaulting, party has certain burdens, and the nondefaulting party has certain rights.

With real estate contracts, if the *seller defaults,* the buyer has three alternatives:

1. The buyer may *rescind, or cancel, the contract* and recover his or her earnest money.
2. The buyer may file a court suit, known as a **suit for specific performance,** to force the seller to perform the contract. Specific performance is ordered only when the subject matter of the contract is not readily available from another source. Since every parcel of real estate is considered unique, a suit for specific performance brought by the buyer under a real estate sales contract may be successful.

3. The buyer may *sue the seller for compensatory damages* (a personal judgment).

If the *buyer defaults,* the seller may pursue one of the following courses:

1. The seller may *declare the contract forfeited.* The right to forfeit is usually provided in the terms of the contract, and the seller is usually entitled to retain the earnest money and all payments received from the buyer as *liquidated damages.*
2. The seller may *rescind the contract;* that is, he or she may cancel, or terminate, the contract as if it had never been made. This requires the seller to return all payments the buyer has made.
3. The seller may *sue for specific performance.* In some cases this may require the seller to offer, or tender, a valid deed to the buyer to show the seller's compliance with the contract terms.
4. The seller may *sue for compensatory damages.*

Statute of limitations. The law of every state allows a specific time limit during which parties to a contract may bring legal suit to enforce their rights. The **statute of limitations** varies for different legal actions, and any rights not enforced within the applicable time period will be lost. (Compare this with the principle of *laches,* discussed in Chapter 19.)

Contracts Used in the Real Estate Business

As mentioned earlier, the types of written agreements most commonly used by brokers and salespeople are listing agreements, real estate sales contracts, option agreements, contracts for deed, leases and escrow agreements.

Broker's Authority to Prepare Documents

In many states, specific guidelines have been drawn, whether by state real estate officials, court decision or statute, regarding the authority of real estate licensees to prepare contracts for their clients and customers. As a rule, a licensed real estate broker is not authorized to practice law—that is, to draft (prepare) legal documents such as deeds and mortgages. A broker or salesperson may, however, be permitted to fill in the blanks on certain approved preprinted documents (such as sales contracts and leases), provided the licensee does not charge a separate fee for completing such forms. You should determine, by questioning your state license officials or local real estate board, the current status, in your state on the use of preprinted forms by real estate licensees.

Contract forms. *Printed forms* are used for all kinds of contracts because most transactions are basically similar in nature. The use of printed forms raises three problems: (1) what to *fill in the blanks,* (2) what printed matter is not applicable to a particular sale and is to be *ruled out* by drawing lines through the unwanted words and (3) what additional clauses or agreements (called *riders* or *addendums*) are to be *added.* All changes and additions are usually initialed in the margin or on the rider by both parties when the contract is executed. The newer forms provide a greater number of alternative provisions, which may be used or ruled out depending upon what the parties wish to express in their agreement.

In Practice...

It is essential that both parties to a contract understand exactly what it is to which they are agreeing. Poorly drafted documents may be subject to various interpreta-

tions and lead to litigation. The parties to a real estate transaction should be advised, before signing them, to have sales contracts and other legal documents examined by their attorneys to ensure that such agreements accurately reflect their intentions. Where preprinted forms do not sufficiently cover special provisions in a transaction, the parties should be encouraged to have an attorney draft a sales contract that properly covers such provisions.

Listing Agreements

Listing agreements are *instruments used by the real estate broker in order to represent a principal legally.* They are contracts that establish the rights of the broker as agent and of the buyer or seller as principal. There are many forms of listing agreements: (1) open listing, (2) net listing, (3) exclusive-agency listing and (4) exclusive-right-to-sell listing. Review the explanations of the types of listing agreements presented in Chapter 6.

Sales Contracts

A **real estate sales contract** sets forth all details of the agreement between a buyer and a seller for the purchase and sale of a parcel of real estate. Depending on the state or locality, this agreement may be known as an *offer to purchase, contract of purchase and sale, purchase agreement, earnest money agreement, deposit receipt* or other variation of these titles. Whatever the contract is called, when it has been prepared and signed by the purchaser it is an offer to purchase the subject real estate. Later, if the document is accepted and signed by the seller, it then becomes, or "ripens into," a contract of sale. An example of a real estate sales contract is figure 11.1.

In a few localities, it is customary to prepare a shorter document, known as a *binder,* for the purchaser to sign. This document states the essential terms of the purchaser's offer and acknowledges receipt of the deposit. It also provides that the parties agree to have a more formal and complete contract of sale drawn up by an attorney upon the seller's acceptance and signing of the binder. Throughout the country, a binder receipt might be used in any situation where the details of the transaction are too complex for the standard sales contract form.

Every sales contract requires at least two parties, a seller and a buyer. The same person cannot be both the buyer and seller, as a person cannot legally contract with him- or herself. *The contract of sale is the most important document in the sale of real estate,* since it sets out in detail the agreement between the buyer and the seller and establishes their legal rights and obligations. It is more important than the deed itself, because *the contract, in effect, dictates the contents of the deed.*

Details to be included in a real estate sales contract are the price, terms, legal description of the land, kind and condition of the title, form of deed the seller will deliver, kind of title evidence required, who will provide title evidence and how defects in the title, if any, are to be eliminated. The contract must state all the terms and conditions of the agreement and spell out all contingencies. In situations where a contract is vague in its terms and one party sues the other based on one of these terms, the courts may refuse to make a contract for the parties. The real estate broker must be aware of the responsibilities and legal rights of the parties to a sale and must see that an adequate contract is prepared.

Contracts in writing. The statute of frauds provides that no action may be brought on any contract for the sale of real estate unless the contract is in writing

Figure 11.1
Real Estate Sales Contract

DUPAGE BOARD OF REALTORS®
STANDARD RESIDENTIAL SALES CONTRACT

1. BUYER(S). _Mary Lou Barton, a single woman_
   Address _2121 Greenside Avenue_ ; City _Sheffield_ ; State _IN_ ; Zip _40000_

   agrees to purchase, and SELLER(S), _Steven and Martha Ann Smithson, husband and wife_
   Address _647 Briar Lane_ ; City _Oak Brook_ ; State _IL_ ; Zip _60000_

   agrees to sell to Buyer(s) at the PRICE of _Two Hundred Sixty Five Thousand and xx/100_ Dollars ($ _265,000_)

   PROPERTY commonly known as _647 Briar Lane_

   (City of _Oak Brook_ County of _Du Page_ Illinois,)
   a complete legal description may be attached as an exhibit by either party, (hereinafter referred to as "the premises") with approximate lot dimensions of _70 feet x 160 feet_ together with all existing improvements and fixtures, if any, which shall be left on the premises, are included in the sale price, and shall be transferred to the Buyer(s) by a Bill of Sale at the time of closing; including, but not limited to: hot water heater; plumbing and electrical fixtures; sump pumps; central heating and cooling; humidifying and filtering equipment; fixed carpeting; built-in kitchen appliances; equipment and cabinets; water softener (except rental units); storm and screen windows and doors; attached shutters, window treatment hardware, blinds and shades, shelving systems, fireplace screen; roof or attic T.V. antenna; all planted vegetation; garage door openers and car units; and the following items of personal property:

   Refrigerator located in kitchen

2. THE EARNEST MONEY: Buyer(s) has paid $ _10,000_ by check/~~note or cash~~ XXXXXXXXXXXXXXXXXXX
   (and will pay within _five_ days the additional sum of $ _17,000_) as earnest money to be applied on the purchase price. The earnest money shall be held by the Listing Broker for the mutual benefit of the parties concerned and upon the closing of the sale, shall be applied first to the payment of any expenses incurred by Listing Broker for the Seller(s) in respect to this transaction, and second to payment of the broker's sales commission, rendering the overplus, if any, to the Seller(s). The balance of the purchase price shall be paid at closing.

3. THE CLOSING DATE: The closing date shall be _September 14_ , 19 _88_ (or on the date, if any, to which said date is extended by reason of paragraphs 6 and 11) at _office of seller's attorney_ , or at Buyer's lending institution, if any.

4. POSSESSION: POSSESSION SHALL BE GRANTED TO BUYER(S) AT THE TIME OF CLOSING, UNLESS OTHERWISE AGREED IN WRITING BY THE PARTIES.

5. THE DEED: Seller(s) shall convey or cause to be conveyed to Buyer(s) (in joint tenancy) or Buyer's nominee, by a recordable, stamped general warranty deed with release of homestead rights, or Trustee's Deed if applicable, good title to the premises subject only to the following "permitted exceptions" if any, none of which shall impair the use of the property as a residence: (a) General real estate taxes not due and payable at time of closing; (b) Special Assessments confirmed after this Contract date; (c) Building, building line and use or occupancy restrictions, conditions and covenants of record; (d) Zoning laws and Ordinances; (e) Easements for public utilities; (f) Drainage ditches, feeders, laterals and drain tile, pipe or other conduit; (g) If the property is other than a detached, single-family home, party walls, party wall rights and agreements; terms, provisions, covenants, and conditions of the declaration of condominium, if any, and all amendments thereto; any easements established by or implied from the said declaration of condominium or amendments thereto, if any; limitations and conditions imposed by the Illinois Condominium Property Act, and if applicable; installments of assessments due after the date of closing.

6. FINANCING CONDITION: (a) This Contract is subject to the condition that on or before _August 20, 1978_ , Buyer(s) shall secure, or there shall be made available to Buyer(s), a written commitment for a loan to be secured by a mortgage or trust deed on the premises in the amount of $ _212,000_ , or such lesser sum as Buyer(s) accepts; (b) If after the Buyer(s) has submitted a true loan application and otherwise made every reasonable effort to procure a loan commitment from any source made available to Buyer(s) and has been unable to do so, and after serving written notice thereof upon Seller(s) or Seller's attorney within 1 day of the time specified herein for securing such commitment, then this Contract shall become null and void, and all monies paid by Buyer(s) hereunder shall be refunded; however, if Seller(s), at Seller's option, notifies Buyer(s) within 10 days of Buyer's notice, that Seller(s) intends to procure for Buyer(s) such a commitment within 45 days, then this Contract shall remain in full force and effect. IN THE EVENT BUYER(S) DOES NOT SERVE NOTICE OF FAILURE TO PROCURE SAID LOAN COMMITMENT UPON SELLER(S) AS HEREIN PROVIDED, THEN THIS CONTRACT SHALL CONTINUE IN FULL FORCE AND EFFECT WITHOUT ANY LOAN CONTINGENCIES; (c) Buyer(s) shall, at Buyer's expense, execute all documents necessary to procure a mortgage loan from any source. Buyer(s) shall be allowed a reasonable time prior to closing to have a mortgage or trust deed placed of record and to arrange for access to the proceeds thereof, and any delays caused by Buyer's Lender shall not constitute a default by Seller(s). Seller(s) shall allow reasonable inspection of the premises by Buyer's Lender and furnish all pertinent information requested by lender's representative; (d) The type of loan Buyer(s) shall secure is as follows:
   (DELETE THOSE ITEMS WHICH DO NOT APPLY)

   (1) Conventional (Fixed or Adjustable Rate) Mortgage. Rider 401 shall be completed, executed by the parties and shall become a part of this Contract.
   ~~(2) ... Rider 402 shall be completed, executed by the parties and shall become a part of this Contract.~~
   ~~(3) ... Rider 403 shall be completed, executed by the parties and shall become a part of this Contract.~~
   ~~(4) ... shall be completed ...~~
   ~~(5) Existing loan ...~~

7. SELLER'S REPRESENTATIONS: Seller(s) represents: (a) that Seller(s) has not received any notice from any governmental body of any ordinance or building code violation or pending rezoning, reassessment, or special assessment proceedings affecting the premises; (b) that all equipment and appliances to be conveyed, including, but not limited to, the following are in operating condition on the date of closing: all mechanical equipment, heating and cooling equipment, water heaters and softeners, septic and plumbing systems, electrical systems, kitchen equipment remaining with the premises, and any miscellaneous mechanical personal property to be transferred to the Buyer(s); (c) if the property is being sold in an "AS IS" condition, Rider 406 shall be attached and made a part of this Contract, and representations contained in paragraph 7(b) of this Contract shall not apply.

8. COMMISSION: Seller(s) agrees that _Fresh Aire Realty, Inc._ , Listing Broker, brought about this sale and agrees to pay a Broker's commission as agreed. COOPERATING BROKER: _Red Arrow Real Estate, Inc._

9. OTHER TERMS AND CONDITIONS: This contract incorporates the Terms and Conditions set forth above, on the reverse side and the Riders signed by the parties and attached hereto numbered: _401_ . THE PRINTED MATTER OF THIS CONTRACT HAS BEEN PREPARED UNDER THE SUPERVISION OF THE DUPAGE BOARD OF REALTORS® AND THE DUPAGE COUNTY BAR ASSOCIATION. THE PARTIES ARE CAUTIONED THAT THIS IS A LEGALLY BINDING CONTRACT AND TO SEEK LEGAL COUNSEL. ALL BROKERS INVOLVED IN THIS TRANSACTION HAVE AN AGENCY RELATIONSHIP WITH THE SELLER(S).

Date of Acceptance _July 10, 1988_
(The date shall be inserted only after the parties have agreed to all the terms and conditions of this Contract)

BUYER(S) _Mary Lou Barton_   SELLER(S) _Steven Smithson_

BUYER(S) _____   SELLER(S) _Martha Ann Smithson_

Form # 100 Copyright 1968 rev. 4/86

Figure 11.1
(cont.)

10. ATTORNEYS MODIFICATION: The terms of this Contract, (and all riders attached) except purchase price are subject to modification by the parties' attorneys within 5 business days from the date of acceptance. Notice of modification, if any, shall be in writing and shall state the specific terms being modified and the suggested revisions. If within 10 business days of the date of acceptance, agreement is not reached, this Contract shall be null and void, and all earnest money shall be returned to Buyer(s).

11. TITLE: (a) At least 1 business day prior to the closing date, Seller(s) shall furnish or cause to be furnished to Buyer(s) at Seller's expense, an Owner's Duplicate Certificate of Title issued by the Registrar of Titles and a Special Tax and Lien Search and a commitment issued by a title insurance company licensed to do business in the State of Illinois, to issue an owner's title insurance policy on the current form of American Land Title Association Owner's Policy (or equivalent policy) including coverage over General Schedule B exceptions in the amount of the purchase price covering the date hereof, subject only to: (1) the "permitted exceptions" as set forth in paragraph 5, (2) title exceptions pertaining to liens or encumbrances of a definite or ascertainable amount, which may be removed by the payment of money at the time of closing (an amount sufficient to secure the release of such title exceptions shall be deducted from the proceeds of sale due Seller(s) at closing), and (3) acts done or suffered by, or judgments against Buyer(s), or those claiming by, through or under Buyer(s). (b) If the title commitment discloses unpermitted exceptions, Seller(s) shall have 30 days from the date of delivery thereof to have the said exceptions waived, or to have the title insurer commit to insure against loss or damage that may be caused by such exceptions and the closing date shall be delayed, if necessary, during said 30-day period to allow Seller(s) time to have said exceptions waived. If Seller(s) fails to have unpermitted exceptions waived, or, in the alternative, to obtain a commitment for title insurance specified above as to such exceptions, within the specified time, Buyer(s) may terminate the Contract between the parties, or may elect, upon notice to Seller(s) within 10 days after the expiration of the 30-day period, to take the title as it then is, with the right to deduct from the purchase price, liens or encumbrances of a definite or ascertainable amount. If Buyer(s) does not so elect, this Contract between the parties shall become null and void, without further action of the parties, and all monies paid by Buyer(s) hereunder shall be refunded. (c) Every title commitment which conforms with subparagraph "a" shall be conclusive evidence of good title as therein shown, as to all matters insured by the policy, subject only to special exceptions therein stated.

12. AFFIDAVIT OF TITLE: Seller(s) shall furnish Buyer(s) at closing with an Affidavit of Title, covering the date of closing, subject only to those permitted special exceptions set forth in paragraph 5, and unpermitted exceptions, if any, as to which the title insurer commits to extend insurance in the manner specified in paragraph 11. In the event that this Contract between the parties calls for title to be conveyed by a Trustee's Deed, the Affidavit of Title required to be furnished by Seller(s) shall be signed by the beneficiaries of said Trust.

13. INSPECTIONS AND WARRANTIES: Buyer(s) shall be permitted reasonable inspection of the premises prior to closing. Buyer(s) is requested to make a preliminary inspection at least 10 days prior to closing and thereafter promptly to serve written notice to Seller(s) of any non-compliance with paragraph 7(b), which Seller(s) shall promptly remedy, at Seller's expense. A final inspection of the premises including all equipment, appliances and systems shall be made, if requested, within 5 days prior to the closing date. The covenants, warranties and other provisions of this Contract shall survive the closing of this transaction; however, nothing contained in paragraph 7(b) shall be construed as a warranty that the items therein mentioned will remain in good repair beyond the closing. IN THE ABSENCE OF WRITTEN NOTICE OF ANY DEFICIENCY FROM BUYER(S) PRIOR TO CLOSING, IT SHALL BE CONCLUDED THAT THE CONDITION OF THE PREMISES AND THE ABOVE EQUIPMENT IS SATISFACTORY TO BUYER(S), AND SELLER(S) SHALL HAVE NO FURTHER RESPONSIBILITY WITH REFERENCE THERETO.

14. PRORATIONS: (a) General real estate taxes shall be prorated as of the closing date on the basis of the tax assessor's latest assessed valuation, the latest known equalization factors, and the latest known tax rate. (b) Premiums on any insurance policies assigned to Buyer(s); rents, if the subject real estate is not owner-occupied; accrued interest on any assumed mortgage, water and sewer charges, fuels, and private service contracts; homeowners and/or condominium association dues and assessments, if any, shall be prorated as of the closing date.

15. CLEAN CONDITION: Seller(s) agrees to leave the premises in broom clean condition. All refuse and personal property not to be conveyed to Buyer(s) shall be removed from the premises at Seller's expense before the date of possession.

16. ESCROW CLOSING: At the election of Seller(s) or Buyer(s), upon notice to the other party not less than 5 days prior to the closing date, the sale shall be closed through an Escrow with a title company licensed to do business in the State of Illinois, in accordance with the general provisions of a deed and money escrow agreement consistent with the terms of this Contract. Upon creation of such an Escrow, anything in this Contract between the parties to the contrary notwithstanding, payment of the purchase price and delivery of the Deed shall be made through the Escrow. The cost of the Escrow shall be divided equally between Seller(s) and Buyer(s), except that Buyer(s) shall pay the money lender's escrow charges.

17. PERFORMANCE: Time is of the essence of this Contract. Should Buyer(s) fail to perform this Contract, then at the option of Seller(s) and upon written notice to Buyer(s), the earnest money shall be forfeited by Buyer(s) as liquidated damages and this Contract shall thereupon become null and void and Seller(s) shall have the right, if necessary and applicable, to re-enter and take possession of the premises aforesaid, and all right in and title to the premises and any and all improvements made upon said premises by Buyer(s) shall vest in Seller(s). Buyer(s) or Seller(s) shall pay all reasonable attorneys' fees and costs incurred by the prevailing party in enforcing the terms and provisions of this Contract, including forfeiture or specific performance, or in defending any proceeding to which Buyer(s) or Seller(s) is made a party as a result of the acts or omissions of the other party.

18. NOTICES: All notices required to be given under this Contract shall be construed to mean notice in writing signed by or on behalf of the party giving same, and served upon the other party or their attorney personally or deposited properly addressed to such party at the address herein set forth in the U.S. mail postage paid, certified or registered mail, return receipt requested.

19. SURVEY: Prior to closing date, Seller(s) shall at Seller's expense deliver to Buyer(s) or Buyer's attorney a spotted survey of the premises, dated not more than 6 months prior to the closing date, certified by a licensed surveyor, having all corners staked and showing all improvements, easements, and building lines existing as of this contract date. (In the event the premises is a condominium, only a copy of the pages showing said premises on the recorded survey attached to the Declaration of Condominium shall be required.) If requested, Seller(s) shall provide an affidavit verifying that no changes in improvements have been made since the date of said survey.

20. RISK OF LOSS: In the event that, prior to closing, the subject premises shall be destroyed by fire or other casualty to an extent that the cost of repair thereof exceeds 10% of the purchase price set forth herein; or in the event any portion of the subject premises shall be taken by condemnation, then, at the option of either party hereto, this Contract shall be declared null and void, and Buyer(s) shall be entitled to a return of all monies paid hereunder.

21. FLOOD PLAIN: Buyer(s) will obtain flood insurance if the premises is located within a designated flood plain as determined by the Flood Plain Maps or the Department of Housing and Urban Development, and if said insurance is required by Buyer's lender.

22. TRANSFER TAX STAMPS: (a) Seller(s) shall pay for the State of Illinois and County Real Estate Transfer Tax Stamps. (b) Any applicable City or Village transfer tax shall be paid by the party designated in the Ordinance of the Municipality imposing the tax except if no party is so designated, then the City or Village transfer tax shall be paid by Buyer(s).

23. WELL AND SEPTIC TEST: In the event the premises has either a well or a septic system, Seller(s) shall provide to Buyer(s) at Seller's expense, prior to closing, test results indicating such system to be in compliance with the applicable state statutes and county health department regulations.

24. STATEMENT OF ASSESSMENTS: In the event the premises is a townhouse, condominium, or otherwise subject to a homeowner's association, Seller(s) shall prior to closing furnish Buyer(s) a statement from the Board of Managers, Treasurer, or Managing Agent of the owner's association certifying payment of assessments for common expenses through the date of closing, and, if applicable, proof of waiver or termination of any right of first refusal or general option contained in the Declaration of Condominium or Declaration of Covenants, Conditions and Restrictions, and any other documents as required by Statute, Declaration, Bylaws, or Covenants as a precondition to transfer of ownership.

25. 1445 COMPLIANCE: Buyer(s) and Seller(s) agree that if Seller(s) is a "foreign person" within the meaning of Section 1445 of Internal Revenue Code, then Buyer(s) shall withhold and deduct from sale proceeds a tax equal to 10% of the amount realized. This provision shall not apply if: (a) Seller(s) furnishes to Buyer(s) an affidavit stating under penalty of perjury, Seller's U.S. Taxpayer I.D. number, and that Seller(s) is not a foreign person as defined by the Internal Revenue Code, or (b) the premises is herein acquired by Buyer(s) for use by Buyer(s) as a primary residence, as defined by the Code, and the amount realized on the sale does not exceed $300,000.00, or (c) such other exceptions as are permitted in Section 1445 of the Internal Revenue Code.

26. MERGER OF AGREEMENTS: This Agreement contains the entire agreement between the parties hereto. All negotiations between the parties are merged in this Agreement, and there are no understandings or agreements other than those incorporated in this Agreement.

This form was developed for use by, and is reproduced with the permission of, the DuPage Board of REALTORS® and the DuPage County Bar Association.

and signed by the parties to be bound by the agreement. A written agreement establishes the interest of the purchaser and the purchaser's rights to enforce that interest by court action. It thus prevents the seller from selling the property to another person who might offer a higher price. The signed contract agreement also obligates the buyer to complete the transaction according to the terms agreed upon in the contract.

Offer and acceptance. A broker lists an owner's real estate for sale at the price and conditions set by the owner. This is considered to be an invitation for prospective buyers to make offers to buy. A prospective buyer who wants to purchase the property, at those terms or some other terms, is found. A contract of sale is drawn up, signed by the prospective buyer and presented by the broker to the seller. This is an *offer* to buy. If the seller agrees to the offer *exactly as it was made* and signs the contract, the offer has been *accepted* and the contract is *valid*. The broker must then advise the buyer of the seller's acceptance, or, preferably, deliver a signed copy of the contract to the buyer.

Any attempt by the seller to change the terms proposed by the buyer creates a **counteroffer.** The buyer is relieved of his or her original offer because the seller has, in effect, rejected it by making a counteroffer. The buyer can accept the seller's counteroffer or can reject it and, if he or she wishes, make another counteroffer. Any change in the last offer results in a counteroffer, until one party finally agrees to the other party's last offer and both parties sign the final contract (see figure 11.2).

Figure 11.2
Offer and Acceptance

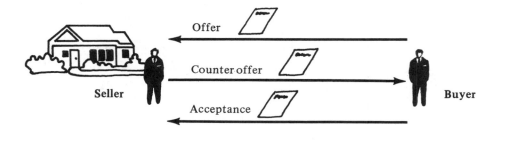

An offer or counteroffer *may be revoked at any time before it has been accepted* (even if the person making the offer or counteroffer agreed to keep the offer open for a set period of time), but the offeree must receive notification of the revocation. The contract should stipulate the manner of acceptance; generally, an offer is not considered to be accepted until the person making the offer has been *notified of the other party's acceptance*. When the parties are communicating through an agent or at a distance, questions may arise regarding whether an acceptance, rejection or counteroffer has effectively taken place. The real estate broker or salesperson should transmit all offers, acceptances or other responses as soon as possible in order to avoid such problems.

Equitable title. When a buyer signs a contract to purchase real estate, he or she does not receive title to the land; only a deed can actually convey title. However, after both buyer and seller have executed a sales contract, the buyer acquires an interest in the land known as **equitable title.** Rights of a holder of equitable title vary from state to state. Acquisition of equitable title may give the buyer an insurable interest in the property. If the parties decide not to go through with the purchase and sale, the buyer may be required, to release the equitable interest in the land, to give the seller a quitclaim deed. (Quitclaim deeds will be discussed in Chapter 12, "Transfer of Title.")

Destruction of premises. In many states, once the sales contract is signed by both parties and unless the contract provides otherwise, the buyer must bear the loss of any damage to or destruction of the property by fire or other casualty. Through laws and court decisions, however, a growing number of states have placed the risk of any loss that occurs before the deed is delivered on the seller. Quite a few of these states have adopted the *Uniform Vendor and Purchaser Risk Act,* which specifically provides that the seller (vendor) bears any loss that occurs before the title passes or the buyer (vendee) takes possession. In any case, the seller may be made to assume the risk of loss when he or she has been negligent, is unable to deliver good title or has delayed the closing of the transaction.

Earnest money deposits. It is customary for a purchaser to put down a cash deposit when making an offer to purchase real estate, generally (and preferably) in the form of a check or note. This cash deposit, commonly referred to as **earnest money,** *gives evidence of the purchaser's intention to carry out the terms of the contract.* The deposit is given to the listing broker. The sales contract typically provides that, upon acceptance of the offer, all monies are to be deposited in a trust account (under the control of the broker or a neutral escrow depository) until the closing.

The amount of the deposit is a matter to be agreed upon by the parties. As agent of the seller, the listing broker (or a cooperating broker as subagent) is obliged to request a reasonable amount as earnest money. Generally, the deposit should be sufficient to discourage the buyer from defaulting, compensate the seller for taking the property off the market and cover any expenses the seller and the broker might incur if the buyer defaults. Most contracts provide that the deposit (less any previously agreed-upon commission that may be owed the broker) becomes the seller's property if the buyer defaults.

Under the laws of most states, earnest money must be held by a broker in a special *trust,* or *escrow, account.* This money cannot be *commingled,* or mixed, with a broker's personal funds. (However, in many states a broker is permitted to place a minimal amount of his or her own money into the trust account in order to keep it open.) Likewise, a broker may not use such funds for his or her own personal use; this illegal act is the tort of *conversion,* a crime of theft, and a violation of all state license laws. A broker need not open a special escrow account for each earnest money deposit received; one such account into which all such funds are deposited is sufficient. A broker should maintain full, complete and accurate records of all earnest money deposits. State license laws usually have strict provisions covering these deposits.

There is some uncertainty as to exactly who owns the earnest money once it is put on deposit. Until the offer is officially accepted, the money is the buyer's. Once the seller accepts the offer, however, the buyer may not demand the money, even though the seller is not entitled to it until the transaction has been completed. Under no circumstances does the money belong to the broker, who must maintain it in his or her trust account. This uncertain nature of earnest money deposits makes it absolutely necessary that such funds be properly protected pending a final decision on their disbursement.

Parts of a sales contract. All real estate sales contracts can be divided into a number of general parts. Although each form of contract will contain these divisions, their location in the contract may vary. Study the sample contract in figure 11.1 to determine the exact terms of the agreement. This contract is divided into the following main sections:

1. Identification of the buyer and the buyer's statement, or obligation.
2. Legal description of the property involved.
3. Identification of the seller and statement of the type of deed the seller agrees to give, including the conditions and provisions (interests of others) to which the deed will be made subject; this is sometimes known as the "subject to" section of the contract.
4. Financial statement of the purchase price and how the purchaser intends to pay for the property, including provision for an earnest money deposit and the conditions of any mortgage financing the purchaser intends to obtain.
5. Provisions for the closing and the purchaser's possession of the property.
6. Provisions for title evidence.
7. Provisions for prorations, which are adjustments for taxes, insurance, fuel and the like.
8. Provisions in the event of destruction or damage to premises.
9. Provisions of default.
10. Provisions for contingencies.
11. Miscellaneous provisions.
12. Dates and signatures.

Option Agreements

An **option** is a *contract by which an* optionor *(generally an owner) gives an* optionee *(a prospective purchaser or lessee) the right to buy or lease the owner's property at a fixed price within a stated period of time.* The optionee pays a fee (the agreed-upon consideration) for the option right and must decide, within the specified time, either to: (1) exercise the option right (to buy or lease the property) or (2) allow the option right to expire. An option is enforceable by only one party—the optionee.

For example, for a consideration of a specified amount of money, a present owner (optionor) agrees to give an optionee an irrevocable right to buy his or her real estate at a certain price for a limited period of time. At the time the option is signed by the parties, the owner does not sell, nor does the optionee buy. They merely agree that the optionee will have the right to buy and the owner will be obligated to sell *if* the optionee decides to exercise the option.

A common application of an option is a lease that includes an option for the tenant to purchase the property. Options on commercial real estate are frequently made dependent upon the fulfillment of specific conditions, such as the obtaining of a zoning change or a building permit. The optionee is usually obligated to exercise the option if the conditions are met. Similar terms could also be included in a sales contract.

Installment Contracts

A real estate sale can be made under an **installment contract,** sometimes called a *contract for deed, land contract* or *articles of agreement for warranty deed.*

Under an installment contract, the seller, also known as the *vendor,* retains fee ownership while the buyer, known as the *vendee,* secures possession and an equitable interest in the property. The buyer usually agrees to give the seller a down payment and pay regular monthly installments of principal and interest over a number of years. The buyer also agrees to pay real estate taxes, insurance premiums, repairs and upkeep on the property. While the buyer obtains possession when the contract is signed by both parties, *the seller is not obligated to execute and deliver a deed to the buyer until a future date, which may not be until all the terms of the contract have been satisfied.*

Real estate is occasionally sold with the new buyer assuming an existing installment contract from the original buyer/vendee. Generally, when a buyer assumes an existing contract, the original buyer/vendee must assign or convey his or her interest to the new buyer and the original seller/vendor must approve the new purchaser.

Default—termination of contract. Historically, installment contracts included a provision that a default by the buyer would permit the seller to forfeit the contract, retain all payments already made and evict the buyer. Most states now offer some legal protection to a defaulting buyer under an installment contract. The seller may be required to refund to the buyer any payments received in excess of a reasonable rental or use value of the property. A defaulted installment contract could require foreclosure in the same manner as a mortgage, and the defaulting buyer may be considered to have an equitable right to a share of sale proceeds.

In Practice...

Legislatures and courts have not looked favorably on the harsh provisions of some real estate installment contracts. A seller contemplating such a sale should first consult an attorney to make sure that the agreement meets all legal requirements.

Leases

A lease is a contract in which the owner agrees to give possession of all or a part of the real estate to another person in exchange for a rental fee. Leases are discussed in detail in Chapter 16.

Escrow Instructions

An escrow is *a means by which the parties to a contract carry out the terms of their agreement.* The parties appoint a disinterested third party to act as the *escrowee,* or *escrow agent.* This escrow agent must be someone who is not a party to the contract and will not benefit in any way from the contract.

Any real estate transaction can be closed through an escrow. The parties to the transaction agree to **escrow instructions** that set forth the duties of the escrow agent and the obligations and requirements of the parties to the transaction. An escrow may be used to close such real estate transactions as a sale, mortgage loan, exchange of property, installment contract (contract for deed) or lease.

Use of an escrow requires the seller to deposit with the escrow agent the deed and other pertinent documents, such as leases, insurance policies and a mortgage payment letter (if the existing mortgage is to be paid in full and released of record). The buyer deposits the purchase price and an executed mortgage and note if he or she is securing mortgage funds to purchase the property. The escrow agent is authorized to have the title examined, and if it is found to meet the conditions of the escrow agreement, the sale is concluded. Title then passes to the buyer, and the seller receives payment. The escrow procedure will be more fully detailed in Chapter 23, "Real Estate Closing."

Local Forms

To gain familiarity with the forms used in your area, go to brokers or real estate companies in your area and ask if they will give (or sell) you copies of the sales contract, listing agreement and other forms they use. Usually such forms can also be obtained at a title or abstract company and some banks and savings and loan associations, or they may be purchased at your local office supply and stationery stores. *Study the forms and compare them to the real estate sales contract printed in this chapter.*

Summary

A *contract* is defined as a legally enforceable promise or set of promises that must be performed and, if a breach occurs, for which the law provides a remedy.

Contracts may be classified according to whether the parties' intentions are *express* or are *implied* by their actions. They may also be classified as *bilateral,* when both parties have obligated themselves to act, or *unilateral,* when one party is obligated to perform only if the other party acts. In addition, contracts may be classified according to their legal enforceability as either *valid, void, voidable* or *unenforceable.*

Many contracts specify a time for performance. In any case, all contracts must be performed within a reasonable time. An *executed* contract is one that has been fully performed. An *executory* contract is one in which some act remains to be performed.

The *essentials of a valid contract* are: (1) legally competent parties; (2) offer and acceptance; (3) legality of object; and (4) consideration. A valid *real estate contract* must include a description of the property, and it should be in writing and signed by all parties.

In a number of circumstances, a contract may be canceled before it is fully performed. Furthermore, in many types of contracts, either of the parties may transfer his or her rights and obligations under the agreement by *assignment* of the contract or *novation* (substitution of a new contract).

If either party to a real estate sales contract defaults, several alternative actions are available. Contracts usually provide that the seller has the right to declare a sale canceled through forfeiture if the buyer defaults. In general, if either party has suffered a loss because of the other's default, the injured party may sue for damages to cover the loss. If one party insists on completing the transaction, that party may sue the defaulter for *specific performance* of the terms of the contract.

Contracts frequently used in the real estate business include listings, sales contracts, options, installment contracts (contracts for deed), leases and escrow agreements.

A *real estate sales contract* binds a buyer and a seller to a definite transaction, as described in detail in the contract. The buyer is bound to purchase the property for the amount stated in the agreement. The seller is bound to deliver a good and marketable title, free from liens and encumbrances (except those allowed by the "subject to" clause of the contract).

Under an *option* agreement, the optionee purchases from the optionor, for a limited time period, the exclusive right to purchase or lease the optionor's property. For a potential purchaser or lessee, an option is a means of buying time to consider or complete arrangements for a transaction. An *installment contract,* or *contract for deed,* is a sales/financing agreement under which a buyer purchases a seller's real estate on time. The buyer may take possession of and responsibility for the property but does not receive the deed until the time stipulated in the contract.

Any real estate transaction may be completed through an *escrow,* a means by which the parties to a contract carry out the terms of their agreement. The parties appoint a third party to act as the *escrowee,* or *escrow agent.* In the sale of real estate, the seller's deed and the buyer's money are deposited with an escrow agent under the escrow instructions that set forth the conditions to be met before the sale will be consummated.

Questions

1. A contract is said to be *bilateral* if:
   a. one of the parties is a minor.
   b. the contract has yet to be fully performed.
   c. only one party to the agreement is bound to act.
   d. all parties to the contract are bound to act.

2. Timothy Smith makes an offer to purchase certain property listed with Olaf Real Estate and leaves a deposit with broker Janice Olaf. Regarding this deposit, Olaf should:
   a. immediately apply it to listing expenses.
   b. deposit it in a trust account or as provided by state law.
   c. give it to the seller along with the offer.
   d. deposit it in her checking account.

3. A contract for the sale of real estate that does not state the consideration to be paid for the property and is not signed by the parties is considered to be:
   a. voidable.
   b. executory.
   c. void.
   d. enforceable.

4. A real estate purchaser is said to have *equitable title:*
   a. when the sales contract is signed by both buyer and seller.
   b. when the transaction is closed.
   c. when escrow is opened.
   d. when a contract for deed is paid off.

5. A seller gave an open listing to several brokers, specifically promising that if one of the brokers found a buyer for the seller's real estate, the seller would then be obligated to pay a commission to that broker. This offer by the seller is a(n):
   a. executed agreement.
   b. discharged agreement.
   c. implied agreement.
   d. unilateral agreement.

6. In the completion of a printed form of sales contract, several words were crossed out and others inserted. In order to eliminate future controversy as to whether the changes were made before or after the contract was signed, the broker should:
   a. write a letter to each party listing the changes.
   b. have each party write a letter to the other approving the changes.
   c. redraw the entire contract.
   d. have both parties initial or sign on the margin near each change.

7. The essential elements of a valid real estate contract include:
   I. legal description of the property.
   II. the signatures of the parties.
   a. I only   c. both I and II
   b. II only   d. neither I nor II

8. If, after the sales contract is signed, the seller decides not to sell:
   a. the seller may cancel the contract and retain the buyer's earnest money deposit.
   b. the buyer may institute a suit for specific performance of the contract or for money damages.
   c. the seller may revoke the original offer.
   d. all of the above

9. Under the statute of frauds of every state, all contracts for the sale of real estate:
   a. must be originated by a real estate broker.
   b. must be on preprinted forms.
   c. must be in writing.
   d. all of the above

10. During the period of time after a real estate sales contract is signed but before title actually passes, the status of the contract is:
    a. voidable.   c. executed.
    b. executory.   d. implied.

11. Which of the following is *not* one of the elements essential to a valid contract?
    a. offer and acceptance
    b. escrow
    c. legality of object
    d. consideration

12. A party may be relieved of contract obligations through which of the following legal processes?
    I. assignment
    II. novation
       a. I only   c. both I and II
       b. II only   d. neither I nor II

13. An earnest money deposit:
    I. is made by a buyer upon signing the sales contract and evidences his or her intention to carry out the contract terms.
    II. is generally held by the seller under the terms of the typical real estate sales contract.
       a. I only   c. both I and II
       b. II only   d. neither I nor II

14. Which one of the following best describes a land installment contract, or contract for deed?
    a. a contract to buy land only
    b. a mortgage on land
    c. a means of conveying title to an escrow while the purchaser pays for the property in installments
    d. a method of selling real estate whereby the purchaser pays for the property in regular installments while the seller retains title to the property

15. When a real estate sales transaction is to be closed in escrow:
    a. the seller and escrow agent execute separate escrow instructions.
    b. the buyer's purchase money is deposited with the escrow agent.
    c. a person who is a party to the contract is usually appointed as the escrow agent.
    d. the escrow instructions set forth only the obligations of the escrow agent.

16. A seller breached a written contract for sale. Some years later, the buyer sued for specific performance but was unsuccessful because of the:
    a. parol evidence rule.
    b. statute of frauds.
    c. statute of limitations.
    d. rule against perpetuities.

17. A contract may be discharged by which of the following means?
    a. impossibility of performance
    b. operation of law
    c. agreement of the parties
    d. all of the above

18. A real estate broker or salesperson helping to complete a real estate sales contract should make sure that all pertinent information is included in the document because:
    I. it establishes the legal rights and obligations of buyer and seller.
    II. it establishes what the contents of the deed of conveyance will be.
       a. I only   c. both I and II
       b. II only   d. neither I nor II

19. Broker Sam Manella has found a buyer for Joe Taylor's home. The buyer has entered into a real estate sales contract for the property for $3,000 less than the asking price and has deposited $2,000 earnest money with broker Manella. Taylor is out of town for the weekend and Manella has been unable to inform him of the signed agreement. At this point, the real estate sales contract is a(n):
    a. voidable contract.
    b. offer.
    c. executory agreement.
    d. implied contract.

20. If, in Question 19, seller Taylor does not agree to the terms of the real estate sales contract as presented to him by broker Manella, he may:
    a. refuse to sign it and ask that Manella return the buyer's earnest money.
    b. present the buyer with a counteroffer.
    c. sign it provisionally.
    d. a and b

21. Caz Krys is selling his home to Burton Timmins. After the sales contract has been signed by both parties, but before the title has passed to the buyer, the home is destroyed in a fire. Generally, who must bear the loss?

    I. Caz Krys, the seller
    II. Burton Timmins, the buyer

        a. I only   c. both I and II
        b. II only   d. neither I nor II

22. When a broker uses a client's earnest money deposit for his or her own personal use, the broker is guilty of:

    a. commingling.
    b. conversion.
    c. violating the parol evidence rule.
    d. a and b

23. An option agreement:

    I. is limited to a specified time period.
    II. must recite a set amount of consideration for purchase of the property.

        a. I only   c. both I and II
        b. II only   d. neither I nor II

24. The purchaser of real estate under an installment contract:

    a. generally pays no interest charge.
    b. is called a vendor.
    c. is not required to pay property taxes for the duration of the contract.
    d. is called a vendee.

25. By local law or court decision, who is usually authorized to draft deeds and other legal contracts?

    a. a licensed real estate broker
    b. an attorney licensed to practice law
    c. a licensed real estate salesperson
    d. all of the above

12

Transfer of Title

Key Terms

Adverse possession
Bargain and sale deed
Deed
Delivery and acceptance
Descent
Escheat
General warranty deed
Grantee
Granting clause
Grantor
Habendum clause
Heir
Intestate
Involuntary alienation

Minor
Probate
Quitclaim deed
Reconveyance deed
Special warranty deed
"Subject to" clause
Testate
Testator
Title
Transfer tax
Trust deed
Trustee's deed
Voluntary alienation
Will

Overview

A parcel of real estate may be transferred from one owner to another in a number of different ways. It may be transferred *voluntarily,* such as by sale or gift, or it may be taken *involuntarily,* by operation of law. It may be transferred by the owner before death, or it may be transferred by will or descent after death. In every instance, however, a transfer of title to a parcel of real estate is a complex legal procedure involving a number of laws and documents. This chapter will discuss the four methods of title transfer, as well as the various legal documents of conveyance with which the real estate broker or salesperson must be familiar.

Title

Title to real estate means the right to or ownership of the land. The word *title* also is used to refer to the documentary evidence of the right of ownership, such as a deed. The term *title* thus has two functions: It represents the "bundle of rights" the owner possesses in the real estate, and it also denotes facts that, if proven, would enable a person to recover or retain ownership or possession of a parcel of real estate.

Titles are either *original* or *derivative.* Original title to real property can be vested only in the state, and is usually obtained through discovery, occupancy, conquest or cession to the state. All other titles are derivative and are vested in individuals (or corporations, partnerships and the like).

The laws of each state govern real estate transactions for land located within its boundaries. Each state has the authority to pass legislative acts that affect the methods of transferring title or other interests in real estate. Title to real estate may be transferred in most states by the following methods: (1) voluntary alienation; (2) involuntary alienation; (3) will; and (4) descent.

Voluntary Alienation

Voluntary alienation (transfer) of title may be made by either gift or sale. To transfer title by voluntary alienation during his or her lifetime, an owner must use some form of deed of conveyance. *seller alienating himself from property.*

A **deed** is a *written instrument by which an owner of real estate intentionally conveys his or her right, title or interest in a parcel of real estate to another.* All deeds must be in writing in accordance with the requirements of the statute of frauds. The owner is referred to as the **grantor**, and the one who acquires title is called the **grantee**. A deed is executed (signed) by the grantor.

Instrument of conveyance

Requirements for a Valid Conveyance

Although the formal requirements for a valid deed are not uniform in all states, certain requirements are basic (see figure 12.1). These are:

1. a *grantor* having the legal capacity to execute (sign) the deed.
2. a *grantee* named with reasonable certainty, so that he or she can be identified.
3. a recital of *consideration.*
4. a *granting clause* (words of conveyance).
5. a habendum clause (to define ownership taken by the grantee).
6. designation of any *limitations* on the conveyance of a full fee simple estate.
7. an accurate *legal description* of the property conveyed.
8. *exceptions and reservations,* if any, affecting the title (**"subject to" clause**).
9. the *signature of the grantor,* sometimes with a seal.
10. *delivery* of the deed and *acceptance* by the grantee to pass title.

Grantor. A grantor must have a legal existence, be of lawful age and be legally competent in order to convey title to real estate. The laws of the state where the real estate is located will control the precise requirements to convey title. The rules governing contracts (discussed in Chapter 11) usually apply to determine if a grantor is competent to convey real property.

Figure 12.1
Elements of a Valid Conveyance

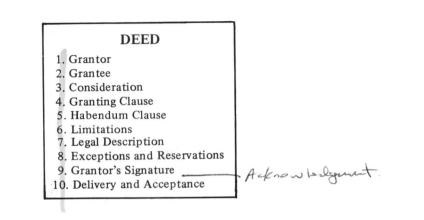

A grantor must be of sound mind and of lawful age, generally at least 18 years old. A **minor** usually does not have legal capacity to transfer title. Any attempted conveyance by a minor is considered to be voidable.

A grantor generally is held to have sufficient mental capacity to execute a deed if he or she is capable of understanding the action. A deed executed by a person while mentally impaired (as by intoxication) is only *voidable*—it is not void. A deed executed by a person who has been judged legally incompetent is considered to be void. Court authority must be secured before real estate owned by a legally incompetent person can be conveyed.

In most states, a grantor's spouse is required to join in and sign any deed of conveyance in order to waive any marital and/or homestead rights. This varies according to state law and the manner in which the title to real estate is held by the conveying parties, as discussed in Chapters 7 and 8.

It is important that a grantor's name be spelled correctly and that there be no variation in its spelling throughout the deed. If for any reason a grantor's name has been changed from that by which title was acquired originally, as when a woman changes her name by marriage, both names must be shown as, for example, "Mary Smith, formerly Mary Jones."

Grantee. To be valid, a deed must name a grantee and do so in such a way that the grantee is readily identifiable. A deed naming as the grantee a wholly fictitious person, a company that does not legally exist, or a society or club that is not properly incorporated is considered void.

Consideration. In order to be valid, all deeds must contain a clause acknowledging the grantor's receipt of a consideration. In most states, the amount of consideration must be stated in dollars. When a deed conveys real estate as a gift to a relative, "love and affection" may be sufficient consideration, but it is customary in most states to recite a *nominal* consideration, such as "$10.00 and other good and valuable consideration." The full dollar amount of consideration is seldom set forth in the deed, except when the instrument is executed by a corporation or trustee, or pursuant to court order.

Granting clause (words of conveyance). A deed of conveyance transfers a present interest in real estate. It must contain words of grant that state the grantor's intention to convey the property at this time. An expression of intent to convey at some future time is inadequate. Such words of grant, or conveyance, are contained in the **granting clause.** Depending on the type of deed and the obligations agreed to by the grantor, the wording is generally either "convey and warrant," "grant," "grant, bargain and sell" or "remise, release and quitclaim."

If more than one grantee is involved, the granting clause should cover the creation of their specific rights in the property. The clause might state, for example, that the grantees will take title as joint tenants or tenants in common. The wording is especially important in states where specific wording is necessary to create a joint tenancy.

The granting clause should also indicate what interest in the property is being conveyed by the grantor. Deeds that convey the entire fee simple interest of the grantor usually contain such wording as "to Jacqueline Smith and to her heirs and assigns forever." If the grantor is conveying less than his or her complete interest, such as a life estate to property, the wording must indicate this limitation on the grantee's interest. For example, a deed creating a life estate would convey property "to Jacqueline Smith for the duration of her natural life."

Habendum clause. Although it is not essential, when it is necessary to define or explain the ownership to be enjoyed by the grantee, a **habendum clause** may follow the granting clause. The habendum clause begins with the words "to have and to hold." Its provisions must agree with those set down in the granting clause. When there is a discrepancy between the two clauses, the provisions in the granting clause are followed.

Description of real estate. For a deed to be valid, it must contain an accurate description of the real estate conveyed. Land is considered adequately described if a competent surveyor can locate the property from the description used. The rules relative to describing real estate were discussed in Chapter 9.

Exceptions and reservations ("subject to" clauses). As mentioned in the discussion of warranties, a deed should specifically note any encumbrances, reservations or limitations that affect the title being conveyed. Such exceptions to clear title may include mortgage liens, taxes, restrictions and easements that run with the land. For example, a deed may grant title to a grantee "subject to general real estate taxes for the year 1982 and subsequent years."

In addition to existing encumbrances, a grantor may reserve some right in the land for his or her own use (an easement, for instance). A grantor may also place certain restrictions on a grantee's use of the property. For example, a developer may restrict the number of houses that may be built on a one-acre lot in a subdivision. A deed must clearly indicate such restrictions. They may be stated in the deed or contained in a previously recorded document (such as the subdivider's master deed) that is expressly cited in the deed. Many deed restrictions have time limits, often including renewal clauses.

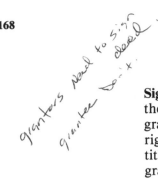

grantors need to sign deed
grantee do not

Signature of grantor. To be valid, a deed must be signed by *all grantors* named in the deed. As discussed previously, when a grantor's spouse has been named as a grantor, the spouse must also sign the deed in order to release marital or other rights. This requirement will vary according to state law and the manner in which title is held by the conveying parties. In some states there must be witnesses to the grantor's signature, but this requirement is not uniform from state to state.

Most states permit a grantor's signature to be signed by an attorney-in-fact acting under a power of attorney. An *attorney-in-fact* is any person who has been given power of attorney (specific written authority) to execute and sign one or more legal instruments for another person. In such cases, it is usually necessary for an authorizing document known as a *power of attorney* to be recorded in the county where the property is located. Since the power of attorney terminates upon the death of the person granting such authority, adequate evidence must be submitted that the grantor was alive at the time the attorney-in-fact signed the deed.

A grantor who is unable to write is permitted to sign by *mark* in most states. With this type of signature, two persons other than the notary public taking the acknowledgment (discussed below) usually must witness the grantor's execution of the deed and sign as witnesses.

In some states, it is still necessary for a seal or the word *seal* to be written or printed after an individual grantor's signature. The corporate seal should always be used by corporations.

Acknowledgment. An acknowledgment is a form of declaration made voluntarily by a person who is signing a formal, written document before a notary public or authorized public officer. An acknowledgment usually states that the person signing the deed or other document is known to the officer or has produced sufficient identification and that the person signing is doing so as his or her own *free and voluntary act*. The acknowledgment provides evidence that the signature is genuine.

Usually an acknowledgment is made before a *notary public*. It can also be taken by a judge, justice of the peace, court clerk, county clerk or one of certain officers in the military as prescribed by state law. The form of a *certificate of acknowledgment* varies from state to state. The certificate form authorized by the state where the property is located should be used even if the party signing is a resident of another ("foreign") state. In other words, the laws of the state where the land is located govern the procedure.

Although it is customary to acknowledge the execution of a deed to real estate, such acknowledgment is not essential to the *validity* of the deed unless state statutes require it. However, in some states, an unacknowledged instrument is not admissible as evidence in court without proof of the genuineness of the signature. The acknowledgment is accepted as such proof.

From a purely practical point of view, a deed that is not acknowledged is not a satisfactory instrument. In some states, an unacknowledged deed is not eligible for recording, an important protection against subsequent innocent purchasers from the same grantor. Recording is discussed in Chapter 13.

Delivery and acceptance. Before a transfer of title by conveyance can take effect, there must be an actual **delivery** of the deed by the grantor and either actual or implied **acceptance** by the grantee. Delivery may be made by the grantor to the grantee personally or to a third party, commonly known as an *escrowee* (discussed in Chapter 23), for ultimate delivery to the grantee upon the completion of certain requirements. *Title is said to pass when a deed is delivered.* The effective date of the transfer of title from the grantor and to the grantee is the date of delivery of the deed itself. When a deed is delivered in escrow, the date of delivery of the conveyance generally is ("relates back" to) the date that it was deposited with the escrow agent. (However, when the real estate is registered under the Torrens system, as discussed in Chapter 13, title does not pass until the deed has been examined and accepted for registration.)

Delivery is a very technical aspect of the validity of a deed and is usually strictly construed by the courts. Brokers should consult legal counsel with questions regarding delivery.

Execution of Corporate Deeds

A corporation is a legal entity. The laws affecting corporations' rights to convey real estate vary from state to state. Some basic rules are:

1. A corporation can convey real estate only by authority granted in its *bylaws* or upon a proper resolution passed by its *board of directors*. If all or a substantial portion of a corporation's real estate is being conveyed, it is usually required that a resolution authorizing the sale can be secured from the *stockholders*.
2. Deeds to real estate can be *signed only by an authorized officer.*
3. The corporate *seal* must be affixed to the conveyance.

Rules pertaining to religious corporations and not-for-profit corporations vary widely. Since the legal requirements must be followed explicitly, it is advisable to consult an attorney for all corporate conveyances.

Types of Deeds

There are several forms of deeds. The most common are:

1. general warranty deed. — grantee greatest protection.
2. special warranty deed.
3. deed of bargain and sale.
4. quitclaim deed.
5. trust deed.
6. trustee's deed.
7. reconveyance deed.
8. deed executed pursuant to a court order.

General warranty deed. For a purchaser of real estate, a **general warranty deed** (shown in figure 12.2) provides the *greatest protection* of any deed. It is referred to as a general warranty deed or simply warranty deed because the grantor is legally bound by certain covenants or warranties. In most states, the warranties are usually implied by the use of certain words specified in the state statutes. Each state law should be examined, but some of the specific words include: "convey and warrant," "warrant generally," and, in some states, "grant, bargain and sell." In some localities, the grantor's warranties are expressly written into the deed itself. The basic warranties are:

1. *Covenant of seisin:* The grantor warrants that he or she is the owner of the property and has the right to convey title to it. The grantee may recover damages up to the full purchase price if this covenant is broken.

2. *Covenant against encumbrances:* The grantor warrants that the property is free from any liens or encumbrances except those specifically stated in the deed. Encumbrances would generally include such items as mortgages, mechanics' liens and easements. If this covenant is breached, the grantee may sue for expenses to remove the encumbrance.

3. *Covenant of quiet enjoyment:* The grantor guarantees that the grantee's title will be good against third parties who might bring court actions to establish superior title to the property. If the grantee's title is found to be inferior, the grantor is liable for damages.

4. *Covenant of further assurance:* The grantor promises to obtain and deliver any instrument needed in order to make the title good. For example, if the grantor's spouse has failed to sign away dower rights, the grantor must deliver a quitclaim deed executed by the spouse to clear the title.

5. *Covenant of warranty forever:* The grantor guarantees that if at any time in the future the title fails, he or she will compensate the grantee for the loss sustained.

These covenants in a general warranty deed are not limited to matters that occurred during the time the grantor owned the property; they extend back to its origins.

Special warranty deed. A conveyance that carries only one covenant is a **special warranty deed,** also referred to as a **limited warranty deed.** The grantor warrants *only* that the property was not encumbered during the time he or she held title except as noted in the deed. Special warranty deeds generally contain the words "remise, release, alienate and convey" in the granting clause. Any additional warranties to be included must be specifically stated in the deed.

A special warranty deed may be used by a fiduciary such as an estate representative or trustee, and thus will usually state the full consideration for the property. A special warranty deed may also be used by a corporation, and sometimes by a grantor who has acquired title at a tax sale. A fiduciary or corporation has no authority to warrant against acts of its predecessors in title. Such unauthorized warranties by a corporation are considered to be beyond the scope and authority of the corporate powers and are referred to as *ultra vires.* Fiduciaries may hold title for a limited time without having a personal interest in the proceeds.

Bargain and sale deed. Deeds using the words "grant and release" or "grant, bargain and sell" in the granting clause are usually **bargain and sale deeds.** A bargain and sale deed contains no warranties against encumbrances; however, it does *imply* that the grantor holds title and possession of the property. Because the warranty is not specifically stated, the grantee has little legal recourse if defects later appear in the title. In some areas, a covenant against encumbrances initiated by the grantor may be added to a standard bargain and sale deed to create a *bargain and sale deed with covenant against the grantor's acts.* This deed is roughly equivalent to a special warranty deed. In other areas, warranties used in general warranty deeds may be inserted into a bargain and sale deed to give the grantee similar protection. A bargain and sale deed, sometimes with a covenant against the grantor's acts, is often used by trustees, estate representatives and officers of the court to convey real property placed under their control.

Figure 12.2
Warranty Deed

GEORGE E. COLE*
LEGAL FORMS

NO. 808
February, 1985

WARRANTY DEED
Statutory (ILLINOIS)
(Individual to Individual)

CAUTION: Consult a lawyer before using or acting under this form. Neither the publisher nor the seller of this form makes any warranty with respect thereto, including any warranty of merchantability or fitness for a particular purpose.

THE GRANTOR

martial status [handwritten]

Walter James Anderson, a (widower)

of the __Village__ of __Rockvale__ County of __Cook__
State of _____Illinois_____ for and in consideration of
__Ten and xx/100----------------------------__
_____ DOLLARS,
_____ in hand paid,

martial status. [handwritten]

CONVEY _s_ and WARRANT _s_ to
Brian Lee Johnson and Susan Roberta Johnson,
husband and wife, of 647 N. Maple, Madison, Ohio,
as joint tenants with right of survivorship
(NAME AND ADDRESS OF GRANTEE)

(The Above Space For Recorder's Use Only)

the following described Real Estate situated in the County of _____Cook_____ in the
State of Illinois, to wit:

Lot 47 and the South half of Lot 48 in Block 5 in the Sunset Subdivision, in the West 1/2 of the East 1/2 of Section 8, Township 23 North, Range 12 East of the Third Principal Meridian, in Cook County, Illinois.

Subject to: General real estate taxes for 1988 and subsequent years including special assessments (if any); building use, and occupancy restrictions, conditions and covenants of record; zoning laws and public and private easements of record.

hereby releasing and waiving all rights under and by virtue of the Homestead Exemption Laws of the State of Illinois.

Permanent Real Estate Index Number(s): __0-88420-76901__

Address(es) of Real Estate: __303 West Iowa Street, Rolling Hills, IL 60000__

DATED this __24th__ day of __March__ 19_88_

PLEASE
PRINT OR
TYPE NAME(S)
BELOW
SIGNATURE(S)

_____(SEAL) _____(SEAL)
_____ _____
_____(SEAL) _____(SEAL)
_____ _____

State of Illinois, County of _____Cook_____ ss. I, the undersigned, a Notary Public in and for said County, in the State aforesaid, DO HEREBY CERTIFY that

Walter James Anderson

IMPRESS
SEAL
HERE

personally known to me to be the same person __ whose name __is__ subscribed to the foregoing instrument, appeared before me this day in person, and acknowledged that __he__ signed, sealed and delivered the said instrument as __his__ free and voluntary act, for the uses and purposes therein set forth, including the release and waiver of the right of homestead.

Given under my hand and official seal, this __24th__ day of __March__ 19_88_

Commission expires __July 31__ 1988 __Rose V. Williams__
NOTARY PUBLIC

This instrument was prepared by __Pioneer Title Co. Oaks, IL__
(NAME AND ADDRESS)

MAIL TO:
Brian Lee Johnson
(Name)
303 West Iowa Street
(Address)
Rolling Hills, IL 60000
(City, State and Zip)

SEND SUBSEQUENT TAX BILLS TO:
Brian Lee Johnson
(Name)
303 West Iowa Street
(Address)
Rolling Hills, IL 60000
(City, State and Zip)

OR RECORDER'S OFFICE BOX NO. _____

AFFIX "RIDERS" OR REVENUE STAMPS HERE

George E. Cole legal forms reprinted with permission of Boise Cascade Office Products Corporation.

Figure 12.3
Types of Deeds

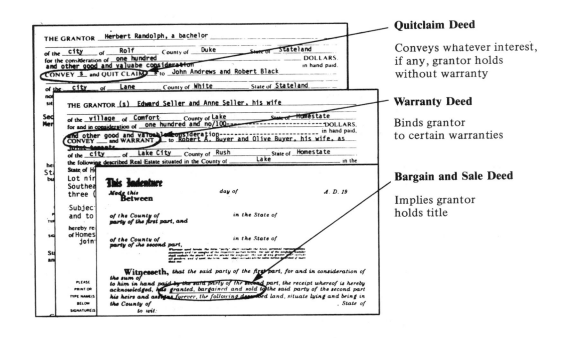

Quitclaim Deed

Conveys whatever interest,
if any, grantor holds
without warranty

Warranty Deed

Binds grantor
to certain warranties

Bargain and Sale Deed

Implies grantor
holds title

Quitclaim deed. A **quitclaim deed** provides the grantee with the least protection of any deed. It carries no covenant or warranties and, in most states, usually conveys only such interest, if any, that the grantor may have when the deed is delivered. By a quitclaim deed, the grantor only "remises, releases, and quitclaims" his or her interest in the property to the grantee. In most states, a quitclaim deed is the only type of deed that may be used to convey less than a fee simple title. For example, it might convey an easement or it might reconvey equitable title back to a seller. Examples of a quitclaim deed, warranty deed, and bargain and sale deed appear in figure 12.3.

If the grantor under a quitclaim deed has no interest in the property described, the grantee will acquire nothing by virtue of the quitclaim deed, nor will he or she acquire any right of warranty claim against the grantor. A quitclaim deed can convey title as effectively as a warranty deed if the grantor has good title when the deed is delivered, but it provides none of the guarantees that a warranty deed does.

A quitclaim deed is frequently used to cure a defect, called a "cloud on the title," in the recorded history of a real estate title. For example, if the name of the grantee is misspelled on a warranty deed placed in the public record, a quitclaim deed with the correct spelling may be executed to the grantee in order to perfect the title. A quitclaim deed is also used when a grantor allegedly has *inherited* property but is not certain of the validity of the title of the decedent from whom the property was inherited. The use of a warranty deed in such an instance could carry with it obligations of warranty, while a quitclaim deed would convey only the grantor's interest.

Trust deed. A **trust deed** is the means by which a **trustor** conveys real estate to a **trustee** for the benefit of a **beneficiary.** The real estate is held by the trustee in order to fulfill the purpose of the trust. In a few states, what is called a *deed in trust* is used to convey full power to sell, mortgage, subdivide and the like, to the trustee under a land trust, which is controlled by the beneficiary under the provisions of the trust agreement. In many states, a *deed of trust* enables the trustor to pledge real estate as security for a loan, and thus serves the same purpose as a mortgage. The deed of trust is discussed in detail in Chapter 15.

Trustee's deed. A deed of conveyance executed by a trustee is a **trustee's deed** and is used when a trustee named in a will, trust agreement or trust deed conveys the trust real estate to anyone other than the trustor. The trustee's deed sets forth the fact that the trustee executes the instrument in accordance with the powers and authority granted to him or her by the trust instrument.

Reconveyance deed. A **reconveyance deed** is used by a trustee under a deed of trust to return title to the trustor. For example, when a loan secured by a trust deed on real estate has been fully paid, the beneficiary notifies the trustee, who then reconveys the property to the trustor. As with any document of title, a reconveyance deed should be recorded to prevent future title problems.

Deeds executed pursuant to court order. This classification covers such deed forms as executors' (or administrators') deeds, masters' deeds, sheriffs' deeds and many others. These statutory deed forms are used to convey title to property that is transferred by court order or by will. The forms of such deeds must conform to the laws of the state where the property is located.

One characteristic of such instruments is that the *full consideration* is usually stated in the deed. This is done because the deed is executed pursuant to a court order, and since the court has authorized the sale of the property for a given amount of consideration, this amount should be *exactly* stated in the document.

Transfer Tax Stamps

Most states have enacted laws providing for a tax, usually referred to as the state **transfer tax,** on conveyances of real estate. In these states, the tax is usually payable when the deed is recorded, through the purchase of *stamps* from the county recorder of the county in which the deed is recorded. The stamps are then affixed to deeds and conveyances before the document can be recorded.

The *transfer tax is usually paid by the seller.* The *tax rate* varies from state to state; examples are rates of 50 cents for each $500, or $1.50 for each $1,000, or fraction thereof of taxable consideration. In *some* states, when real estate is transferred subject to the unpaid balance of an existing mortgage that was made by the seller before the time of transfer and that is being assumed by the buyer, the amount of the assumed mortgage may be deducted from the full consideration to determine the taxable consideration.

In many states, a *transfer declaration form* (or *transfer statement*) must be signed by both the buyer and the seller or their agents. This form usually requires such information as: the full sales price of the property; the legal description of the property; the address, date and type of deed; and the type of improvement. If the transfer is between relatives or is a compulsory transaction in accordance with a court order, this must also be specified in the transfer declaration form.

Certain deeds may be *exempted* from the tax, such as: gifts of real estate; deeds not made in connection with a sale (such as a change in the form of cotenancy); conveyances to or from or between governmental bodies; deeds by charitable, religious or educational institutions; deeds securing debts or releasing property as security for a debt; partitions; tax deeds; deeds pursuant to mergers of corporations; and deeds from subsidiary to parent corporations for cancellations of stock.

See your state supplement for *Modern Real Estate Practice* or check with local officials to determine the conditions and cost of the transfer tax in your area.

Involuntary Alienation	Title to property can be transferred by **involuntary alienation**; that is, without the owner's consent (see figure 12.4). Such transfers are usually carried out by operation of law and range from government condemnation of land for public use to the sale of property to satisfy delinquent tax or mortgage liens. When a person dies intestate and leaves no heirs, the title to his or her real estate passes to the state by the state's power of *escheat*.

Federal, state and local governments, school boards, some government agencies and certain public and quasi-public corporations and utilities (railroads and gas and electric companies) have the power of *eminent domain*. Under this power, private property may be taken for public use through a *suit for condemnation*. The exercise of eminent domain is subject to a court's determination of three necessary conditions: (1) that the use is for the benefit of the public; (2) that an equitable amount of compensation, as set by the court, will be paid to the owner; and (3) that the rights of the property owner will be protected by due process of law.

Land may also be transferred without an owner's consent in order to satisfy debts contracted by the owner. In such cases the debt is foreclosed, the property is sold and the proceeds of the sale are applied to pay off the debt. Debts that could be foreclosed include mortgage loans, real estate taxes, mechanics' liens or general judgments against the property owner. (See Chapters 10 and 15.)

In addition to the involuntary transfer of land by legal processes, land may be transferred by natural forces. As discussed in Chapter 7, owners of land bordering on rivers, lakes and other bodies of water may acquire additional land through the process of *accretion,* the slow accumulation of soil, rock or other matter deposited by the movement of water on an owner's property. The opposite of accretion is *erosion,* the gradual wearing away of land by the action of water and wind. In addition, property may be lost through *avulsion,* the sudden tearing away of land by such natural means as earthquakes or tidal waves.

Adverse possession is another means of involuntary transfer. An owner who does not use his or her land or does not inspect it for a number of years may lose title to another person who makes some claim to the land, takes possession and, most importantly, uses the land. Usually the possession of the claimant must be open, notorious, continuous (uninterrupted for the number of years set by state law—as long as 20 years in some states), hostile and adverse to the true owner's possession (ONCHA). Through the principle of *tacking,* successive periods of adverse possession can be combined by successive adverse possessors taking possession under *color of title*—that is, by a deed that appears on its face to be valid, but is not

**Figure 12.4
Involuntary
Alienation**

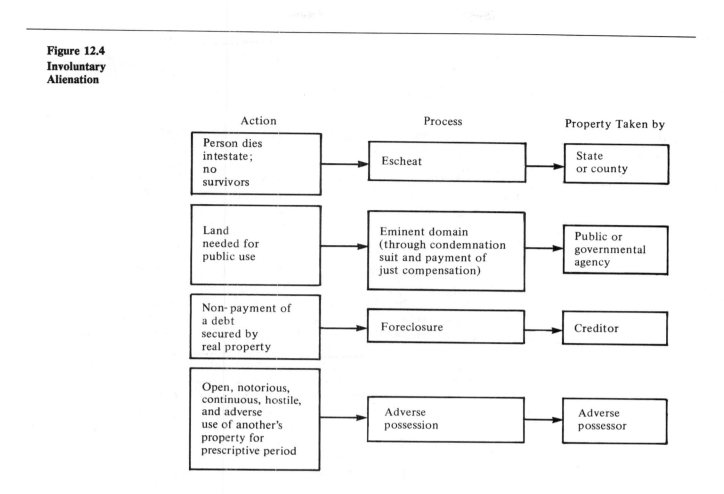

Action	Process	Property Taken by
Person dies intestate; no survivors	Escheat	State or county
Land needed for public use	Eminent domain (through condemnation suit and payment of just compensation)	Public or governmental agency
Non-payment of a debt secured by real property	Foreclosure	Creditor
Open, notorious, continuous, hostile, and adverse use of another's property for prescriptive period	Adverse possession	Adverse possessor

but is not (such as a forgery). A person who is not in possession for the entire required time can thus establish a claim of adverse possession.

Through adverse possession, the law recognizes that the use of land is an important function of its ownership. The subject of adverse possession is extremely technical because the right is statutory, and state requirements must be carefully followed in order to establish ownership. A claimant who does not receive title may acquire an easement by prescription (see Chapter 7). When a transaction involves the possibility of title by adverse possession, the parties should seek legal counsel.

Transfer of a Deceased Person's Property

Every state has a law known as the *statute of descent and distribution*. When a person dies **intestate** (without having left a will), the decedent's real estate and personal property pass to the decedent's heirs according to this statute. In effect, the state makes a will for anyone who did not do so. A person who dies **testate** has prepared a will indicating the way that person's property will be disposed of after death.

Legally, when a person dies, title to the real estate owned by that person immediately passes either to the heirs by descent or to the persons named in the will. Before the heirs can take possession of the property, however, the estate must be probated, and all claims against it must be satisfied.

Probate Proceedings

Probate is a legal process by which a court determines the assets of a deceased person and who will inherit those assets. Probate court proceedings must take place in the county where the real estate in question is located. In the case of a person who has died testate, the court also rules on the validity of the will. If the will is upheld, the property is distributed according to the will's provisions. If a person has died intestate, the court determines who inherits by reviewing a *proof of heirship*. This statement, usually prepared by an attorney, gives personal information regarding the decedent's spouse, children and other relatives.

To initiate probate proceedings, the custodian of the will, an heir or another interested party must petition the court. The court then holds a hearing to determine the validity of the will and/or the order of descent, should no valid will exist. If for any reason a will is declared invalid by the court, any property owned by the decedent will pass by the laws of descent. Once the heirs are established, the court will appoint an *administrator* (called an *administratrix* if a woman) to oversee the administration and distribution of the estate [if no *executor (executrix)* was named in the will]. In some states the person who oversees an estate is called the *personal representative,* however appointed. Probate proceedings vary from state to state, and local procedures must be followed.

The court gives the administrator or executor the authority to appraise the assets of the estate and satisfy all debts that were owed by the decedent. The estate representative is also responsible for paying federal estate taxes and, in most states, state inheritance taxes. Once all these liens against the property have been satisfied, the executor distributes the remaining assets of the estate according to the provisions of the will or the state law of descent.

In Practice...

A broker entering into a listing agreement with the executor or administrator of an estate in probate should be aware that the amount of commission will be fixed by the court and that such commission is payable only from the proceeds of the sale. The broker will not be able to collect a commission unless the court approves the sale.

Transfer of Title by Will

A **will** is an instrument made by an owner to convey title to property after the owner's death. A will takes effect only after death; until that time, any property covered by the will can be conveyed by the owner and thus be removed from the owner's estate.

The gift of real property by will is known as a *devise,* and a person who receives property by will is known as a *devisee*. Technically, an *heir* is one who takes property by the law of descent, but the term is commonly used to include devisees, as well. A *legacy* or *bequest* is a gift of (usually) personal property; the person receiving the property is known as a *legatee.*

The privilege of disposing of property by will is statutory and a will must conform to all the statutory requirements of the state in which the real estate is located. In addition, a will cannot supersede the state laws of dower and curtesy, which were enacted to protect the inheritance rights of the surviving spouse. In a case where a will does not provide the minimum statutory inheritance, the surviving spouse has the option of choosing the minimum statutory share rather than the lesser share provided in the will. This practice, called *renouncing the will,* is a right reserved only to a surviving spouse.

A will differs from a deed in that a deed conveys a present interest in real estate during the lifetime of the grantor, while a will conveys no interest in the property until after the death of the testator. To be valid, a deed *must* be delivered during the lifetime of the grantor. The parties named in a will have no rights or interests so long as the party who has made the will is still alive; they acquire interest or title only after the owner's death. State laws usually require that upon the death of a testator, the will must be filed with the court and *probated* in order for title to pass to the devisees.

Legal requirements for making a will. Because a will must be valid and admitted to probate in order to effectively convey title to real estate, it must be executed and prepared in accordance with the laws of the state where the real estate is located. A testator must have legal capacity to make a will (see figure 12.5). Usually, a person must be of *legal age* and of *sound mind*. There are no rigid tests to determine the capacity to make a will. Usually, the courts hold that to make a valid will, the testator must have sufficient mental capacity to understand the nature and extent of the property owned, the identity of natural heirs and that execution of the will means that at the testator's death the property will go to those named in the will. The drawing of a will must be a voluntary act, free of any undue influence by other people.

Figure 12.5
Requirements for a
Valid Will

```
WILL

1. Legal Age
2. Sound Mind
3. Proper Wording ✓
4. No Undue Influence
5. Witnesses
```

In most states, a written will must be signed by its testator before two or more witnesses, who must also sign the document. The witnesses should not be people who are named as devisees in the will.

The testator may modify the will. A modification or amendment of, or addition to, a previously executed will is called a *codicil*.

A *holographic will* is one that is in the testator's handwriting but is not witnessed or acknowledged. A *nuncupative will* is one that is given orally by a testator.

Certain states do not permit the use of holographic and/or nuncupative wills to convey title to property.

Transfer of Title by Descent

By law, the title to real estate and personal property of a person who dies intestate passes to the decedent's heirs. Under the **descent** statutes, the primary **heirs** of the deceased are the spouse and close blood relatives, such as children, parents, brothers, sisters, aunts, uncles, and, in some cases, first and second cousins, and so on. The closeness of the relationship to the decedent determines the specific rights of the heirs. As previously discussed, the relative's right to inherit must be established by proof of heirship during the probate process.

The right to inherit under laws of descent varies from state to state, and intestate property is distributed according to the laws of the state in which the property is located. When a husband dies leaving a wife and one child, the wife and child usually take the entire estate between them, some states dividing it equally and some allowing one-third to the surviving spouse. If, however, a wife and two or more children survive, it is customary for the wife to take one-third and the children to divide the remaining two-thirds equally among them. If a wife but no children or descendants of children exist, some state laws give the wife one-half of the estate and divide the other half equally among collateral heirs, such as parents and brothers and sisters of the decedent; in other states the wife receives all the property.

When children have been legally adopted, most states consider them to be heirs of the adopting parents but not heirs of ancestors of the adopting parents.

In most states, illegitimate children inherit from the mother but do not inherit from the father unless he has admitted parentage in writing or parentage has been established legally. If the father legally adopts such a child, that child will inherit as an adoptee.

Summary

Title to real estate is the right to and evidence of ownership of the land. It may be transferred in four ways: (1) voluntary alienation, (2) involuntary alienation, (3) will and (4) descent.

The voluntary transfer of an owner's title is made by a *deed,* executed (signed) by the owner as *grantor* to the recipient as *grantee.* The form and execution of a deed must comply with the statutory requirements of the state in which the land is located.

Among the most common of these requirements are: a grantor with legal capacity to contract, a readily identifiable grantee, a granting clause, a legal description of the property, a recital of consideration, exceptions, reservations on the title ("subject to" clause) and the signature of the grantor, properly witnessed if necessary. In addition, the deed should be acknowledged before a notary public or other officer in order to provide evidence that the signature is genuine and to allow recording. If required by state law, deeds are subject to state transfer taxes when they are recorded. Title to the property passes when the grantor delivers a deed to the grantee and it is accepted.

The obligation of a grantor is determined by the form of the deed; that is, whether it is a general warranty deed, special warranty deed, bargain and sale deed, or quitclaim deed. The words of conveyance in the granting clause are important in determining the form of deed.

A *general warranty deed* provides the greatest protection of any deed by binding the grantor to certain covenants or warranties. A *special warranty deed* warrants only that the real estate is not encumbered except as stated in the deed. A *bargain and sale deed* carries with it no warranties, but implies that the grantor holds title to the property. A *quitclaim deed* carries with it no warranties whatsoever and conveys only the interest, *if any,* the grantor possesses in the property.

An owner's title may be transferred without his or her permission by a court action, such as a *foreclosure* or judgment sale, a tax sale, *condemnation* under the right of eminent domain, *adverse possession* or *escheat*. Land may also be transferred by the natural forces of water and wind, which either increase property by *accretion* or decrease it through *erosion* or *avulsion*.

The real estate of an owner who makes a valid *will* (who dies testate) passes to the devisees through the probating of the will. The title of an owner who dies without a will (intestate) passes according to the provisions of the *law of descent* of the state in which the real estate is located.

Questions

1. Title to real estate may be transferred during a person's lifetime by which of the following means?
   a. voluntary alienation
   b. descent
   c. involuntary alienation
   d. a and c

2. Who is required to sign a deed in order to make it valid?
   I. grantor
   II. grantee
     a. I only   c. both I and II
     b. II only   d. neither I nor II

3. Harry Hughes, age 15, recently inherited many parcels of real estate from his late father and has decided to sell one of them in order to pay inheritance taxes. If Hughes entered into a deed conveying his interest in the property to a purchaser, such a conveyance would be:
   a. valid.   c. invalid.
   b. void.   d. voidable.

4. A deed that an owner of real estate may use to voluntarily transfer a right, title or interest in real estate may be a:
   a. sheriff's deed.
   b. warranty deed.
   c. foreclosure deed.
   d. all of the above

5. Title to real estate can be transferred at death by which of the following documents?
   a. warranty deed
   b. special warranty deed
   c. trustee's deed
   d. will

6. Determination of the type of deed used in conveying title can be made by examining the:
   a. grantor's name.
   b. grantee's name.
   c. granting clause.
   d. acknowledgment.

7. Matilda Fairbanks bought acreage in a distant county, never went to see the acreage and did not use the ground. Harold Sampson moved his mobile home onto the land, had a water well drilled and lived there for many years. Sampson may become the owner of the land if he has complied with the state law regarding:
   I. requirements for a valid conveyance.
   II. adverse possession.
     a. I only   c. both I and II
     b. II only   d. neither I nor II

8. All deeds should be:
   a. recorded.
   b. signed by the grantee.
   c. surveyed.
   d. all of the above

9. Alvin Rosewell executes a deed to Sylvia Plat as grantee, has it acknowledged and receives payment from the buyer. Rosewell holds the deed, however, and arranges to meet Plat the next morning at the courthouse to deliver the deed to her. In this situation at this time:
   a. Plat owns the property since she has paid for it.
   b. title to the property will not officially pass until Plat has been given the deed the next morning.
   c. title to the property will not pass until Plat has received the deed and recorded it the next morning.
   d. Plat will own the property when she has signed the deed the next morning.

10. Claude Johnson, a bachelor, died owning real estate that he devised by his will to his niece, Annette. At what point does title pass to his niece?
   a. immediately upon Johnson's death
   b. after his will has been probated
   c. after Annette has paid all inheritance taxes
   d. when Annette executes a new deed to the property

11. A person who pays for and receives a quitclaim deed:
    I. will receive whatever title the grantor possessed in the property.
    II. can force the grantor to make the title good by a suit in court.
    - a. I only
    - c. both I and II
    - b. II only
    - d. neither I nor II

12. Which of the following types of deeds most often recites the full, actual consideration paid for the property?
    - a. warranty deed
    - b. trustee's deed
    - c. deed in trust
    - d. deed executed pursuant to court order

13. A grantor in a special warranty deed is bound by which of the following warranties?
    - a. warranty of quiet enjoyment
    - b. warranty against encumbrances
    - c. warranty against encumbrances by the grantor
    - d. special warranty

14. The basic requirements for a valid conveyance are governed by:
    - a. state law.
    - b. local custom.
    - c. national law.
    - d. law of descent.

15. An owner of real estate who was adjudged legally incompetent made a will during his stay at a nursing home. He later died and was survived by a wife and three children. His real estate will pass:
    - a. to his wife.
    - b. to the heirs mentioned in his will.
    - c. according to the state law of descent.
    - d. to the state.

16. A general warranty deed usually obligates the grantor to the covenants of:
    - a. seisin.
    - b. quiet enjoyment.
    - c. escheat.
    - d. a and b

17. Which of the following types of deeds implies but does not specifically warrant that the grantor holds good title to the property?
    - a. special warranty deed
    - b. bargain and sale deed
    - c. quitclaim deed
    - d. trustee's deed

18. Local transfer taxes on real estate conveyances are usually paid:
    - a. by the grantee.
    - b. to the state real estate commission.
    - c. by the grantor.
    - d. by the real estate agent.

19. Entrepreneur Harley Wilcox is purchasing a large apartment building in a choice urban location. For financial and professional reasons, Wilcox wants to hold the property as beneficiary under a land trust. Which of the following instruments would be used to create this trust?
    - a. deed of trust
    - c. trustee's deed
    - b. deed in trust
    - d. a or c

20. Which of the following is *not* a way by which title to real estate is transferred by involuntary alienation?
    - a. eminent domain
    - c. erosion
    - b. escheat
    - d. seisin

21. A person who has died leaving a valid will is called a(n):
    - a. devisee.
    - c. legatee.
    - b. testator.
    - d. intestate.

22. A statute or act that creates the need for a deed to be in writing is:
    I. the law of descent and distribution
    II. in effect in all states.
    - a. I only
    - c. both I and II
    - b. II only
    - d. neither I nor II

23. Which of the following best describes the covenant of quiet enjoyment?

    a. The grantor promises to obtain and deliver any instrument needed to make the title good.
    b. The grantor guarantees that if the title fails in the future, he or she will compensate the grantee.
    c. The grantor warrants that he or she is the owner and has the right to convey title to it.
    d. The grantor assures that the title will be good against the title claims of third parties.

24. Which of the following instruments would *not* be given to convey title to a purchaser?

    a. executor's deed
    b. trust deed
    c. quitclaim deed
    d. a and b

25. An instrument authorizing one person to act for another is called a(n):

    a. power of attorney.
    b. release deed.
    c. quitclaim deed.
    d. acknowledgment.

13

Title Records

Key Terms

Abstract of title
Actual notice
ALTA policy
Attorney's opinion of title
Bulk transfer
Certificate of title
Chain of title
Constructive notice
Evidence of title
Financing statement

Marketable title
Priority
Recording
Security agreement
Subrogation
Suit to quiet title
Title insurance
Torrens system
Uniform Commercial Code

Overview

For the protection of real estate owners, taxing bodies, creditors and the general public, public records are maintained in every city, county, parish or borough in the United States. Such records help to establish official ownership, give notice of encumbrances, and establish priority of liens. The placing of documents in the public record is known as **recording.** This chapter will discuss the necessity for recording and the various types of title evidence that may be determined by an examination of the public records.

Public Records and Recording

In all states, public records are maintained by designated officials as required by state law. These include records maintained by the recorder of deeds, county clerk, county treasurer, tax collector, city clerk and clerks of various courts of record. Records involve land titles, property taxes, special assessments, ordinances, and zoning and building codes.

The principle expressed by the original statute of frauds has long been enacted by all states. Written instruments are thus required for all transfers of title or interest, whether by deed, mortgage or lease.

In addition to the statute of frauds, many state legislatures have also passed laws that require owners or parties interested in real estate to record, or file, in the public records all documents affecting their interests in real estate in order to give *public notice* to the world of those interests. These statutory enactments are commonly referred to as *recording acts*.

Necessity for Recording

An individual planning to purchase a fee simple estate to a parcel of real estate wants to be sure that the seller will be able to convey good title to the property. The same question of *kind and condition* of title probably has been inquired into many times in the past—as often, in fact, as the property has changed hands. As long as taxes are paid and liens do not become delinquent, it is expected that a fee simple title will remain a marketable title.

All states provide that a *deed or mortgage may not be effective as far as later purchasers* are concerned unless such documents have been *recorded*. The public records thus should reveal the condition of the title, and a purchaser should be able to rely on a search of such public records.

Recording Acts

Under the recording acts, in order to serve as public notice, all instruments in writing affecting any estate, right, title or interest in land *must be recorded in the county where the land is located*. Everyone interested in the title to a parcel of property can thus receive notice of the various interests of all other parties. From a practical point of view, the recording acts may give legal **priority** to those interests that are recorded first.

To be *eligible for recording,* an instrument must be drawn and executed in conformity with the provisions of the recording statutes of the state in which the real estate is located. The prerequisites for recording are not uniform. For example, many states require that the names be typed below the signatures on a document and that the instrument be acknowledged before a notary public or other officer. In a few states, the instrument must also be witnessed. A number of states require that the name of the attorney who prepared the document must also appear on it.

Notice

The courts charge a prospective real estate buyer or mortgagee (lender) with the responsibility of inspecting the property and searching the public records to ascertain the interests, if any, of other parties. **Constructive notice** is a presumption of law that charges a buyer with knowledge of what could be learned by such an inspection and search. The information is available; therefore, the buyer or lender is responsible for learning it. Failure to do so is no defense for not knowing of a right or interest, since the recording of that interest in the public records or possession of the real estate gives constructive, or legal, notice to the world of an individual's rights in the property.

Constructive notice, or what a buyer is charged with knowing, is distinguished from **actual notice,** or what the person actually knows (see figure 13.1). An individual who has searched the public records and inspected the property has actual notice—*direct knowledge*—of the information learned. If it can be proved that an individual has actual knowledge of information concerning a parcel of real estate, he or she cannot rely on a lack of constructive notice, as when a deed is unrecorded or an owner is not in possession. For example, Bill Wilson mortgaged his land to Jane Fry, and she failed to record the mortgage. Wilson later mortgaged the same land to Edgar Morse, who *knew* of the existence of the earlier mortgage. In this case, Morse is charged with actual knowledge of the existing mortgage, so in a dispute with Fry over priority of claims, Fry's mortgage will have a prior claim on the property.

**Figure 13.1
Notice**

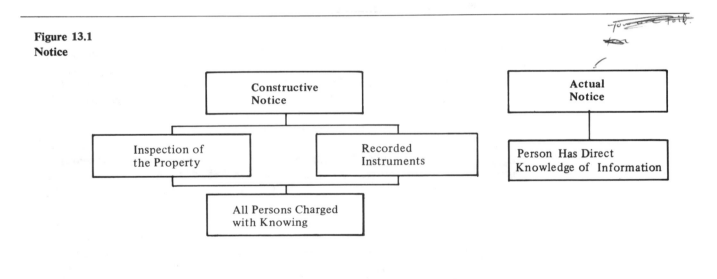

Real estate taxes and special assessments are direct liens on specific parcels of real estate and need not be recorded in the recorder's office. Other liens, such as inheritance taxes and franchise taxes, are placed by statutory authority against all real estate owned either by a decedent at the time of death or by a corporation at the time the franchise tax became a lien; these liens are not recorded either.

Priorities. Many complicated situations can arise that affect the priority of rights in a parcel of real estate. For example, a purchaser may receive a deed and take possession of the property but not record the deed. By taking possession, a purchaser gives constructive notice of an interest in the land. Such a purchaser's rights would be considered superior to the rights of a subsequent purchaser who acquired a deed from the original owner at a later date and recorded the deed but did not inspect the property to determine who was in possession. How the courts rule in any situation depends, of course, on the specific facts of the case. These are strictly legal questions that should be referred by the parties to their lawyers.

Foreign Language Documents

Deeds or mortgages written in a foreign language, although valid between the parties to a transaction, usually do not impart constructive notice when recorded. Recorded documents must be in the English language. An official translation by a consulate of the country in which the language is used, when attached to a foreign language document, may meet state recording requirements. Both the original document and the translation are then recorded and become part of the public record.

Chain of Title

State statutes generally require that recorded instruments must be within the **chain of title,** so that a search of the grantor-grantee indexes will reveal the document and the interest. The grantor index references titles by the grantors' names; the grantee index uses grantees' names.

The chain of title shows the record of ownership of the property over a period of time, depending on the length of the title search. An **abstract of title** is a condensed history of all the instruments affecting a particular parcel of land. In the United States, chains of title in colonial states frequently date back to a grant from the king of England. In those states admitted to the Union after the formation of the United States, the deeds of conveyance in the chain of title generally stem from the *patent* issued by the U.S. government. In a few states, such as Louisiana and Texas, the chains of title date back to a point prior to acquisition of the land by the federal government.

Through the chain of title, the ownership of the property can be traced backward from its present owner to its source. If there is a period for which ownership is unaccounted, there is a *gap* in the chain. In such cases, it is usually necessary to establish ownership by a court action called a **suit to quiet title.** The court's judgment, following a proceeding in which all possible claimants are allowed to present evidence, can then be filed. A suit to quiet title may be required when, for instance, a grantor acquired title under one name and conveyed title under a different name. Title acquired by adverse possession can also be established of record by a quiet title action.

Evidence of Title

Under the terms of the usual real estate sales contract, the seller is required to deliver **marketable title** to the buyer at the closing. In order for title to be marketable it must: (1) be free from any significant liens and encumbrances; (2) disclose no serious defects and not be dependent on doubtful questions of law or fact to prove its validity; (3) not expose a purchaser to the hazard of litigation or threaten the quiet enjoyment of the property; and (4) convince a reasonably well-informed and prudent person, acting upon business principles and willful knowledge of the facts and their legal significance, that he or she could, in turn, sell or mortgage the property at a fair market value.

Although an unmarketable title (one that does not meet these requirements) does not mean that the property cannot be transferred under any circumstances, it does mean that there are *certain defects in the title that may limit or restrict its ownership.* A buyer cannot be forced to accept a conveyance that is materially different from the one bargained for in the sales contract; the buyer cannot be forced to buy a lawsuit. Note that questions of marketable title must be raised by a buyer (or the buyer's broker or attorney) prior to acceptance of the deed. Once a buyer has accepted a deed with unmarketable title, the only available legal recourse is to sue the seller under the covenants of warranty (if any) contained in the deed.

Proper **evidence of title** is proof that title is, in fact, marketable. A buyer can be satisfied that such evidence exists by acquiring a(n): (1) abstract of title and lawyer's opinion, (2) certificate of title, (3) Torrens certificate or (4) title insurance policy.

Sometimes the question is raised as to whether a recorded warranty deed or other form of conveyance is evidence of title. A deed by itself is not considered sufficient evidence of title; while it conveys the interest of the grantor, even a warranty deed contains no proof of the kind or condition of the grantor's title. The only effective proof is based upon an adequate search of the public records to *ascertain the ownership interests and condition of the title.*

Abstract of Title and Lawyer's Opinion

An abstract of title is a brief history (in abstract, or brief, form) of the instruments appearing in the county record that affect title to the parcel in question. The legal description of the property is in the abstract's caption. Abstracts usually commence with the government's ownership of the land. They ordinarily consist of several sections, or continuations, and each section covers a specific period of time. It is therefore necessary for each succeeding section of the abstract to begin with the public record from a date immediately following the date of the previous section. If this were not done, there would be a gap in the abstract.

When an abstract is first prepared or is continued, the abstractor lists and summarizes each instrument in chronological order along with information relative to taxes, judgments, special assessments and the like. The abstractor concludes with a certificate indicating which records were examined and when, and then signs the abstract. Abstractors must exercise due care, since they can be liable for negligence for any failure to include or accurately record all pertinent data. Note, however, that an *abstractor does not pass judgment on or guarantee the condition of the title.*

In a sale of land, the seller's attorney usually orders the abstract continued to cover the current date. When the abstractor has completed the abstract, it is submitted to the buyer's attorney, who must *examine the entire abstract.* This means that the lawyer must examine each section from the origin of that title. Following a detailed examination, the attorney must evaluate all the facts and material in order to prepare a written report for the purchaser on the condition of the ownership; this report is called an **attorney's opinion of title.**

As transfers of title accumulate through the years, the abstract of title to a particular parcel becomes more and more voluminous, and the time needed by an attorney to examine the abstract increases correspondingly.

Certificate of Title

In some localities, a *certificate of title* is used, and no abstract is prepared. A title examiner checks the public records and prepares a certificate of title stating the property's owner of record and listing any present encumbrances—usually without an attorney's opinion.

In many ways, use of an abstract examination and opinion or certificate of title is imperfect and open to objection. For example, it is difficult to detect forged deeds or false statements, including incorrect marital information and transfers involving incompetent parties or minors. Or an honest mistake could be made against which the owner of real estate has no recourse. To provide purchasers with protection against this type of error and to provide defense of the title, title insurance became available.

Title Insurance

A title insurance policy is a contract by which a title insurance company agrees, subject to the terms of its policy, to indemnify (that is, to compensate or reimburse) the insured (the owner, mortgagee or other interest holder) against any losses sustained as a result of defects in that title other than those exceptions listed in the policy. A title insurance policy may also be used in addition to an abstract or certificate of title.

A *standard coverage* policy usually insures against defects that may be found in the public records plus such items as forged documents, documents of incompetent grantors, incorrect marital statements and improperly delivered deeds. The *extended coverage* provided by an **American Land Title Association (ALTA) policy,** includes all the protection of a standard policy plus additional protection to cover risks that may be discovered only through inspection of the property, including rights of persons in actual possession of the land, even if unrecorded, or that would be revealed by examination of an accurate survey. The company does not agree to insure against any defects in or liens against the title that are found by the title examination and listed in the policy.

Table 13.1
Owner's Title
Insurance Policy

Standard Coverage	Extended Coverage	Not Covered by Either Policy
1. Defects found in public records 2. Forged documents 3. Incompetent grantors 4. Incorrect marital statements 5. Improperly delivered deeds	Standard coverage plus defects discoverable through: 1. Property inspection, including unrecorded rights of persons in possession 2. Examination of survey 3. Unrecorded liens not known of by policyholder	1. Defects and liens listed in policy 2. Defects known to buyer 3. Changes in land use brought about by zoning ordinances

Upon completion of the examination, the title company usually issues what may be called a *preliminary report* of title, or a *commitment* to issue a title policy or a *binder.* The policy that will be issued is described and the following are given: (1) the name of the insured party, (2) the legal description of the real estate, (3) the estate or interest covered, (4) a schedule of all exceptions, consisting of encumbrances and defects found in the public records and (5) conditions and stipulations under which the policy is issued. An *owner's policy will usually exclude coverage* against the following exceptions: unrecorded documents, unrecorded defects of which the policyholder has knowledge, rights of parties in possession and questions of survey. Under the contract, the title insurance company promises to defend the title as insured as well as to pay any claims against the property if the title proves to be defective.

The consideration for the policy (the *premium*) is paid once for the life of the policy. The maximum loss for which the company may be liable cannot exceed the face amount of the policy (unless the amount of coverage has been extended by use of what is called an *inflation rider*). When a title company makes a payment to settle a claim covered by a policy, the company acquires by the right of **subrogation** all the remedies and rights of the insured party against anyone responsible for the settled claim.

Title companies issue various forms of title insurance policies, the most common of which are the *owner's* title insurance policy, the *mortgagee* title insurance policy, the *leasehold* title insurance policy and the *certificate of sale* title insurance policy. As the names indicate, each of these policies is issued to insure specific interests. For example, a mortgagee title insurance policy insures a mortgage company or lender that it has a valid first lien against the property. A leasehold title insurance policy insures a lessee that he or she has a valid lease. A certificate of sale policy is issued to a purchaser in a court sale.

Title search. The examination undertaken by an abstractor or title insurance company to determine what, if any, defects there are in a property's chain of title is called a *title search*. The title searcher could begin the examination with the original source of title, which often dates from a government patent grant or award of title, or the search might begin with title records dating back no more than 40 years, or it might begin with the date of issuance of a prior title insurance policy. The searcher then checks the title in the recorder's office and searches the records in other governmental offices such as the tax offices and assessment offices (for sewer or special assessment liens that might be in effect).

In Practice...

Before a lender will forward money on a loan secured by real estate, it will normally order a title search at the expense of a borrower to assure itself that there are no liens superior in priority to its mortgage on the property.

In addition, in some states a preliminary title report is ordered upon acceptance of an offer to purchase, and copies are given to the buyers, agents and sellers. In fact, the entire contract may depend upon the buyers' written approval of this document within a given number of days after receiving it. Sellers usually are also given a copy, to ensure that the correct property has been researched.

If the sale or loan is not completed, a minimal fee may be charged.

The Torrens System

The **Torrens system** of land title registration was developed in 1857 by an Australian, Sir Robert Torrens, who took the idea from the system of registering title to shipping vessels. Approximately 10 states have adopted the Torrens system; it is also used in Canada. In the states that have adopted the Torrens system, the established recording system is also still in use. Registration of land titles is not compulsory. The owner of real estate may continue under the standard recording system or may register title under the Torrens system.

Although the provisions of the Torrens system are not uniform, the procedures to be followed in registering land titles in the various states are substantially the same. A written application to register a title to real estate is made with the county court of the county in which the real estate is located. The application lists all facts regarding the title and liens against the real estate. A court hearing is held, and all persons known to have an interest in the real estate are given notice. Any interested person may appear to present a claim. If the applicant proves ownership, the court enters an order for the registration of the real estate, and the *registrar of titles,* also known as the *title examiner,* is directed to register the title.

Transferring title under the Torrens system. Once real estate is registered under the Torrens system, a certificate is prepared by the registrar, who keeps the original and issues a duplicate to the owners of the property. At the same time, signature cards are signed by the owners in order to protect them from forgery.

When title to registered property is conveyed, mortgaged or encumbered in any way, the owner delivers the deed, mortgage or other instrument to the grantee, mortgagee or encumbrancer, together with the owner's duplicate certificate of title. When these documents are presented to the registrar for examination and approval, the registrar checks the signatures against the signature cards. When everything is in order, the registrar registers the transfer or document. A deed to Torrens registered land does not pass ownership. It is the *registration* that transfers title to the grantee. If such property is mortgaged, the registrar of titles issues a mortgagee's duplicate certificate of title to the lender. Torrens registrars usually retain all original documents delivered to them for registration.

At any time, the Torrens original certificate of title in the registrar's office reveals the owner of the land and all mortgages, judgments and similar liens. This record exists because a mortgage judgment or other *lien is not valid until it has been entered on the original title certificate* by the registrar.

Under most state land registration acts, title to Torrens registered property *can never be acquired through a claim of adverse possession.* This gives an owner of registered land protection against such claims.

Under the Torrens system, it may be necessary to verify the payment of taxes and special assessments, since the county treasurer and county collector are not usually required to register their tax liens on the Torrens records. Usually judgments or decrees of the federal courts are not required to be registered, so a separate federal court search is required. Searches for unpaid taxes, special assessments and federal liens can be obtained from the registrar of titles.

State laws generally provide that a certificate holder who has suffered a loss as a result of a registrar's mistake may file a claim against an indemnity fund established to compensate people financially for bona fide losses. If a claim or suit regarding title arises, the holder of a Torrens certificate must stand the expense of defending the suit and prove loss in order to gain a right to any compensation from the registrar.

Some state laws permit an owner to remove the title to his or her land from Torrens registration. In other states, land once so registered must remain under the Torrens system.

| Uniform Commercial Code | The **Uniform Commercial Code** (UCC) is a codification of commercial law that has been adopted, wholly or in part, in all states. While this code generally does not apply directly to real estate, it has replaced state laws relating to chattel mort- |

gages, conditional sales agreements, and liens on chattels, crops or items that are to become fixtures. In many areas, UCC filings have replaced chattel mortgages as financing instruments for personal property.

To create a security interest in a chattel, including chattels that will become fixtures, Article 9 of the UCC requires the use of a **security agreement,** which must contain a complete description of the items against which the lien applies. A short notice of this agreement, called a **financing statement,** must be filed of record. The type of property dictates where the filing must be made. A security interest in timber to be cut, minerals, or goods that are or are to become fixtures is "perfected" by filing in the office where mortgages on real estate are recorded. The recording of the financing statement constitutes notice to subsequent purchasers and mortgagees of the security interest. Many mortgagees require the signing and recording of a financing statement when the mortgaged premises include chattels or readily removable fixtures (washers, dryers and the like) as part of the security for the mortgage debt. If the financing statement has been properly recorded, upon the borrower's default the creditor could repossess the chattels and remove them from the property.

Article 6 of the UCC covers **bulk transfers,** which are defined as the sale *not* made in the ordinary course of the transferor's business of the major part of the materials, supplies, merchandise or other inventory of an enterprise. The purpose of this article is to outlaw the fraud perpetrated when a businessperson who is in debt sells all stock in trade (personal property) and disappears without having paid his or her creditors. Under Article 6, a bulk sale does not give the purchaser of such goods a clear title unless the purchaser complies with the article's requirements, which include giving notice of the sale to the seller's creditors. Some sales of business property involve the sale of the business and all of the owner's stock in trade, which may constitute a bulk sale.

Summary

The purpose of the recording acts is to give legal, public and *constructive notice* to the world of parties' interests in real estate. The recording provisions have been adopted to create system and order in the transfer of real estate. Without them, it would be virtually impossible to transfer real estate from one party to another. The interests and rights of the various parties in a particular parcel of land must be recorded so that such rights will be legally effective against third parties who do not have knowledge or notice of the rights.

Possession of real estate is generally interpreted as conveying notice of the rights of the person in possession. *Actual notice* is knowledge acquired directly.

Title evidence shows whether or not a seller is conveying *marketable title.* Marketable title is generally one that is so free from significant defects that the purchaser can be assured against having to defend the title.

There are four forms of providing title evidence commonly in use throughout the United States: (1) abstract of title and lawyer's opinion, (2) certificate of title, (3) Torrens certificate and (4) title insurance policy.

A deed of conveyance is evidence that a grantor has conveyed his or her interest in land, but it is not evidence of the kind or condition of the title. The purpose of a deed is to transfer a grantor's interest in real estate to a grantee. It does not *prove* that the grantor has any interest at all, even if the conveyance is by means of a deed that carries with it the implied covenants of warranty.

A Torrens certificate, title insurance policy, certificate of title and abstract of title reveal the history of a title. Each must be *later dated*, or continued or reissued, to cover a more recent date.

Under the Uniform Commercial Code, security interests in chattels must be recorded using a *security agreement* and *financing statement*. The recording of a financing statement gives notice to purchasers and mortgagees of the security interests in chattels and fixtures on the specific parcel of real estate.

Questions

1. John Anderson bought Jim Cleaver's home, and Cleaver delivered his deed to Anderson. Because it was a general warranty deed, Anderson can assume which of the following?

   I. He has evidence of title.
   II. There are no outstanding mortgages or liens on the property, unless specified.

      a. I only   c. both I and II
      b. II only   d. neither I nor II

2. A title insurance policy with standard coverage generally covers all but which of the following?

   a. forged documents
   b. incorrect marital statements
   c. rights of parties in possession
   d. incompetent grantors

3. Actual notice refers to:

   a. the facts a person may ascertain by examining the public records.
   b. what a person has actual knowledge of.
   c. what could be found by a property inspection.
   d. all of the above

4. Phil Simpson bought Larry Fine's house, received a deed and moved into the residence, but neglected to record the document. One week later, Fine died, and his heirs in another city, unaware that the property had been sold, conveyed title to Melvin Howard, who recorded the deed. Who owns the property?

   a. Phil Simpson
   b. Melvin Howard
   c. Larry Fine's heirs
   d. both Simpson and Howard

5. Marketable title refers to:

   a. a property that can command a fair market value.
   b. a property that is free from significant title defects.
   c. the certificate issued under the Torrens system.
   d. a and b

6. The Torrens system of property registration:

   a. is used in all states.
   b. is mandatory where it is in effect.
   c. is a voluntary system.
   d. registers only titles—liens and encumbrances are not noted on the certificate of title.

7. A purchaser went to the county building to check the recorder's records. She found that the seller was the grantee in the last recorded deed and that no mortgage was on record against the property. Thus, the purchaser may assume which of the following?

   a. All taxes are paid and no judgments are outstanding.
   b. The seller has good title.
   c. The seller did not mortgage the property.
   d. all of the above

8. When a title insurance policy is being issued, the public records are searched, and the title company's record of title is continued to date. When the title examination is completed, the title company notifies the parties in writing of the condition of the title. This notification is referred to as:

   a. a chain of title.
   b. a preliminary report of title, binder or commitment for title insurance.
   c. a Torrens certificate.
   d. an abstract.

9. In locations where the abstract system is used, an abstract is usually examined by the:

   a. broker.
   b. abstract company.
   c. purchaser.
   d. attorney for the purchaser.

10. The person who prepares an abstract of title for a parcel of real estate:
    a. writes a brief history of the title after inspecting the county records for documents affecting the title.
    b. insures the condition of the title.
    c. inspects the property.
    d. all of the above

11. A purchaser of real estate is charged with knowledge of all recorded documents. The purchaser is also charged with the responsibility to:
    I. make improvements on the property.
    II. learn the rights of the parties in possession.
       a. I only   c. both I and II
       b. II only   d. neither I nor II

12. Which *one* of the following statements *best* explains why instruments affecting real estate are recorded with the recorder of deeds of the county where the property is located?
    a. Recording gives constructive notice to the world of the rights and interests in a particular parcel of real estate.
    b. The law requires that such instruments be recorded.
    c. The instruments must be recorded to comply with the terms of the statute of frauds.
    d. Recording proves the execution of the instrument.

13. When a claim is settled by a title insurance company, the company acquires all rights and claims of the insured against any other person who is responsible for the loss. This is called:
    a. escrow.   c. subordination.
    b. abstract of title.   d. subrogation.

14. The documents referred to as title evidence include:
    a. certificate of title.
    b. warranty deeds.
    c. security agreements.
    d. a and c

15. Which of the following provides evidence of the kind of estate and all liens against an interest in a parcel of real estate?
    a. a recorded deed
    b. a court suit for specific performance
    c. Torrens certificate
    d. a foreclosure suit

16. Written instruments affecting real estate should be recorded:
    a. in the county where the real estate is located.
    b. to give actual notice of the owner's interest in the property.
    c. to give constructive notice of the owner's interest in the property.
    d. a and c

17. A title insurance policy usually includes:
    I. a legal description of the insured parcel of real estate.
    II. the exceptions that are not covered by the policy.
       a. I only   c. both I and II
       b. II only   d. neither I nor II

18. To give notice of a security interest in a fixture, a creditor must record which of the following?
    a. security agreement
    b. financing statement
    c. bulk transfer
    d. quitclaim deed

19. *Chain of title* refers to which of the following?
    a. a summary or history of all instruments and legal proceedings affecting a specific parcel of land
    b. a series of links measuring 7.92 inches each
    c. an instrument or document that protects the insured parties (subject to specific exceptions) against defects in the examination of the record and hidden risks such as forgeries, undisclosed heirs, errors in the public records and so forth
    d. the succession of conveyances from some starting point whereby the present owner derives title

20. The date and time a document was recorded establish which of the following?
    a. priority of filing   c. subrogation
    b. chain of title   d. marketable title

14

Real Estate License Laws

Key Terms
Branch office
Broker
Broker-salesperson
Denial, suspension or revocation of license
Irrevocable consent
NARELLO
Real estate commission
Real estate education
Real estate license law
Real estate recovery fund
Rules and regulations
Salesperson

Overview
Generally, broker and salesperson license applicants are required to pass an examination designed to test their knowledge of real estate principles and laws. Foremost among these laws is each state's *real estate license law*, which sets forth strict operating restrictions for licensees and penalties for noncompliance. This chapter will introduce you to some of the provisions that are basic to most state license laws. It is recommended that you read through this chapter, then study your state law and the license law chapter in your state supplement for *Modern Real Estate Practice* (where available). In addition, you should complete the license law analysis form that takes the place of end-of-chapter questions, to help you identify and learn key provisions in your state law.

Real Estate License Laws in All States	All states, the District of Columbia and Canadian provinces have enacted **real estate license laws** that provide the state with the authority to license and regulate the activities of real estate brokers and salespeople. Certain details of the laws vary from state to state, but the main provisions of many state laws are similar and are based on the so-called *pattern law* recommended by the License Law Committee of the NATIONAL ASSOCIATION OF REALTORS®. In addition, uniform policies and standards in the fields of license law administration and enforcement are promoted by an organization of state license law officials known as **NARELLO**—the National Association of Real Estate License Law Officials.
Purposes of License Laws	The purposes of the real estate license laws are: (1) to protect the public from dishonest or incompetent brokers or salespeople, (2) to prescribe certain standards and qualifications for licensing brokers and salespeople and (3) to maintain high standards in the real estate profession.

Basic Provisions of License Laws	The authority that controls the licensing of real estate brokers and salespeople is usually the state **real estate commission.** The commission generally has the power to issue licenses, make real estate information available to licensees and the public, and enforce the real estate license law. The law is usually enforced through the **denial, suspension or revocation of licenses,** although certain officials may be able to bring civil and/or criminal court actions against violators in serious cases.
	Most state real estate commissions have adopted a series of administrative **rules and regulations** that further define the basic law, provide for its administration and set forth additional operating guidelines for brokers and salespeople. These rules and regulations usually have the *same force and effect as the law* itself. Throughout this chapter, all discussions of the license law also include the typical provisions of state real estate commissions' rules and regulations.
Who Must Be Licensed	Generally, the state license laws stipulate that any person who, for another and for compensation or promise of compensation, performs any of the following acts with regard to real estate (and in some states, business opportunities) must be licensed as a real estate **broker:**

1. sells.
2. lists.
3. buys.
4. rents or leases.
5. collects rents.
6. deals in options.
7. exchanges.
8. offers to perform or negotiate one of these activities.
9. represents that he or she engages in any of these activities.

The specific provisions vary from state to state, and many states cite additional activities that a person must be licensed to perform. In some states, for example, a person who, for others and for a fee, auctions real estate, negotiates a mortgage loan or deals in cemetery lots may be required to have a broker's license. It is important to identify the specific requirements for your state.

Any person who performs any of the previously listed activities while employed by or associated with a real estate broker must be licensed as a real estate **salesperson**. In addition, some states have a special name or issue a special license for an individual who has qualified as a real estate broker and passed the broker's exam but is currently acting as a salesperson associated with and responsible to another licensed broker. Such person may be known as a **broker-salesperson** or an *associate broker*. To summarize, a broker is authorized to operate his or her own real estate business; a salesperson can operate only in the name of and under the supervision of a licensed broker.

Exceptions. The real estate license laws *generally do not apply* to certain persons and situations, including:

1. a person or firm who sells his, her or its own property when this is not the person's or firm's principal vocation.
2. a person acting under a power of attorney.
3. a salaried employee of a property owner who acts on behalf of the property owner, when dealing in real estate is not the owner's principal vocation.
4. an attorney-at-law performing his or her regular duties.
5. a receiver, trustee, guardian, administrator, executor or other person acting under court order.
6. an auctioneer performing his or her regular duties (although, as previously mentioned, such person must be licensed in some states).
7. a public official or employee performing his or her regular duties.

Licensing Procedure   All states vary in their specific requirements for licensing. However, most require that an applicant be of legal age, a high school graduate and a state resident for a certain period of time. In addition, he or she must not have had a real estate license revoked for a certain period of time in any state, not have been convicted of a serious crime for a certain period of time and so forth. Some states may also require credit reports, fingerprint cards or FBI clearance and/or personal references. In addition, most states require a salesperson applicant to be sponsored by a licensed broker who operates within the state and for whom the salesperson will work. A broker applicant usually will be required to have a minimum amount of experience as a salesperson.

Educational requirements. Many states require license applicants to complete a certain number of hours of **real estate education** as a prerequisite to obtaining a license. These requirements vary from state to state, but generally broker applicants are required to complete more hours of classroom time than salesperson applicants. In addition, a number of states have enacted *continuing education* requirements that licensees must complete in order to qualify for license renewal.

Examinations. All states require license applicants to pass a written real estate examination prior to licensing. State requirements vary as to the length, manner and passing grade for such exams, but generally the broker's exam is more inclusive and longer than the salesperson's exam. The states also vary in their regulations regarding retests and appeals for applicants who have failed the exams.

Licensing of nonresidents. Most state licensing agencies have reciprocity agreements with the licensing agencies of certain other states. These agreements provide that out-of-state brokers will be allowed to operate within the state upon meeting certain requirements. Generally, reciprocity agreements are made between states that have similar licensing requirements or states that adjoin each other. Some states require out-of-state brokers to take the local state real estate licensing exam; others do not. In addition, most states require nonresident brokers to file an **irrevocable consent** agreement with the state licensing agency. This document states that suits and actions may be brought against the out-of-state broker within the state in which the agreement is filed and that the outcome of such suits will be valid and binding.

Licensing of corporations and partnerships. In most cases, a real estate brokerage may be established as a corporation if at least one officer of the corporation is a licensed real estate broker. It may be required that all members of a partnership be brokers. Some states require that all officers or partners who are not participating in the business be registered as nonactive brokers. The license laws usually provide that no officer or partner may be registered as a real estate salesperson.

Real Estate Recovery Fund

Many states have instituted a special **real estate recovery fund** from which members of the general public may collect if they have suffered financial loss as a result of the actions of a real estate licensee. The fund is usually maintained by part of the fees that licensees must pay. Generally people who seek reimbursement from the fund can do so only after they have filed a court suit and won a money judgment against the licensee. If the aggrieved individual cannot collect the judgment from the licensee in any other way, he or she can apply for payment from the recovery fund. The registrant's license is usually suspended until he or she repays the recovery fund for the amount paid to the injured party, plus interest.

General Operation of a Real Estate Business

The state license laws regulate many of the everyday operations of real estate brokers and salespeople. Generally, every resident real estate broker must maintain a definite place of business within the state and may operate one or more **branch offices.** The licenses of salespeople are dependent on that of the employing broker. Termination, suspension or revocation of the broker's license means that all activities of salespeople must cease.

Usually brokers must keep detailed accounting records and retain copies of the documents used in all listings and transactions for a specified period of time. In addition, many license laws include specific provisions regarding the contents of contracts and documents used in transactions. Each broker must also either maintain a special trust account for the deposit of funds belonging to clients and customers or make use of a neutral escrow depository.

Brokers must never *commingle* a client's funds with their own money. In some states, however, a broker is permitted to deposit a small amount of personal cash in a trust account in order to pay banking charges and keep the account open.

Brokers cannot use any misleading or fraudulent advertising in the course of business, and they generally cannot use blind ads (that is, advertising that does not specifically indicate that the advertiser of the property is a real estate broker). In addition, salespeople usually cannot advertise in their own names, but only in the name of their supervising broker.

Suspension or Revocation of a Real Estate License

Most state license laws detail the various violations of the license law and other reasons for which a real estate license may be suspended or revoked. You should study the rules for your state and know them thoroughly.

Summary

The *real estate license laws* were enacted by the various states to protect the public from dishonest brokers and salespeople, prescribe certain licensing standards and maintain high standards in the real estate profession.

Each state law stipulates who must be licensed and who is exempt from licensing, sets forth certain operating standards to which brokers and salespersons must adhere and creates certain licensing procedures and requirements.

Note, however, that each state law is different. *You must know your own state license law.* If you do not have a copy of your state real estate license law, secure one immediately.

The analysis form that takes the place of questions in this chapter will help you to determine and learn the requirements of your state law. Use it as a study device while you read through your state law and state supplement (where available), or use it as a testing device *after* studying the license law. (Be sure to check your answers against the provisions of the law.)

Remember, you will be operating and working under your state real estate license law—*you must know it well.*

Analysis Form: Real Estate Broker's and Salesperson's Law
State (or province) of

Instructions: After studying your state law, answer the questions and fill in the information indicated. If the question or point does not apply in your state, indicate this fact by some statement such as *no, none, not required* or *does not apply.* If you complete this form carefully, the information will be invaluable when you prepare for your state license examination and for future use.

1. When was your state law originally passed? _____

2. Has it been amended? _____ If so, when was the last amendment passed?

3. What are the requirements for licensure in your state?

	For Broker's License	For Salesperson's License
Minimum age	_____	_____
Apprenticeship (years)	_____	_____
Education	_____	_____
Examination required?	_____	_____
Bond required (if any)	_____	_____
Number and type of recommendations required	_____	_____
Photograph required?	_____	_____

4. Copy exactly the definition of a *broker* as given by your law. Know this definition and be able to list the activities that it includes.

   _____

   _____

   _____

5. Copy exactly the definition of a *salesperson* as given by your law. Learn this definition.

   _____

   _____

   _____

6. What persons or groups are *exempt* from licensure in your state?

   _____

   _____

   _____

7. What fees are required in your state?

	For Broker	For Salesperson
For original license application	_____	_____
Additional fee for examination	_____	_____
Periodic renewal fee	_____	_____
Recovery fund, if separate	_____	_____

8. For what period is the license certificate issued? _____ _____

On what date does it expire? _____ _____

During what month or by what date must the certificate be renewed? _____ _____

9. Following are some of the reasons why a state may discipline a broker or salesperson, refuse to issue a license, or revoke or suspend a license. Place a check mark in front of the reasons given in your state law. Cross out reasons that do not apply and add other reasons that are not listed here. When you have compiled your list, memorize the reasons. *Almost every state examination will require you to know these grounds for discipline.* Be absolutely sure you know them.

_____ Filing for record any papers to cloud title as claim for commission

_____ Making false affidavits or committing perjury in any court proceeding

_____ Pursuing a continued and flagrant course of misrepresentation

_____ Making false promises through salespeople, advertising and the like

_____ Acting for more than one party without approval of all parties (dual agency)

_____ Failing to remit or account for funds belonging to others

_____ Misleading advertising or an ad without the broker's name

_____ Misusing the term REALTOR® or other insignia of membership

_____ Procuring license by fraud, such as by filing a fraudulent application

_____ Willfully disregarding or violating provisions of the licensing act or regulations

_____ Paying a commission to any unlicensed person in violation of the act

_____ Representing a broker other than one's employer

_____ Being convicted of embezzlement, fraud and similar crimes, or state or federal felonies

_____ Displaying "For Sale" signs without proper authorization from a seller

_____ Not clearly explaining to a principal the duration of an exclusive listing agreement

_____ Engaging in conduct that constitutes bad faith or improper, incompetent, fraudulent or dishonest dealing

_____ Employing unlicensed salespeople

_____ Accepting a commission in violation of the licensing act

_____ Operating an office or branch office from an unregistered location

_____ Commingling funds or property of a principal with a broker's personal funds

_____ Failing to deposit the money of others in an escrow or trust account

_____ Other:

10. What penalties are provided in your state law for operating without a license?

| | Individuals | | Corporations | |
	1st Offense	2nd Offense	1st Offense	2nd Offense
Fine	_____	_____	_____	_____
Imprisonment	_____	_____	_____	_____

Are other penalties or fines provided and, if so, for what offenses?

11. What is the name of the state department, board, commission or office that is responsible for administering the real estate law in your state?

12. If there is a real estate commission or advisory committee, how many members are there? What is their term of office?

13. What are the requirements in regard to a broker's maintaining an office and/or a sign?

14. What provisions and/or requirements are made for the discharge or termination of employment of a real estate salesperson by a broker?

15. List the main requirements for issuance of a certificate to a nonresident broker.

16. Does your state have a real estate recovery fund?

15

Real Estate Financing

Overview

Rarely is a parcel of real estate purchased on a cash basis. Since almost every real estate transaction involves some type of financing, an understanding of real estate financing is of prime importance to the real estate licensee. Usually the buyer in a real estate transaction borrows the major portion of the purchase price by securing a loan and pledging the real property involved as security (collateral) for the loan. This chapter will discuss the basic types of financing instruments, as well as alternative types of financing and payment plans. In addition, the chapter will examine the various sources of real estate loan funds and the role of the federal government in real estate financing.

Mortgage Theory

The earliest form of lending using real estate as collateral was the **mortgage** used in England under Anglo-Saxon law. A borrower who needed to finance the purchase of land (the *mortgagor*) was forced to convey title to the property to the lender (the *mortgagee*), to ensure payment of the debt. If the obligation was not paid, the mortgagor automatically forfeited the land to the creditor, who was already the legal owner of the property.

Through the years, English courts began to acknowledge that a mortgage was only a *security device* and the mortgagor was the true owner of the mortgaged real estate. Under this concept, real estate was merely pledged by use of the mortgage document as *security* for the payment of a debt. The debt itself was represented by a *note*.

United States Mortgage Law

Upon gaining independence from England, the original 13 colonies adopted the English laws as their own basic body of law. From their inception, American courts of equity considered a mortgage as a voluntary lien on real estate, given to secure the payment of a debt or the performance of an obligation.

Even so, some of the states recognized—and still do recognize—a lender as the owner of mortgaged land. This ownership is subject to defeat upon full payment of the debt or performance of the obligation. These states are called **title theory** states. Under title theory, a mortgagee has the right to possession of and rents from the mortgaged property immediately upon default by the mortgagor.

Those states that interpret a mortgage purely as a lien on real property are called **lien theory** states. In such states, if a mortgagor defaults, the lender may foreclose the lien (generally through a court action), offer the property for sale and apply the funds received from the sale to reduce or extinguish the obligation. As protection to the borrower, these states generally allow a statutory redemption period during which a defaulted mortgagor can redeem the property.

Today, a number of states have modified the strict interpretation of title and lien theories. These *intermediary,* or *modified lien theory,* states allow a lender to take possession of the mortgaged real estate upon default.

Regardless of whether a state follows the title or lien theory of mortgages, the security interest that the mortgagee has in the real estate is legally considered *personal property*. This interest can be transferred *only* with a transfer of the debt that the mortgage secures. In reality, *the differences between the rights of the parties to a mortgage loan in a lien theory state and a title theory state are more theoretical than actual.*

Security and Debt

Generally, any interest in real estate that may be sold may be pledged as security for a debt. The basic principle of the property law, that a person cannot convey greater rights in property than he or she actually has, applies equally to the right to mortgage. So the owner of a fee simple estate can mortgage the fee, and the owner of a leasehold or subleasehold can mortgage that leasehold interest. For example, a large retail corporation renting space in a shopping center may mortgage its leasehold interest in order to finance some remodeling work.

As discussed in Chapter 8, the owner of a cooperative interest holds a personal property interest, not an interest in real estate. Although a cooperative owner has a leasehold interest, the nature of that leasehold is not generally acceptable to lenders as collateral. The owner of a condominium unit, however, does own a mortgageable interest.

Mortgage Loan Instruments

There are two parts to a mortgage loan—the debt itself and the security for the debt. When a property is to be mortgaged, the owner must execute, or sign, two separate instruments:

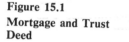

1. The **note,** or *financing instrument,* is the promise, or agreement, to repay a debt in definite installments with interest. The mortgagor executes one or more promissory notes to total the amount of the debt.

Figure 15.1
Mortgage and Trust Deed

2. The **mortgage,** or *security instrument,* is the document that creates the lien, or conveys the property to the mortgagee as *security* for the debt.

Hypothecation is the term used to describe the pledging of property as security for payment of a loan. A pledge of security—a mortgage—cannot be legally effective unless there is a debt to secure. *Both note and mortgage must be executed in order to create an enforceable mortgage loan.*

Trust deeds. In some areas of the country, and in certain situations, lenders prefer to use a three-party instrument known as a **trust deed,** or *deed of trust,* rather than a mortgage document. A trust deed conveys "naked title" or "bare legal title" (title without the right of possession) to the real estate as security for the loan to a third party, called the *trustee.* The trustee then holds title on behalf of the lender, known as the *beneficiary,* who is the legal owner and holder of the note. The wording of the conveyance sets forth actions that the trustee may take if the borrower, the *trustor,* defaults under any of the trust deed terms. (See figure 15.1 for a comparison of mortgages and trust deeds.) In states where trust deeds are generally preferred, foreclosure procedures for defaulted trust deeds are usually simpler and faster than those for mortgage loans.

Usually the lender chooses the trustee and reserves the right to substitute trustees in the event of death or dismissal. State law usually dictates who may serve as trustee. Although the trust deed is particularly popular in certain states, it is used all over the country. For example, in the financing of a commercial or industrial real estate venture that involves a large loan and several lenders, the borrower generally executes a single trust deed to secure as many notes as are necessary.

Provisions of the Financing Instrument

In general, the financing instrument executed by a borrower states the amount of the debt, the time and method of payment and the rate of interest. If a promissory note is used with a mortgage, the borrower (mortgagor) is the *maker* or *payor* and the lender (mortgagee) is the payee. If it is used with a trust deed, the note may be made payable to the bearer. It may also refer to or repeat several of the clauses that appear in the mortgage document or trust deed. The note, like the mortgage or trust deed, should be signed by all parties who have an interest in the property. In states where dower and curtesy are in effect or where homestead or community property is involved, both spouses may have an interest in the property and both should sign the note. Figure 15.2 is an example of a note commonly used with a mortgage.

A note is a **negotiable instrument,** that is, a written promise or order to pay a specific sum of money. An instrument is said to be negotiable when its holder, the payee, may transfer the right to receive payment to a third party. This may be accomplished by signing the instrument over to the third party or, in some cases, by merely delivering the instrument to that person. Other examples of negotiable instruments include checks and bank drafts.

To be negotiable, or freely transferable, an instrument must meet certain requirements of Article 3 of the Uniform Commercial Code. The instrument must be in writing, made by one person to another and signed by the maker. It must contain an unconditional promise to pay a sum of money on demand or at a set date in the future. In addition, the instrument must be payable to the order of a specifically named person or to the bearer (whoever has possession of the note). Instru-

Figure 15.2
Note (Used with Mortgage)

NOTE

........April 12........................, 19..88..   ....Chicago........, ...Illinois........
                                                              [City]   [State]

........222 Kelly Street, Chicago, Illinois 60601..
                                    [Property Address]

1. BORROWER'S PROMISE TO PAY

In return for a loan that I have received, I promise to pay U.S. $..79,000.00................ (this amount is called "principal"), plus interest, to the order of the Lender. The Lender is ..First City Savings and Loan Association of Chicago, Illinois.. I understand that the Lender may transfer this Note. The Lender or anyone who takes this Note by transfer and who is entitled to receive payments under this Note is called the "Note Holder."

2. INTEREST

Interest will be charged on unpaid principal until the full amount of principal has been paid. I will pay interest at a yearly rate of ....9.5......%.

The interest rate required by this Section 2 is the rate I will pay both before and after any default described in Section 6(B) of this Note.

3. PAYMENTS

(A) Time and Place of Payments

I will pay principal and interest by making payments every month.

I will make my monthly payments on the ....1st.. day of each month beginning on ....May 1............................, 19..88.... I will make these payments every month until I have paid all of the principal and interest and any other charges described below that I may owe under this Note. My monthly payments will be applied to interest before principal. If, on ....April 1, 2018............., I still owe amounts under this Note, I will pay those amounts in full on that date, which is called the "maturity date."

I will make my monthly payments at ....130 North LaSalle Street, Chicago, Illinois.. or at a different place if required by the Note Holder.

(B) Amount of Monthly Payments

My monthly payment will be in the amount of U.S. $..664.29........................

4. BORROWER'S RIGHT TO PREPAY

I have the right to make payments of principal at any time before they are due. A payment of principal only is known as a "prepayment." When I make a prepayment, I will tell the Note Holder in writing that I am doing so.

I may make a full prepayment or partial prepayments without paying any prepayment charge. The Note Holder will use all of my prepayments to reduce the amount of principal that I owe under this Note. If I make a partial

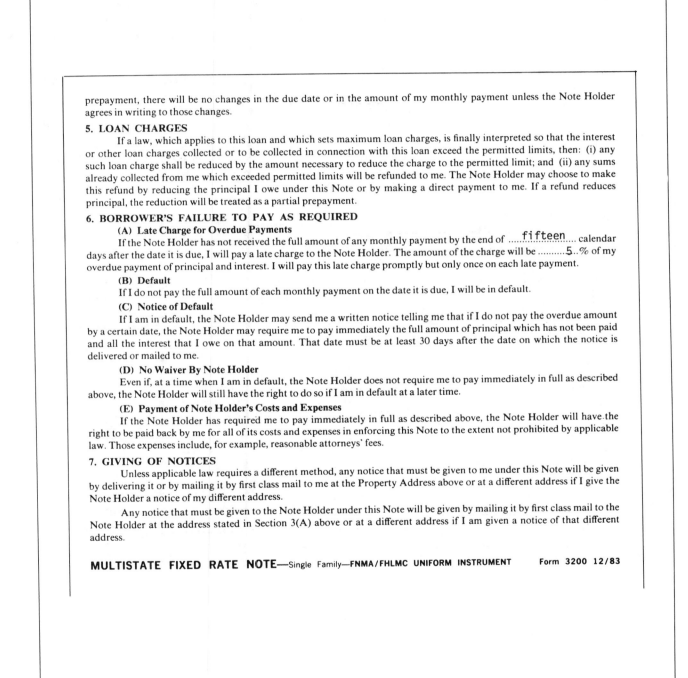

prepayment, there will be no changes in the due date or in the amount of my monthly payment unless the Note Holder agrees in writing to those changes.

5. LOAN CHARGES

If a law, which applies to this loan and which sets maximum loan charges, is finally interpreted so that the interest or other loan charges collected or to be collected in connection with this loan exceed the permitted limits, then: (i) any such loan charge shall be reduced by the amount necessary to reduce the charge to the permitted limit; and (ii) any sums already collected from me which exceeded permitted limits will be refunded to me. The Note Holder may choose to make this refund by reducing the principal I owe under this Note or by making a direct payment to me. If a refund reduces principal, the reduction will be treated as a partial prepayment.

6. BORROWER'S FAILURE TO PAY AS REQUIRED

(A) Late Charge for Overdue Payments

If the Note Holder has not received the full amount of any monthly payment by the end of .....fifteen.... calendar days after the date it is due, I will pay a late charge to the Note Holder. The amount of the charge will be ....5..% of my overdue payment of principal and interest. I will pay this late charge promptly but only once on each late payment.

(B) Default

If I do not pay the full amount of each monthly payment on the date it is due, I will be in default.

(C) Notice of Default

If I am in default, the Note Holder may send me a written notice telling me that if I do not pay the overdue amount by a certain date, the Note Holder may require me to pay immediately the full amount of principal which has not been paid and all the interest that I owe on that amount. That date must be at least 30 days after the date on which the notice is delivered or mailed to me.

(D) No Waiver By Note Holder

Even if, at a time when I am in default, the Note Holder does not require me to pay immediately in full as described above, the Note Holder will still have the right to do so if I am in default at a later time.

(E) Payment of Note Holder's Costs and Expenses

If the Note Holder has required me to pay immediately in full as described above, the Note Holder will have the right to be paid back by me for all of its costs and expenses in enforcing this Note to the extent not prohibited by applicable law. Those expenses include, for example, reasonable attorneys' fees.

7. GIVING OF NOTICES

Unless applicable law requires a different method, any notice that must be given to me under this Note will be given by delivering it or by mailing it by first class mail to me at the Property Address above or at a different address if I give the Note Holder a notice of my different address.

Any notice that must be given to the Note Holder under this Note will be given by mailing it by first class mail to the Note Holder at the address stated in Section 3(A) above or at a different address if I am given a notice of that different address.

MULTISTATE FIXED RATE NOTE—Single Family—**FNMA/FHLMC UNIFORM INSTRUMENT**   Form 3200 12/83 ments that are payable *to order* must be transferred by endorsement; those payable *to bearer* may be transferred by delivery.

Interest

[handwritten: Charge/Rent use of the money]

A charge for the use of money is called **interest.** Interest may be due either at the end of each payment period (known as payment *in arrears*) or at the beginning of each payment period (payment *in advance*). Whether interest is charged in arrears or in advance is specified in the note. In practice, the distinction becomes important if the property is sold before the debt is repaid in full, as will become evident in Chapter 23, "Closing the Real Estate Transaction."

Usury. The maximum rate of interest that may be charged on loans may be set by state law (with the exception we will note later in this discussion). Charging interest in excess of this rate is called **usury,** and lenders are penalized for making usurious loans. In some states, a lender who makes a usurious loan will be permitted to collect the borrowed money, but only at the legal rate of interest. In other states, a usurious lender may lose the right to collect any interest or may lose the entire amount of the loan in addition to the interest. Loans made to corporations are generally exempt from usury laws.

Usury laws were enacted primarily to protect consumers from unscrupulous lenders who would charge unreasonably high interest rates. Some states specifically limit the legal maximum interest rate to a fixed amount, while other states have what is known as a *floating interest rate.* In such states, the maximum rate that may be charged is adjusted up or down at specific intervals based on a certain economic standard, such as the prime lending rate or the rate of return on government bonds. *The rate of interest charged on any one loan, however, remains constant throughout the term of the loan* (except for variable interest loans).

Usury laws are state laws, but federal law preempts state law, and the Depository Institutions Deregulation and Monetary Control Act of 1980 specifically exempts from state interest limitations *all* federally related residential first mortgage loans made after March 31, 1980. Federally related loans are those made by federally chartered institutions or insured or guaranteed by a federal agency. The exemption includes loans used to finance manufactured housing (the federal term for mobile homes) and the acquisition of stock in a cooperative housing corporation. The federal act effectively limits state usury laws to private lenders.

Points. When a mortgage or trust deed is originated, the mortgage company's commission fee or service charge is computed as a percentage of the loan amount. This **loan fee,** or *loan origination fee,* is commonly referred to as **points;** one point equals approximately one percent (1%) of the loan amount. For example, a service charge of two points on an $80,000 mortgage loan would be two percent of $80,000, or $1,600.

Note that, in some areas, a service charge based on a percentage of the loan amount and included in the loan origination fee is termed *prepaid interest,* rather than points.

In Practice...

Interest payments made under a mortgage loan secured by a first or second home are deductible for federal income-tax purposes. This deduction, in effect, reduces the borrower's total cost of housing for the year. Interest deductions are limited, however, to the interest paid on an initial loan amount or refinancing no greater than the purchase price of the home plus capital improvements, unless the loan proceeds are used for qualified medical or educational purposes. Points (prepaid interest) paid at the time of financing a home purchase are fully deductible for the year paid. Points on a loan to finance property improvements are also fully deductible for the year paid. Points paid on a loan refinancing are deductible, but only in portions each year over the stated term of the loan. If advance payments of loan principal are made, there is no increase in the deduction. If the entire loan is repaid, however, any undeducted points may be deducted for that year. Tax deductions for the homeowner were discussed in greater detail in Chapter 4.

Prepayment

When a loan is paid in installments over a long term, the total interest paid by the borrower can be a larger amount of money than the principal of the loan. If such a loan is paid off ahead of its full term, the lender will collect less interest from the borrower. For this reason, some mortgage and trust deed notes contain a *prepayment clause* requiring the borrower to pay a **prepayment penalty,** against the unearned portion of the interest for any payments made ahead of schedule.

The premium charged may run from one percent of the balance due at the time of prepayment to all interest due for the first ten years of the loan. Some lenders allow the borrower to pay off 20 percent of the original loan in any one year without paying a premium; but if the loan is paid off in full, the borrower may be charged a percentage of the principal paid in excess of that allowance. Some states either limit or do not permit a lender to charge a penalty on prepaid residential mortgage or trust deed loans. Other states allow a lender to charge a prepayment penalty *only* if the loan is paid off with funds borrowed from another source.

Payment Plans

Most mortgage and trust deed loans are **amortized loans.** That is, regular payments are made—each payment being applied first to the interest owed and the balance to the principal amount—over a term of perhaps 15 to 30 years. At the end of the term, the full amount of the principal and all interest due will be reduced to zero. Such loans are also called *direct reduction loans.*

Most amortized mortgage and trust deed loans are paid in monthly installments; some, however, are payable quarterly or semiannually. These payments may be computed based on a number of payment plans, which tend alternately to gain and lose favor with lenders and borrowers as the cost and availability of mortgage money fluctuate. Such payment plans include the following (some of which are illustrated in figure 15.3). Note that, while these are commonly referred to as "mortgages," they are loans that may be secured either by mortgage or trust deed.

Fully amortized mortgage. The most frequently used plan, the *fully amortized mortgage,* requires the mortgagor to pay a *constant amount,* usually monthly. This may be referred to as a *level payment* loan. The mortgagee credits each payment first to the interest due and then applies the balance to reduce the principal of the loan. Thus, while each payment is the same, the portion applied toward repayment of the principal grows and the interest due declines as the unpaid balance of the loan is reduced.

Straight-line amortized mortgage. With *straight-line amortization,* the mortgagor may pay a *different amount for each installment,* with each payment consisting of a fixed amount credited toward the principal plus an additional amount for the

Figure 15.3
Payment Plans

Fully Amortized Mortgage

Payment
Amount

Principal and Interest on 30 year Mortgage

▨ **Principal**   ■ **Interest**

Straight Line Amortization

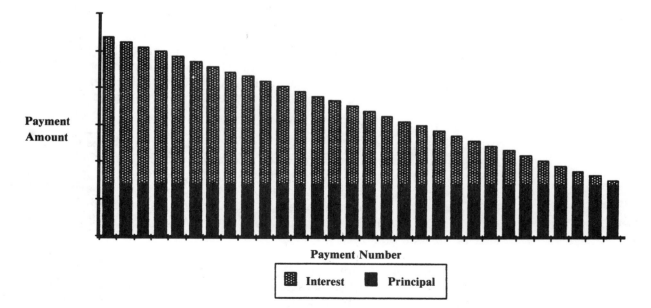

Payment
Amount

Payment Number

▨ **Interest**   ■ **Principal**

interest due on the balance of the principal outstanding since the last payment was made.

Straight payment mortgage. A mortgagor may choose a *straight payment plan* that calls for periodic payments of interest, with the principal to be *paid in full at the end of the loan term.* This is known as a straight, or term, loan. Such plans are generally used for home-improvement loans and second mortgages rather than for residential first mortgage loans. Prior to the 1930s, the only form of mortgage loan available was the straight payment loan, payable after a relatively short term, such as three to five years. The high rate of foreclosure of such loans in the Depression years prompted the use of the more manageable amortized loans that are now the norm.

Adjustable rate mortgage (ARM). *Adjustable rate loans* are generally originated at one rate of interest, with the rate fluctuating up or down during the loan term based on a certain economic indicator, such as the cost-of-funds index for federally chartered savings and loan associations. Details of how and when the rate of interest on the loan will change are included in the provisions of the note. Generally, interest rate adjustments are limited to one each year, and there is a set maximum number of increases that may be made over the life of the loan. Certain regulations may enable a lender to adjust the interest rate on a monthly basis. The borrower is usually given the right to prepay the loan in full without penalty (see the discussion on prepayment penalties in this chapter) whenever the interest rate is changed.

Graduated payment mortgage (GPM). The mortgagor may elect to take advantage of a *flexible payment plan,* such as a *graduated payment mortgage,* generally used to enable younger buyers and buyers in times of high interest rates to purchase real estate. Under this plan, a mortgagor makes lower monthly payments for the first few years of the loan (typically the first five years), and larger payments for the remainder of the term, when the mortgagor's income is expected to have increased.

Balloon payment loan. When a mortgage or trust deed loan requires periodic payments that will not fully amortize the amount of the loan by the time the final payment is due, the final payment is a larger amount than the others. This is called a **balloon payment,** and this type of loan is a *partially amortized loan.* For example, a loan made for $80,000 at 11½ percent interest may be computed on a 30-year amortization schedule but paid over a 20-year term with a final balloon payment due at the end of the twentieth year. In this case, each monthly payment would be $792.24 (the amount taken from a 30-year amortization schedule), with a final balloon payment of $56,340 (the amount of principal still owing after 20 years). It is frequently assumed that if the payments are promptly made, the lender will extend the balloon payment for another limited term. The lender, however, is in no way legally obligated to grant this extension and can require payment in full when the note is due.

Growing equity mortgage (GEM). The *growing equity mortgage,* or *rapid-payoff mortgage,* makes use of a fixed interest rate, but payments of principal are increased according to an index or schedule. The total payment thus increases, but the borrower's income is expected to keep pace, and the loan is paid off more quickly.

Renegotiable rate mortgage (RRM). *Renegotiable rate loans* are long-term loans that are renewable every three, four or five years, at which time the interest rate is increased or decreased. These adjustments are based on a national index—for instance, the interest rates on previously occupied homes as compiled by the Federal Home Loan Bank Board. Interest rates may change at a maximum rate of one-half percent per year, with a five percent maximum over the life of the loan; specifics are included in the provisions of the note. Often such limitations are self-imposed by lenders. Borrowers must be notified of any rate change at least 30 days in advance of the change. Downward interest adjustments are mandatory, while upward adjustments are optional. Borrowers are usually allowed to prepay without penalty within a reasonable time after receiving notice of a rate change.

Shared-appreciation mortgage (SAM). A *shared-appreciation mortgage* is one in which the lender originates a mortgage or trust deed loan at a favorable interest rate (several points below the going rate) in return for a guaranteed share of the gain (if any) the borrower will realize when the property is eventually sold. This type of loan was originally made to developers of large real estate projects, but in times of expensive mortgage money it has appeared in the residential financing market. The specific details of the shared-appreciation agreement are set forth in the mortgage or trust deed and note documents.

Reverse annuity mortgage (RAM). A *reverse annuity mortgage* is one in which regular monthly payments are made *to the borrower,* based on the equity the homeowner has invested in the property given as security for the loan. A reverse loan allows senior citizens on fixed incomes to realize the equity buildup in their homes without having to sell. The borrower is charged a fixed rate of interest and the loan is eventually paid from the sale of the property or from the borrower's estate upon his or her death.

Provisions of the Mortgage Document or Trust Deed	The mortgage document or trust deed refers to the terms of the note and clearly establishes that the conveyance of land is security for the debt. It identifies the lender as well as the borrower, and it includes an accurate legal description of the property. It should be signed by all parties who have an interest in the real estate. (Figure 15.4 is a sample mortgage; figure 15.5, a trust deed.)
Duties of the Mortgagor or Trustor	The borrower is required to fulfill many obligations. These usually include the following:

1. payment of the debt in accordance with the terms of the note.
2. payment of all real estate taxes on the property given as security.
3. maintenance of adequate insurance to protect the lender if the property is destroyed or damaged by fire, windstorm or other hazard.
4. maintenance of the property in good repair at all times.
5. lender authorization before making any major alterations on the property.

Failure to meet any of these obligations can result in a borrower's default on the note. When this happens, the loan documents may provide for a grace period (30 days, for example) during which the borrower can meet the obligation and cure the default. If the borrower does not do so, the lender has the right to foreclose the mortgage or trust deed and collect on the note. The most frequent cause of default is the borrower's failure to meet monthly installments.

**Figure 15.4
Mortgage**

———————————— [Space Above This Line For Recording Data] ————————————

MORTGAGE

THIS MORTGAGE ("Security Instrument") is given on ....April 12..,
19.88..... The mortgagor is ...Thomas..Perkins..and..Celia..Perkins,..husband..and..wife..................
.... ("Borrower"). This Security Instrument is given to ....
.. First City Savings and Loan Association ...., which is organized and existing
under the laws of ...Illinois..and..the..United..States....., and whose address is .130..North..La..Salle.........
..Chicago, Illinois... ("Lender").
Borrower owes Lender the principal sum of .....Seventy..Nine..Thousand..and..xx/100---------------------
--------------------------------- Dollars (U.S. $..79,000.00...........). This debt is evidenced by Borrower's note
dated the same date as this Security Instrument ("Note"), which provides for monthly payments, with the full debt, if not
paid earlier, due and payable on ....April..1,..2018.................................... This Security Instrument
secures to Lender: (a) the repayment of the debt evidenced by the Note, with interest, and all renewals, extensions and
modifications; (b) the payment of all other sums, with interest, advanced under paragraph 7 to protect the security of this
Security Instrument; and (c) the performance of Borrower's covenants and agreements under this Security Instrument and
the Note. For this purpose, Borrower does hereby mortgage, grant and convey to Lender the following described property
located in ....Cook... County, Illinois:

Lot 4 in Block 5 of the Daley Subdivision, a subdivision located in
the Southeast 1/4 of Section 17, Township 5 North, Range 12 East of
the Third Principal Meridian.
Permanent Tax Index No. 17-09-788-971

which has the address of ....222..Kelly..Street.., ...Chicago..........................,
                                                              [Street]   [City]
Illinois ....60601... ("Property Address");
                          [Zip Code]

TOGETHER WITH all the improvements now or hereafter erected on the property, and all easements, rights,
appurtenances, rents, royalties, mineral, oil and gas rights and profits, water rights and stock and all fixtures now or
hereafter a part of the property. All replacements and additions shall also be covered by this Security Instrument. All of the
foregoing is referred to in this Security Instrument as the "Property."

BORROWER COVENANTS that Borrower is lawfully seised of the estate hereby conveyed and has the right to
mortgage, grant and convey the Property and that the Property is unencumbered, except for encumbrances of record.
Borrower warrants and will defend generally the title to the Property against all claims and demands, subject to any
encumbrances of record.

THIS SECURITY INSTRUMENT combines uniform covenants for national use and non-uniform covenants with
limited variations by jurisdiction to constitute a uniform security instrument covering real property.

UNIFORM COVENANTS. Borrower and Lender covenant and agree as follows:
    1. Payment of Principal and Interest; Prepayment and Late Charges. Borrower shall promptly pay when due
the principal of and interest on the debt evidenced by the Note and any prepayment and late charges due under the Note.
    2. Funds for Taxes and Insurance. Subject to applicable law or to a written waiver by Lender, Borrower shall pay
to Lender on the day monthly payments are due under the Note, until the Note is paid in full, a sum ("Funds") equal to
one-twelfth of: (a) yearly taxes and assessments which may attain priority over this Security Instrument; (b) yearly
leasehold payments or ground rents on the Property, if any; (c) yearly hazard insurance premiums; and (d) yearly
mortgage insurance premiums, if any. These items are called "escrow items." Lender may estimate the Funds due on the
basis of current data and reasonable estimates of future escrow items.
    The Funds shall be held in an institution the deposits or accounts of which are insured or guaranteed by a federal or
state agency (including Lender if Lender is such an institution). Lender shall apply the Funds to pay the escrow items.
Lender may not charge for holding and applying the Funds, analyzing the account or verifying the escrow items, unless
Lender pays Borrower interest on the Funds and applicable law permits Lender to make such a charge. Borrower and
Lender may agree in writing that interest shall be paid on the Funds. Unless an agreement is made or applicable law
requires interest to be paid, Lender shall not be required to pay Borrower any interest or earnings on the Funds. Lender
shall give to Borrower, without charge, an annual accounting of the Funds showing credits and debits to the Funds and the
purpose for which each debit to the Funds was made. The Funds are pledged as additional security for the sums secured by
this Security Instrument.
    If the amount of the Funds held by Lender, together with the future monthly payments of Funds payable prior to
the due dates of the escrow items, shall exceed the amount required to pay the escrow items when due, the excess shall be,
at Borrower's option, either promptly repaid to Borrower or credited to Borrower on monthly payments of Funds. If the
amount of the Funds held by Lender is not sufficient to pay the escrow items when due, Borrower shall pay to Lender any
amount necessary to make up the deficiency in one or more payments as required by Lender.
    Upon payment in full of all sums secured by this Security Instrument, Lender shall promptly refund to Borrower
any Funds held by Lender. If under paragraph 19 the Property is sold or acquired by Lender, Lender shall apply, no later
than immediately prior to the sale of the Property or its acquisition by Lender, any Funds held by Lender at the time of
application as a credit against the sums secured by this Security Instrument.

ILLINOIS—Single Family—**FNMA/FHLMC UNIFORM INSTRUMENT**

Form 3014 12/83
44713 SAF SYSTEMS AND FORMS
CHICAGO, IL

Figure 15.4 (cont.)

3. Application of Payments. Unless applicable law provides otherwise, all payments received by Lender under paragraphs 1 and 2 shall be applied: first, to late charges due under the Note; second, to prepayment charges due under the Note; third, to amounts payable under paragraph 2; fourth, to interest due; and last, to principal due.

4. Charges; Liens. Borrower shall pay all taxes, assessments, charges, fines and impositions attributable to the Property which may attain priority over this Security Instrument, and leasehold payments or ground rents, if any. Borrower shall pay these obligations in the manner provided in paragraph 2, or if not paid in that manner, Borrower shall pay them on time directly to the person owed payment. Borrower shall promptly furnish to Lender all notices of amounts to be paid under this paragraph. If Borrower makes these payments directly, Borrower shall promptly furnish to Lender receipts evidencing the payments.

Borrower shall promptly discharge any lien which has priority over this Security Instrument unless Borrower: (a) agrees in writing to the payment of the obligation secured by the lien in a manner acceptable to Lender; (b) contests in good faith the lien by, or defends against enforcement of the lien in, legal proceedings which in the Lender's opinion operate to prevent the enforcement of the lien or forfeiture of any part of the Property; or (c) secures from the holder of the lien an agreement satisfactory to Lender subordinating the lien to this Security Instrument. If Lender determines that any part of the Property is subject to a lien which may attain priority over this Security Instrument, Lender may give Borrower a notice identifying the lien. Borrower shall satisfy the lien or take one or more of the actions set forth above within 10 days of the giving of notice.

5. Hazard Insurance. Borrower shall keep the improvements now existing or hereafter erected on the Property insured against loss by fire, hazards included within the term "extended coverage" and any other hazards for which Lender requires insurance. This insurance shall be maintained in the amounts and for the periods that Lender requires. The insurance carrier providing the insurance shall be chosen by Borrower subject to Lender's approval which shall not be unreasonably withheld.

All insurance policies and renewals shall be acceptable to Lender and shall include a standard mortgage clause. Lender shall have the right to hold the policies and renewals. If Lender requires, Borrower shall promptly give to Lender all receipts of paid premiums and renewal notices. In the event of loss, Borrower shall give prompt notice to the insurance carrier and Lender. Lender may make proof of loss if not made promptly by Borrower.

Unless Lender and Borrower otherwise agree in writing, insurance proceeds shall be applied to restoration or repair of the Property damaged, if the restoration or repair is economically feasible and Lender's security is not lessened. If the restoration or repair is not economically feasible or Lender's security would be lessened, the insurance proceeds shall be applied to the sums secured by this Security Instrument, whether or not then due, with any excess paid to Borrower. If Borrower abandons the Property, or does not answer within 30 days a notice from Lender that the insurance carrier has offered to settle a claim, then Lender may collect the insurance proceeds. Lender may use the proceeds to repair or restore the Property or to pay sums secured by this Security Instrument, whether or not then due. The 30-day period will begin when the notice is given.

Unless Lender and Borrower otherwise agree in writing, any application of proceeds to principal shall not extend or postpone the due date of the monthly payments referred to in paragraphs 1 and 2 or change the amount of the payments. If under paragraph 19 the Property is acquired by Lender, Borrower's right to any insurance policies and proceeds resulting from damage to the Property prior to the acquisition shall pass to Lender to the extent of the sums secured by this Security Instrument immediately prior to the acquisition.

6. Preservation and Maintenance of Property; Leaseholds. Borrower shall not destroy, damage or substantially change the Property, allow the Property to deteriorate or commit waste. If this Security Instrument is on a leasehold, Borrower shall comply with the provisions of the lease, and if Borrower acquires fee title to the Property, the leasehold and fee title shall not merge unless Lender agrees to the merger in writing.

7. Protection of Lender's Rights in the Property; Mortgage Insurance. If Borrower fails to perform the covenants and agreements contained in this Security Instrument, or there is a legal proceeding that may significantly affect Lender's rights in the Property (such as a proceeding in bankruptcy, probate, for condemnation or to enforce laws or regulations), then Lender may do and pay for whatever is necessary to protect the value of the Property and Lender's rights in the Property. Lender's actions may include paying any sums secured by a lien which has priority over this Security Instrument, appearing in court, paying reasonable attorneys' fees and entering on the Property to make repairs. Although Lender may take action under this paragraph 7, Lender does not have to do so.

Any amounts disbursed by Lender under this paragraph 7 shall become additional debt of Borrower secured by this Security Instrument. Unless Borrower and Lender agree to other terms of payment, these amounts shall bear interest from the date of disbursement at the Note rate and shall be payable, with interest, upon notice from Lender to Borrower requesting payment.

If Lender required mortgage insurance as a condition of making the loan secured by this Security Instrument, Borrower shall pay the premiums required to maintain the insurance in effect until such time as the requirement for the insurance terminates in accordance with Borrower's and Lender's written agreement or applicable law.

8. Inspection. Lender or its agent may make reasonable entries upon and inspections of the Property. Lender shall give Borrower notice at the time of or prior to an inspection specifying reasonable cause for the inspection.

9. Condemnation. The proceeds of any award or claim for damages, direct or consequential, in connection with any condemnation or other taking of any part of the Property, or for conveyance in lieu of condemnation, are hereby assigned and shall be paid to Lender.

In the event of a total taking of the Property, the proceeds shall be applied to the sums secured by this Security Instrument, whether or not then due, with any excess paid to Borrower. In the event of a partial taking of the Property, unless Borrower and Lender otherwise agree in writing, the sums secured by this Security Instrument shall be reduced by the amount of the proceeds multiplied by the following fraction: (a) the total amount of the sums secured immediately before the taking, divided by (b) the fair market value of the Property immediately before the taking. Any balance shall be paid to Borrower.

If the Property is abandoned by Borrower, or if, after notice by Lender to Borrower that the condemnor offers to make an award or settle a claim for damages, Borrower fails to respond to Lender within 30 days after the date the notice is given, Lender is authorized to collect and apply the proceeds, at its option, either to restoration or repair of the Property or to the sums secured by this Security Instrument, whether or not then due.

Unless Lender and Borrower otherwise agree in writing, any application of proceeds to principal shall not extend or postpone the due date of the monthly payments referred to in paragraphs 1 and 2 or change the amount of such payments.

Figure 15.4 (cont.)

10. Borrower Not Released; Forbearance By Lender Not a Waiver. Extension of the time for payment or modification of amortization of the sums secured by this Security Instrument granted by Lender to any successor in interest of Borrower shall not operate to release the liability of the original Borrower or Borrower's successors in interest. Lender shall not be required to commence proceedings against any successor in interest or refuse to extend time for payment or otherwise modify amortization of the sums secured by this Security Instrument by reason of any demand made by the original Borrower or Borrower's successors in interest. Any forbearance by Lender in exercising any right or remedy shall not be a waiver of or preclude the exercise of any right or remedy.

11. Successors and Assigns Bound; Joint and Several Liability; Co-signers. The covenants and agreements of this Security Instrument shall bind and benefit the successors and assigns of Lender and Borrower, subject to the provisions of paragraph 17. Borrower's covenants and agreements shall be joint and several. Any Borrower who co-signs this Security Instrument but does not execute the Note: (a) is co-signing this Security Instrument only to mortgage, grant and convey that Borrower's interest in the Property under the terms of this Security Instrument; (b) is not personally obligated to pay the sums secured by this Security Instrument; and (c) agrees that Lender and any other Borrower may agree to extend, modify, forbear or make any accommodations with regard to the terms of this Security Instrument or the Note without that Borrower's consent.

12. Loan Charges. If the loan secured by this Security Instrument is subject to a law which sets maximum loan charges, and that law is finally interpreted so that the interest or other loan charges collected or to be collected in connection with the loan exceed the permitted limits, then: (a) any such loan charge shall be reduced by the amount necessary to reduce the charge to the permitted limit; and (b) any sums already collected from Borrower which exceeded permitted limits will be refunded to Borrower. Lender may choose to make this refund by reducing the principal owed under the Note or by making a direct payment to Borrower. If a refund reduces principal, the reduction will be treated as a partial prepayment without any prepayment charge under the Note.

13. Legislation Affecting Lender's Rights. If enactment or expiration of applicable laws has the effect of rendering any provision of the Note or this Security Instrument unenforceable according to its terms, Lender, at its option, may require immediate payment in full of all sums secured by this Security Instrument and may invoke any remedies permitted by paragraph 19. If Lender exercises this option, Lender shall take the steps specified in the second paragraph of paragraph 17.

14. Notices. Any notice to Borrower provided for in this Security Instrument shall be given by delivering it or by mailing it by first class mail unless applicable law requires use of another method. The notice shall be directed to the Property Address or any other address Borrower designates by notice to Lender. Any notice to Lender shall be given by first class mail to Lender's address stated herein or any other address Lender designates by notice to Borrower. Any notice provided for in this Security Instrument shall be deemed to have been given to Borrower or Lender when given as provided in this paragraph.

15. Governing Law; Severability. This Security Instrument shall be governed by federal law and the law of the jurisdiction in which the Property is located. In the event that any provision or clause of this Security Instrument or the Note conflicts with applicable law, such conflict shall not affect other provisions of this Security Instrument or the Note which can be given effect without the conflicting provision. To this end the provisions of this Security Instrument and the Note are declared to be severable.

16. Borrower's Copy. Borrower shall be given one conformed copy of the Note and of this Security Instrument.

17. Transfer of the Property or a Beneficial Interest in Borrower. If all or any part of the Property or any interest in it is sold or transferred (or if a beneficial interest in Borrower is sold or transferred and Borrower is not a natural person) without Lender's prior written consent, Lender may, at its option, require immediate payment in full of all sums secured by this Security Instrument. However, this option shall not be exercised by Lender if exercise is prohibited by federal law as of the date of this Security Instrument.

If Lender exercises this option, Lender shall give Borrower notice of acceleration. The notice shall provide a period of not less than 30 days from the date the notice is delivered or mailed within which Borrower must pay all sums secured by this Security Instrument. If Borrower fails to pay these sums prior to the expiration of this period, Lender may invoke any remedies permitted by this Security Instrument without further notice or demand on Borrower.

18. Borrower's Right to Reinstate. If Borrower meets certain conditions, Borrower shall have the right to have enforcement of this Security Instrument discontinued at any time prior to the earlier of: (a) 5 days (or such other period as applicable law may specify for reinstatement) before sale of the Property pursuant to any power of sale contained in this Security Instrument; or (b) entry of a judgment enforcing this Security Instrument. Those conditions are that Borrower: (a) pays Lender all sums which then would be due under this Security Instrument and the Note had no acceleration occurred; (b) cures any default of any other covenants or agreements; (c) pays all expenses incurred in enforcing this Security Instrument, including, but not limited to, reasonable attorneys' fees; and (d) takes such action as Lender may reasonably require to assure that the lien of this Security Instrument, Lender's rights in the Property and Borrower's obligation to pay the sums secured by this Security Instrument shall continue unchanged. Upon reinstatement by Borrower, this Security Instrument and the obligations secured hereby shall remain fully effective as if no acceleration had occurred. However, this right to reinstate shall not apply in the case of acceleration under paragraphs 13 or 17.

BY SIGNING BELOW, Borrower accepts and agrees to the terms and covenants contained in this Security Instrument and in any rider(s) executed by Borrower and recorded with it.

Thomas Perkins ....(Seal)
—Borrower

Celia Perkins ....(Seal)
—Borrower

**Figure 15.5
Trust Deed**

GEORGE E. COLE·
LEGAL FORMS

FORM NO. 2604
February, 1985

TRUST DEED AND NOTE
(ILLINOIS)

CAUTION: Consult a lawyer before using or acting under this form. *Neither the publisher nor the seller of this form makes any warranty with respect thereto, including any warranty of merchantability or fitness for a particular purpose.*

THIS INDENTURE WITNESSETH, That the undersigned as grantors, of _Chicago_ , County of _Cook_ and State of _Illinois_ , for and in consideration of the sum of One Dollar and other good and valuable considerations, in hand paid, convey and warrant to _First Security Title and Trust_ , of _Chicago_ , County of _Cook_ and State of _Illinois_ , as trustee, the following described Real Estate, with all improvements thereon, situated in the County of _Cook_ in the State of Illinois, to-wit:

Lot 7, Block 23, Uptown Subdivision of the Northwest quarter of Section 14, Township 9 North, Range 3 east of the Third Principal Meridian in Cook County, Illinois,

Above Space For Recorder's Use Only

hereby releasing and waiving all rights under and by virtue of the homestead exemption laws of the State of Illinois.

Permanent Real Estate Index Number(s): _1-006699-74311_

Address(es) of Real Estate: _4830 Uptown Road, Chicago, Illinois 60000_

GRANTORS AGREE to pay all taxes and assessments upon said property when due, to keep the buildings thereon insured to their full insurable value, to pay all prior incumbrances and the interest thereon and to keep the property tenantable and in good repair and free of liens. In the event of failure of grantors to comply with any of the above covenants, then grantee is authorized to attend to the same and pay the the bills therefor, which shall, with 9% interest thereon, become due immediately, without demand. On default in any payments hereunder, grantee may declare the whole indebtedness due and proceed accordingly.

AS FURTHER SECURITY grantors hereby assign, transfer and set over to grantee all the rents, issues and profits of said premises, from and after this date, and authorize him to sue for, collect and receipt for the same, to serve all necessary notices and demands, to bring forcible detainer proceedings to recover possession thereof, to rent the said premises as he may deem proper and to apply the money so arising to the payment of this indebtedness, or to any advancements made as aforesaid, and it shall not be the duty of grantee to inquire into the validity of any such taxes, assessments, liens, incumbrances, interest or advancements.

In trust, nevertheless, for the purpose of securing performance of the following obligation, to-wit:

$ _137,000.00_ _June 26_ 19_87_ after date for value received I (we) promise to pay to the order of _One City Savings and Loan Association_ the sum of _One Hundred thirty-seven thousand and xx/100————————————————————_ Dollars at the office of the legal holder of this instrument with interest at _10_ per cent per annum after date hereof until paid, payable at said office, as follows: _180 monthly payments of $1,472.22 each including interest and principal, one payment being due on the first day of each month beginning on August 1_, 1987.

And to secure the payment of said amount I (we) hereby authorize, irrevocably any attorney of any court of record in any County or State in the United States to appear for us in such court, in term time or vacation, at any time after maturity hereof, and confess a judgment without process in favor of the holder of this instrument for such amount as may appear to be unpaid thereon, together with costs, and reasonable attorney's fees, and to waive and release all errors which may intervene in any such proceedings, and to consent to immediate execution upon such judgment, hereby ratifying and confirming all that my (our) said attorney may do by virtue hereof.

IN THE EVENT of the trustee's death, inability, or removal from said _Cook_ County, or of his resignation, refusal or failure to act, then _Pioneer Title Company_ , of said County, is hereby appointed to be the first successor in this trust; and if for any like cause first successor fails or refuses to act, the person who shall then be the acting Recorder of Deeds of said County is hereby appointed to be second successor in this trust. And when all the aforesaid covenants and agreements are performed the trustee, or his successor in trust, shall release the premises to the party entitled thereto on receiving his reasonable charges.

If any provision of this indenture shall be prohibited by or invalid under applicable law, such provision shall be ineffective to the extent of such prohibition or invalidity, without invalidating or affecting the remainder of such provision or the remaining provisions of this indenture.

Witness our hands and seals this _26th_ day of _June_ , 19_87_ .

PLEASE
PRINT OR
TYPE NAME(S)
BELOW
SIGNATURE(S)

J. W. Baker (SEAL)

Rebecca Ann Taylor Baker (SEAL)

This instrument was prepared by _Carey Eileen Carpenter, Attorney-at-Law, 75 State St. Chicago, IL._
(NAME AND ADDRESS)

George E. Cole legal forms are reprinted with permission of Boise Cascade Office Products Corporation.

Provisions for Default

The provisions typically include an **acceleration clause** to assist the lender in foreclosure. If a borrower defaults, the lender has the right to accelerate the maturity of the debt—to declare the *entire* debt due and payable *immediately*—even though the terms of the mortgage or trust deed allow the borrower to amortize the debt in regular payments over a period of years. Without the acceleration clause, the lender would have to sue the borrower every time a payment became due and in default.

Other clauses in a mortgage or trust deed enable the lender to take care of the property in the event of the borrower's negligence or default. If the borrower does not pay taxes or insurance premiums or make necessary repairs on the property, the lender may step in and do so to protect the security (the real estate). Any money advanced by the lender to cure such defaults is either added to the unpaid debt or declared immediately due and owing from the borrower.

Assignment of the Mortgage

As mentioned earlier, a note is a negotiable instrument; as such, it may be sold to a third party. The mortgagee will endorse the note to the third party and also execute an *assignment of mortgage* or *assignment of deed of trust*. The assignee becomes the new owner of the debt and security instrument. This assignment must be recorded. Upon payment in full, or satisfaction of the debt, the assignee is required to execute the satisfaction, or release, of the security instrument as discussed in the following section. In the event of a foreclosure, the assignee is required to file the suit.

Release of the Mortgage Lien

When all mortgage loan payments have been made and the note paid in full, the mortgagor wants the public record to show that the debt has been paid and the mortgage released. By the provisions of the **defeasance clause** in the usual mortgage document, when the note has been fully paid the mortgagee is required to execute a **satisfaction of mortgage,** also known as a *release of mortgage* or *mortgage discharge*. This document reconveys to the mortgagor all interest in the real estate that was conveyed to the mortgagee by the original recorded mortgage document. By having this release entered in the public record, the owner shows that the mortgage lien has been removed from the property.

If a mortgage has been assigned by a recorded assignment, the release must be executed by the assignee mortgagee.

When a real estate loan secured by a trust deed has been completely repaid, the beneficiary requests in writing that the trustee convey the property back to the grantor. The trustee then executes and delivers a **release deed,** sometimes called a *deed of reconveyance,* to the grantor conveying the same rights and powers that the trustee was given under the trust deed. The release deed should be acknowledged and recorded in the public records of the county where the property is located.

Tax and Insurance Reserves

Many lenders require borrowers to provide a reserve fund, called an *impound* or *escrow account,* to meet future real estate taxes and insurance premiums. When the mortgage or trust deed loan is made, the borrower starts the reserve by depositing funds to cover the amount of unpaid real estate taxes prorated from the lien date to the end of the current month. If a new insurance policy has just been purchased, the insurance premium reserve will be started with the deposit of one-twelfth of the annual tax and insurance premium liability. Thereafter, the monthly loan payments required of the borrower will include interest, principal, and tax and insurance reserves.

RESPA, the federal Real Estate Settlement Procedures Act (discussed in Chapter 23), limits the total amount of reserves that may be required by a lender.

Federal flood insurance program. As described in Chapter 4, this subsidized plan authorized by Congress requires property owners in certain areas to obtain flood-damage insurance on properties financed by mortgages or other loans, grants or guarantees obtained from federal agencies and federally insured or regulated lending institutions. The program seeks to improve future management and planning of flood-plain areas through land-use and control measures.

Assignment of Rents

The borrower may make an assignment of rents to the lender, to be effective upon the borrower's default. The rent assignment may be included in the mortgage or trust deed, or it may be made as a separate document. In either case, the rent assignment should be drafted in language that clearly indicates that the parties intend to assign the rents, and not merely to pledge them as security for the loan. In title theory states, the lender is, in most cases, automatically entitled to any rents if the borrower defaults.

Buying Subject to or Assuming a Seller's Mortgage or Trust Deed

A person who purchases real estate that has an outstanding mortgage or trust deed on it may take the property subject to the mortgage or may assume it and agree to pay the debt. This technical distinction becomes important if the buyer defaults and the mortgage or trust deed is foreclosed.

When the property is sold *subject to* the mortgage, the courts frequently hold that the purchaser is not personally obligated to pay the debt in full. The purchaser has bought the real estate knowing that he or she must make the loan payments and that, upon default, the lender will foreclose and the property will be sold by court order to pay the debt. If the sale does not pay off the entire debt, the purchaser is not liable for the difference; however, the original seller might still be liable for that difference. In contrast, when the grantee purchases the property and *assumes and agrees to pay* the seller's debt, then the grantee becomes personally obligated for the payment of the *entire debt.* If the mortgage is foreclosed in such a case and the court sale does not bring enough money to pay the debt in full, a deficiency judgment against the assumer may be obtained for the unpaid balance of the note. Note that the lender must agree to the assumption, and a release of liability must be given to the original borrower; otherwise, the original borrower is also liable for the unpaid balance. Most states recognize this distinction.

Before a conventional mortgage may be assumed, most lending institutions require the assumer to qualify financially. The lender will usually charge a transfer fee to cover the costs of changing their records. This charge is customarily borne by the purchaser.

A desirable feature of FHA-insured and VA-guaranteed loans is their easy assumability. These types of loans are discussed later in this chapter.

Alienation clause. Frequently, when a conventional real estate loan is made, the lender wishes to prevent some future purchaser of the property from being able to assume that loan, particularly at its old rate of interest. For this reason, some lenders include an **alienation clause** (also known as a *resale clause, due-on-sale clause* or *call clause*) in the note. An alienation clause provides that upon the sale of the property by the borrower to a buyer who wants to assume the loan, the lender has the choice of either declaring the entire debt to be immediately due and owing or permitting the buyer to assume the loan at current market interest rates. Government-backed loans generally prohibit use of alienation clauses.

Recording Mortgages and Trust Deeds

The mortgage document or trust deed must be recorded in the recorder's office of the county in which the real estate is located. The recordation gives constructive notice to the world of the borrower's obligations and establishes the lien's priority. If the property is registered in Torrens, notice of the lien must be entered on the original certificate of title on file at the registrar's office. *First Recorded First in Line.*

First and Second Mortgages or Trust Deeds

Mortgages and other liens normally have priority in the order in which they have been recorded. A mortgage or trust deed on land that has no prior mortgage lien on it is a *first mortgage* or *first trust deed*. When the owner of this land later executes another loan for additional funds, the new loan becomes a *second mortgage or trust deed,* or a *junior lien,* when recorded. The second lien is subject to the first lien; the first has prior claim to the value of the land pledged as security. Because second loans represent a greater risk to the lender, they are usually issued at higher interest rates.

The priority of mortgage or trust deed liens may be changed by the execution of a *subordination agreement,* in which the first lender subordinates his or her lien to that of the second lender. To be valid, such an agreement must be signed by both lenders.

Foreclosure

When a borrower defaults in making payments or fulfilling any of the obligations set forth in the mortgage or trust deed, the lender can enforce his or her rights through a foreclosure. A **foreclosure** is a legal procedure whereby the property that is pledged as security in the mortgage document or trust deed is sold to satisfy the debt. The foreclosure procedure brings the rights of the parties and all junior lienholders to a conclusion and passes title in the subject property to either the person holding the mortgage document or trust deed or to a third party who purchases the realty at a *foreclosure sale*. Property thus sold is *free of the mortgage and all junior liens.*

Methods of Foreclosure

There are three general types of foreclosure proceedings—judicial, nonjudicial and strict foreclosure. The specific provisions of these vary from state to state.

Court ordered

Judicial foreclosure. A judicial foreclosure proceeding provides that the property pledged as security may be sold by court order after the mortgagee has given sufficient public notice. Upon a borrower's default, the lender may *accelerate* the due date of all remaining monthly payments. The lender's attorney can then file a suit to foreclose the lien. Upon presentation of the facts in court, the property is ordered sold. A public sale is advertised and held, and the real estate is sold to the highest bidder.

Nonjudicial foreclosure. Other states allow nonjudicial foreclosure procedures to be used when a *power-of-sale clause* is contained in the security instrument. In those states that recognize trust deed loans, the trustee is generally given the power of sale. Some states allow a similar power of sale to be used with a mortgage loan.

To institute a nonjudicial foreclosure, the trustee (or mortgagee) must record a notice of default at the county recorder's office within a designated time period in order to give notice to the public of the intended auction. This official notice is generally accompanied by advertisements published in local newspapers that state the total amount due and the date of the public sale. The purpose of this notice is to publicize the sale. After selling the property, the trustee (or mortgagee) may be required to file a copy of a notice of sale or affidavit of foreclosure.

Strict foreclosure. Although the judicial and nonjudicial foreclosure procedures are the prevalent practices today, in some states it is still possible for a lender to acquire the mortgaged property by a strict foreclosure process. After appropriate notice has been given to the delinquent borrower and the proper papers have been prepared and filed, the court establishes a specific time period during which the balance of the defaulted debt must be paid in full. If this is not done, the court usually awards full legal title to the lender.

Deed in Lieu of Foreclosure

An alternative to foreclosure would be for the lender to accept, or "buy," a *deed in lieu of foreclosure* from the borrower. This is sometimes known as a *friendly foreclosure,* for it is by agreement rather than by civil action. The major disadvantage to this manner of default settlement is that the mortgagee takes the real estate subject to all junior liens; foreclosure eliminates all such liens.

Redemption

Most states give defaulting borrowers a chance to redeem their property. In most such cases redemption takes one of two forms—equitable redemption or statutory redemption.

Historically, the **right of redemption** is inherited from the old common-law proceedings in which the court sale ended the *equitable right of redemption.* Carried over to statutory law, this concept provides that if, during the course of a foreclosure proceeding but *before the foreclosure sale,* the borrower or any other person who has an interest in the real estate (such as another creditor) pays the lender the amount currently due, plus costs, the debt will be reinstated as before. In some cases, the person who redeems may be required to repay the accelerated loan in full. If some person other than the mortgagor or trustor redeems the real estate, the borrower becomes responsible to that person for the amount of the redemption.

As discussed earlier, many states also allow defaulted borrowers a period in which to redeem their real estate *after the sale.* During this *statutory redemption* period (which may be as long as one year) the court may appoint a receiver to take charge of the property, collect rents, pay operating expenses and so forth. The mortgagor or trustor who can raise the necessary funds to redeem the property within the statutory period pays the redemption money to the court. Since the debt was paid from the proceeds of the sale, the borrower then can take possession free and clear of the former defaulted loan.

Deed to Purchaser at Sale

If redemption is not made or if no redemption period is allowed by state law, then the successful bidder at the sale receives a deed to the real estate. This is a statutory form of deed that may be executed by a sheriff or master-in-chancery to *convey such title as the borrower had* to the purchaser at the sale. There are no warranties with such a deed; the title passes as is, but free of the former defaulted debt. It is possible to procure a title insurance policy in such a case, however.

Deficiency Judgment

If the foreclosure sale of the real estate secured by a mortgage or trust deed does not produce a sufficient sales price to pay the loan balance in full after deducting expenses and accrued unpaid interest, the mortgagee may be entitled to a *personal judgment* against the maker of the note for the unpaid balance. Such a judgment is called a **deficiency judgment.** It may also be obtained against any endorsers or guarantors of the note and any owners of the mortgaged property who may have assumed the debt by written agreement. If there are any surplus proceeds from the foreclosure sale after the debt and all junior liens (second mortgage, mechanic's lien and so on) are paid off and expenses and interest are deducted, these proceeds are paid to the borrower.

Loans

Most mortgage and trust deed loans are classified as to whether or not they are conventional loans. Loans are classified as **conventional** when the payment of the debt rests primarily upon the ability of the borrower to pay, with security provided by the mortgage or trust deed. Repayment of other loans is additionally secured through insurance issued by the Federal Housing Administration (FHA) or by a guarantee made by the Veterans Administration (VA).

Conventional Loans

In making conventional loans, lenders rely primarily on their own appraisal of the security and their own credit reports and information concerning the credit reliability of the prospective borrower. Because such loans are increasingly sold in the secondary mortgage market (discussed later), borrower qualifications have become somewhat stricter in recent years.

FHA-Insured Loans

The Federal Housing Administration (FHA) was created in 1934 under the National Housing Act to encourage improvement in housing standards and conditions, provide an adequate home-financing system through insurance of housing credit and to exert a stabilizing influence on the mortgage market. The FHA was the government's response to the lack of housing, excessive foreclosures and the collapsed building industry that occurred during the Depression.

The FHA, which operates under the Department of Housing and Urban Development (HUD), neither builds homes nor lends money itself. Rather, *it insures loans on real property made by approved lending institutions.* It does not insure the property, but it does insure the lender against loss. The common term **FHA loan,** then, refers to a loan that is not made by the agency but insured by it.

The most popular FHA program is Title II, Section 203(b), which applies to loans on one- to four-family residences. Although interest rates on these loans are no longer fixed by the FHA, such rates generally are one-half percent lower than those charged under conventional loans. These rates are usually lower because the protection of the FHA mortgage insurance makes them a lesser risk to the lender. Technical requirements established under congressional authority must be met before the FHA will issue the insurance. Three of these requirements are:

Paid by Buyer

1. In addition to paying interest, the *borrower is now charged a one-time mortgage insurance premium for the FHA insurance.* This amount may be paid at closing by the borrower or someone else, or it may be added to the loan amount.

2. The mortgaged real estate must be appraised by an *approved FHA appraiser.* The loan amount insured generally cannot exceed 97 percent on the first $25,000 of appraised value or purchase price, whichever is less, and 95 percent of the remainder. For a single-family owner-occupied house or condominium with a maximum appraised value or purchase price (whichever is less) of $50,000 (including closing costs), the maximum loan is 97 percent of the entire appraised value. For houses less than one year old, and not insured prior to the beginning of construction, the loan ratio is 90 percent of the appraised value or selling price, whichever is less. Note that if the purchase price exceeds the FHA-appraised value, the buyer may pay the difference in cash as part of the down payment. In addition, the FHA has set maximum loan amounts for various regions of the country. Contact your local FHA office for such amounts in your area. FHA regulations require that both buyer and seller sign a statement indicating that they have examined the FHA appraisal.

3. The FHA regulations set *standards* for type and construction of buildings, quality of neighborhood, and credit requirements for borrowers.

Prepayment privileges. When a mortgage or trust deed loan is insured by the FHA and the real estate given as security is a single-family dwelling or an apartment building with no more than four units, the borrower retains the privilege of prepaying the debt without penalty. On the first day of any month before the loan matures, the borrower may pay the entire debt or an amount equal to one or more monthly payments on the principal. The borrower must give the lender written notice of intention to exercise this privilege at least 30 days beforehand, or the lender has the option of charging up to 30 days' interest in lieu of such notification.

Other FHA loan programs. In addition to loans made under Title II, Section 203(b), as previously discussed, FHA loans are also granted under the following programs:

1. Title I: Home improvement loans are covered under this title; such loans are for relatively low amounts with a repayment term of no longer than seven years and 32 days.
2. Title II, §234: Loans made to purchase condominiums are covered under this program, which in most respects is similar to the basic 203(b) program.
3. Title II, §245: Graduated payment mortgages, as discussed in this chapter, are allowed under this program; depending on interest rates, the loan-to-value ratio of such loans might range from 87 to 93 percent.

Points. Since December 1, 1983, a lender of an FHA-insured loan can charge *points* in addition to a one percent loan fee. A point is one percent of the loan amount. The effective yield to the lender is increased by roughly one-eighth of one percent for each point charged. The FHA limits seller contributions (including discount points, temporary buydown costs and closing costs) to five percent of the property's acquisition cost. With that limitation, payment of points is a matter of negotiation between buyer and seller.

Private Mortgage Insurance

Aside from the FHA, mortgage insurance may also be obtained through private sources. Under the provisions of such privately insured lending programs, home purchasers can obtain conventional mortgage or trust deed loans of up to 95 percent of the appraised property value at prevailing interest rates and reasonable insurance premium costs. The leader in this field is the *Mortgage Guaranty Insurance Corporation (MGIC)* of Milwaukee, Wisconsin, which instituted the program in 1957.

VA-Guaranteed (GI) Loans

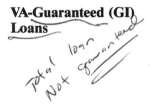

Under the Servicemen's Readjustment Act of 1944 and subsequent federal legislation, the Veterans Administration is authorized to guarantee loans to purchase or construct homes for eligible veterans—those who have served a minimum of 181 days' active service since September 16, 1940 (90 days for veterans of World War II, the Korean War, and the Viet Nam conflict; two full years for those enlisting for the first time after September 7, 1980). The VA also guarantees loans to purchase mobile homes and plots on which to place them. GI loans assist veterans in financing the purchase of homes with little or no down payments, at comparatively low interest rates. Rules and regulations are issued from time to time by the VA, setting forth the qualifications, limitations and conditions under which a loan may be guaranteed. (Table 15.1 is a comparison of VA and FHA loan programs.)

Like the term *FHA loan,* **VA loan** is something of a misnomer. The VA does not normally lend money itself; it guarantees loans made by lending institutions approved by the agency. The term *VA loan,* then, refers to a loan that is not made by the agency but guaranteed by it.

There is no VA limit on the amount of the loan a veteran can obtain; this is determined by the lender. The VA does, however, set a limit on the amount of the loan that it will guarantee, currently 60 percent of the loan amount or $27,500, whichever is less, in the purchase, construction, repair or alteration of a house, condominium or farm residence.

Note that the $27,500 figure (or 60 percent) is the amount of the guarantee and refers to the amount the lender would receive from the VA in the case of a default and foreclosure if the sale did not bring enough to cover the outstanding balance.

To determine what portion of a mortgage loan the VA will guarantee, the veteran must apply for a *certificate of eligibility.* This certificate does not mean that the veteran will automatically receive a mortgage. It merely sets forth the maximum guarantee the veteran is entitled to.

The VA will also issue a *certificate of reasonable value* (CRV) for the property being purchased, stating its current market value based on a VA-approved appraisal. The CRV places a ceiling on the amount of a VA loan allowed for the property; if the purchase price is greater than the amount cited in the CRV, the veteran may pay the difference in cash.

Only in certain situations (such as in isolated rural areas) where financing is not reasonably available does the VA actually lend money; ordinarily, a veteran obtains a loan from a VA-approved lending institution. The VA does not require a down payment. Although the VA guarantee is never more than $27,500, in practice the veteran may be able to obtain a 100 percent loan if the appraised valuation of the property is $110,000 or less and the veteran is entitled to a full $27,500 (the usual 25 percent down payment) guarantee.

Table 15.1 Comparison of FHA and VA Loan Programs	Federal Housing Administration	Veterans Administration
	1. Financing is available to veterans and nonveterans alike	1. Financing available only to veterans and certain unremarried widows and widowers
	2. Financing programs for owner-occupied, rental and other types of construction; owner-occupied has greater loan-to-value ratio	2. VA financing limited to owner-occupied residential (one- to four-family) dwellings—must sign occupancy certificate on two separate occasions
	3. Requires a larger down payment than VA	3. Does not normally require down payment, though lender may require small down payment
	4. Different evaluation methods; like VA, there are prescribed valuation procedures for the approved appraisers to follow	4. Methods of valuation differ—VA issues a certificate of reasonable value
	5. FHA valuation sets the maximum loan FHA will insure but does not limit the sales price	5. With regard to home loans, the VA loan may not exceed the appraised value of the home
	6. No prepayment penalty	6. No prepayment penalty
	7. On default, foreclosure and claim, the FHA lender usually gets U.S. debentures	7. Following default, foreclosure and claim, the lender usually receives cash
	8. Insures the loan by way of mutual mortgage insurance; premiums paid by borrower	8. Guarantees up to 60 percent of the loan or $27,500, whichever is less
	9. Discount points can be charged, payable by either seller (no more than 5 points) or buyer	9. Borrower prohibited from paying discount points (except in refinancing and certain defined circumstances)
	10. Borrower is subject to one percent loan origination fee; 2½ percent for buildings to be constructed	10. VA loan can be assumed by nonveteran without VA approval
	11. FHA loan can be assumed without FHA approval after two years	11. Borrower must pay VA a one percent funding fee at closing

Maximum loan terms are 30 years for one- to four-family dwellings and 40 years for farm loans. The interest rate cannot exceed the rate set periodically by the VA Administrator. Residential property purchased with a VA loan must be owner-occupied.

VA loans can be assumed by purchasers who do not qualify as veterans. The original veteran borrower remains liable for the loan unless a release of the liability is approved by the VA. A release would be possible if, for example, another veteran used his or her own entitlement in assuming the loan.

Prepayment. As with an FHA loan, the borrower under a VA loan can prepay the debt at any time without penalty. Also, the veteran will not be required to pay more than a one percent origination fee.

Points. Points are generally not payable by a veteran, but the VA allows lenders to charge reasonable closing costs plus a loan origination fee that may not exceed one percent of the loan amount. There is also a one percent funding fee which the veteran pays the VA at closing.

In Practice... *Regulations and requirements regarding FHA and VA loans change frequently. Check with local lenders, as well as with your local FHA and VA offices, from time to time for current information regarding these government-backed loan programs.*

Other Financing Techniques

By altering the terms of the basic mortgage or trust deed and note, a borrower and a lender can tailor financing instruments to best suit the type of transaction and the financial needs of both parties. Especially in times of tight, expensive mortgage money, such "creative financing" gains prominence. In addition, real estate may be financed using instruments other than mortgages and trust deeds, as will be discussed in the following section.

Purchase-Money Mortgages or Trust Deeds

[handwritten: Short period of time with a balloon payment]

A purchase-money mortgage or purchase-money deed of trust is given at the time of purchase to facilitate the sale. The term is used in two ways—to refer to *any* security instrument originating at the time of sale and (most often) to refer to the instrument *given by the purchaser to a seller who "takes back" a note for part or all of the purchase price.* It may be a first or second mortgage, and it becomes a lien on the property when the title passes. In the event of the foreclosure of a purchase-money mortgage or trust deed, the lien takes priority over judgment liens against the borrower, homestead exemptions of the borrower and spouse and (in some states) dower rights of the spouse.

Package Mortgages or Trust Deeds

A package loan not only includes the real estate, but also *expressly includes all fixtures and appliances installed on the premises.* In recent years, this kind of loan has been used extensively in financing furnished condominium units. Such loans usually include the kitchen range, refrigerator, dishwasher, garbage disposal unit, washer and dryer, food freezer and other appliances, as well as furniture, drapes and carpets, as part of the real estate in the sales price of the home.

Not all state courts agree that personal property (such as a washer and dryer) becomes real estate under these circumstances and thus subject to the package mortgage. You must determine whether or not the package mortgage is used in your state. The rights of a person who acquires a security interest in fixtures or in personal property that will become attached to real estate and thus become a fixture are usually defined in the *Uniform Commercial Code* (see Chapter 13).

Blanket Mortgages or Trust Deeds

[handwritten: One mortgage covering two or more lot coverage]

A blanket loan covers *more than one parcel or lot* and is usually used to finance subdivision developments (though it can be used to finance the purchase of improved properties as well). These loans usually include a provision, known as a *partial release clause,* that the borrower may obtain the release of any one lot or parcel from the lien by repaying a definite amount of the loan. The lender issues a partial release for each parcel released from the mortgage lien. This release form includes a provision that the lien will continue to cover all other unreleased lots.

Wraparound Encumbrances

A wraparound mortgage or trust deed, also known as an *overriding* or *all-inclusive mortgage* or *trust deed,* enables a borrower who is paying off an existing mortgage or trust deed loan to obtain additional financing from a second lender. *The new lender assumes payment of the existing loan and gives the borrower a new, increased loan at a higher interest rate.* The total amount of the new loan

[handwritten: have a mortgage and wrap a second mortgage around it.]

includes the existing loan as well as the additional funds needed by the borrower. The borrower makes payments to the new lender on the larger loan, and the new lender makes the payments on the original loan.

A wraparound mortgage is frequently used as a method of refinancing real property or financing the purchase of real property when an existing mortgage cannot be prepaid. It is also used to finance the sale of real estate when the buyer wishes to put up a minimum of initial cash for the sale. The buyer executes a wraparound document to the seller, who will collect payments on the new loan and continue to make payments on the old loan. The buyer should require a protective clause in the document granting the right to make payments directly to the original lender in the event of a potential default on the old loan by the seller.

In Practice...

A wraparound loan is possible only if the original loan permits such a refinancing. An acceleration, alienation or due-on-sale clause in the original loan documents may prevent a sale under such terms. A real estate licensee should neither encourage nor assist in any financing that violates loan provisions. To do so could result in suspension or revocation of the agent's license.

Open-End Mortgages or Trust Deeds

An open-end loan, a type which is being used with increasing frequency, secures a *note* executed by the borrower to the lender, as well as any future *advances* of funds made by the lender to the borrower or to the borrower's successors in title. The interest rate on the initial amount borrowed is fixed, but interest on future advances may be the market rate then in effect.

The mortgage or trust deed usually includes a statement of the maximum amount to be secured. Any sums the lender may have to pay to protect the security as a result of the borrower's neglect—for such items as taxes, assessments or insurance premiums—are added to this maximum amount.

Open-end mortgages frequently are used by borrowers to obtain additional funds in order to improve their property. The borrower "opens" the mortgage or trust deed to increase the debt to its original amount—after the debt has been reduced by payments over a period of time. The terms of an open-end mortgage usually restrict the increase in debt to a limit of either the original amount of the debt or a stipulated amount set forth in the mortgage or trust deed. The lender is not obligated to advance the additional funds.

Construction Loans

A construction loan is made to *finance the construction of improvements* on real estate (homes, apartments, office buildings and so forth). Under a construction loan, the lender commits the full amount of the loan but makes partial *progress payments* as the building is being constructed.

Progress payments are made to the *general contractor* for that part of the construction work that has been completed since the previous payment. Prior to each payment, the lender inspects the work. The general contractor must provide the lender with adequate waivers of lien releasing all mechanics' lien rights (see Chapter 10) for the work covered by the payment. This kind of loan generally bears a higher interest rate because of the risks assumed by the lender. These risks include the inadequate releasing of mechanics' liens just referred to, possible delays in completing the building or the financial failure of the contractor or subcontractors. This type of financing is generally *short-term, or interim, financing.* The borrower is expected to arrange for a permanent loan (also known as an *end loan* or *take-out loan*) that will repay or "take-out" the construction financing lender when the work is completed.

Sale and Leaseback

Sale-and-leaseback arrangements are used rather extensively as a means of financing large commercial or industrial plants. The land and building, usually used by the seller for business purposes, are sold to an investor, such as an insurance company. The real estate is then leased back by the buyer (the investor) to the seller, who continues to conduct business on the property as a tenant. The buyer becomes the lessor, and the original owner becomes the lessee. This enables a business firm that has money invested in a plant to free that money so it can be used as working capital.

Sale-and-leaseback arrangements are very complex. They involve complicated legal procedures, and their success is usually related to the effects the transaction has on the firm's tax situation. A real estate broker should advise the parties to consult with legal and tax experts when involved in this type of transaction.

Installment Contracts (Land Contracts)

As discussed in Chapter 11, real estate can be purchased under an *installment contract,* also known as a contract for deed, land contract or articles of agreement for warranty deed. Real estate is often sold on contract in one of two situations: (1) when mortgage financing is unavailable or too expensive and (2) when the purchaser does not have a sufficient down payment to cover the difference between a mortgage or trust deed loan and the selling price of the real estate.

Investment Group Financing

Large real estate projects, such as highrise apartment buildings, office complexes and shopping centers, are often financed as a joint venture through group financing arrangements, such as syndicates, limited partnerships and real estate investment trusts. These complex investment agreements are discussed in Chapter 22, "Real Estate Investment."

Sources of Real Estate Financing— The Primary Mortgage Market

Few people could afford, or would want, to pay all cash for real estate. Yet, real estate is a much-desired asset, and its desirability coupled with its scarcity have historically made it an appreciating and profitable investment.

The funds used to finance the purchase of real estate come from a variety of sources that comprise the **primary mortgage market**—lenders who supply funds to borrowers as an investment. Lenders may originate loans for the purpose of selling them to other investors as part of what is termed the *secondary mortgage market.* We will take a look at the secondary mortgage market later in this chapter.

By the 1980s, the total mortgage debt in the United States on residential and commercial property and farms exceeded $1,600 billion dollars. Savings and loan associations held approximately 29 percent of that debt; commercial banks, 18 percent; life insurance companies, 8½ percent; mutual savings banks, 6 percent; various federal agencies, 8½ percent; mortgage pools or trusts, 13 percent; and individuals, real estate investment trusts, credit unions, noninsured pension funds and others combined held 17 percent. The primary sources of real estate financing are discussed in this section.

Savings and Loan Associations

Savings and loan associations are the most active participants in the home-loan mortgage market, specializing in long-term residential loans. A savings and loan earns money by paying less for the funds it receives than it charges for the loans it makes. Loan income includes more than interest however—there are loan origination fees, loan assumption fees and others.

Services offered by savings and loan associations were given a boost by the Depository Institutions Deregulation and Monetary Control Act of 1980, which became fully effective in April, 1986. Deregulation has enabled the savings and loans to increase the interest rates paid to depositors and offer services previously unavailable, such as interest-bearing checking (NOW) accounts. The Garn-St. Germain Depository Act of 1982 allows federally chartered savings and loans to make overdraft loans on both business and NOW accounts, and has broadened the range of loans that can be offered.

Traditionally, savings and loan associations are the most flexible of all the lending institutions with regard to their mortgage lending procedures, and they are generally local in nature. In addition, they participate in FHA-insured and VA-guaranteed loans, though only to a limited extent.

All savings and loan associations must be chartered, either by the federal government or by the states in which they are located. *All* savings and loans are regulated by the Federal Home Loan Bank system (FHLB). The FHLB sets up mandatory guidelines for member associations and provides depositors with savings insurance through the Federal Savings and Loan Insurance Corporation (FSLIC).

Commercial Banks

Commercial banks are an important source of real estate financing. Primarily, bank loan departments handle such short-term loans as construction, home-improvement and mobile-home loans. In some areas, however, commercial banks are originating an increasing number of home mortgages. Commercial banks usually issue a larger proportion of VA and FHA loans than do savings and loan associations. Like the savings and loan associations, banks must be chartered by the state or federal government. Bank deposits are insured by the Federal Deposit Insurance Corporation (FDIC).

Mutual Savings Banks

These institutions, which operate like savings and loan associations, are located primarily in the northeastern section of the United States. They issue no stock and are mutually owned by their investors. Although mutual savings banks do offer limited checking account privileges, they are primarily savings institutions and are highly active in the mortgage market, investing in loans secured by income property as well as residential real estate. In addition, since mutual savings banks usually seek low-risk loan investments, they often prefer to originate FHA-insured or VA-guaranteed loans.

Life Insurance Companies

Insurance companies amass large sums of money from the premiums paid by their policyholders. While a certain portion of this money is held in reserve to satisfy claims and cover operating expenses, much of it is invested in profit-earning enterprises, such as long-term real estate loans.

Most insurance companies like to invest their money in large, long-term loans that finance commercial and industrial properties. They also invest in residential mortgage and trust deed loans by purchasing large blocks of government-backed loans (FHA-insured and VA-guaranteed loans) from the Federal National Mortgage Association and other agencies that warehouse such loans for resale in the secondary mortgage market (as discussed later in this chapter).

In addition, many life insurance companies seek to further ensure the safety of their investments by insisting on equity positions (known as *equity kickers*) in many projects they finance. This means that the company requires a partnership arrangement with, for example, a project developer or subdivider as a condition of making a loan. This is called *participation financing*.

Mortgage Banking Companies

Mortgage banking companies use money borrowed from other institutions and funds of their own to make real estate loans that may later be sold to investors (with the mortgage company receiving a fee for servicing the loans). Mortgage bankers are involved in all types of real estate loan activities and often serve as middlemen between investors and borrowers, but they are not mortgage brokers.

Mortgage banking companies are usually organized as stock companies. As a source of real estate financing, they are subject to considerably fewer lending restrictions than are commercial banks or savings and loans.

Credit Unions

Credit unions are cooperative organizations in which members place money in savings accounts, usually at higher interest rates than other savings institutions offer. In the past, most credit unions made only short-term consumer and home-improvement loans, but in recent years they have been branching out to originating longer-term first and second mortgage and trust deed loans.

Mortgage Brokers

This discussion ends with a group who are not lenders, but are often instrumental in obtaining financing. Mortgage brokers are individuals who are licensed to act as intermediaries in bringing borrowers and lenders together. They locate potential borrowers, process preliminary loan applications and submit the applications to lenders for final approval. Frequently, they work with or for mortgage banking companies in these activities. They are not involved in servicing a loan once it is made. Many mortgage brokers are also real estate brokers who offer these financing services in addition to their regular brokerage activities.

Application for Credit

All mortgage lenders require prospective borrowers to file an application for credit that provides the lender with the basic information needed to evaluate the acceptability of the proposed loan. The application includes information regarding the purpose of the loan, the amount, rate of interest and the proposed terms of repayment. This is considered a preliminary offer of a loan agreement; final terms may require lengthy negotiations.

A prospective borrower must submit personal information to the lender, including employment, earnings, assets and financial obligations. Details of the real estate that will be the security for the loan must be provided, including legal description, improvements, title, survey and taxes. For loans on income property or those made to corporations, additional information is required, such as financial and operating statements, schedules of leases and tenants, and balance sheets.

The lender carefully investigates the application information, studying credit reports and an appraisal of the property before deciding whether or not to grant the loan. The lender's acceptance of the application is written in the form of a *loan commitment,* which creates a contract to make a loan and sets forth the details. With borderline cases, a commitment may be made based on the lender's current financial position.

In Practice...   *Since interest rates and loan terms change frequently, you should check with local sources of real estate financing on a regular basis to learn of specific loan rates and terms. As a licensee, you can better serve your customers—and thus more effectively sell your clients' properties—if you can knowledgeably refer buyers to local lenders offering the most favorable terms.*

Government Influence in Mortgage Lending

Aside from FHA-insured and VA-guaranteed loan programs, the federal government influences mortgage lending through the Federal Reserve System as well as through various federal agencies, such as the Farmer's Home Administration. It also deals in the secondary mortgage market through the Government National Mortgage Association, the Federal Home Loan Mortgage Corporation and the Federal National Mortgage Association.

Federal Reserve System

Established in 1913 under President Woodrow Wilson, the Federal Reserve System (also known as "the Fed") operates to maintain sound credit conditions, help counteract inflationary and deflationary trends, and create a favorable economic climate. The Federal Reserve System divides the country into 12 federal reserve districts, each served by a federal reserve bank. All nationally chartered banks must join the Federal Reserve and purchase stock in its district reserve banks.

The Federal Reserve regulates the flow of money and interest rates in the marketplace indirectly, through its member banks, by controlling their *reserve requirements* and *discount rates.*

Reserve controls. The Federal Reserve requires each member bank to keep a certain amount of its assets on hand as reserve funds unavailable for loans or any other use. This requirement was designed primarily to protect customer deposits, but it also provides a means of manipulating the flow of cash in the money market. By increasing its reserve requirements, the Federal Reserve, in effect, limits the amount of money that member banks can use to make loans, thus causing interest rates to increase.

In this manner, the government can slow down an overactive economy by limiting the number of loans that would have been directed toward major purchases of goods and services. The opposite is also true—by decreasing the reserve requirements, the Federal Reserve can allow more loans to be made, thus increasing the amount of money circulated in the marketplace and causing interest rates to decline.

Discount rates. Federal Reserve member banks are permitted to borrow money from the district reserve banks to expand their lending operations. The interest rate that the district banks charge for the use of this money is called the discount rate. This rate is the basis on which the banks determine the percentage rate of interest that they, in turn, charge their loan customers. Theoretically, when the Federal Reserve discount rate is high, bank interest rates are high; therefore, fewer loans will be made and less money will circulate in the marketplace. Conversely, a lower discount rate results in lower interest rates, more bank loans and more money in circulation.

Government Influence in the Secondary Market

Mortgage lending takes place in both the primary and secondary mortgage markets. This chapter has principally dealt thus far with the primary market, lenders who originate loans. Loans are bought and sold in the **secondary mortgage market** only after they have been funded. For example, a lender may wish to sell a number of loans in order to raise immediate funds when it needs more money to meet the mortgage demands in its area. Secondary market activity is especially desirable when money is in short supply, because it provides a great stimulant to the housing construction market as well as to the mortgage market.

Generally, when a loan has been sold the original lender continues to collect the payments from the borrower. The lender then passes the payments along to the investor who has purchased the loan and charges the investor a fee for servicing the loan.

A major source of secondary mortgage market activity is a warehousing agency, which purchases a number of mortgage loans and assembles them into one or more packages of loans for resale to investors. The major warehousing agencies are the Federal National Mortgage Association (FNMA), the Government National Mortgage Association (GNMA) and the Federal Home Loan Mortgage Corporation (FHLMC).

Federal National Mortgage Association. The Federal National Mortgage Association (FNMA), often referred to as **Fannie Mae,** is a quasi-governmental agency, now organized as a privately owned corporation that issues its own common stock and provides a secondary market for mortgage loans—conventional as well as FHA and VA loans. FNMA will buy a *block* or *pool* of mortgages from a lender in exchange for *mortgage-backed securities* that the lender may keep or sell. FNMA guarantees payment of all interest and principal to the holder of the securities.

Mortgage banking firms are generally actively involved with FNMA, originating loans and selling them to FNMA while retaining the servicing functions.

Government National Mortgage Association. The common name for the Government National Mortgage Association (GNMA) is **Ginnie Mae.** It exists as a corporation without capital stock and is a division of the Department of Housing and Urban Development (HUD). GNMA is designed to administer special assistance programs and work with FNMA in secondary market activities. Fannie Mae and Ginnie Mae can join forces in times of tight money and high interest rates through their tandem plan. Basically, the *tandem plan* provides that FNMA can purchase high-risk, low-yield (usually FHA) loans at full market rates, with GNMA guaranteeing payment and absorbing the difference between the low yield and current market prices.

Ginnie Mae also guarantees investment securities issued by private offerors (such as banks, mortgage companies, and savings and loan associations) and backed by pools of FHA and VA mortgage loans. The *Ginnie Mae pass-through certificate* is a security interest in a pool of mortgages that provides for a monthly "pass-through" of principal and interest payments directly to the certificate holder. Such certificates are guaranteed by Ginnie Mae.

Federal Home Loan Mortgage Corporation. The Federal Home Loan Mortgage Corporation (FHLMC), or **Freddie Mac,** provides a secondary market for mortgage loans, primarily conventional loans. Freddie Mac has the authority to purchase mortgages, pool them and sell bonds in the open market with the mortgages as security. Note, however, that FHLMC does not guarantee payment of Freddie Mac mortgages.

Many lenders use the standardized forms and follow the guidelines issued by Freddie Mac, since use of FHLMC forms is mandatory for lenders who wish to sell mortgages in the agency's secondary mortgage market. The standardized documents include loan applications, credit reports and appraisal forms.

Farmer's Home Administration

The Farmer's Home Administration (FmHA) is a federal agency of the Department of Agriculture that was originally designed to handle emergency farm financing and that channels credit to farmers and rural residents, as well as to certain small communities. FmHA loan programs fall into two categories: (1) guaranteed loans, made and serviced by a private lender and guaranteed for a specific percentage by the FmHA and (2) insured loans that are originated, made and serviced by the agency.

Financing Legislation

The federal government regulates the lending practices of mortgage lenders through the Truth-in-Lending Act, Equal Credit Opportunity Act and the Real Estate Settlement Procedures Act.

Truth-in-Lending Act and Regulation Z

The **Truth-in-Lending Act** was put into effect on July 1, 1969, and was implemented by **Regulation Z** of the Federal Reserve Board. Regulation Z requires credit institutions to disclose to borrowers the true cost of obtaining credit so that the borrower can compare the costs of various lenders and avoid the uninformed use of credit. When credit is extended to individuals for personal, family or household uses, and the amount of credit is $25,000 or less, Regulation Z applies. If a credit transaction is secured by a residence, Regulation Z always applies, regardless of the amount. The regulation does not apply to business or commercial loans, nor to agricultural loans over $25,000.

The regulation requires that the consumer be fully informed of all finance charges, as well as the true annual interest rate, before a transaction is consummated. The finance charges must include any loan fees, finders' fees, service charges and points, as well as interest. In the case of a mortgage loan made to finance the purchase of a dwelling, the lender must compute and disclose the *annual percentage rate (APR)* but does not have to indicate the total interest payable during the term of the loan. Also, the lender does not have to include as part of the finance charge such actual costs as title fees, legal fees, appraisal fees, credit reports, survey fees and closing expenses.

Creditor. A *creditor,* for purposes of Regulation Z, is a person who extends consumer credit more than 25 times a year, or more than five times a year if the transaction involves a dwelling as security. The credit must be subject to a finance charge or payable in more than four installments by written agreement.

Disclosure statement. Truth-in-lending disclosures must be grouped together in a *disclosure statement,* with certain information set off by a box, a different type style, bold type or a different background color.

Three-day right of rescission. In the case of most consumer credit transactions covered by Regulation Z, the borrower has three days in which to rescind the transaction by merely notifying the lender. This right of rescission does not apply to residential purchase money, first mortgage or trust deed loans. In an emergency, the right to rescind may be waived in writing to prevent a delay in funding.

Advertising. Regulation Z provides strict regulation of real estate advertisements that include mortgage financing terms. General phrases like "liberal terms available" may be used, but if specifics are given they must comply with this act. By the provisions of the act, the APR—which includes all charges—rather than the interest rate alone *must be stated.* The total finance charge must be specified as well.

Specific credit terms, such as the down payment, monthly payment, dollar amount of the finance charge or term of the loan, may not be advertised unless the following information is set forth as well: cash price; required down payment; number, amounts and due dates of all payments; and annual percentage rate. The total of all payments to be made over the term of the mortgage must also be specified unless the advertised credit refers to a first mortgage or trust deed to finance acquisition of a dwelling.

Penalties. Regulation Z provides penalties for noncompliance. The penalty for violation of an administrative order enforcing Regulation Z is $10,000 for each day the violation continues. A fine of up to $10,000 may be imposed for engaging in an unfair or deceptive practice. In addition, a creditor may be liable to a consumer for twice the amount of the finance charge, for a minimum of $100 and a maximum of $1,000, plus court costs, attorney's fees and any actual damages. Willful violation is a misdemeanor punishable by a fine of up to $5,000 or one year's imprisonment, or both.

Federal Equal Credit Opportunity Act

The federal Equal Credit Opportunity Act (ECOA), in effect since 1975, prohibits lenders and others who grant or arrange credit to consumers from discriminating against credit applicants on the basis of race, color, religion, national origin, sex, marital status, age (provided the applicant is of legal age) or dependency upon public assistance. In addition, lenders and other creditors must inform all rejected credit applicants, in writing, within 30 days, of the principal reasons why credit was denied or terminated.

Real Estate Settlement Procedures Act

The federal Real Estate Settlement Procedures Act (RESPA) was created to ensure that the buyer and seller in a residential real estate transaction involving a new first mortgage loan have knowledge of all settlement costs. This important federal law will be discussed in detail in Chapter 23.

Summary

Mortgage and trust deed loans provide the principal sources of financing for real estate operations. Mortgage loans involve a borrower, called the *mortgagor,* and a lender, the *mortgagee.* Trust deed loans involve a third party, called the *trustee,* in addition to the borrower (the *trustor*) and the lender (the *beneficiary*).

Some states recognize the lender as the owner of mortgaged property; these are known as *title theory states.* Others recognize the borrower as the owner of mortgaged property and are known as *lien theory states.* A few *intermediary states* recognize modified versions of these theories.

After a lending institution has received, investigated and approved a loan application, it issues a commitment to make the mortgage loan. The borrower is required to execute a *note,* agreeing to repay the debt, and a *mortgage* or *trust deed,* placing a lien on the real estate to secure the note. The security instrument is recorded in order to give notice to the world of the lender's interest.

The note for the amount of the loan usually provides for *amortization* of the loan. The note also sets the rate of *interest* at which the loan is made and that the mortgagor or trustor must pay as a charge for borrowing the money. Types of loans include fully amortized, straight-line amortized and straight payment mortgages as well as adjustable rate mortgages, graduated payment mortgages, growing equity mortgages, renegotiable rate mortgages, shared appreciation mortgages and reverse annuity mortgages. The mortgage document or trust deed secures the debt and sets forth the obligations of the borrower and the rights of the lender. Payment in full of the note by its terms entitles the borrower to a satisfaction, or *release,* which is recorded to clear the lien from the public records. Default by the borrower may result in *acceleration* of payments, a *foreclosure* sale and, after the *redemption period* (if provided by state law), *loss of title.*

There are many types of mortgage and trust deed loans, including *conventional loans* and those *insured by the FHA or guaranteed by the VA.* FHA and VA loans must meet certain requirements in order for the borrower to obtain the benefits of the government backing, which induces the lender to lend its funds. The interest rates for these loans may be lower than those charged for conventional loans. Lenders may also charge *points.*

Other types of real estate financing include seller-financed purchase-money mortgages or trust deeds, blanket mortgages, package mortgages, wraparound mortgages, open-end mortgages, construction loans, sale-and-leaseback agreements, land contracts and investment group financing.

The federal government affects real estate financing money and interest rates through the Federal Reserve Board's *discount rate* and *reserve requirements;* it also participates in the *secondary mortgage market.* The secondary market is generally composed of the investors who ultimately purchase and hold the loans as investments. These include insurance companies, investment funds and pension plans. *Fannie Mae* (Federal National Mortgage Association), *Ginnie Mae* (Government National Mortgage Association) and *Freddie Mac* (Federal Home Loan Mortgage Corporation) take an active role in creating a secondary market by regularly purchasing mortgage and trust deed loans from originators and retaining, or warehousing, them until investment purchasers are available.

Regulation Z, implementing the federal Truth-in-Lending Act, requires lenders to inform prospective borrowers who use their homes as security for credit of *all finance charges* involved in such a loan. Severe penalties are provided for noncompliance. The federal *Equal Credit Opportunity Act* prohibits creditors from discriminating against credit applicants on the basis of race, color, religion, national origin, sex, marital status, age or dependency upon public assistance. The *Real Estate Settlement Procedures Act* requires lenders to inform both buyers and sellers in advance of all fees and charges required for the settlement or closing of a residential real estate transaction.

Questions

1. The McBains are purchasing a lakefront summer home in a new resort development. The house is completely equipped, and the McBains have obtained a trust deed loan that covers the purchase price of the residence, including furnishings and appliances. This kind of financing is called:

   a. a wraparound trust deed.
   b. a package trust deed. ✓
   c. a blanket trust deed.
   d. an unconventional trust deed.

2. In general, a promissory note:

   I. is a negotiable instrument.
   II. may be sold by the lender to a third party.

      a. I only   c. both I and II ✓
      b. II only   d. neither I nor II

3. With a fully amortized mortgage or trust deed loan:

   a. interest may be charged in arrears, meaning at the end of each period for which interest is due.
   b. the interest portion of each payment remains the same throughout the entire term of the loan.
   c. interest only is paid each period.
   d. a and b

4. Freddie Mac:

   a. mortgages are guaranteed by the full faith and credit of the federal government.
   b. buys and pools blocks of conventional mortgages, selling bonds with such mortgages as security.
   c. can tandem with GNMA to provide special assistance in times of tight money.
   d. buys and sells VA and FHA mortgages.

5. A loan charge of three points on a $120,000 loan is:

   a. $450.   c. $4,500.
   b. $116,400.   d. $3,600.

6. A developer has obtained a large loan in order to finance the construction of a planned unit development.

   I. This is a short-term loan, and the developer has arranged for long-term financing in order to repay it when the construction is completed.
   II. The borrowed money is disbursed in installments, and the lender inspects the construction that has been completed to date and ensures that all subcontractors and laborers have been properly paid before disbursing each installment of the loan.

      a. I only   c. both I and II ✓
      b. II only   d. neither I nor II

7. The Carters purchased a residence for $95,000. They made a down payment of $15,000 and agreed to assume the seller's existing mortgage, which had a current balance of $23,000. The Carters financed the remaining $57,000 of the purchase price by executing a mortgage and note to the seller. This type of loan, by which the seller becomes the mortgagee, is called a:

   a. wraparound mortgage.
   b. package mortgage.
   c. balloon note.
   d. purchase-money mortgage. ✓

8. In a sale and leaseback:

   I. the seller/vendor retains title to the real estate.
   II. the buyer/vendee gets possession of the property.

      a. I only   c. both I and II
      b. II only   d. neither I nor II ✓

9. In theory, when the Federal Reserve Board raises its discount rate, which of the following should happen?

   I. Interest rates will rise.
   II. Interest rates will fall.
   III. Mortgage money will become scarce.

      a. I only   c. I and III ✓
      b. II only   d. II and III

10. Which of the following best defines the *secondary market?*

    a. lenders who exclusively deal in second mortgages
    b. where loans are bought and sold after they have been originated
    c. the major lender of residential mortgages and trust deeds
    d. the major lender of FHA and VA loans

11. A loan at 9½% interest, originated with a charge of two points, has an effective rate of approximately:

    a. 11½ percent.   c. 9¾ percent.
    b. 9¼ percent.   d. 9.625 percent.

12. Which of the following is a participant in the secondary market?

    a. FNMA
    b. GNMA
    c. RESPA
    d. a and b

13. The person who obtains a real estate loan by signing a note and a mortgage is called the:

    a. mortgagor.
    b. beneficiary.
    c. mortgagee.
    d. vendor.

14. A borrower obtains a mortgage loan in order to make repairs on her home. The loan is not insured or guaranteed by a government agency, and the mortgage document secures the amount of the loan as well as any future funds advanced to the borrower by the lender. This borrower has obtained:

    a. a wraparound mortgage.
    b. a conventional loan.
    c. a land contract.
    d. a growing equity mortgage.

15. A graduated payment mortgage:

    a. allows for smaller payments to be made in the early years of the loan.
    b. allows for the debt's interest rate to increase or decrease from time to time, depending on certain economic factors.
    c. is also called a growing equity mortgage.
    d. all of the above

16. The borrower under a trust deed is known as the:

    a. trustor.   c. beneficiary.
    b. trustee.   d. vendee.

17. FHA-insured loans are made from funds furnished by:

    a. the FHA.
    b. private lenders approved by the FHA.
    c. the Fed.
    d. a and b

18. A borrower obtains a $76,000 mortgage loan at 10½ percent interest. If the monthly payments of $695.21 are credited first on interest and then on principal, what will the balance of the principal be after the borrower makes the first payment?

    a. $75,335.00   c. $75,969.79
    b. $75,943.33   d. $75,304.79

19. Regulation Z requires lenders to:

    I. properly inform buyers and sellers of commercial property of all settlement costs in a real estate transaction.
    II. inform prospective borrowers of all charges, fees and interest involved in making a home mortgage or trust deed loan.

    a. I only   c. both I and II
    b. II only   d. neither I nor II

20. The federal Equal Credit Opportunity Act prohibits lenders from discriminating against potential borrowers on the basis of which of the following?

    a. race   c. national origin
    b. sex   d. all of the above

21. Which of the following is an example of a conventional loan?

    a. a mortgage loan insured by the Federal Housing Administration
    b. a second loan for home improvements secured through a credit union
    c. a trust deed obtained through a private lender with a VA guarantee
    d. all of the above

22. A renegotiable rate mortgage is one in which:

    I. the lender profits from the property's appreciation when it is sold.
    II. the interest rate is lower in the early years of the loan and higher in later years, when the mortgagor's salary is expected to rise.

    a. I only   c. both I and II
    b. II only   d. neither I nor II

23. Which of the following is *not* a necessary element of a mortgage?
    a. signature of mortgagor
    b. date
    c. legal capacity of parties
    d. document in writing

24. Which of the following is true of a second mortgage?
    a. It has priority over a first mortgage.
    b. It cannot be used as a security instrument.
    c. It is not negotiable.
    d. It is usually issued at a higher rate of interest than a first mortgage.

25. Aunt Fran continues to live in the home she purchased 30 years ago, but she now receives monthly checks thanks to her:
    a. shared appreciation mortgage.
    b. adjustable rate mortgage.
    c. reverse annuity mortgage.
    d. overriding trust deed.

16

Leases

Overview

An owner of real property who does not wish to use the property personally or who wants to derive some measure of income from its ownership can allow it to be used by another person in exchange for consideration. The person who pays for the use of the property *leases* it from the owner. Generally, any type of real property may be leased. The apartment dweller as well as the commercial or industrial tenant may find it advantageous to lease real estate for a given period of time rather than purchase it. This chapter will examine the various leasehold estates a landlord and a tenant may enter into and the types and specific provisions of lease agreements commonly used in the real estate business.

Leasing Real Estate

A **lease** is a contract between an owner of real estate (known as the *lessor)* and a tenant (the *lessee*) that transfers the right to exclusive possession and use of the owner's property to the tenant for a specified period of time. This agreement generally sets forth the length of time the contract is to run, the amount to be paid by the lessee for the right to use the property, and other rights and obligations of the parties.

In effect, the lease agreement is a combination of a conveyance (of an interest in the real estate) and a contract (to pay rent and assume other obligations). The landlord (lessor) grants the tenant (lessee) the right to occupy the premises and use them for purposes stated in the lease. In return, the landlord retains the right to receive payment for the use of the premises as well as a reversionary right to retake possession after the lease term has expired. The lessor's interest in leased property is called a *leased fee estate plus reversionary right.*

The statute of frauds in most states requires that an agreement to lease real estate be in writing if it will not be performed within one year of the date of making. In other words, *a lease that will end more than one year from the day it was agreed to must be written.* It should also be signed by both lessor and lessee. A lease that will end in one year or less is usually enforceable if it is entered into orally.

In Practice...

Even though a particular lease may be enforceable if agreed to orally, such as a lease for one year commencing the day of agreement, it is always better practice to put lease agreements in writing and to have the writing signed by all parties to the agreement. The lease document should be as inclusive as possible, for reasons that will become apparent as you read this chapter.

Leasehold Estates

When a landowner leases his or her real estate to a tenant, the tenant's right to occupy the land for the duration of the lease is called a **leasehold estate.** A leasehold estate is an estate in land that is generally considered personal property. However, when the contract is a lease for life or for more than 99 years, under which the tenant assumes many of the landowner's obligations, certain states give the tenant some of the benefits and privileges of a property owner.

In the discussion of interests and estates in Chapter 7, freehold estates were differentiated from leasehold estates. Just as there are several types of freehold (ownership) estates, there are also various leasehold estates. The four most important are: (1) estate for years, (2) estate from period to period, (3) estate at will and (4) estate (tenancy) at sufferance (see table 16.1).

Estate for Years

A leasehold estate that continues for a *definite period of time*, whether for years, months, weeks or even days, is an **estate for years.** An estate for years (sometimes referred to as an *estate for term*) always has a specific starting and ending time and does not automatically renew itself at the end of the lease period. When that period expires, the lessee is required to vacate the premises and surrender possession to the lessor. No notice is required to terminate such a lease at the end of the lease period. A lease for years may be terminated prior to the expiration date by the mutual consent of both parties, but otherwise neither party may terminate without showing that the lease agreement has been breached. As is characteristic of all leases, a lease, or estate, for years gives the lessee the right to occupy and use the leased property—subject, of course, to the terms and covenants contained in the lease agreement itself, which is generally a written document.

Table 16.1 Leasehold Estates	Type of Estate	Distinguishing Characteristics
	Estate for Years	For definite period of time
	Estate from Period to Period	Automatically renews
	Estate at Will	For indefinite period of time
	Estate at Sufferance	Without landlord's consent

Estate from Period to Period

An **estate from period to period,** or *periodic tenancy,* is created when the landlord and tenant enter into an agreement that continues for a specific period, being *automatically renewed for an indefinite time without a specific ending date.* Rent is payable at definite intervals. Such a tenancy is generally created by agreement or operation of law to run for a certain amount of time; for instance, month to month, week to week, or year to year. The agreement is automatically renewed for similar succeeding periods until one of the parties gives notice to terminate. In effect, the payment and acceptance of rent extend the lease for another period.

A tenancy from period to period is usually created when a tenant with an estate for years remains in possession, or holds over, after the expiration of the lease term. If no new lease agreement has been made, the landlord may evict the tenant, or treat the holdover tenant as under a periodic tenancy. Acceptance of rent is usually considered conclusive proof of the landlord's acquiescence in a periodic tenancy. The courts customarily hold that a tenant who holds over can do so for a term equal to the term of the original lease, providing the period is for one year or less. (A longer term would require a written agreement.) Thus, if the original lease were for six months and the tenant held over, the courts would usually consider the new term to be for a like period, that is, six months. If the original lease were for five years, the new term could not exceed one year.

A **month-to-month tenancy** is generally created when a tenant takes possession with no definite termination date and pays rent on a monthly basis. Some leases stipulate that in the absence of a renewal agreement, a tenant who holds over does so as a month-to-month tenant. This is usually a valid agreement. In a few states, a holdover tenancy is considered a tenancy at will. (See the following discussion.)

In order to *terminate* a periodic estate, either the landlord or the tenant must give *proper notice.* The form of the notice and the time at which it must be given are usually set out in detail in the statutes of the various states. Normally, to terminate an estate from week to week, one week's notice is required; to terminate an estate from month to month, one month's notice is required. Notices of termination for an estate from year to year vary widely and usually require a minimum of two months' and a maximum of six months' notice.

Estate at Will

An estate that gives the tenant the right to possess with the *consent of the land-lord for a term of unspecified or uncertain duration,* is an **estate at will**, or *tenancy at will*. It may be created by express agreement or by operation of law, and during its existence the tenant has all the rights and obligations of a lessor-lessee relationship, including the payment of rent at regular intervals.

For example, at the end of a lease period, a landlord informs a tenant that in a few months the city is going to demolish the apartment building to make way for an expressway. The landlord gives the tenant the option to occupy the premises until demolition begins. If the tenant agrees to stay, a tenancy at will is created.

The term of an estate at will is indefinite, but the estate may be terminated by giving proper notice in accordance with the statutes of the state where the land is located. An estate at will is automatically terminated by the death of either the landlord or the tenant.

Estate at Sufferance

An **estate at sufferance**, or *tenancy at sufferance,* arises when a tenant who lawfully came into possession of real property continues, after his or her rights have expired, to hold possession of the premises *without the consent of the landlord.* Two examples of estates at sufferance are: (1) when a tenant for years *fails to surrender* possession at the expiration of the lease and (2) when a mortgagor, without consent of the purchaser, continues in possession after the foreclosure sale and expiration of the redemption period. The latter example is a tenancy at sufferance *by operation of law.* In some states, a tenant may be charged up to double rent for the period of possession as a tenant at sufferance.

Standard Lease Provisions

In determining the validity of a lease, the courts apply the rules governing contracts. If the intention to convey temporary possession of a certain parcel of real estate from one person to another is expressed, the courts generally hold that a lease has been created. Most states require no special wording to establish the landlord-tenant relationship. The lease may be written, oral or implied, depending on the circumstances and the requirements of the statute of frauds. The law of the state where the real estate is located must be followed to assure the validity of the lease. An example of a typical residential lease is figure 16.1.

Once a valid lease has been executed, the lessor, as the owner of the real estate, is usually bound by the **covenant of quiet enjoyment** that is implied by law. Under this covenant, the lessor guarantees that the lessee may take possession of the leased premises and that the landlord will not interfere in the tenant's possession or use of the property.

The requirements for a valid lease are essentially the same as those for any other contract. Generally, the essentials of a valid lease are:

1. *Offer and acceptance.* The parties must reach a mutual agreement on all the terms of the contract.
2. *Consideration.* All leases, being contracts, must be supported by valid consideration. In leasing real estate, *rent* is the normal consideration granted for the right to occupy the leased premises; however, the payment of rent is not essen-

Figure 16.1
Residential Lease
Agreement

APARTMENT LEASE — UNFURNISHED
(For Use In Illinois)

GEORGE E. COLE®
LEGAL FORMS

NO. L-17
FEBRUARY 1986

CAUTION: Consult a lawyer before using or acting under this form.
Neither the publisher nor the seller of this form makes any warranty with respect
thereto, including any warranty of merchantability or fitness for a particular purpose.

IF UNHEATED, CHECK HERE: ___
(SEE PARAGRAPH 11)

APARTMENT LEASE
UNFURNISHED

DATE OF LEASE	TERM OF LEASE		MONTHLY RENT	SECURITY DEPOSIT *
	BEGINNING	ENDING		
April 1, 1988	May 1, 1988	April 30, 1989	$800.00	$600.00

* IF NONE, WRITE "NONE". Paragraph 2 of this Lease then INAPPLICABLE.

LESSEE

NAME • J.P. Smithers

APT. NO. • 305

ADDRESS OF PREMISES • 248 West Windsor Drive
Chicago, Illinois 60000

LESSOR

NAME • Maddox Management

BUSINESS ADDRESS • 1309 West 45th Street
Chicago, Illinois 60000

In consideration of the mutual covenants and agreements herein stated, Lessor hereby leases to Lessee and Lessee hereby leases from Lessor for a private dwelling the apartment designated above (the "Premises"), together with the appurtenances thereto, for the above Term.

ADDITIONAL COVENANTS AND AGREEMENTS *(if any)*

Lessee will maintain smoke detector.

LEASE COVENANTS AND AGREEMENTS

RENT

1. Lessee shall pay Lessor or Lessor's agent as rent for the Premises the sum stated above, monthly in advance, until termination of this lease, at Lessor's address stated above or such other address as Lessor may designate in writing.

SECURITY DEPOSIT

2. Lessee has deposited with Lessor the Security Deposit stated above for the performance of all covenants and agreements of Lessee hereunder. Lessor may apply all or any portion thereof in payment of any amounts due Lessor from Lessee, and upon Lessor's demand Lessee shall in such case during the term of the lease promptly deposit with Lessor such additional amounts as may then be required to bring the Security Deposit up to the full amount stated above. Upon termination of the lease and full performance of all matters and payment of all amounts due by Lessee, so much of the Security Deposit as remains unapplied shall be returned to Lessee. This deposit does not bear interest unless and except as required by law. Where all or a portion of the Security Deposit is applied by Lessor as compensation for property damage, Lessor when and as required by law shall provide to Lessee an itemized statement of such damage and of the estimated or actual cost of repairing same. If the building in which Premises are located (the "Building") is sold or otherwise transferred, Lessor may transfer or assign the Security Deposit to the purchaser or transferee of the Building, who shall thereupon be liable to Lessee for all of Lessor's obligations hereunder, and Lessee shall look thereafter solely to such purchaser or transferee for return of the Security Deposit and for other matters (including any interest or accounting) relating thereto.

CONDITION OF PREMISES; REDELIVERY TO LESSOR

3. Lessee has examined and knows the condition of Premises and has received the same in good order and repair except as herein otherwise specified, and no representations as to the condition or repair thereof have been made by Lessor or his agent prior to, or at the execution of this lease, that are not herein expressed or endorsed hereon; and upon the termination of this lease in any way, Lessee will immediately yield up Premises to Lessor in as good condition as when the same were entered upon by Lessee, ordinary wear and tear only excepted, and shall then return all keys to Lessor.

Figure 16.1 (cont.)

LIMITATION OF LIABILITY

4. Except as provided by Illinois statute, Lessor shall not be liable for any damage occasioned by failure to keep Premises in repair, and shall not be liable for any damage done or occasioned by or from plumbing, gas, water, steam or other pipes, or sewerage, or the bursting, leaking or running of any cistern, tank, wash-stand, water-closet, or waste-pipe, in, above, upon or about the Building or Premises, nor for damage occasioned by water, snow or ice being upon or coming through the roof, skylight, trap-door or otherwise, nor for damages to Lessee or others claiming through Lessee for any loss or damage of or to property wherever located in or about the Building or Premises, nor for any damage arising from acts or neglect of co-tenants or other occupants of the Building, or of any owners or occupants of adjacent or contiguous property.

USE; SUBLET; ASSIGNMENT

5. Lessee will not allow Premises to be used for any purpose that will increase the rate of insurance thereon, nor for any purpose other than that hereinbefore specified, nor to be occupied in whole or in part by any other persons, and will not sublet the same, nor any part thereof, nor assign this lease, without in each case the written consent of the Lessor first had, and will not permit any transfer, by operation of law, of the interest in Premises acquired through this lease, and will not permit Premises to be used for any unlawful purpose or purpose that will injure the reputation of the same or of the Building or disturb the tenants of the Building or the neighborhood.

USE AND REPAIR

6. Lessee will take good care of the apartment demised and the fixtures therein, and will commit and suffer no waste therein; no changes or alterations of the Premises shall be made, nor partitions erected, nor walls papered, nor locks on doors installed or changed, without the consent in writing of Lessor; Lessee will make all repairs required to the walls, ceilings, paint, plastering, plumbing work, pipes and fixtures belonging to Premises, whenever damage or injury to the same shall have resulted from misuse or neglect; no furniture filled or to be filled wholly or partially with liquids shall be placed in the Premises without the consent in writing of Lessor; the Premises shall not be used as a "boarding" or "lodging" house, nor for a school, nor to give instructions in music, dancing or singing, and none of the rooms shall be offered for lease by placing notices on any door, window or wall of the Building, nor by advertising the same directly or indirectly, in any newspaper or otherwise, nor shall any signs be exhibited on or at any windows or exterior portions of the Premises or of the Building without the consent in writing of Lessor; there shall be no lounging, sitting upon, or unnecessary tarrying in or upon the front steps, the sidewalk, railing, stairways, halls, landing or other public places of the Building by Lessee, members of the family or others persons connected with the occupancy of Premises; no provisions, milk, ice, marketing, groceries, furniture, packages or merchandise shall be taken into the Premises through the front door of the Building except where there is no rear or service entrance; cooking shall be done only in the kitchen and in no event on porches or other exterior appurtenances; Lessee, and those occupying under Lessee, shall not interfere with the heating apparatus, or with the lights, electricity, gas, water or other utilities of the Building which are not within the apartment hereby demised, nor with the control of any of the public portions of the Building; use of any master television antenna hookup shall be strictly in accordance with regulations of Lessor or Lessor's agent; Lessee and those occupying under Lessee shall comply with and conform to all reasonable rules and regulations that Lessor or Lessor's agent may make for the protection of the Building or the general welfare and the comfort of the occupants thereof, and shall also comply with and conform to all applicable laws and governmental rules and regulations affecting the Premises and the use and occupancy thereof.

ACCESS

7. Lessee will allow Lessor free access to the Premises at all reasonable hours for the purpose of examining or exhibiting the same or to make any needful repairs which Lessor may deem fit to make for the benefit of or related to any part of the Building; also Lessee will allow Lessor to have placed upon the Premises, at all times, notice of "For Sale" and "To Rent," and will not interfere with the same.

RIGHT TO RELET

8. If Lessee shall abandon or vacate the Premises, the same may be re-let by Lessor for such rent and upon such terms as Lessor may see fit, subject to Illinois statute, and if a sufficient sum shall not thus be realized, after paying the expenses of such reletting and collecting, to satisfy the rent hereby reserved, Lessee agrees to satisfy and pay all deficiency.

HOLDING OVER

9. If the Lessee retains possession of the Premises or any part thereof after the termination of the term by lapse of time or otherwise, then the Lessor may at Lessor's option within thirty days after the termination of the term serve written notice upon Lessee that such holding over constitutes either (a) renewal of this lease for one year, and from year to year thereafter, at double the rental specified under Section 1 for such period, or (b) creation of a month to month tenancy, upon the terms of this lease except at double the monthly rental specified under Section 1, or (c) creation of a tenancy at sufferance, at a rental of ___$30.00___ dollars per day for the time Lessee remains in possession. If no such written notice is served then a tenancy at sufferance with rental as stated at (c) shall have been created, and in such case if specific per diem rental shall not have been inserted herein at (c), such per diem rental shall be one-fifteenth of the monthly rental specified under Section 1 of this lease. Lessee shall also pay to Lessor all damages sustained by Lessor resulting from retention of possession by Lessee.

RESTRICTIONS ON USE

10. Lessee will not permit anything to be thrown out of the windows, or down the courts or light shafts in the Building; nothing shall be hung from the outside of the windows or placed on the outside window sills of any window in the Building; no parrot, dog or other animal shall be kept within or about the Premises; the front halls and stairways and the back porches shall not be used for the storage of carriages, furniture or other articles.

WATER AND HEAT

11. The provisions of subsection (a) only hereof shall be applicable and shall form a part of this lease unless this lease is made on an unheated basis and that fact is so indicated on the first page of this lease, in which case the provisions of subsection (b) only hereof shall be applicable and form a part of this lease.

(a) Lessor will supply hot and cold water to the Premises for the use of Lessee at all faucets and fixtures provided by Lessor therefor. Lessor will also supply heat, by means of the heating system and fixtures provided by Lessor, in reasonable amounts and at reasonable hours, when necessary, from October 1 to April 30, or otherwise as required by applicable municipal ordinance. Lessor shall not be liable or responsible to Lessee for failure to furnish water or heat when such failure shall result from causes beyond Lessor's control, nor during periods when the water and heating systems in the Building or any portion thereof are under repair.

(b) Lessor will supply cold water to the Premises for the use of Lessee at all faucets and fixtures provided by Lessor therefor. Lessor shall not be liable or responsible to Lessee for failure to furnish water when such failure shall result from causes beyond Lessor's control, nor during periods when the water system in the Building or any portion thereof is under repair. All water heating and all heating of the Premises shall be at the sole expense of Lessee. Any equipment provided by Lessee therefor shall comply with applicable municipal ordinances.

Figure 16.1 (cont.)

STORE ROOM	12. Lessor shall not be liable for any loss or damage of or to any property placed in any store room or any storage place in the Building, such store room or storage place being furnished gratuitously and not as part of the obligations of this lease.
DEFAULT BY LESSEE	13. If default be made in the payment of the above rent, or any part thereof, or in any of the covenants herein contained to be kept by the Lessee, Lessor may at any time thereafter at his election declare said term ended and reenter the Premises or any part thereof, with or (to the extent permitted by law) without notice or process of law, and remove Lessee or any persons occupying the same, without prejudice to any remedies which might otherwise be used for arrears of rent, and Lessor shall have at all times the right to distrain for rent due, and shall have a valid and first lien upon all personal property which Lessee now owns, or may hereafter acquire or have an interest in, which is by law subject to such distraint, as security for payment of the rent herein reserved.
NO RENT DEDUCTION OR SET OFF	14. Lessee's covenant to pay rent is and shall be independent of each and every other covenant of this lease. Lessee agrees that any claim by Lessee against Lessor shall not be deducted from rent nor set off against any claim for rent in any action.
RENT AFTER NOTICE OR SUIT	15. It is further agreed, by the parties hereto, that after the service of notice or the commencement of a suit or after final judgment for possession of the Premises, Lessor may receive and collect any rent due, and the payment of said rent shall not waive or affect said notice, said suit, or said judgment.
PAYMENT OF COSTS	16. Lessee will pay and discharge all reasonable costs, attorney's fees and expenses that shall be made and incurred by Lessor in enforcing the covenants and agreements of this lease.
RIGHTS CUMULATIVE	17. The rights and remedies of Lessor under this lease are cumulative. The exercise or use of any one or more thereof shall not bar Lessor from exercise or use of any other right or remedy provided herein or otherwise provided by law, nor shall exercise nor use of any right or remedy by Lessor waive any other right or remedy.
FIRE AND CASUALTY	18. In case the Premises shall be rendered untenantable during the term of this lease by fire or other casualty, Lessor at his option may terminate the lease or repair the Premises within 60 days thereafter. If Lessor elects to repair, this lease shall remain in effect provided such repairs are completed within said time. If Lessor shall not have repaired the Premises within said time, then at the end of such time the term hereby created shall terminate. If this lease is terminated by reason of fire or casualty as herein specified, rent shall be apportioned and paid to the day of such fire or other casualty.
SUBORDINATION	19. This lease is subordinate to all mortgages which may now or hereafter affect the real property of which Premises form a part.
PLURALS; SUCCESSORS	20. The words "Lessor" and "Lessee" wherever herein occurring and used shall be construed to mean "Lessors" and "Lessees" in case more than one person constitutes either party to this lease; and all the covenants and agreements herein contained shall be binding upon, and inure to, their respective successors, heirs, executors, administrators and assigns and be exercised by his or their attorney or agent.
SEVERABILITY	21. Wherever possible each provision of this lease shall be interpreted in such manner as to be effective and valid under applicable law, but if any provision of this lease shall be prohibited by or invalid under applicable law, such provision shall be ineffective to the extent of such prohibition or invalidity, without invalidating the remainder of such provision or the remaining provisions of this lease.

WITNESS the hands and seals of the parties hereto, as of the Date of Lease stated above.

LESSEE: ___*J P Smithers*___ (seal)   LESSOR: ___*J W Maddox*___ (seal)

_____ (seal)   _____ (seal)

ASSIGNMENT BY LESSOR

On this _____ , 19 _____ , for value received, Lessor hereby transfers, assigns and sets over to

_____ all right, title and interest in and to the above lease and the rent thereby reserved,

except rent due and payable prior to _____ , 19 _____ .

_____ (seal)

_____ (seal)

GUARANTEE

On this _____ , 19 _____ , in consideration of Ten Dollars ($10.00) and other good and valuable consideration, the receipt and sufficiency of which is hereby acknowledged, the undersigned Guarantor hereby guarantees the payment of rent and performance by Lessee, Lessee's heirs, executors, administrators, successors or assigns of all covenants and agreements of the above lease.

_____ (seal)

_____ (seal)

tial as long as consideration was granted in creation of the lease itself. The courts consider a lease to be a contract and not subject to subsequent changes in the rent or other terms unless these changes are in writing and executed in the same manner as the original lease.

3. *Capacity to contract.* The parties must have the legal capacity to contract.
4. *Legal objectives.* The objectives of the lease must be legal.

When the statute of frauds applies, an oral lease is considered to be *unenforceable.* A description of the leased premises should be clearly stated. If the lease covers land, the legal description of the real estate should be used. If, on the other hand, the lease is for a part of a building, such as office space or an apartment, the space itself or the apartment designation should be clearly and carefully described. If supplemental space is to be included, the lease should clearly identify it.

To be valid, a lease for more than a year's duration must be signed by the landlord, since the courts consider a lease to be a conveyance of an interest in real estate. The tenant's signature is usually *not essential if the tenant has actually taken possession.* Of course, it is preferable for both parties to sign the lease.

Use of Premises

A lessor may restrict a lessee's use of the premises through provisions included in the lease. This is most important in leases for stores or commercial space. For example, a lease may provide that the leased premises are to be used *only* for the purpose of a real estate office *and for no other.* In the absence of such limitations, a lessee may use the premises for any lawful purpose.

Term of Lease

The term of a lease is the period for which the lease will run, and it should be set out precisely. The date of the beginning of the term and the date of its ending should be stated together with a statement of the total period of the lease: for example, "for a term of thirty years beginning June 1, 1986 and ending May 31, 2016." Courts do not favor leases with an indefinite term and will hold that such perpetual leases are not valid unless the language of the lease and the surrounding circumstances clearly indicate that such is the intention of the parties. In some states, terms of agricultural leases are limited by statute. Some states prohibit leases that run for 100 years or more.

Security Deposit

Most leases require the tenant to provide some form of **security deposit** to be held by the landlord during the lease term and kept, wholly or partially, in the event of the tenant's default in payment of rent or destruction of the premises. State law may set maximum amounts for security deposits and specify how they must be handled. Some prohibit security deposits from being used *both* for nonpayment of rent and property damage. Some require that lessees receive annual interest on their security deposits.

Other safeguards against nonpayment of rent may include an advance rental payment, contracting for a lien on the tenant's property and/or requiring the tenant to have a third person guarantee payment.

In Practice...

A lease should specify whether a payment is a security deposit or an advance rental. If it is a security deposit, the tenant is usually not entitled to apply it to the final month's rent. If it is an advance rental, the landlord must treat it as income for tax purposes.

Confession of Judgment Clause

A **confession of judgment** clause is included in many commercial leases to assist the landlord in forcing *collection of rent*. The tenant by this clause authorizes any attorney of record to appear in court in the tenant's name and to confess judgment, or agree that a judgment be entered against the tenant in favor of the landlord for the delinquent rent, court costs and attorney's fees. Such a clause may be called a *cognovit*. Many states have now declared confession of judgment clauses illegal when used in residential leases.

Legal Principles of Leases

Most states provide that leases can be filed for record in the county in which the property is located. But unless the lease is for a relatively long term, it *usually is not recorded.* Possession of the property by the lessee is notice to the world of his or her rights, and an inspection of the property will result in *actual notice* of the lessee's leasehold interest.

When a lease runs for a period of *three years* or longer, recording is more common. The recording of a *long-term lease* places the world on notice of the long-term rights of the lessee. The recordation of such a lease is usually required if the lessee intends to mortgage the leasehold interest.

In some states, only a *memorandum of lease* is filed for record. The terms of the lease are not disclosed to the public, but the objective of giving public notice of the rights of the lessee is still accomplished. The memorandum of lease must set forth the names of the parties and a description of the property being leased.

[handwritten margin note: Memorandum copy theirs is highlights that there is a lease on the property]

Possession of Leased Premises

As noted earlier, leases carry the implied covenant that the landlord will give the tenant enjoyment (possession) of the premises. If the premises are occupied by a holdover tenant, or adverse claimant, at the beginning of the new lease period, in most states it is the landlord's duty to bring whatever action is necessary to recover actual possession and to bear the expense of this action. In a few states, however, the landlord is bound only to give the tenant the right of possession; it is the tenant's obligation to bring any court action necessary to secure actual possession.

Improvements

Neither the landlord nor the tenant is required to make any improvements to the leased property. In the absence of an agreement to the contrary, the tenant may make improvements with the landlord's permission. Any such alterations generally become the property of the landlord; that is, they become fixtures. However, as discussed in Chapter 2, a tenant may be given the right by the terms of the lease to install trade fixtures or chattel fixtures. It is customary to provide that such trade fixtures may be removed by the tenant before the lease expires, provided the tenant restores the premises to their previous condition.

Maintenance of Premises

Historically, a landlord was not obligated to make any repairs to leased premises. However, many states now require a residential lessor to maintain dwelling units in a habitable condition and to make any necessary repairs to common elements, such as hallways, stairs or elevators. The tenant does not have to make any repairs, but he or she must return the premises in the same condition they were received, with allowances for ordinary use.

Assignment and Subleasing

The lessee may assign the lease or may sublease if the lease terms do not prohibit it. A tenant who transfers all of his or her leasehold interests *assigns* the lease. One who transfers less than all of the leasehold interests by leasing them to a new tenant **subleases** (see figure 16.2). In most cases, the sublease or assignment of a lease does not relieve the original lessee of the obligation to make rental payments unless the landlord agrees to waive such liability. Most leases prohibit the lessee from assigning or subletting without the lessor's consent. The lessor thus retains control over the occupancy of the leased premises, but must not unreasonably withhold consent. The sublessor's (original lessee's) interest in the real estate is known as a *sandwich lease*.

Figure 16.2
Assignment versus Subletting

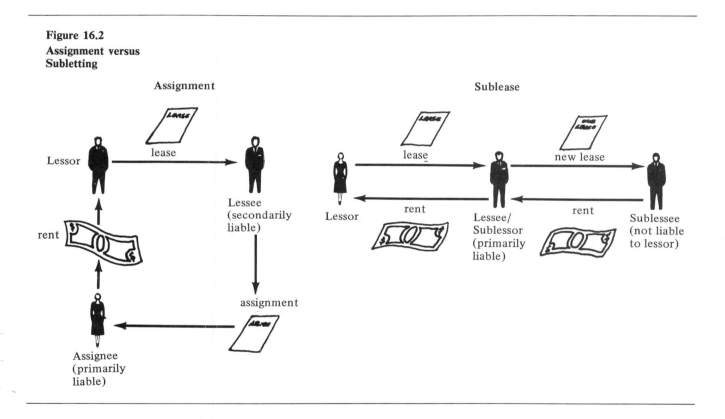

Options

Many leases contain an *option* that grants the lessee the privilege of *renewing* or extending the lease but requires that the lessee give *notice* on or before a specific date of intention to exercise the option. Some leases grant to the lessee the option to purchase the leased premises; the provisions for the option to purchase vary widely. Options to purchase are becoming more common (see Chapter 11).

Destruction of Premises

In land leases involving *agricultural land,* the courts have held that damage to or destruction of the improvements, even if not the tenant's fault, does not relieve the tenant from the obligation to pay rent to the end of the term. This ruling has been extended in most states to include *ground leases* upon which the tenant has constructed a building and, in many instances, leases that give possession of an entire building to the tenant. When the tenant leases an entire building, the courts have held that he or she is also leasing the land upon which that building is located.

In those cases where the leased premises are only a part of the building (such as office or commercial space or an apartment in an apartment building), the tenant is *not* required to continue to pay rent upon destruction of the leased premises. In some states, if the property was destroyed as a result of the landlord's negligence, the tenant can recover damages from the landlord.

In Practice...   *All of these general statements concerning destruction of leased premises are controlled largely by terms of the lease. Printed lease forms and all carefully prepared leases usually include a provision covering the subject of destruction of the premises. Great care must be exercised in reading the entire lease document before signing it.*

Termination of Lease

A written lease for a definite period of time expires at the end of that time period; no separate notice is required to terminate the lease when it expires. Oral and written leases that do not specify a definite expiration date (such as a month-to-month or year-to-year tenancy or a tenancy at will) may be terminated by giving proper notice in advance as required by state law. Generally, the laws specify a minimum time period or number of days' notice that must be given by the party who wishes to terminate the lease.

When the conditions of a lease are breached, or broken, by the tenant, a landlord may terminate the lease and evict the tenant. This kind of action must be handled through a court proceeding according to state law.

It is possible that the parties to a lease will mutually agree to cancel the lease. The tenant may offer to surrender the leasehold interest; if so, acceptance by the landlord will result in termination. A tenant who abandons leased property, however, remains liable for the terms of the lease—including the rent. The terms of the specific lease will usually indicate whether or not the landlord is obligated to try to rerent the space. If the landlord intends to sue for unpaid rent, however, most states will require an attempt to limit the amount owed (to "mitigate damages") by rerenting the premises.

When the owner of leased property dies or the property is sold, *the lease does not terminate.* There are two exceptions: (1) a lease from the owner of a life estate terminates on the death of that person and (2) the death of either party terminates a tenancy at will. The heirs of a deceased landlord are bound by the terms of existing valid leases. In addition, if a landlord conveys leased real estate, the new landlord takes the property subject to the rights of the tenants. If a tenant under an estate for years or from year to year dies, the lease will remain in effect; the deceased lessee's heirs will be bound by the terms of the lease agreement.

A tenancy may be terminated by operation of law, as in a bankruptcy or condemnation proceeding.

Breach of Lease

When a tenant breaches any lease provision, the landlord may sue the tenant to obtain a judgment to cover rent past due, damages to the premises or other defaults. Likewise, when a landlord breaches any lease provision, the tenant is entitled to certain remedies.

Suit for possession—actual eviction. When a tenant breaches a lease or improperly retains possession of leased premises, the landlord may regain possession through a **suit for possession.** This process is known as **actual eviction.** Law requires the landlord to serve *notice* on the tenant before commencing the suit. Most lease terms require at least a ten-day notice in case of a *default*, but in many states, only a five-day notice must be given before filing a suit for possession based on a default in payment of rent. When a court issues a judgment for possession to a landlord, the tenant must peaceably leave and take all belongings, or the landlord can have the judgment enforced by a *bailiff* or other court officer, who will *forcibly remove* the tenant and the tenant's possessions.

Tenants' remedies—constructive eviction. If a landlord breaches any clause of a lease agreement, the tenant has the right to sue, claiming a judgment for damages against the landlord. If an action or omission on the landlord's part results in the leased premises becoming uninhabitable for the purpose intended in the lease, the tenant may have the right to abandon the premises. This action, called **constructive eviction,** terminates the lease agreement if the tenant can prove that the premises have become uninhabitable because of the conscious neglect of the landlord. In order to claim constructive eviction, *the tenant must actually remove him- or herself from the premises* while the uninhabitable condition exists.

For example, a lease (and, in our example, state law) requires the landlord to furnish heat; because of the landlord's failure to repair a defective heating plant, the heat is not provided. If this results in the leased premises becoming uninhabitable, the tenant may abandon them. It should be noted that some leases provide that if the failure to furnish heat is accidental and not the landlord's fault, it is not grounds for constructive eviction.

Pro-Tenant Legislation

For the most part, leases are drawn up primarily for the benefit of the landlord. However, consumer awareness has fostered the belief that a valid lease is dependent on both parties' fulfillment of certain obligations. To provide laws outlining such obligations, several states have adopted some variation of the *Uniform Residential Landlord and Tenant Act.* This model law addresses such issues as the landlord's right of entry, maintenance of premises, the tenant's protection against retaliation by the landlord for complaints and the disclosure of the property owners' names and addresses to the tenants. The act further sets down specific remedies available to both the landlord and the tenant if a breach of the lease agreement occurs.

The federal government also took steps to increase tenants' protection with the implementation of the Tenants' Eviction Procedures Act in 1976. This act establishes standardized eviction procedures for people living in *government-subsidized housing.* It requires that the landlord have a valid reason for evicting the tenant and that the landlord give the tenant proper notice of eviction. This act does not supersede state laws in this area; however, it does provide recourse for tenants in states that have no such laws. The act applies only to multiunit residential buildings that are owned or subsidized by the Department of Housing and Urban Development and to buildings that have government-insured mortgages.

| **Types of Leases** | The manner in which rent is determined indicates the type of lease that is in force. The three primary types of leases are: (1) the gross lease, (2) the net lease and (3) the percentage lease (see table 16.2). |

| **Gross Lease** | In a **gross lease,** the tenant's obligation is to pay a *fixed rental*, and the landlord pays all taxes, insurance, mortgage payments, repairs and the like connected with the property (usually called *property charges*). This type of lease is most often used for residential apartment rentals. |

	Type of Lease	Lessee Pays	Lessor Pays
Table 16.2 **Types of Leases**	Gross Lease Residential (also small Commercial)	Basic Rent	Property Charges (taxes, repairs, insurance, etc.)
	Net Lease Commercial/Industrial	Basic Rent Plus All or Most Property Charges	May Pay Some Property Charges
	Percentage Lease Commercial/Industrial	Basic Rent Plus Percent of Gross Sales (may pay property costs)	May Pay Some or All Property Charges

| **Net Lease** | The **net lease** provides that in addition to the rent, the *tenant pays all or some of the property charges.* The monthly rental paid to the landlord is in addition to these charges and so is net income for the landlord after operating costs have been paid. Leases for entire commercial or industrial buildings and the land on which they are located, ground leases and long-term leases are usually net leases.

In a **triple net lease,** or *net-net-net lease,* the tenant pays all operating and other expenses, such as taxes, insurance, assessments, maintenance and other charges. |

| **Percentage Lease** | Either a gross lease or a net lease may be a **percentage lease.** A percentage lease provides that the rental is based on a *percentage of the gross or net income* received by the tenant doing business on the leased property. This type of lease is usually used in the rental of retail business locations.

The percentage lease usually provides for a minimum fixed rental fee plus a percentage of that portion of the tenant's business income that exceeds a stated minimum. For example, a lease might provide for a minimum monthly rental of $1,500, with the further agreement that the tenant pay an additional amount each month equivalent to four percent of all gross sales in excess of $30,000. The percentage charged in such leases varies widely with the nature of the business, and is negotiable between landlord and tenant. A tenant's bargaining power is determined by the volume of the business. Percentages vary with the location of the property and general economic conditions. |

| **Other Lease Types** | **Variable leases.** There are several types of leases that allow for increases in the fixed rental charge during the lease period. Two of the more common ones are the *graduated lease*, which provides for increases in rent at set future dates, and |

the *index lease*, which allows rent to be increased or decreased periodically based on changes in the government cost-of-living index or some other index.

Ground leases. When a landowner leases land to a tenant who agrees to *erect a building* on the land, the lease is usually referred to as a **ground lease.** Ground leases usually involve separate ownership of land and building. Such a lease must be for a long enough term to make the transaction desirable to the tenant making the investment in the building. These leases are generally *net leases* that require the lessee to pay rent as well as real estate taxes, insurance, upkeep and repairs. Such leases often run for terms of 50 years or longer, and a lease for 999 years is not impossible. Although such leases are considered to be personal property, certain states' laws may give leaseholders some of the rights and obligations of real property owners. Some early state laws considered leases for more than 99 years to be fee estates.

Oil and gas leases. When oil companies lease land to explore for oil and gas, a special lease agreement must be negotiated. Usually, the landowner receives a cash payment for executing the lease. If no well is drilled within a year or other period stated in the lease, the lease expires; however, most oil and gas leases provide that the oil company may continue its rights for another year by paying another flat rental fee. Such rentals may be paid annually until a well is produced. If oil and/or gas is found, the landowner usually receives one-eighth of its value as a royalty. In this case, the lease will continue for as long as oil or gas is obtained in significant quantities.

Summary

A *lease* is an agreement that grants one person the right to use the property of another for a certain period in return for consideration. The lease agreement is a combination of a conveyance creating a leasehold interest in the property and a contract outlining the rights and obligations of the landlord and the tenant.

A leasehold estate that runs for a specific length of time creates an *estate for years;* one that runs for an indefinite number of terms creates a *periodic estate* (year to year, month to month). An *estate at will* runs as long as the landlord permits, and an estate at sufferance is possession without the consent of the landlord. A leasehold estate is generally classified as personal property.

The requirements of a valid lease include offer and acceptance, consideration, capacity to contract and legal objectives. In addition, the state statute of frauds generally requires that any lease that will not be executed within one year of the date of agreement must be in writing. Most leases also include clauses relating to such rights and obligations of the landlord and tenant as the use of the premises, subletting, judgments, maintenance of the premises and termination of the lease period.

Leases may be terminated by the expiration of the lease period, the mutual agreement of the parties or a breach of the lease by either landlord or tenant. It is important to note that in most cases neither the death of the tenant nor the landlord's sale of the rental property terminates a lease.

Upon a tenant's default on any of the lease provisions, a landlord may sue for a money judgment or for *actual eviction* in a case where a tenant has improperly retained possession of the premises. If the premises have become uninhabitable due to the landlord's negligence, the tenant may have the right of *constructive eviction,* that is, the right to abandon the premises and refuse to pay rent until the premises are repaired.

There are several basic types of leases, including *net leases, gross leases* and *percentage leases*. These leases are classified according to the method used in determining the rental rate of the property.

Questions

1. Alvin Yates's lease will expire in two weeks. At that time, he will move to larger quarters on the other side of town. In order to terminate this lease agreement:

   I. Yates must give the landlord prior notice.

   II. the landlord must give Yates prior notice.

   a. I only
   b. II only
   c. both I and II
   d. neither I nor II

2. A tenant's right to occupy, or take possession of, leased premises is:

   a. a reversionary interest.
   b. an estate in land.
   c. a leasehold interest.
   d. b and c

3. A ground lease is usually:

   a. short term.
   b. for 100 years or longer.
   c. long term.
   d. a gross lease.

4. A percentage lease is a lease that provides for:

   a. a rental of a percentage of the value of a building.
   b. a definite periodic rent not exceeding a stated percentage.
   c. a definite monthly rent plus a percentage of the tenant's gross receipts in excess of a certain amount.
   d. a graduated amount due monthly and not exceeding a stated percentage.

5. If several renting tenants moved out of a store building because the building collapsed:

   a. this would be an actual eviction.
   b. the tenants would be liable for the rent until the expiration date of their leases.
   c. the landlord would have to provide substitute space.
   d. this would be a constructive eviction.

6. Today Jane agreed to a one-year lease on a new apartment, to begin in one week. The agreement:

   a. must be written.
   b. may be oral or written.
   c. must be signed by Jane.
   d. a and c

7. A lease for two years must be in writing because:

   a. either party may forget the terms.
   b. the tenant must sign the agreement to pay rent.
   c. the statute of frauds requires it.
   d. it is the customary procedure to protect the tenant.

8. A lease calls for a minimum rent of $1,200 per month plus 4 percent of the annual gross business over $150,000. If the total rent paid at the end of the year was $19,200, how much business did the tenant do during the year?

   a. $159,800
   b. $25,200
   c. $270,000
   d. $169,200

9. Paul Robinson's written five-year lease with monthly rental payments expired last month, but Robinson has remained in possession and the landlord has accepted his most recent rent payment without comment. At this point:

   a. Robinson is a holdover tenant.
   b. Robinson's lease has been renewed for another five years.
   c. Robinson's lease has been renewed for another month.
   d. Robinson is a tenant at sufferance.

10. Albert Franzen rented an apartment to Wilbur Post under a one-year written lease. Three months into the lease term, Franzen died. With regard to the written lease between Post and his late landlord:

    I. Post continues to be bound by its terms.

    II. Franzen's heirs are now bound by its terms.

    a. I only
    b. II only
    c. both I and II
    d. neither I nor II

11. A tenant's legal right to possession of leased property against the ownership claims of third parties is:

    a. tenancy at will.
    b. cognovit.
    c. covenant of quiet enjoyment.
    d. constructive eviction.

12. A tenant's lease has expired, the tenant has neither vacated nor negotiated a renewal lease, and the landlord has declared that she does not want the tenant to remain in the building. The tenancy is called:

    a. estate for years.
    b. periodic estate.
    c. estate at will.
    d. estate at sufferance.

13. The requirements of a valid lease include:

    a. offer and acceptance.
    b. consideration.
    c. capacity to contract.
    d. all of the above

14. When a tenant holds possession of a landlord's property without a current lease agreement and without the landlord's approval:

    a. the tenant is maintaining a gross lease.
    b. the landlord may file suit for possession.
    c. the tenant has no obligation to pay rent.
    d. b and c

15. Which of the following best describes a *net lease?*

    a. an agreement in which the tenant pays a fixed rent and the landlord pays all taxes, insurance and so forth on the property
    b. a lease in which the tenant pays rent in addition to some or all property charges
    c. a lease in which the tenant pays the landlord a percentage of the monthly income derived from the property
    d. an agreement granting an individual a leasehold interest in fishing rights to shoreline properties

16. If there is no special lease provision regarding permanent improvements made by a tenant on leased property, such improvements:

    a. are called fixtures.
    b. remain the property of the tenant after the lease expires.
    c. may be removed by a new tenant.
    d. all of the above

17. If a residential tenant is unable to receive hot water because of a faulty hot-water heater, which of the following remedies may the tenant take if the landlord is obliged by the lease terms to fix the equipment?

    a. The tenant may sue the landlord for damages.
    b. The tenant may abandon the premises.
    c. The tenant may terminate the lease agreement.
    d. all of the above

18. Actual eviction occurs when:

    a. a tenant peaceably vacates a property upon termination of a lease.
    b. a landlord regains possession through a legal action.
    c. a court officer removes a tenant from the premises.
    d. b and c

19. A tenant who transfers the entire remaining term of the lease to a third party is:

    a. a sublettor.
    b. assigning the lease.
    c. automatically relieved of any further obligation under it.
    d. giving the third party a sandwich lease.

20. Which of the following leases would probably be recorded?

    I. a two-year residential lease
    II. a five-year net lease for commercial property with provisions for yearly rental increases and an option to purchase the property at the end of the lease term

    a. I only   c. both I and II
    b. II only   d. neither I nor II

Part Three

Practices

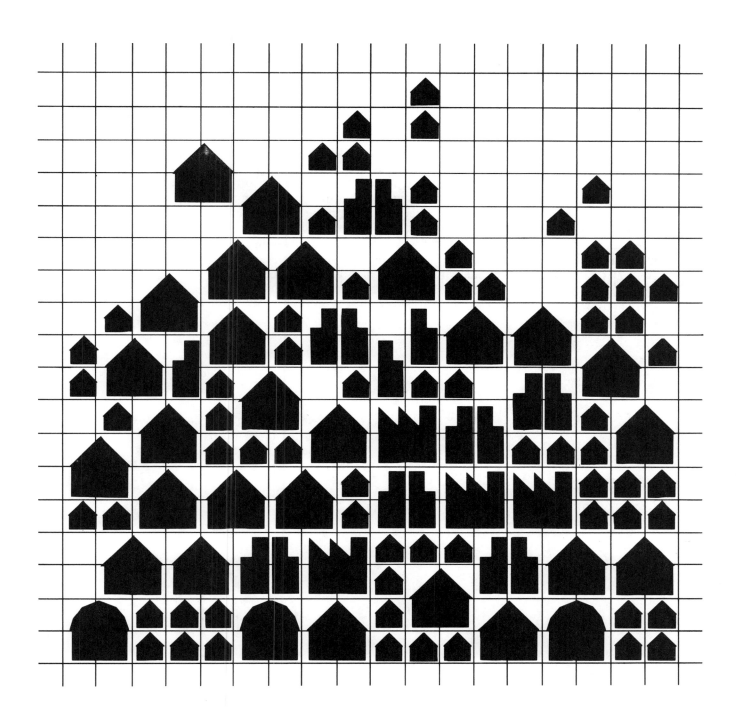

17

Property Management

Key Terms

Management agreement
Management considerations
Multiperil policies
Property manager
Risk management
Surety bond
Tenant improvements
Workers' Compensation Acts

Overview

A real estate owner who rents the upstairs apartment in the building in which he or she resides ordinarily has no problem with property management—setting and collecting rents, maintenance and repairs are easy enough with only one tenant. But the owners of large, multiunit developments often lack the time and/or expertise to successfully manage their properties. Enter the *property manager,* a real estate professional hired to maintain the property and ensure the profitability of the owner's investment. This chapter will examine the growing property management profession and will also include discussions of one of the many duties of a property manager—handling the various types of property insurance available to further protect an owner's real estate investment.

Property Management	The need for specialized property managers became apparent during the 1930s as lending institutions took possession of numerous foreclosed income properties. Lacking the expertise to administer these properties, they looked to the real estate industry for expert management assistance. In recent years the increased size of buildings; the technical complexities of construction, maintenance and repair; and the trend toward absentee ownership by individual investors and investment groups have led to the expanded use of professional property managers for both residential and commercial properties.

Property management has become so important that many brokerage firms maintain separate management departments staffed by carefully selected, well-trained people. Many corporate and institutional owners of real estate have also established property management departments. Many real estate investors still manage their own property, however, and thus must acquire the knowledge and skills of a property manager. In some states, property managers must be licensed real estate brokers. In others, property managers must be licensed as such.

Functions of the Property Manager

In the simplest terms, a **property manager** is someone who *preserves the value of an investment property while generating income as an agent for the owners.* A property manager is expected to merchandise the property and control operating expenses so as to maximize income. A property manager chooses the best possible means to carry out an agent's responsibilities—and has more authority and discretion than an employee. A manager should maintain and modernize the property to preserve and enhance the owner's capital investment. The manager carries out these objectives by: (1) securing suitable tenants, (2) collecting the rents, (3) caring for the premises, (4) budgeting and controlling expenses, (5) hiring and supervising employees and (6) keeping proper accounts and making periodic reports to the owner. — *Run a smooth operation, show profit to owners with little or no problems.*

Securing Management Business

In today's market, property managers may look to corporate owners, apartment and condominium associations, homeowners' associations, investment syndicates, trusts and absentee owners as possible sources of management business. In securing business from any of these sources, word of mouth is often the best advertising. A manager who consistently demonstrates the ability to increase property income over previous levels should have no difficulty finding new business.

The Management Agreement

The first step in taking over the management of any property is to enter into a **management agreement** with the owner (see figure 17.1). This agreement creates an agency relationship between the owner and the property manager. A property manager is usually considered to be a *general agent,* whereas a real estate broker is usually considered to be a *special agent.* As agent, the property manager is charged with the same agency responsibilities as the listing broker—care, obedience, accounting, loyalty and disclosure (COALD). (Agency responsibilities were discussed at length in Chapter 5.)

Figure 17.1
Property Management Agreement

OWNER ___Elinor Q. Franks_____

and

AGENT ___Don Silver Management_____

For Property located at

___312 West East Street_____

___Clinton, Iowa   50000_____

Beginning ___January 1,_____ 19 _87_

Ending ___June 1,_____ 19 _88_

MANAGEMENT
AGREEMENT

IN CONSIDERATION of the covenants herein contained, __Elinor Q. Franks__
_____ (hereinafter called "OWNER), and _____
___Don Silver Management_____ (hereinafter called "AGENT"), **agree as**
follows:

1. The OWNER hereby employs the AGENT exclusively to rent and manage the property
(hereinafter called the "Premises") known as _____
_____312 West End Street_____
_____Clinton, Iowa 50000_____
upon the terms and conditions hereinafter set forth, for a term of __1½ yrs__ beginning on
the __1st__ day of __January_____, 19 _87___, and ending on the ___1st__
day of _____June_____, 19 _88___, and thereafter for yearly periods from
time to time, unless on or before_____90___ days prior to the date last above mentioned or on
or before _____90_____ days prior to the expiration of any such renewal period, either party
hereto shall notify the other in writing that it elects to terminate this Agreement, in which case
this Agreement shall be thereby terminated on said last mentioned date. (See also Paragraph
6.3 below.)

2. THE AGENT AGREES:

2.1 To accept the management of the Premises, to the extent, for the period, and upon
the terms herein provided and agrees to furnish the services of its organization for the rental
operation and management of the Premises.

2.2 To render a monthly statement of receipts, disbursements, and charges to the
following person(s) at the address(es) shown:

Name	Address
Regina Stump, CPA, on behalf of owner	211 North Blvd., Ste 601 Burton, Iowa 50000

and to remit each month the net proceeds (provided AGENT is not required to make any
mortgage, escrow, or tax payment on the first day of the following month). AGENT will remit
the net proceeds or the balance thereof after making allowance for such payments to the
following persons, in the percentages specified, and at the addresses shown:

**Figure 17.1
(cont.)**

Name	Percentage	Address
Elinor Q. Franks	100	912 Knowles, Suite 900
		Burton, Iowa 50000

In case the disbursements and charges shall be in excess of the receipts, the OWNER agrees to pay such excess promptly, but nothing herein contained shall obligate the AGENT to advance its own funds on behalf of the OWNER.

2.3 To cause all employees of the AGENT who handle or are responsible for the safe-keeping of any monies of the OWNER to be covered by a fidelity bond in an amount and with a company determined by the AGENT _____

3. THE OWNER AGREES:

To give the AGENT the following authority and powers (all or any of which may be exercised in the name of the OWNER) and agrees to assume all expenses in connection therewith:

3.1 To advertise the Premises or any part thereof; to display signs thereon and to rent the same; to cause references of prospective tenants to be investigated; to sign leases for terms not in excess of _____two_ years and to renew and/or cancel the existing leases and prepare and execute the new leases without additional charge to the OWNER; provided, however, that the AGENT may collect from tenants all or any of the following: a late rent administrative charge, a non-negotiable check charge, credit report fee, a subleasing administrative charge and/or broker's commission and need not account for such charges and/or commission to the OWNER; to terminate tenancies and to sign and serve such notices as are deemed needful by the AGENT; to institute and prosecute actions to oust tenants and to recover possession of the Premises; to sue for and recover rent; and, when expedient, to settle, compromise, and release such actions or suits, or reinstate such tenancies. OWNER shall reimburse AGENT for all expenses of litigation including attorneys' fees, filing fees, and court costs which AGENT does not recover from tenants. AGENT may select the attorney of its choice to handle such litigation.

3.2 To hire, discharge, and pay all engineers, janitors, and other employees; to make or cause to be made all ordinary repairs and replacements necessary to preserve the Premises in its present condition and for the operating efficiency thereof and all alterations required to comply with lease requirements, and to do decorating on the Premises; to negotiate contracts for nonrecurring items not exceeding $ 5,000.00 and to enter into agreements for all necessary repairs, maintenance, minor alterations, and utility services; and to purchase supplies and pay all bills. AGENT shall secure the approval of the OWNER for any alterations of expenditures in excess of $ 5,000.00 for any one item, except monthly or recurring operating charges and emergency repairs in excess of the maximum, if, in the opinion of the AGENT, such repairs are necessary to protect the property from damage or to maintain services to the tenants as called for by their tenancy.

3.3 To collect rents and/or assessments and other items due or to become due and give receipts therefor and to deposit all funds collected hereunder in the AGENT's custodial account.

3.4 To handle tenants' security deposits and to comply, on the OWNER's behalf, with applicable state or local laws concerning the AGENT's responsibility for security deposits and interest thereon, if any.

3.5 To execute and file all returns and other instruments and do and perform all acts required of the OWNER as an employer with respect to the Premises under the Federal Insurance Contributions Acts, the Federal Unemployment Tax Act, and Subtitle C of the Internal Revenue Code of 1954 with respect to wages paid by the AGENT on behalf of the OWNER and under any similar federal and state law now or hereafter in force (and in connection therewith the OWNER agrees upon request to promptly execute and deliver to the AGENT all necessary powers of attorney, notices of appointment, and the like).

Figure 17.1
(cont.)

3.6 The AGENT shall not be required to advance any monies for the care or management of said property, and the OWNER agrees to advance all monies necessary therefor. If the AGENT shall elect to advance any money in connection with the property, the OWNER agrees to reimburse the AGENT forthwith and hereby authorizes the AGENT to deduct such advances from any monies due the OWNER. The AGENT shall, upon instruction from the OWNER, impound reserves each month for the payment of real estate taxes, insurance, or any other special expenditure. In addition, the OWNER agrees to establish a permanent Operating Reserve Account with the AGENT in the amount of $ __10,000.00__

4. THE OWNER FURTHER AGREES:

4.1 To indemnify, defend, and save the AGENT harmless from all suits in connection with the Premises and from liability for damage to property and injuries to or death of any employee or other person whomsoever, and to carry at his (its) own expense public liability, elevator liability (if elevators are part of the equipment of the Premises), and workmen's compensation insurance naming the OWNER and the AGENT and adequate to protect their interests and in form, substance, and amounts reasonably satisfactory to the AGENT, and to furnish to the AGENT certificates evidencing the existence of such insurance. Unless the OWNER shall provide such insurance and furnish such certificate within ___30___ days from the date of this Agreement, the AGENT may, but shall not be obligated to, place said insurance and charge the cost thereof to the account of the OWNER. All such insurance policies shall provide that the AGENT shall receive thirty (30) days' written notice prior to cancellation of the policy.

4.2 To pay all expenses incurred by the AGENT, including, but not limited to, reasonable attorneys' fees and AGENT's costs and time in connection with any claim, proceeding, or suit involving an alleged violation by the AGENT or the OWNER, or both, of any law pertaining to fair employment, fair credit reporting, environmental protection, rent control, taxes, or fair housing, including, but not limited to, any law prohibiting, or making illegal, discrimination on the basis of race, sex, creed, color, religion, national origin, or mental or physical handicap, provided, however, that the OWNER shall not be responsible to the AGENT for any such expenses in the event the AGENT is finally adjudicated to have personally, and not in a representative capacity, violated any such law. Nothing contained herein shall obligate the AGENT to employ counsel to represent the OWNER in any such proceeding or suit, and the OWNER may elect to employ counsel to represent the OWNER in any such proceeding or suit. The OWNER also agrees to pay reasonable expenses (or an apportioned amount of such expenses where other employers of AGENT also benefit from the expenditure) incurred by the AGENT in obtaining legal advice regarding compliance with any law affecting the premises or activities related thereto.

4.3 To indemnify, defend, and save the AGENT harmless from all claims, investigations, and suits, or from actions or failures to act of the OWNER, with respect to any alleged or actual violation of state or federal labor laws, it being expressly agreed and understood that as between the OWNER and the AGENT, all persons employed in connection with the Premises are employees of the OWNER, not the AGENT. However, it shall be the responsibility of the AGENT to comply with all applicable state or federal labor laws. The OWNER's obligation under this paragraph 4.3 shall include the payment of all settlements, judgments, damages, liquidated damages, penalties, forfeitures, back pay awards, court costs, litigation expense, and attorneys' fees.

4.4 To give adequate advance written notice to the AGENT if the OWNER desires that the AGENT make payment, out of the proceeds from the premises, of mortgage indebtedness, general taxes, special assessments, or fire, steam boiler, or any other insurance premiums. In no event shall the AGENT be required to advance its own money in payment of any such indebtedness, taxes, assessments, or premiums.

5. THE OWNER AGREES TO PAY THE AGENT EACH MONTH:

5.1 FOR MANAGEMENT: __$1,500.00__ per month or ___seven___ percent (__7__%) of the monthly gross receipts from the operation of the Premises during

**Figure 17.1
(cont.)**

the period this Agreement remains in full force and effect, whichever is the greater amount. Gross receipts are all amounts received from the operation of the Premises including, but not limited to, rents, parking fees, deposits, laundry income, and fees.

5.2 **APARTMENT LEASING** ___$150 per unit for each new rental___
___or lease renewal___

5.3 **COMMERCIAL LEASING** ___

5.4 **MODERNIZATION (REHABILITATION/CONSTRUCTION)**___two and___
___one-half percent (2½%) of total costs___

5.5 **FIRE RESTORATION** ___four percent (4%) of total costs___

5.6 **OTHER ITEMS OF MUTUAL AGREEMENT**___

6. **IT IS MUTUALLY AGREED THAT:**

6.1 The OWNER expressly withholds from the AGENT any power or authority to make any structural changes in any building or to make any other major alterations or additions in or to any such building or equipment therein, or to incur any expense chargeable to the OWNER other than expenses related to exercising the express powers above vested in the AGENT without the prior written direction of the following person:

Name _____ Address _____
___Elinor Q. Franks___   ___912 Knowles, Suite 900___
                               ___Burton, Iowa   50000___

except such emergency repairs as may be required because of danger to life or property or which are immediately necessary for the preservation and safety of the Premises or the safety of the tenants and occupants thereof or are required to avoid the suspension of any necessary service to the Premises.

6.2 The AGENT does not assume and is given no responsibility for compliance of any building on the Premises or any equipment therein with the requirements of any statute, ordinance, law, or regulation of any governmental body or of any public authority or official thereof having jurisdiction, except to notify the OWNER promptly or forward to the OWNER promptly any complaints, warnings, notices, or summonses received by it relating to such matters. The OWNER represents that to the best of his (its) knowledge the Premises and

**Figure 17.1
(cont.)**

such equipment comply with all such requirements and authorizes the AGENT to disclose the ownership of the Premises to any such officials and agrees to indemnify and hold harmless the AGENT, its representatives, servants, and employees, of and from all loss, cost, expense, and liability whatsoever which may be imposed on them or any of them by reason of any present or future violation or alleged violation of such laws, ordinances, statutes, or regulations.

6.3   In the event it is alleged or charged that any building on the Premises or any equipment therein or any act or failure to act by the OWNER with respect to the Premises or the sale, rental, or other disposition thereof fails to comply with, or is in violation of, any of the requirements of any constitutional provision, statute, ordinance, law, or regulation of any governmental body or any order or ruling of any public authority or official thereof having or claiming to have jurisdiction thereover, and the AGENT, in its sole and absolute discretion, considers that the action or position of the OWNER or registered managing agent with respect thereto may result in damage or liability to the AGENT, the AGENT shall have the right to cancel this Agreement at any time by written notice to the OWNER of its election so to do, which cancellation shall be effective upon the service of such notice. Such notice may be served personally or by registered mail, on or to the person named to receive the AGENT's monthly statement at the address designated for such person as provided in Paragraph 2.2 above, and if served by mail shall be deemed to have been served when deposited in the mails. Such cancellation shall not release the indemnities of the OWNER set forth in Paragraphs 4 and 6.2 above and shall not terminate any liability or obligation of the OWNER to the AGENT for any payment, reimbursement, or other sum of money then due and payable to the AGENT hereunder.

7.   This Agreement may be cancelled by OWNER before the termination date specified in paragraph 1 on not less than _____30_____ days' prior written notice to the AGENT, provided that such notice is accompanied by payment to the AGENT of a cancellation fee in an amount equal to _____30_____ % of the management fee that would accrue over the remainder of the stated term of the Agreement. For this purpose the monthly management fee for the remainder of the stated term shall be presumed to be the same as that of the last month prior to service of the notice of cancellation.

8.   The OWNER shall pay or reimburse the AGENT for any sums of money due it under this Agreement for services for actions prior to termination, notwithstanding any termination of this Agreement. All provisions of this Agreement that require the OWNER to have insured or to defend, reimburse, or indemnify the AGENT (including, but not limited to, Paragraphs 4.1, 4.2, and 4.3) shall survive any termination and, if AGENT is or becomes involved in any proceeding or litigation by reason of having been the OWNER's AGENT, such provisions shall apply as if this Agreement were still in effect. The parties understand and agree that the AGENT may withhold funds for thirty (30) days after the end of the month in which this Agreement is terminated to pay bills previously incurred but not yet invoiced and to close accounts.

This Agreement shall be binding upon the successors and assigns of the AGENT and their heirs, administrators, executors, successors, and assigns of the OWNER.

IN WITNESS WHEREOF, the parties hereto have affixed or caused to be affixed

their respective signatures this ___16th___ day of ___December___, 19_86__

WITNESSES: OWNER:

Michael J. Frey   _Elinor J. Franks_

Rachel F. Phillips   _____

_____

                                                    AGENT:

                                                    Firm __Don Silver Management__

                                                    By __Don Silver__

_____
Submitted by

The management agreement should be in writing and should cover the following points:

1. *Description* of the property.
2. *Time period* the agreement will cover.
3. *Definition of management's responsibilities.* All of the manager's duties should be stated in the contract; exceptions should be noted.
4. *Extent of manager's authority as an agent.* This provision should state what authority the manager is to have in such matters as hiring, firing and supervising employees, fixing rental rates for space, making expenditures and authorizing repairs within the limits established previously with the owner. (Repairs that exceed a certain expense limit may require the owner's written approval.)
5. *Reporting.* Agreement should be reached on the frequency and detail of the manager's periodic reports on operations and financial position. These reports serve as a means for the owner to monitor the manager's work and as a basis for both the owner and the manager to assess trends that can be used in shaping future management policy.
6. *Management fee.* The fee can be based on a percentage of gross or net income, a commission on new rentals, a fixed fee or a combination of these.
7. *Allocation of costs.* The agreement should state which of the property management expenses, such as custodial and other help, advertising, supplies and repairs, are to be charged to the property's expenses and paid by the owner.

After entering into an agreement with a property owner, a manager handles the property as the owner would. In all activities, the manager's first responsibility is to *realize the highest return on the property that is consistent with the owner's instructions.*

Before contracting to manage any property, the professional property manager should be certain that the building owner has realistic income expectations and is willing to spend money on necessary maintenance. Attempting to meet impossible owner demands by dubious methods can endanger the manager's reputation and prove detrimental to obtaining future business.

Management Considerations

A property manager must live up to both the letter and the spirit of the management agreement. The owner must be kept well informed on all matters of policy as well as on the financial condition of the property and its operation. A manager must keep in contact with others in the field, thus becoming increasingly knowledgeable on the subject and keeping informed on current policies pertaining to the profession.

The day-to-day responsibilities of the property manager are discussed next.

Budgeting Expenses

Before attempting to rent any property, a property manager should develop an operating budget based on anticipated revenues and expenses and reflecting the long-term goals of the owner. In preparing a budget, a manager should begin by allocating money for such continuous, fixed expenses as employees' salaries, real estate taxes, property taxes and insurance premiums.

Rents — expenses

Next, the manager should establish a cash reserve fund for such variable expenses as repairs, decorating and supplies. The amount allocated for the reserve fund can be computed from the previous yearly costs of the variable expenses.

Capital expenditures. If an owner and a property manager decide that modernization or renovation of the property would enhance its value, the manager should budget money to cover the costs of remodeling. The property manager should be thoroughly familiar with the *principle of contribution* (discussed in Chapter 18, "Real Estate Appraisal") or seek expert advice when estimating any increase in value expected by an improvement. In the case of large-scale construction, the expenses charged against the property's income should be spread over several years. Although budgets should be as accurate an estimate of cost as possible, adjustments may sometimes be necessary, especially in the case of new properties.

Renting the Property

Effective rental of the property is essential to the success of a property manager. However, the role of the manager in managing a property should not be confused with that of a broker acting as a leasing agent and solely concerned with renting space. The property manager may use the services of a leasing agent, but that agent does not undertake the full responsibility of maintenance and management of the property.

Setting rental rates. In establishing rental rates for a property, a basic concern must be that, in the long term, the income from the rentable space cover the fixed charges and operating expenses and also provide a fair return on the investment. Consideration must also be given to the prevailing rates in comparable buildings and the current level of vacancy in the property to be rented—supply and demand. Following a detailed survey of the competitive space available in the neighborhood, prices should be noted and adjusted for differences between neighboring properties and the property being managed. Annual rent adjustments are usually warranted.

Note that while apartment rental rates are stated in monthly amounts, office and commercial space rentals are usually stated according to either the annual or the monthly rate per square foot of space.

If a high level of vacancy exists, an immediate effort should be made to determine why. *A high level of vacancy does not necessarily indicate that rents are too high.* The trouble may be inept management or defects in the property. The manager should attempt to identify and correct the problems first, rather than immediately lower rents. Conversely, *while a high percentage of occupancy may appear to indicate an effective rental program, it could also mean that rental rates are too low.* With an apartment house or office building, any time the occupancy level exceeds 95 percent serious consideration should be given to raising the rents.

Tenant selection. Generally, the highest rents can be secured from satisfied tenants. While a broker may sell a property and then have no further dealings with the purchaser, a building manager's success is greatly dependent on retaining sound, long-term relationships. In selecting prospective commercial or industrial tenants, a manager should be sure that each person will "fit the space." The manager should be certain that: (1) the *size of the space* meets the tenant's requirements, (2) the tenant will have the *ability to pay* for the space for which he or she contracts, (3) the *tenant's business will be compatible* with the building and the other tenants and (4) if the tenant is likely to expand in the future, there will be *expansion space available.* After a prospect becomes a tenant, *the manager must be sure that the tenant remains satisfied in all respects commensurate with fair business dealing.*

Note that in selecting residential tenants, the property manager must comply with all federal and local fair housing laws (see Chapter 21).

Collecting rents. A building will not be a profitable operation unless the property manager can collect all rents when they are due. Any substantial loss resulting from nonpayment of rent will quickly eliminate the margin of profitability in an operation.

The best way to minimize problems with rent collection is to make a *careful selection* of tenants in the first place. A property manager's desire to have a high level of occupancy should not override good judgment in accepting only those tenants who can be expected to meet their financial obligations to the property owner. A property manager should investigate financial references given by the prospect, local credit bureaus and, when possible, the prospective tenant's former landlord.

The terms of rental payment should be spelled out in detail in the lease agreement. A *firm and consistent collection plan* with a sufficient system of notices and records should be established by the property manager. In cases of delinquency, every attempt must be made to make collections without resorting to legal action. For those cases in which it is required, a property manager must be prepared to initiate and follow through with the necessary steps in conjunction with legal counsel.

Maintaining the Property

One of the most important functions of a property manager is the supervision of property maintenance. A manager must learn to balance the provided services with the costs they entail so as to satisfy the tenants' needs while minimizing operating expenses. *Maintenance* actually covers several types of activities. First, the manager must *protect the physical integrity of the property* to ensure that the condition of the building and its grounds are kept at present levels over the long term. Preserving the property by repainting the exterior or replacing the heating system will help to keep the building functional and decrease routine maintenance costs.

A property manager must also *supervise the routine cleaning and repairs* of the building, including such day-to-day duties as cleaning common areas, minor carpentry and plumbing, and regularly scheduled upkeep of heating, air conditioning and landscaping.

In addition, especially when dealing with commercial or industrial space, a property manager will be called on to make **tenant improvements**—alterations to the interior of the building to meet the functional demands of the tenant. These alterations range from repainting to completely gutting the interior and redesigning the space. Tenant improvements are especially important when renting new buildings, since the interior is usually left incomplete so that it can be adapted to the needs of the individual tenants.

Supervision of modernization or renovation of buildings that have become functionally obsolete and thus unsuited to today's building needs is also important.

(See Chapter 18 for a definition of *functional obsolescence.*) The renovation of a building often increases the building's marketability and thus its possible income.

Hiring employees versus contracting for services. One of the major decisions a property manager faces is whether to contract for maintenance services from an outside firm or hire on-site employees to perform such tasks. This decision should be based on a number of factors, including size of the building, complexity of tenants' requirements and availability of suitable labor.

The Management Profession

For those interested in pursuing a career in property management, most metropolitan areas have local associations of building and property owners and managers that are affiliates of regional and national associations. The Institute of Real Estate Management was founded in 1933 and is part of the NATIONAL ASSOCIATION OF REALTORS®. The Institute awards the designation of *Certified Property Manager* (CPM) to persons who have met certain requirements. The Building Owners and Managers Association International (BOMA International) is a federation of local associations of owners and managers, primarily of office buildings. Training courses leading to the designation *Real Property Administrator* are offered by the Building Owners and Managers Institute International (BOMI International), an independent institute affiliated with BOMA. In addition, there are many specialized professional organizations for apartment managers, community association managers, shopping center managers and others.

Participation in groups such as these allows property managers to gain valuable professional knowledge, to discuss their problems with other managers facing similar issues and to promote the interests of the profession.

Risk Management

One of the most critical areas of responsibility for a property manager, because of the enormous dollar losses that can result from certain occurrences, is the field of insurance. Awareness of the purposes of insurance coverage, and how to make best use of the many types of insurance available are part of what is called **risk management.**

Risk management involves answering the question, "What will happen if something goes wrong?" The perils of any risk must be evaluated in terms of options. In considering the possibility of a loss, the property manager must decide whether it is better to:

- *avoid it,* by removing the source of risk, such as a swimming pool;
- *retain it,* to a certain extent, by insuring with a large *deductible* (loss not covered by the insurer);
- *control it,* by installing sprinklers, fire doors and other preventive measures; or
- *transfer it,* by taking out an insurance policy.

When insurance is considered, a competent, reliable insurance agent should be selected to survey the property and make recommendations. (The property manager, or a member of the management firm, may even be a licensed insurance broker and able to perform this task.) Additional insurance surveys should be obtained if any questions remain. Final decisions, however, must be made by the property owner. Note that *in most states, an insurance broker must be licensed as such.*

Types of Insurance Coverage

There are many kinds of insurance coverage available to income-property owners and managers. Some of the more common types are:

1. *Fire and hazard.* Fire insurance policies provide coverage against direct loss or damage to property from a fire on the premises. Standard fire coverage can be extended to cover hazards such as windstorm, hail, smoke damage or civil insurrection.
2. *Consequential loss, use and occupancy.* Consequential loss insurance, which can include rent loss, covers the loss of revenue to a business that occurs if the business's property cannot be used.
3. *Contents and personal property. Inland marine insurance* covers building contents and personal property during periods when they are not actually located on the business premises.
4. *Liability.* Public liability insurance covers the risks an owner assumes when the public enters the building. Claims are used to pay medical expenses for a person injured in the building as a result of the landlord's negligence. Another liability risk is that of medical or hospital payments for injuries sustained by building employees hurt in the course of their employment. These claims are covered by state laws known as **Workers' Compensation Acts.** These laws require a building owner who is an employer to obtain a workers' compensation policy from a private insurance company.
5. *Casualty.* Casualty insurance policies include coverage against theft, burglary, vandalism, machinery damage, and health and accident insurance. Casualty policies are usually written on specific risks, such as theft, rather than being all-inclusive.
6. *Surety bonds.* **Surety bonds** cover an owner against financial losses resulting from an employee's criminal acts or negligence while performing assigned duties.

Today, many insurance companies offer **multiperil policies** for apartment and business buildings. These policies offer the property manager an insurance package that includes such standard types of commercial coverage as fire, hazard, public liability and casualty.

Claims

When a claim is made under a policy insuring a building or other physical object, there are two possible methods of determining the amount of the claim. One is the *depreciated* actual or cash value of the damaged property, and the other is current replacement cost. When purchasing insurance, a manager must assess whether the property should be insured at full replacement cost or at a depreciated cost. As with the homeowners' policies discussed in Chapter 4, commercial policies include *coinsurance clauses* that require the insured to carry fire coverage, usually in an amount equal to 80 percent of the building's replacement value.

Summary

Property management is a specialized service to owners of income-producing properties in which the managerial function may be delegated to an individual or a firm with particular expertise in the field. The manager, as agent of the owner, becomes the administrator of the project and assumes the executive functions required for the care and operation of the property.

A management agreement establishing the agency relationship between owner and manager must be carefully prepared to define and authorize the manager's duties and responsibilities.

Projected expenses, combined with the manager's analysis of the condition of the building and the rent patterns in the neighborhood, will form the basis on which rental rates for the property are determined. Once a rent schedule is established, the property manager is responsible for soliciting tenants whose needs are suited to the available space and who are financially capable of meeting the proposed rents. The manager is generally obligated to collect rents, maintain the building, hire necessary employees, pay taxes for the building and deal with tenant problems.

Maintenance includes safeguarding the physical integrity of the property and performing routine cleaning and repairs as well as making tenant improvements— adapting the interior space and overall design of the property to suit the tenants' needs and meet the demands of the market.

In addition, the manager is expected to secure adequate insurance coverage for the premises. The basic types of coverage applicable to commercial structures include *fire and hazard insurance* on the property and fixtures, *consequential loss, use and occupancy insurance* to protect the owner against revenue losses and *casualty insurance* to provide coverage against such losses as theft, vandalism and destruction of machinery. The manager should also secure *public liability insurance* to insure the owner against claims made by people injured on the premises and *workers' compensation policies* to cover the claims of employees injured on the job.

Questions

1. Which of the following types of insurance coverage insures the property owner against the claims of employees injured while on the job?
   a. consequential loss
   b. workers' compensation
   c. casualty
   d. surety bond

2. In renting units in an apartment building, a property manager must comply with which of the following?
   a. the terms of the management agreement
   b. the lawful instructions of the owner
   c. fair housing laws
   d. all of the above

3. From a management point of view, apartment building occupancy that reaches as high as 98 percent would tend to indicate that:
   a. the building is poorly managed.
   b. the building has reached its maximum potential.
   c. the building is a desirable place to live.
   d. rents should be raised.

4. A guest slips on an icy apartment building stair and is hospitalized. A claim against the building owner for medical expenses may be paid under which of the following policies held by the owner?
   a. workers' compensation
   b. casualty
   c. liability
   d. fire and hazard

5. The relationship between a building owner and a property manager is:
   I. an agency relationship.
   II. established in the management agreement.
   a. I only
   b. II only
   c. both I and II
   d. neither I nor II

6. Which of the following should *not* be a consideration in selecting a tenant?
   a. the size of the space versus the tenant's requirements
   b. the tenant's ability to pay
   c. the racial and ethnic backgrounds of the tenants
   d. the compatibility of the tenant's business to other tenants' businesses

7. Risk management alternatives include:
   a. avoiding losses.
   b. controlling losses.
   c. transferring losses.
   d. all of the above

8. Tenant improvements are:
   a. fixtures.
   b. adaptations of space to suit tenants' needs.
   c. removable by the tenant.
   d. all of the above

9. In drawing up an operating budget, the property manager should consider:
   a. the variable expenses.
   b. the long-range desires of the owner.
   c. anticipated revenues.
   d. all of the above

10. Generally, the provisions of the manager-owner agreement should include:
    I. a definition of the manager's responsibilities.
    II. a listing of previous owners of the property.
    a. I only
    b. II only
    c. both I and II
    d. neither I nor II

11. Rents should be determined on the basis of:
    a. prevailing rental rates in the area.
    b. operating expenses, fixed charges and a proper net profit to the owner.
    c. current level of vacancy.
    d. all of the above

12. Property manager Frieda Jacobs hires Albert Weston as the full-time maintenance person for one of the buildings she manages. While repairing a faucet in one of the apartments, Weston steals a television set. Jacobs could protect the owner against this type of loss by purchasing:
    a. liability insurance.
    b. workers' compensation insurance.
    c. a surety bond.
    d. casualty insurance.

13. Before accepting a commercial tenant, the property manager should:
    a. determine if the available space fits the tenant's needs.
    b. check the tenant's ability to pay.
    c. check whether the tenant's business is compatible with the businesses of the other tenants.
    d. all of the above

14. The possible methods of determining the amount of a claim under an insurance policy covering damage to a building include the:
    I. replacement cost method.
    II. actual cash value method.
       a. I only   c. both I and II
       b. II only   d. neither I nor II

15. In assuming responsibility for the maintenance of a property, the manager is expected to:
    I. directly or indirectly supervise the routine cleaning and repair work of the building.
    II. adapt the interior space of the building to meet the requirements of individual tenants.
       a. I only   c. both I and II
       b. II only   d. neither I nor II

18

Real Estate Appraisal

Key Terms

Anticipation
Appraisal
Assemblage
Capitalization rate
Change
Competition
Conformity
Contribution
Cost approach
Depreciation
Direct market comparison approach
Environmental obsolescence
Functional obsolescence
Gross rent multiplier
Highest and best use

Income approach
Index method
Physical deterioration
Plottage
Progression
Quantity-survey method
Reconciliation
Regression
Replacement cost
Reproduction cost
Square-foot method
Substitution
Supply and demand
Unit-in-place method
Value

Overview

As stated earlier in the text, real estate is the business of value. Members of the general public informally estimate this value when they buy, sell or invest in real estate. A formal estimate of value is usually conducted by a professional real estate appraiser and serves as a basis for the pricing, financing, insuring or leasing of real property. This chapter will examine value—what determines it, adds to it and detracts from it. It will also discuss in detail the various methods professional appraisers use to estimate the value of residential as well as commercial and industrial real estate.

Appraising

An **appraisal** is an estimate or opinion of value. Formal appraisal reports are relied upon in important decisions made by mortgage lenders, investors, public utilities, governmental agencies, businesses and individuals.

Although the highest level of appraisal activity is conducted by skilled professionals, in most states, a person does not have to be licensed to appraise real estate. Some states require an appraiser to be a licensed broker or salesperson, and a handful of states require an appraisal license. The tumultuous real estate market of the 1980s has brought renewed attention to the absolute necessity for competent appraisals, and more controls may be expected on both state and national levels.

Not all estimates of real estate value are made by professional appraisers; often the real estate agent must help a seller arrive at a market value for property without the aid of a formal appraisal report. Thus, it is necessary for everyone engaged in the real estate business, even those who are not experts in appraisal, to possess at least a fundamental knowledge of real estate valuation.

Value

Value is an abstract word with many acceptable definitions. In a broad sense, **value** may be defined as the relationship between an object desired and a potential purchaser. It is the power of a good or service to command other goods or services in exchange. In terms of real estate appraisal, value may be described as the *present worth of future benefits arising from the ownership of real property.*

For a property to have value in the real estate market, it must have four characteristics that can be remembered by the acronym DUST:

1. *Demand.* The need or desire for possession or ownership backed up by the financial means to satisfy that need.
2. *Utility.* The capacity to satisfy human needs and desires.
3. *Scarcity.* A finite supply.
4. *Transferability.* The relative ease of transfer of ownership rights from one person to another.

Market Value

While a given parcel of real estate may have many different kinds of value at the same time (as illustrated in figure 18.1), generally the goal of an appraiser is an estimate of *market value.* The market value of real estate is the most probable price that a property should bring in a competitive and open market, allowing a reasonable time to find a purchaser who buys the property with knowledge of all the uses to which it is adapted and for which it is capable of being used. Included in this definition are the following key points:

1. Market value is the *most probable* price a property will bring—not the average price or the highest price.
2. Payment must be made in *cash* or its equivalent.

Market value - is what the buyer wants to pay and the seller wants to sell for

3. Buyer and seller are unrelated and are acting without *undue pressure*.

4. A *reasonable length of time* must be allowed for the property to be exposed in the *open market*.

**Figure 18.1
Kinds of Value**

Market Value	Salvage Value
Insurance Value *(handwritten: what it takes to repair or replace.)*	Book Value *(handwritten: specific price of property)*
Assessed Value *(handwritten: value of what you will pay for real estate value.)*	Depreciated Value
Mortgage Value *(handwritten: 80% Loan to value ratio. Bank 80% = 20% down.)*	Condemnation Value *(handwritten: court determines the value of property.)*

(handwritten: higher than market value)

---

5. Both buyer and seller must be *well informed* of the property's use and potential, including its assets and defects.

Market value versus market price. Market value is an estimate based on an analysis of comparable sales and other pertinent market data. *Market price,* on the other hand, is what a property has *actually* sold for—its sale price. Theoretically, the market price would be the same as market value. Market price can be taken as accurate evidence of current market value, however, only after considering all of the factors listed above. A sale from father to daughter, for instance, might well have been designed to favor one of the parties.

Basic Principles of Value

There are always a number of economic principles at work that affect the value of real estate. The most important of these principles are defined in the following paragraphs.

Highest and best use. The most profitable single use to which the property is adapted and needed or the use that is likely to be in demand in the reasonably near future is its **highest and best use.** Highest and best use is noted in every appraisal, but may also be the object of a more extensive analysis. For example, a highest-and-best-use study may show that a parking lot in a busy downtown area is not the highest and best use of the land.

Substitution. The principle of **substitution** states that the maximum value of a property tends to be set by the cost of purchasing an equally desirable and valuable substitute property.

Supply and demand. This principle states that the value of a property will increase if the supply decreases and the demand either increases or remains constant—and vice versa. For example, the last lot to be sold in a residential area where the demand for homes is high would probably be worth more than the first lot sold in that area.

Conformity. This means that maximum value is realized if the use of land conforms to existing neighborhood standards. In residential areas of single-family houses, for example, buildings should be similar in design, construction, size and age to other buildings in the neighborhood. Subdivision restrictions rely on the principle of conformity to ensure maximum future value.

Anticipation. This principle holds that value can increase or decrease in anticipation of some future benefit or detriment affecting the property. For example, the value of a house may be affected if there are rumors that an adjacent parcel may be converted to commercial use in the near future.

Increasing and diminishing returns. Improvements to land and structures will eventually reach a point at which they will no longer have an effect on property values. As long as money spent on improvements produces an increase in income or value, the *law of increasing returns* is applicable. But at the point where additional improvements will not produce a proportionate increase in income or value, the *law of diminishing returns* applies.

Regression and progression. The principle that, between dissimilar properties, the worth of the better property is adversely affected by the presence of the lesser-quality property is known as **regression.** Thus, in a neighborhood of modest homes, a structure that is larger, better maintained, and/or more luxurious, would tend to be valued in the same range as the others. Conversely, the principle of **progression** states that the worth of a lesser property tends to increase if it is located among better properties.

Plottage. The principle of **plottage** holds that the merging or consolidation of adjacent lots held by separate land owners into one larger lot may produce a higher total land value than the sum of the two sites valued separately. For example, if two adjacent lots are valued at $35,000 each, their total value if consolidated into one larger lot under a single use might be $90,000. The process of merging the two lots under one owner is known as **assemblage.**

Contribution. The value of any component of a property is what its addition contributes to the value of the whole or what its absence detracts from that value. For example, the cost of installing an air-conditioning system and remodeling an older office building may be greater than is justified by the increase in market value (a function of expected net increases) that may result from the improvement to the property.

Competition. This principle states that excess profits tend to attract competition. For example, the success of a retail store may attract investors to open similar stores in the area. This tends to mean less profit for all stores concerned unless the purchasing power in the area increases substantially.

Change. No physical or economic condition remains constant. Real estate, is subject to natural phenomena, such as tornadoes, fires, and routine wear and tear of the elements. The real estate business is also subject to the demands of its market, just as is any business. It is an appraiser's job to be knowledgeable about the past and, therefore perhaps predictable, effects of natural phenomena and the behavior of the marketplace.

| **The Three Approaches to Value** | In order to arrive at an accurate estimate of value, three basic approaches, or techniques, are traditionally used by appraisers: the direct market comparison approach, the cost approach and the income approach. Each method serves as a check against the others and narrows the range within which the final estimate of value will fall. Each method is generally considered most reliable for specific types of property. |

| **The Direct Market Comparison Approach** | In the **direct market comparison approach**, an estimate of value is obtained by comparing the subject property (the property under appraisal) with recently sold comparable properties (properties similar to the subject). This approach is most often used by brokers and salespeople when helping a seller to set a price for residential real estate in an active market. Since no two parcels of real estate are exactly alike, each comparable property must be compared to the subject property, and the sales prices must be adjusted for any dissimilar features. The principal factors for which adjustments must be made fall into four basic categories: |

1. *Date of sale.* An adjustment must be made if economic changes occur between the date of sale of the comparable property and the date of the appraisal.
2. *Location.* An adjustment may be necessary to compensate for locational differences. For example, similar properties might differ in price from neighborhood to neighborhood, or even in more desirable locations within the same neighborhood.
3. *Physical features.* Physical features that may require adjustments include age of building, size of lot, landscaping, construction, number of rooms, square feet of living space, interior and exterior condition, presence or absence of a garage, fireplace, or air conditioner and so forth.
4. *Terms and conditions of sale.* This consideration becomes important if a sale is not financed by a standard mortgage procedure.

After a careful analysis of the differences between comparable properties and the subject property, the appraiser assigns a dollar value to each of these differences. On the basis of their knowledge and experience, appraisers estimate dollar adjustments that reflect actual values assigned in the marketplace. The value of a feature present in the subject property but not in the comparable property is *added* to the total sales price. This presumes that, all other features being equal, a property having a feature (such as a fireplace or wet bar) not present in the comparable property would tend to have a higher market value solely because of this feature. (The feature need not be a physical amenity; it may be a locational or aesthetic feature.) Likewise, the value of a feature present in the comparable but not the subject property is *subtracted*. The adjusted sales prices of the comparables represent the probable value range of the subject property. From this range, a single market value estimate can be selected.

The market comparison approach is essential in almost every appraisal of real estate. It is considered the most reliable of the three approaches in appraising residential property, where the amenities (intangible benefits) may be difficult to measure. An example of the market data approach is shown in table 18.1.

Same = Similar.
= inferior.

**Table 18.1
Direct Market
Comparison
Approach to
Value**

	Subject Property	Comparables				
		A	B	C	D	E
Sale Price		$118,000	$112,000	$121,000	$116,500	$110,000
Location	good	same	poorer +4,500	same	same	same
Age	6 years	same	same	same	same	same
Size of Lot	60' × 135'	same	same	larger −5,000	same	larger −5,000
Landscaping	good	same	same	same	same	same
Construction	brick	same	same	same	same	same
Style	ranch	same	same	same	same	same
No. of Rooms	6	same	same	same	same	same
No. of Bedrooms	3	same	same	same	same	same
No. of Baths	1½	same	same	same	same	same
Sq. Ft. of Living Space	1500	same	same	same	same	same
Other Space (basement)	full basement	same	same	same	same	same
Condition— Exterior	average	better −1,500	poorer +1000	better −1,500	same	poorer +2,000
Condition— Interior	good	same	same	better −500	same	same
Garage	2-car attached	same	same	same	same	none +5,000
Other Improvements						
Financing						
Date of Sale		current	1 yr. ago +3,500	current	current	current
Net Adjustments		−1,500	+9,000	−7,000	-0-	+2,000
Adjusted Value		$116,500	$121,000	$114,000	$116,500	$112,000

Note: Since the value range of the properties in the comparison chart (excluding comparable B) is close, and comparable D required no adjustment, an appraiser would conclude that the indicated market value of the subject is $116,500.

The Cost Approach

The **cost approach** to value is based on the principle of substitution, which states that the maximum value of a property tends to be set by the cost of acquiring an equally desirable and valuable substitute property. The cost approach is sometimes called appraisal by summation. The cost approach consists of five steps:

1. Estimate the value of the land as if it were vacant and available to be put to its highest and best use.
2. Estimate the current cost of constructing the building(s) and site improvements.
3. Estimate the amount of accrued depreciation resulting from physical deterioration, functional obsolescence and/or locational obsolescence.
4. Deduct accrued depreciation from the estimated construction cost of new building(s) and site improvements.
5. Add the estimated land value to the depreciated cost of the building(s) and site improvements to arrive at the total property value.

Land value (step 1) is estimated by using the market comparison approach; that is, the location and improvements of the subject site are compared to those of similar nearby sites, and adjustments are made for significant differences.

There are two ways to look at the construction cost of a building for appraisal purposes (step 2): reproduction cost and replacement cost. **Reproduction cost** is the dollar amount required to construct an *exact duplicate* of the subject building at current prices. **Replacement cost** of the subject property would be the construction cost at current prices of a property that is not necessarily an exact duplicate, but serves the same purpose or function as the original. Replacement cost is most often used in appraising, since it eliminates obsolete features and takes advantage of current construction materials and techniques.

An example of the cost approach to value is shown in table 18.2.

Table 18.2 **Cost Approach to Value**		
Land Valuation: Size 60′ × 135′ @ $450 per front foot		= $27,000
Plus site improvements: driveway, walks, landscaping, etc.		= 8,000
Total Land Valuation		$35,000
Building Valuation: Replacement Cost		
1,500 sq. ft. @ $65 per sq. ft. =		$97,500
Less Depreciation:		
Physical depreciation,		
curable		
(items of deferred maintenance)		
exterior painting	$4,000	
incurable (structural deterioration)	9,750	
Functional obsolescence	2,000	
Environmental obsolescence	–0–	
Total Depreciation		–15,750
Depreciated Value of Building		$ 81,750
Indicated Value by Cost Approach		$116,750

Determining reproduction or replacement cost. An appraiser using the cost approach computes the reproduction or replacement cost of a building using one of the following methods:

1. **Square-foot method.** The cost per square foot of a recently built comparable structure is multiplied by the number of square feet in the subject building; this is the most common method of cost estimation. The example in table 18.2 uses the square-foot method.

   For some property, the cost per *cubic* foot of a recently built comparable structure is multiplied by the number of cubic feet in the subject structure.

2. **Unit-in-place method.** The replacement cost of a structure is estimated based on the construction cost per unit of measure of individual building components including material, labor, overhead and builder's profit. Most components are measured in square feet, although items like plumbing fixtures are estimated by unit cost.

3. **Quantity-survey method.** An estimate is made of the quantities of raw materials needed to replace the subject structure (lumber, plaster, brick and so on),

as well as of the current price of such materials and their installation costs. These factors are added to indirect costs (building permit, survey, payroll taxes, builder's profit) to arrive at the total replacement cost of the structure.

4. **Index method.** A factor representing the percentage increase to the present time of construction costs is applied to the original cost of the subject property.

Depreciation. In a real estate appraisal, **depreciation** refers to any condition that adversely affects the value of an *improvement* to real property. Land usually does not depreciate, except in such rare cases as misused farmland, downzoned urban parcels or improperly developed land. For appraisal purposes (as opposed to depreciation for tax purposes, which will be discussed in Chapter 22), depreciation is divided into three classes according to its cause:

1. **Physical deterioration**—*curable:* Repairs that are economically feasible and would result in an increase in appraised value equal to or exceeding their cost. Routine maintenance, such as painting, falls in this category.

   Physical deterioration—*incurable:* Repairs to the separate structural components of a building, which deteriorate at different rates. Roof, electrical system and plumbing fall in this category.

2. **Functional obsolescence**—*curable:* Physical or design features that are no longer considered desirable by property buyers, but could be replaced or redesigned at low cost. Outmoded fixtures, such as plumbing, are usually easily replaced. Room function might be redefined at no cost if the basic room layout allows for it. A bedroom adjacent to a kitchen, for instance, may be converted to a family room.

   Functional obsolescence—*incurable:* Currently undesirable physical or design features that could not be easily remedied. Many older multistory industrial buildings are considered less suitable than one-story buildings. An office building that cannot be air-conditioned suffers from functional obsolescence.

3. **Environmental (economic) obsolescence**—*incurable only:* Caused by factors not on the subject property, so that this type of obsolescence cannot usually be considered curable. Proximity to a nuisance, such as a polluting factory, would be an unchangeable factor that could not be expected to be cured by the owner of the subject property.

In determining a property's depreciation, most appraisers use the *breakdown method,* in which depreciation is broken down into all three classes, with separate estimates for curable and incurable factors in each class. Depreciation is difficult to measure, and the older the building, the more difficult it is to estimate. Much of functional obsolescence and all of environmental obsolescence can be evaluated only by considering the actions of buyers in the marketplace.

In Practice... *The cost approach is most helpful in the appraisal of special-purpose buildings such as schools, churches and public buildings. Such properties are difficult to appraise using other methods because there are seldom many local sales to use as comparables, and the properties do not ordinarily generate income.*

The Income Approach

The **income approach** to value is based on the present worth of the future rights to income. It assumes that the income derived from a property will control the value of that property. The income approach is used for valuation of income-producing properties—apartment buildings, office buildings, shopping centers and the like. In using the income approach to estimate value, an appraiser must go through the following steps:

1. Estimate annual potential *gross rental income.*
2. Based on market experience, deduct an appropriate allowance for vacancy and rent collection losses, and add income from other sources, such as concessions and vending machines, in order to arrive at the *effective gross income.*
3. Based on appropriate operating standards, deduct the annual *operating expenses* of the real estate from the effective gross income in order to arrive at the annual *net operating income.* Management costs are always included as operating expenses, even if the current owner also manages the property. Mortgage payments, however (including principal and interest), are debt service and *not* considered operating expenses.
4. Estimate the price a typical investor would pay for the income produced by this particular type and class of property. This is done by estimating the rate of return (or yield) that an investor will demand for the investment of capital in this type of building. This rate of return is called the **capitalization** (or "cap") **rate** and is determined by comparing the relationship of net operating income to the sales prices of similar properties that have sold in the current market. For example, a comparable property that is producing an annual net income of $15,000 is sold for $187,500. The capitalization rate is $15,000 ÷ 187,500, or eight percent. If other comparable properties sold at prices that yield substantially the same rate, it may be assumed that eight percent is the rate that the appraiser should apply to the subject property.
5. Finally, the capitalization rate is applied to the property's annual net income, resulting in the appraiser's estimate of the property value.

With the appropriate capitalization rate and the projected annual net operating income, the appraiser can obtain an indication of value by the income approach in the following manner:

$$\text{Net Operating Income} \div \text{Capitalization Rate} = \text{Value}$$

$$\text{Example: } \$15,000 \text{ income} \div 8\% \text{ cap rate} = \$187,500 \text{ value}$$

This formula and its variations are important in dealing with income property.

$$\frac{\text{Income}}{\text{Rate}} = \text{Value} \qquad\qquad \frac{\text{Income}}{\text{Value}} = \text{Rate} \qquad\qquad \text{Value} \times \text{Rate} = \text{Income}$$

A very simplified version of the computations used in applying the income approach is illustrated in table 18.3.

In Practice...

The most difficult step in the income approach to value is determining the appropriate capitalization rate for the property. This rate must be selected to recapture the original investment over the building's economic life, give the owner an acceptable rate of return on investment and provide for the repayment of borrowed capi-

Table 18.3
Income Approach to Value

Gross Annual Rental Income Estimate		$60,000
Less vacancy and collection losses (estimated) @ 6%		– 3,600
		$56,400
Income from other sources		+ 600
Effective Gross Income		$57,000
Expenses:		
Real estate taxes	$9,000	
Insurance	1,000	
Heat	2,800	
Maintenance	6,400	
Utilities, electricity, water, gas	800	
Repairs	1,200	
Decorating	1,400	
Replacements of equipment	800	
Legal and accounting	600	
Management	3,000	
Total Expenses		$27,000
Annual Net Operating Income		$30,000

Capitalization Rate = 10%

Capitalization of annual net income: $\dfrac{\$30,000}{.10}$

Indicated Value by Income Approach = $300,000

---

tal. *Note that an income property that carries with it a great deal of risk as an investment generally requires a higher rate of return than would a property considered a safe investment.*

Gross rent or income multipliers. Certain properties, such as single-family homes or two-flat buildings, are not purchased primarily for income. As a substitute for a more elaborate income analysis, the **gross rent multiplier** (GRM) method is often used in appraising such properties. The GRM relates the sales price of a property to its expected rental income. (Gross *monthly* income is used for residential property; gross *annual* income is used for commercial and industrial property.) The formula is as follows:

$$\frac{\text{Sale Price}}{\text{Rental Income}} = \text{Gross Rent Multiplier}$$

For example, if a home recently sold for $82,000 and its monthly rental income was $650, the GRM for the property would be computed thus:

$$\frac{\$82,000}{\$650} = \textit{126.2 GRM}$$

To establish an accurate GRM, an appraiser should have recent sales and rental data from at least four properties similar to the subject property. The most appropriate GRM can then be applied to the estimated fair market rental of the subject property in order to arrive at its market value. The formula would then be:

$$\text{Rental Income} \times \text{GRM} = \text{Estimated Market Value}$$

Table 18.4 shows some examples of GRM comparisons.

**Table 18.4
Gross Rent
Multiplier**

Comparable No.	Sale Price	Monthly Rent	GRM
1	$93,600	$650	144
2	78,500	450	174
3	95,500	675	141
4	82,000	565	145
Subject	?	625	?

Note: Based on an analysis of these comparisons, a GRM of 145 seems reasonable for homes in this area. In the opinion of an appraiser, then, the estimated value of the subject property would be $625 × 145, or $90,625.

If a property's income also comes from non-rental sources (such as sales concessions), a **gross income multiplier** (GIM) is similarly used.

In Practice...

Much skill is required to use multipliers accurately, because there is no fixed multiplier for all areas or all types of properties. Therefore, many appraisers view the technique simply as a quick, informal way to check the validity of a property value obtained by one of the other appraisal methods.

Reconciliation

If more than one of the three approaches to value are applied to the same property, they will normally produce as many separate indications of value. **Reconciliation** is the art of analyzing and effectively weighing the findings from the different approaches used.

Although each approach may serve as an independent guide to value, whenever possible all three approaches should be used as a check on the final estimate of value. The process of reconciliation is more complicated than simply taking the average of the derived value estimates. An average implies that the data and logic applied in each of the approaches are equally valid and reliable, and should therefore be given equal weight. In fact, however, certain approaches are more valid and reliable with some kinds of properties than with others.

For example, in appraising a home the income approach is rarely used, and the cost approach is of limited value unless the home is relatively new; therefore, the market data approach is usually given greatest weight in valuing single-family residences. In the appraisal of income or investment property, the income approach would normally be given the greatest weight. In the appraisal of churches, libraries, museums, schools and other special-use properties where there is little or no income or sales revenue, the cost approach would usually be assigned the greatest weight. From this analysis, or reconciliation, a single estimate of market value is produced.

**The Appraisal
Process**

The key to an accurate appraisal lies in the methodical collection of data. The appraisal process is an orderly set of procedures used to collect and analyze data in order to arrive at an ultimate value conclusion. The data are divided into two basic classes:

1. *Specific data,* covering details of the subject property as well as comparative data relating to costs, sales, and income and expenses of properties similar to and competitive with the subject property.
2. *General data,* covering the nation, region, city and neighborhood. Of particular importance is the neighborhood, where an appraiser finds the physical, economic, social and political influences that directly affect the value and potential of the subject property.

Figure 18.2 outlines the steps an appraiser takes in carrying out an appraisal assignment. The numbers in the following list correspond to the numbers on the flowchart.

1. *State the problem.* The kind of value to be estimated must be specified, and the valuation approach(es) most valid and reliable for the kind of property under appraisal must be selected.
2. *List the data needed and their sources.* Based on the approach(es) the appraiser will be using, the types of data needed and the sources to be consulted are listed.
3. *Gather, record and verify the general data.* Detailed information must be obtained concerning the economic, political and social conditions of the nation, region, city and neighborhood, and comments on the effects of these data on the subject property also must be obtained.
4. *Gather, record and verify the specific data on the subject property.* Specific data include information about the subject site and improvements.
5. *Gather, record and verify the data for the valuation approach used.* Depending upon the approach(es) used, comparative information relating to sales, income and expenses, and construction costs of comparable properties must be collected. As with steps 3 and 4, all data should be verified, usually by checking the same information against two different sources. In the case of sales data, one source should be a person directly involved in the transaction.
6. *Analyze and interpret the data.* All information collected must be reviewed to ensure that all relevant facts have been considered and handled properly and that no errors have been made in calculations.
7. *Reconcile data for final value estimate.* The appraiser makes a definite statement of conclusions reached. This is usually in the form of a value estimate of the property.
8. *Prepare appraisal report.* After the three approaches have been reconciled and an opinion of value reached, the appraiser prepares a formal written report for the client. The statement may be a completed *form,* a *letter* or a lengthy written *narrative.* The most complete appraisal report would contain the following information:
   a. the estimate of value and the date to which it applies.
   b. the purpose for which the appraisal was made.
   c. a description of the neighborhood and the subject property.
   d. factual data covering costs, sales, and income and expenses of similar, recently sold properties.
   e. an analysis and interpretation of the data collected.
   f. a presentation of one or more of the three approaches to value in enough detail to support the appraiser's final value conclusion.
   g. any qualifying conditions.
   h. supportive material, such as charts, maps, photographs, floor plans, leases and contracts.
   i. the certification and signature of the appraiser.

Figure 18.2
The Appraisal
Process

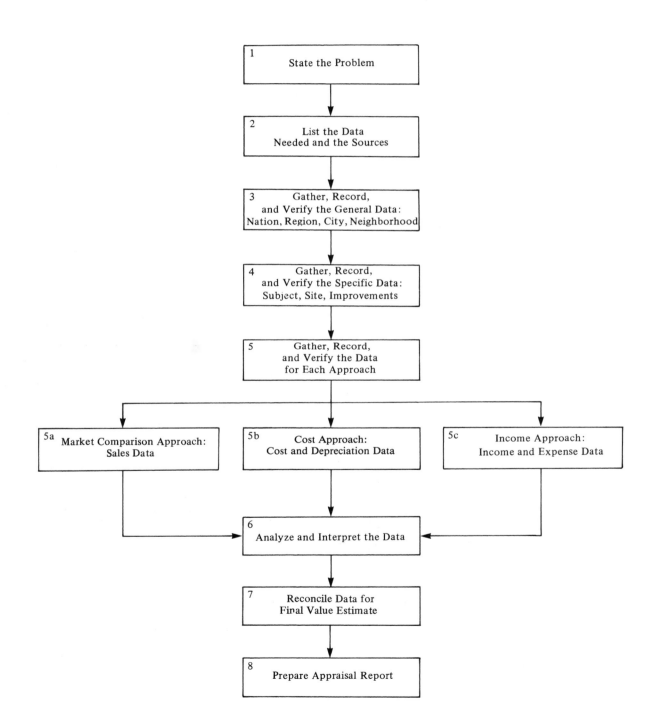

**Figure 18.3
Residential Appraisal
Report**

Property Description & Analysis **UNIFORM RESIDENTIAL APPRAISAL REPORT** File No.

SUBJECT

Property Address	Census Tract	LENDER DISCRETIONARY USE
City	County	State	Zip Code	Sale Price $
Legal Description		Date
Owner/Occupant	Map Reference	Mortgage Amount $
Sale Price $	Date of Sale	PROPERTY RIGHTS APPRAISED	Mortgage Type
Loan charges/concessions to be paid by seller $	☐ Fee Simple	Discount Points and Other Concessions
R.E. Taxes $	Tax Year	HOA $/Mo.	☐ Leasehold	Paid by Seller $
Lender/Client	☐ Condominium (HUD/VA)	
	☐ De Minimis PUD	Source

NEIGHBORHOOD

LOCATION	☐ Urban	☐ Suburban	☐ Rural
BUILT UP	☐ Over 75%	☐ 25-75%	☐ Under 25%
GROWTH RATE	☐ Rapid	☐ Stable	☐ Slow
PROPERTY VALUES	☐ Increasing	☐ Stable	☐ Declining
DEMAND/SUPPLY	☐ Shortage	☐ In Balance	☐ Over Supply
MARKETING TIME	☐ Under 3 Mos.	☐ 3-6 Mos.	☐ Over 6 Mos.

NEIGHBORHOOD ANALYSIS — Good Avg. Fair Poor
- Employment Stability
- Convenience to Employment
- Convenience to Shopping
- Convenience to Schools
- Adequacy of Public Transportation
- Recreation Facilities
- Adequacy of Utilities
- Property Compatibility
- Protection from Detrimental Cond.
- Police & Fire Protection
- General Appearance of Properties
- Appeal to Market

PRESENT LAND USE	%	LAND USE CHANGE	PREDOMINANT OCCUPANCY	SINGLE FAMILY HOUSING
Single Family		Not Likely	☐ Owner	PRICE $ (000) — AGE (yrs)
2-4 Family		Likely	☐ Tenant	
Multi-family		In process	☐ Vacant (0-5%)	Low
Commercial		To:	☐ Vacant (over 5%)	High
Industrial				Predominant
Vacant				—

Note: Race or the racial composition of the neighborhood are not considered reliable appraisal factors.
COMMENTS:

SITE

Dimensions		Topography
Site Area		Size
Zoning Classification		Shape
HIGHEST & BEST USE: Present Use	Other Use	Drainage

Corner Lot
Zoning Compliance

UTILITIES	Public	Other	SITE IMPROVEMENTS	Type	Public	Private
Electricity	☐		Street		☐	☐
Gas	☐		Curb/Gutter		☐	☐
Water	☐		Sidewalk		☐	☐
Sanitary Sewer	☐		Street Lights		☐	☐
Storm Sewer	☐		Alley			

View
Landscaping
Driveway
Apparent Easements
FEMA Flood Hazard Yes* ___ No ___
FEMA* Map/Zone

COMMENTS (Apparent adverse easements, encroachments, special assessments, slide areas, etc.):

IMPROVEMENTS

GENERAL DESCRIPTION	EXTERIOR DESCRIPTION	FOUNDATION	BASEMENT	INSULATION
Units	Foundation	Slab	Area Sq. Ft.	Roof ☐
Stories	Exterior Walls	Crawl Space	% Finished	Ceiling ☐
Type (Det./Att.)	Roof Surface	Basement	Ceiling	Walls ☐
Design (Style)	Gutters & Dwnspts.	Sump Pump	Walls	Floor ☐
Existing	Window Type	Dampness	Floor	None ☐
Proposed	Storm Sash	Settlement	Outside Entry	Adequacy
Under Construction	Screens	Infestation		Energy Efficient Items:
Age (Yrs.)	Manufactured House			
Effective Age (Yrs.)				

ROOM LIST

ROOMS	Foyer	Living	Dining	Kitchen	Den	Family Rm.	Rec. Rm.	Bedrooms	# Baths	Laundry	Other	Area Sq. Ft.
Basement												
Level 1												
Level 2												

Finished area **above** grade contains: Rooms; Bedroom(s); Bath(s); Square Feet of Gross Living Area

INTERIOR

SURFACES	Materials/Condition
Floors	
Walls	
Trim/Finish	
Bath Floor	
Bath Wainscot	
Doors	
Fireplace(s)	#

HEATING		KITCHEN EQUIP.	ATTIC
Type		Refrigerator	None ☐
Fuel		Range/Oven	Stairs ☐
Condition		Disposal	Drop Stair ☐
Adequacy		Dishwasher	Scuttle ☐
COOLING		Fan/Hood	Floor ☐
Central		Compactor	Heated ☐
Other		Washer/Dryer	Finished ☐
Condition		Microwave	
		Intercom	

IMPROVEMENT ANALYSIS — Good Avg. Fair Poor
- Quality of Construction
- Condition of Improvements
- Room Sizes/Layout
- Closets and Storage
- Energy Efficiency
- Plumbing-Adequacy & Condition
- Electrical-Adequacy & Condition
- Kitchen Cabinets-Adequacy & Cond.
- Compatibility to Neighborhood
- Appeal & Marketability
- Estimated Remaining Economic Life ___ Yrs.
- Estimated Remaining Physical Life ___ Yrs.

AUTOS

CAR STORAGE:			
	Garage ☐	Attached ☐	Adequate ☐	House Entry
No. Cars	Carport ☐	Detached ☐	Inadequate ☐	Outside Entry
Condition	None	Built-In ☐	Electric Door ☐	Basement Entry

COMMENTS

Additional features:

Depreciation (Physical, functional and external inadequacies, repairs needed, modernization, etc.):

General market conditions and prevalence and impact in subject/market area regarding loan discounts, interest buydowns and concessions:

Figure 18.3 (cont.)

Valuation Section · **UNIFORM RESIDENTIAL APPRAISAL REPORT** File No.

Purpose of Appraisal is to estimate Market Value as defined in the Certification & Statement of Limiting Conditions.

COST APPROACH

BUILDING SKETCH (SHOW GROSS LIVING AREA ABOVE GRADE)
If for Freddie Mac or Fannie Mae, show only square foot calculations and cost approach comments in this space.

ESTIMATED REPRODUCTION COST–NEW–OF IMPROVEMENTS:

Dwelling _____ Sq. Ft. @ $ _____	=	_____
_____ Sq. Ft. @ $ _____	=	_____
Extras _____	=	_____
	=	_____
Special Energy Efficient Items _____	=	_____
Porches, Patios, etc. _____	=	_____
Garage/Carport _____ Sq. Ft. @ $ _____	=	_____
Total Estimated Cost New	= $	_____

	Physical	Functional	External
Less			
Depreciation			

Depreciated Value of Improvements	= $	_____
Site Imp. "as is" (driveway, landscaping, etc.)	= $	_____
ESTIMATED SITE VALUE	= $	_____
(If leasehold, show only leasehold value.)		
INDICATED VALUE BY COST APPROACH	= $	_____

(Not Required by Freddie Mac and Fannie Mae)
Does property conform to applicable HUD/VA property standards? ☐ Yes ☐ No
If No, explain: _____

Construction Warranty ☐ Yes ☐ No
Name of Warranty Program _____
Warranty Coverage Expires _____

The undersigned has recited three recent sales of properties most similar and proximate to subject and has considered these in the market analysis. The description includes a dollar adjustment, reflecting market reaction to those items of significant variation between the subject and comparable properties. If a significant item in the comparable property is superior to, or more favorable than, the subject property, a minus (−) adjustment is made, thus reducing the indicated value of subject; if a significant item in the comparable is inferior to, or less favorable than, the subject property, a plus (+) adjustment is made, thus increasing the indicated value of the subject.

SALES COMPARISON ANALYSIS

ITEM	SUBJECT	COMPARABLE NO. 1		COMPARABLE NO. 2		COMPARABLE NO. 3	
Address							
Proximity to Subject							
Sales Price	$	$		$		$	
Price/Gross Liv. Area	$ ☑	$ ☑		$ ☑		$ ☑	
Data Source							
VALUE ADJUSTMENTS	DESCRIPTION	DESCRIPTION	+ (−) $ Adjustment	DESCRIPTION	+ (−) $ Adjustment	DESCRIPTION	+ (−) $ Adjustment
Sales or Financing Concessions							
Date of Sale/Time							
Location							
Site/View							
Design and Appeal							
Quality of Construction							
Age							
Condition							
Above Grade Room Count	Total · Bdrms · Baths	Total · Bdrms · Baths		Total · Bdrms · Baths		Total · Bdrms · Baths	
Gross Living Area	Sq. Ft.	Sq. Ft.		Sq. Ft.		Sq. Ft.	
Basement & Finished Rooms Below Grade							
Functional Utility							
Heating/Cooling							
Garage/Carport							
Porches, Patio, Pools, etc.							
Special Energy Efficient Items							
Fireplace(s)							
Other (e.g. kitchen equip., remodeling)							
Net Adj. (total)		☐ + ☐ − $		☐ + ☐ − $		☐ + ☐ − $	
Indicated Value of Subject		$		$		$	

Comments on Sales Comparison: _____

INDICATED VALUE BY SALES COMPARISON APPROACH .... $ _____
INDICATED VALUE BY INCOME APPROACH (If Applicable) Estimated Market Rent $ _____ /Mo. x Gross Rent Multiplier _____ = $ _____
This appraisal is made ☐ "as is" ☐ subject to the repairs, alterations, inspections or conditions listed below ☐ completion per plans and specifications.
Comments and Conditions of Appraisal: _____

RECONCILIATION

Final Reconciliation: _____

This appraisal is based upon the above requirements, the certification, contingent and limiting conditions, and Market Value definition that are stated in
☐ FmHA, HUD &/or VA instructions.
☐ Freddie Mac Form 439 (Rev. 7/86)/Fannie Mae Form 1004B (Rev. 7/86) filed with client _____ 19 _____ ☐ attached.
I (WE) ESTIMATE THE MARKET VALUE, AS DEFINED, OF THE SUBJECT PROPERTY AS OF _____ 19 _____ to be $ _____
I (We) certify: that to the best of my (our) knowledge and belief the facts and data used herein are true and correct; that I (we) personally inspected the subject property, both inside and out, and have made an exterior inspection of all comparable sales cited in this report; and that I (we) have no undisclosed interest, present or prospective therein.

Appraiser(s) SIGNATURE _____   Review Appraiser SIGNATURE _____   ☐ Did ☐ Did Not
NAME _____   (if applicable) NAME _____   Inspect Property

Freddie Mac Form 70 10/86   Fannie Mae Form 1004 10/86

Figure 18.3 is a typical appraisal report form. Note that, even in such a brief report, detailed descriptions of the neighborhood and property being appraised are required.

The Profession of Appraising

In 1932 the American Institute of Real Estate Appraisers was founded. A few years later another organization, now known as the Society of Real Estate Appraisers, was formed. Through the years a number of other professional appraisal organizations have come into existence; they include the American Society of Appraisers, the National Association of Review Appraisers, the National Association of Independent Fee Appraisers, and the American Society of Farm Managers and Rural Appraisers. The American Institute and the Society are the most recognized of these appraisal organizations.

The American Institute offers the professional designations of RM (Residential Member) and the MAI (Member of the Appraisal Institute). The Society offers the designations of SRA (Senior Residential Appraiser), SRPA (Senior Real Property Appraiser) and SREA (Senior Real Estate Analyst). The National Association of Independent Fee Appraisers offers the designations of IFA (member) and IFAS (senior member).

Through these groups, courses have been established in universities and colleges, and books, journals and other publications devoted to various aspects of appraising have come into existence. Appraising has now become the most specialized branch of real estate.

Summary

To *appraise* real estate means to *estimate its value.* Although there are many types of value, the most common objective of an appraisal is to estimate *market value*—the most probable sale price of a property. Basic to appraising are certain underlying economic principles, such as highest and best use, substitution, supply and demand, conformity, anticipation, increasing and diminishing returns, regression, progression, plottage, contribution, competition and change.

A professional appraiser analyzes a property through three approaches to value. In the *direct market comparison approach,* the value of the subject property is compared with the values of others like it that have sold recently. Since no two properties are exactly alike, adjustments must be made to account for any differences. With the *cost approach,* an appraiser calculates the cost of building a similar structure on a similar site. The appraiser then subtracts depreciation (loss in value), which reflects the differences between new properties of this type and the present condition of the subject property. The *income approach* is an analysis based on the relationship between the rate of return that an investor requires and the net income that a property produces.

A special, informal version of the income approach, called the *gross rent multiplier* (GRM), is often used to estimate the value of single-family residential properties that are not usually rented but could be. The GRM is computed by dividing the sales price of a property by its gross monthly rent.

Normally, the application of the different approaches will result in as many different estimates of value. In the process of *reconciliation,* the validity and reliability of each approach are weighed objectively to arrive at the single best and most supportable conclusion of value.

Questions

1. Which of the following approaches to value makes use of a cap rate?

   a. market comparison
   b. cost
   c. income
   d. all of the above

2. The elements of value include which of the following?

   a. utility
   b. scarcity
   c. demand
   d. all of the above

3. The principle of value that states that two adjacent parcels of land combined into one larger parcel could have a greater value than the two parcels valued separately is called:

   a. substitution.
   b. plottage.
   c. regression.
   d. progression.

4. The amount of money a property commands in the marketplace is its:

   a. market price.
   b. market value.
   c. capitalization rate.
   d index.

5. Joe Hamel has his "dream house" constructed for $100,000 in an area where most newly constructed houses are not as well-equipped as his and typically sell for only $80,000. The value of Hamel's house is likely to be affected by the principle of:

   a. progression.   c. change.
   b. assemblage.   d. regression.

6. In Question 5, the owners of the lesser-valued houses in Hamel's immediate area are likely to be affected by the principle of:

   a. progression.   c. competition.
   b. increasing returns.   d. regression.

7. Depreciation, as used in real estate appraisals, can be caused by which of the following?

   a. functional obsolescence
   b. physical deterioration
   c. environmental obsolescence
   d. all of the above

8. *Reconciliation* refers to which of the following?

   a. loss of value due to any cause
   b. separating the value of the land from the total value of the property in order to compute depreciation
   c. analyzing the results obtained by the different approaches to value to determine a final estimate of value
   d. the process by which an appraiser determines the highest and best use for a parcel of land

9. One method an appraiser uses to determine a building's replacement cost involves the estimated cost of the raw materials needed to build the structure, plus labor and indirect costs. This is called the:

   a. square-foot method.
   b. quantity-survey method.
   c. cubic-foot method.
   d. unit-in-place method.

10. If a property's annual net income is $24,000 and it is valued at $300,000, what is its capitalization rate?

    a. 12.5 percent   c. 15 percent
    b. 10.5 percent   d. 8 percent

11. Certain figures must be determined by an appraiser before value can be computed by the income approach. Which one of the following is *not* required for this process?

    a. annual net operating income
    b. capitalization rate
    c. accrued depreciation
    d. annual gross income

12. The ceiling, or top limit, of value of an improved parcel of real estate usually is:
    a. the sales price paid for a similar property.
    b. the cost of buying a lot and erecting a similar building on it.
    c. the capitalized value of present net rents.
    d. the depreciation value of the building plus the cost of land.

13. The income approach would be given the most weight in the valuation of a(n):
    a. single-family residence.
    b. industrial property.
    c. strip shopping center.
    d. school.

14. The market value of a parcel of real estate is:
    I. an estimate of its future benefits.
    II. the amount of money paid for the property.
       a. I only   c. both I and II
       b. II only   d. neither I nor II

15. Capitalization is the process by which annual net operating income is used as the basis to:
    a. determine cost.
    b. estimate value.
    c. establish depreciation.
    d. determine potential tax value.

16. From the reproduction or replacement cost of the building, an appraiser deducts depreciation, which represents:
    a. the remaining economic life of the building.
    b. remodeling costs to increase rentals.
    c. loss of value due to any cause.
    d. costs to modernize the building.

17. In the direct market comparison approach to value, the probable sales price of a building may be estimated by:
    I. capitalizing net operating income.
    II. considering sales of similar properties.
       a. I only   c. both I and II
       b. II only   d. neither I nor II

18. Which of the following factors would *not* be important in comparing properties under the direct market comparison approach to value?
    a. difference in dates of sale
    b. difference in real estate taxes
    c. difference in appearance and condition
    d. difference in original cost

19. In the income approach to value:
    I. the reproduction or replacement cost of the building must be computed.
    II. the capitalization rate must be estimated.
       a. I only   c. both I and II
       b. II only   d. neither I nor II

20. In the cost approach to value, it is necessary to:
    a. determine a dollar value for depreciation.
    b. estimate future expenses and operating costs.
    c. check sales prices of recently sold homes in the area.
    d. a and b

21. The appraised value of a residence with four bedrooms and one bathroom would probably be reduced because of:
    a. economic obsolescence.
    b. functional obsolescence.
    c. physical deterioration—curable.
    d. physical deterioration—incurable.

22. A factor representing the percentage increase in construction costs over time is used in the:
    a. square-foot method.
    b. quantity-survey method.
    c. unit-in-place method.
    d. index method.

19

Control of Land Use

Overview

The various ownership rights a person possesses in a parcel of real estate are subject to certain public and private land-use controls, such as zoning ordinances, building codes and deed restrictions. The purpose of these controls is to ensure that our limited supply of land is being put to its most beneficial use, considering the needs of the general public as well as private owners. This chapter will discuss the three types of land-use controls and how they help shape and preserve the physical surface of our nation.

| Land-Use Controls | The control and regulation of land use is accomplished through: (1) public land-use controls, (2) private land-use controls through deed restrictions and (3) public ownership of land—including parks, schools and expressways—by federal, state and local governments. |

Public Controls

What is referred to as the "police power" of the states is their inherent authority to adopt regulations necessary to protect the public health, safety and general welfare. The states, in turn, allow counties, cities and towns to make regulations in keeping with general laws. Our largely urban population and the increasing demands placed on our limited natural resources have made it necessary for cities, towns and villages to increase their limitations on the private use of real estate. We now have controls over noise, air and water pollution, as well as population density.

Regulations on privately owned real estate include the following:

1. planning
2. zoning
3. subdivision regulations
4. codes that regulate building construction, safety and public health
5. environmental protection legislation

The Master Plan

The primary method by which local governments recognize development goals is through the formulation of a comprehensive **master plan**, also commonly referred to as a *general plan*. Cities and counties develop master plans to insure that social and economic needs are balanced against environmental and aesthetic concerns.

The master plan is both a statement of policies and a presentation of how those policies can be realized. As created by the city, county or regional *planning commission*, a typical master plan provides for:

- *land use*, including standards of population density and economic development;
- *public facilities*, including schools, civic centers and utilities;
- *circulation*, including public transportation and highways;
- *conservation* of natural resources; and
- *noise problems*.

Economic and physical surveys both are essential in preparing a master plan. County-wide plans must also include the coordination of numerous civic plans and developments to ensure orderly city growth with stabilized property values.

City plans are put into effect by enactment and enforcement of zoning ordinances, our next topic.

Zoning   **Zoning ordinances** are laws of local government authorities (such as cities and counties) that regulate and control the use of land and structures within designated districts or zones. Zoning regulates and affects such things as use of the land, lot sizes, types of structures permitted, building heights, setbacks (the minimum distance away from streets or sidewalks that structures may be built) and density (the ratio of land area to structure area or population). The purpose of zoning is to implement a local master plan.

Zoning powers are conferred on municipal governments by state **enabling acts.** There are no nationwide zoning ordinances; with the exception of Hawaii, no states have statewide zoning ordinances. (State and federal governments may, however, regulate land use through special legislation, such as scenic easement and coastal management laws).

Zoning ordinances generally divide land use into use classifications: (1) residential, (2) commercial, (3) industrial and (4) agricultural. A fourth use now included by many communities is *cluster zoning*, or *multiple-use zoning*, which permits planned unit developments.

To ensure adequate control, land-use areas are further divided into subclasses. For example, residential areas may be subdivided to provide for detached single-family dwellings, semidetached structures containing not more than four dwelling units, walk-up apartments, high-rise apartments and so forth. In addition, some communities require the use of **buffer zones**—such as landscaped parks and playgrounds—to separate and screen residential areas from nonresidential areas.

Adoption of zoning ordinances. Today, almost all cities with populations in excess of 10,000 have enacted comprehensive zoning ordinances governing the utilization of land located *within corporate limits*. Many states have enacted legislation that provides that the use of land located *within one to three miles* of an incorporated area must receive the approval and consent of the incorporated area, even if the property is not contiguous to the village, town or city.

Zoning ordinances must not violate the rights of individuals and property holders (as provided under the due process provisions of the Fourteenth Amendment of the U.S. Constitution) or the various provisions of the state constitution of the state in which the real estate is located. If the means used to regulate the use of property are destructive, unreasonable, arbitrary or confiscatory, the legislation is usually considered void. *Tests* commonly applied in determining the validity of ordinances require that:

1. The power must be exercised in a reasonable manner.
2. The provisions must be clear and specific.
3. The ordinance must be free from discrimination.
4. The ordinance must promote public health, safety and general welfare under the police power concept.
5. The ordinance must apply to all property in a similar manner.

When land is taken for public use by the government's power of eminent domain, the owner must receive compensation. When *downzoning* occurs in an area—for instance, when land zoned for residential construction is rezoned for conservation or recreational purposes only—the state is ordinarily not responsible for compensating property owners for any resulting loss of value. However, if the courts find that a "taking" has occurred, then the downzoning will be held to be an unconstitutional attempt to use the power of eminent domain without providing fair compensation to the property owner.

Zoning laws are generally enforced through local requirements that building permits must be obtained before property owners can build on their land. A permit will not be issued unless a proposed structure conforms to the permitted zoning, among other requirements.

Nonconforming use. In the enforcement of a zoning ordinance, a frequent problem is the situation in which an improvement does not conform to the zoning use because it was erected prior to the enactment of the zoning law. This problem is most common in the case of sign ordinances. Such **nonconforming uses** may be allowed to continue for a specific number of years or until: (1) the improvements are destroyed or torn down; (2) the current use is discontinued; or (3) the ownership of the property is transferred. If the nonconforming use is allowed to continue indefinitely, it is considered to be "grandfathered in" to the new zoning.

Zoning boards of appeal. **Zoning appeal boards** have been established in most communities for the specific purpose of hearing complaints about the effects of zoning ordinances on specific parcels of property. Petitions may be presented to the appeal board for variances or exceptions in the zoning law.

Zoning variations. Each time a plan is created or a zoning ordinance enacted, some owners are inconvenienced and want to change the use of a property. Generally, such owners may appeal for either a conditional-use permit or a variance to allow a use that does not meet zoning requirements.

A **conditional-use permit** is usually granted a property owner to allow a special use of property if that is in the public interest—such as a church in a residential district. A **variance** may be sought to provide a deviation from an ordinance. For example, if an owner's lot is level next to a road, but slopes steeply 30 feet away from the road, the zoning board may be willing to allow a variance so the owner can build closer to the road than would normally be allowed.

In addition, a property owner can change the zoning classification of a parcel of real estate by obtaining an *amendment* to the official *zoning map,* which is part of the original zoning ordinance for the area. The proposed amendment must be brought before a public hearing on the matter and approved by the governing body of the community.

When local officials fail to grant the desired relief from zoning regulations, the unhappy property owner can appeal to the courts.

Subdivision Regulations

Most communities have adopted **subdivision regulations,** often as part of a master plan. These will be covered in detail in Chapter 20. Subdivision regulations usually provide for the following:

1. location, grading, alignment, surfacing and widths of streets, highways and other rights of way.
2. installation of sewers and water mains.
3. minimum dimensions of lots and length of blocks.

4. building and setback lines.

5. areas to be reserved or dedicated for public use, such as parks or schools.

6. easements for public utilities.

Subdivision regulations, like all other forms of zoning or building regulations, cannot be static. They must remain flexible to meet the ever-changing needs of society.

Building Codes

Most cities and towns have enacted ordinances to *specify construction standards* that must be met when repairing or erecting buildings. These are called **building codes,** and they set the requirements for kinds of materials, sanitary equipment, electrical wiring, fire prevention standards and the like.

Most communities require the issuance of a **building permit** by the city clerk or other official before a person can build a structure or alter or repair an existing building on property within the corporate limits of the municipality. Through the permit requirement, city officials are made aware of new construction or alterations and can verify compliance with building codes and zoning ordinances by examining the plans and inspecting the work. Once the completed structure has been inspected and found satisfactory, the city inspector issues a *certificate of occupancy.*

If the construction of a building or an alteration violates a deed restriction (discussed later in this chapter), the issuance of a building permit will *not* cure this violation. A building permit is merely evidence of the applicant's compliance with municipal regulations.

In Practice...

The subject of city planning, zoning and restriction of the use of real estate is extremely technical, and the interpretation of the law is not altogether clear. Questions concerning any of these subjects in relation to real estate transactions should be referred to legal counsel.

Environmental Protection Legislation

Federal and state legislators have passed a number of environmental protection laws in an attempt to respond to the growing public concern over the improvement and preservation of America's natural resources.

The various states have responded to the environmental issue by passing a variety of localized environmental protection laws regarding all forms of pollution—air, water, noise and solid waste disposal. For example, many states have enacted laws that prevent builders or private individuals from constructing septic tanks or other effluence-disposal systems in certain areas, particularly where public bodies of water—streams, lakes and rivers—are affected.

In addition to the states and federal government, cities and counties also frequently pass environmental legislation.

Private Land-Use Controls

A real estate owner can include in the deed, when property is conveyed, **a deed restriction** limiting the use of the property. ← must be lawful

There is a distinction between restrictions on the grantee's right to *sell* and restrictions on the grantee's right to *use*. In general, provisions in a deed conveying a fee simple estate with restrictions that the grantee will not sell, mortgage or convey it are void. Such restrictions attempt to limit the basic principle of the *free alienation (transfer) of property;* the courts consider them against public policy and therefore unenforceable.

A subdivider may establish restrictions on the right to *use* land through a **covenant** in a deed or by reference to a separate recorded declaration. When a lot in that subdivision is conveyed by an owner's deed, the deed refers to the plat or declaration of restrictions and incorporates these restrictions as limitations on the title conveyed by the deed. In this manner, the restrictive covenants are included in the deed by reference and become binding on all grantees. Such covenants or restrictions usually relate to: (1) type of building; (2) use to which the land may be put; (3) type of construction, height, setbacks and square footage; and (4) cost.

These use restrictions are usually considered valid if they are reasonable restraints and are for the benefit of all property owners in the subdivision. If, however, such restrictions are too broad in their terms, they prevent the free transfer of property. If they are "repugnant" to the estate granted, such restrictions will probably not be enforceable. If any restrictive covenant or condition is considered ineffective by a court, the estate will then stand free from the invalid covenant or condition.

Deed restrictions may be more restrictive of an owner's use than a zoning ordinance. The more restrictive of the two takes precedence.

Subdivision restrictions give each lot owner the right to apply to the court for an *injunction* to prevent a neighboring lot owner from violating the recorded restrictions. If granted, the court injunction will direct the violator to stop or remove the violation upon penalty of being in contempt of court. The court retains the power to punish the violator for failure to obey the court order. If adjoining lot owners stand idly by while a violation is being committed, they can *lose the right* to the court's injunction by their inaction; the court might claim their right was lost through **laches,** that is, loss of a right through undue delay or failure to assert it.

Conditions in a deed are different from restrictions or covenants. A grantor's deed of conveyance of land can be subject to certain stated conditions whereby the grantee's title may return to the grantor. (This was discussed in Chapter 7 as a defeasible fee estate.) For example, Bill Potter conveys a lot to Jane Knish by a deed that includes a condition forbidding the sale, manufacture or giving away of intoxicating liquor on the lot. In case of violation Potter has a right of reentry, that is, the right to retake possession of the property. If Knish operates a tavern on the lot, Potter can file suit and obtain title to the property.

Direct Public Ownership

Over the years, the government's general policy has been to encourage private ownership of land. It is necessary, however, for a certain amount of land to be owned by the government for such uses as municipal buildings, state legislative houses, schools and military stations. Such **direct public ownership** is a means of land control.

There are other examples of necessary public ownership. Urban renewal efforts, especially government-owned housing, are one way that public ownership serves the public interest. Publicly owned streets and highways serve a necessary function for the entire population. In addition, public land is often used for such recreational purposes as parks. National and state parks and forest preserves create areas for public use and recreation, and at the same time help to conserve our natural resources.

At present, the federal government owns approximately 775 million acres of land, nearly one-third of the total area of the United States. At times the federal government has held title to as much as 80 percent of the nation's total land area.

Summary

The control of land use is exercised in two ways: through public controls and private (or nongovernment) controls.

Public controls are ordinances based upon the states' *police powers* to protect the public health, safety and welfare. Through power conferred by state enabling acts, local governments enact comprehensive *master plans*.

Zoning ordinances carrying out the provisions of the master plan segregate residential areas from business and industrial zones and control not only land use, but height and bulk of buildings and density of populations. Zoning enforcement problems involve boards of appeal, conditional-use permits, variances and exceptions, as well as nonconforming uses. *Subdivision regulations* are required to maintain control of the development of expanding community areas so that growth will be harmonious with community standards.

Building codes specify standards for construction, plumbing, sewers, electrical wiring and equipment.

In addition to land-use control on the local level, the state and federal governments have occasionally intervened when necessary to preserve natural resources through *environmental legislation*.

Private controls are exercised by owners, generally subdividers, who control use of subdivision lots by carefully planned *deed restrictions* that are made to apply to all lot owners. The usual recorded restrictions may be enforced by adjoining lot owners obtaining a court *injunction* to stop a violator. *Conditions* are imposed by grantors and their violation may allow the grantors or their heirs the *right of reentry*.

Public ownership is a means of land-use control that provides land for such public benefits as parks, highways, schools and municipal buildings.

Questions

1. A provision in a subdivision declaration used as a means of forcing the grantee to live up to the terms under which he or she holds title to the land is a:
   a. restriction.
   b. reverter.
   c. laches.
   d. conditional-use clause.

2. For a zoning ordinance to be valid, the courts have decided that the ordinance must:
   I. not violate the due process provisions of the Fourteenth Amendment of the U.S. Constitution.
   II. be free from discrimination.
   III. not result in a loss of property values.
   a. I and II
   b. II and III
   c. I and III
   d. I, II and III

3. If a land owner wants to use property in a manner that is prohibited by a local zoning ordinance but would be of benefit to the community, the property owner can ask for which of the following?
   a. variance
   b. downzoning
   c. conditional-use permit
   d. dezoning

4. A new building is erected; it does not conform to local zoning ordinances and the builder did not seek prior permission to construct the building in this manner. This building is an example of a:
   I. nonconforming use.
   II. variance.
   a. I only
   b. II only
   c. both I and II
   d. neither I nor II

5. Public land-use controls include all but which of the following?
   a. subdivision regulations
   b. deed restrictions
   c. environmental protection laws
   d. master plan specifications

6. The police power allows regulation of:
   a. the number of buildings.
   b. building sizes.
   c. building ownership.
   d. a and b

7. To determine whether or not a location can be used for a retail store, one would examine:
   I. the city building code.
   II. the city's list of permitted nonconforming uses.
   a. I only
   c. both I and II
   b. II only
   d. neither I nor II

8. The purpose of a building permit is:
   a. to override a deed restriction.
   b. to maintain municipal control over the volume of building.
   c. to provide evidence of compliance with municipal regulations.
   d. all of the above

9. Which of the following would probably be included in a list of deed restrictions?
   I. types of buildings that may be constructed on the property
   II. minimum requirements for setbacks and square footage
   a. I only
   c. both I and II
   b. II only
   d. neither I nor II

10. The goals of a city planning commission include:
    a. formulation of policy.
    b. determination of land uses.
    c. conservation of natural resources.
    d. all of the above

11. The grantor of a deed may place effective restrictions on:
    a. the right to sell the land.
    b. use of the land.
    c. who the next purchaser will be.
    d. a and b

12. Zoning powers are conferred on municipal governments:
    a. by state enabling acts.
    b. through police power.
    c. by eminent domain.
    d. a and b

13. A restriction in a seller's deed may be enforced by which of the following?
    I. court injunction
    II. zoning board of appeal

    a. I only   c. both I and II
    b. II only   d. neither I nor II

14. Zoning laws are generally enforced by:
    a. zoning boards of appeal.
    b. ordinances stipulating that building permits will not be issued unless the proposed structure conforms to the zoning ordinance.
    c. deed restrictions.
    d. a and b

15. Zoning boards of appeal are established to hear complaints about:
    a. restrictive covenants.
    b. the effects of a zoning ordinance.
    c. building codes.
    d. a and c

20

Subdividing and Property Development

Key Terms

Clustering
Curvilinear system
Density zoning
Developer
Gridiron pattern
Interstate Land Sales Full Disclosure Act
Minimum standards
Plat of subdivision
Property report
Subdivider
Subdivision

Overview

Subdividers and property developers convert raw land or property that is no longer serving its highest and best use into subdivisions for residential and other uses. These subdividers and developers, working with local officials, can contribute to the orderly growth of communities. This chapter will deal with the process of developing and subdividing property and will also discuss some of the legal aspects of selling subdivided land.

Land Development

Land in large tracts must receive special attention before it can be converted into sites for homes, stores or other uses. As our cities and towns grow in size, additional land is required for their expansion. In order for such new areas to develop soundly, the services of competent subdividers and land developers working closely with city planners are required. A **subdivider** buys undeveloped acreage and divides it into smaller lots for sale to individuals or developers or for the subdivider's own use. A **developer** (who may also be a subdivider) builds homes or other buildings on the lots and sells them. Developing is generally a much more extensive activity than is subdividing. A developer may have a sales staff or may use the services of local real estate brokerage firms.

Regulation of Land Development

There is *no uniform planning and land development legislation that affects the entire country.* Laws governing subdividing and land planning are controlled by the state and local governing bodies (county, city, town or village) where the land is located. Rules and regulations developed by governmental agencies such as the Federal Housing Administration have, however, provided certain **minimum standards** that have served as usable guides. Local regulations are by no means uniform throughout the country, but reflect customs and local climate, health and hazard conditions. Some of the major FHA minimum standards will be discussed later in this chapter. A large number of local governments have established higher standards for subdividers of land under their jurisdiction.

Although the recording of a plat of subdivision of land prior to public sale for residential or commercial use is usually required, land planning precedes the actual subdividing process. The land development plan must comply with the overall *master plan* adopted by the county, city, village or town. The basic city plan and zoning requirements are not inflexible, but long, expensive and frequently complicated hearings are usually required before alterations can be authorized. Approval of the subdivision plat is, however, a necessary step before recording.

As discussed in Chapter 19, most villages, cities and other areas that are incorporated under state laws have *planning commissions*. Depending upon how the particular group was organized, such committees or commissions may have only an advisory status to the aldermen or trustees of the community. In other instances, the commission can have authority to approve or disapprove plans. Communities establish strict criteria before approving new subdivisions. The following are frequently included: (1) *dedication* of land for streets, schools and parks; (2) assurance by *bonding* that sewer and street costs will be paid, or completion of such improvements before construction begins; and (3) *compliance with zoning ordinances* governing use and lot size, along with fire and safety ordinances.

Because of the fear that they may pollute streams, rivers, lakes and underground water sources, septic systems are no longer authorized in most areas, and an approved sewage-disposal arrangement must be included in a land development plan. The shortage of water has caused great concern, and local authorities usually require land planners to submit information on how they intend to satisfy sewage-disposal and water-supply requirements. Development and/or septic tank installation may first require a *percolation test* of the soil's absorption and drainage capacities. Frequently a planner will also have to submit an *environmental impact report*.

When property to be subdivided is located outside the limits of cities, villages and incorporated towns, most state laws require that the proposed land plan be submitted to county authorities (county, borough or parish) for approval, and also to all incorporated communities (cities, towns or villages) located within a radius of one to three miles. If there is more than one such incorporated area, each must review and approve the plan.

Subdividing

The process of **subdivision** normally involves three distinct stages of development: (1) the initial planning stage, (2) the final planning stage and (3) the disposition, or start-up.

During the *initial planning stage,* the subdivider seeks out raw land in a suitable area. Once the land is located, the property is analyzed for its highest and best use, and preliminary subdivision plans are drawn up accordingly. As previously discussed, close contact is initiated between the subdivider and local planning and zoning officials. If the project requires zoning variances, negotiations begin along these lines. The subdivider also locates financial backers and initiates marketing strategies.

The final planning stage is basically a follow-up of the initial stage. Final plans are prepared, approval is sought from local officials, permanent financing is obtained, the land is purchased, final budgets are prepared and marketing programs are designed.

The *disposition,* or *start-up,* carries the subdividing process to a conclusion. Subdivision plans are recorded with local officials, and streets, sewers and utilities are installed. Buildings, open parks and recreational areas are constructed and landscaped if they are part of the subdivision plan. Marketing programs are then initiated, and title to the individual parcels of subdivided land is transferred as the lots are sold.

Subdivision Plans

In plotting out a subdivision according to local planning and zoning controls, a subdivider usually determines the size as well as the location of the individual lots. The size of the lots, both in front footage and in depth, together with the total amount of square footage, is generally regulated by local ordinances and must be taken into careful consideration. Frequently ordinances regulate both the minimum and the maximum size of a lot.

The land itself must be studied, usually in cooperation with a surveyor, so that the subdivision can be laid out with consideration of natural drainage and land contours. A subdivider should provide for *utility easements,* as well as easements for water and sewer mains.

Most subdivisions are laid out by use of *lots and blocks.* An area of land is designated as a block, and the area making up this block is divided into lots. Usually, lots and blocks are both numbered consecutively, but if a developer does not intend to subdivide an entire tract of land at one time, some variation from consecutive numbering may be granted.

Although subdividers customarily designate areas reserved for schools, parks and future church sites, this is usually not considered good practice. Once a subdivision has been recorded, the purchasers of the lots have a vested interest in those areas reserved for schools, parks and churches. If for any reason in the future, any such purpose is not appropriate, it will become difficult for the developer to abandon the original plan and use that property for residential purposes. To get around this situation, many developers designate such areas as *out-lot A, out-lot B* and so forth. Such a designation does not vest any rights in these out-lots in the purchasers of the homesites. If one of these areas is to be used for church purposes, it can be so conveyed and so used. If, on the other hand, the out-lot is not to be used for such a purpose, it can be resubdivided into residential properties without the burden of securing the consent of the lot owners in the area.

Plat of subdivision. The subdivider's completed **plat of subdivision,** a map of the development indicating the location and boundaries of individual properties, must contain all necessary approvals of public officials and must be recorded in the county where the land is located. *Have it recorded.*

Since the plat will be the basis for future conveyances, the subdivided land should be carefully measured, with all lot sizes and streets noted by the surveyor and accurately entered on the document. Survey monuments should be established, and measurements should be made from these monuments, with the location of all lots carefully marked.

Covenants and restrictions. Deed restrictions, discussed in Chapters 7 and 19, are usually originated and recorded by a subdivider as a means of *controlling and maintaining the desirable quality and character of the subdivision.* These restrictions can be included in the subdivision plat, or they may be set forth in a separate recorded instrument, commonly referred to as a *declaration of restrictions.*

FHA standards. FHA minimum standards have been established for residential area subdivisions that are to be submitted for approval for FHA loan insurance. The primary minimum standards established by the FHA are the following:

1. Streets must comply with approved widths and must be paved.
2. The area must be free from hazards, such as airplane landing fields, heavy through traffic and excessive noise or air pollution.
3. Each lot must have access to all utilities.
4. Provisions for shopping, schools, churches, recreation and transportation must be available.
5. Lots must comply with minimum, and in some cases maximum, size requirements.
6. Plans for construction must be approved and must meet minimum standards.
7. Uniform building setbacks and lot lines are usually required.
8. Minimum landscaping is usually required.

There are also FHA standards applicable to building construction. Since 1986, in recognition of the more stringent local codes in effect, FHA has allowed local building codes (where pre-approved by HUD—the Department of Housing and Urban Development) to serve as the standards. Exceptions generally include site conditions, thermal (insulation) standards and certain other material standards.

Subdivision Density   Zoning ordinances control land use. Such controls often include minimum lot sizes and population density requirements for subdivisions and land developments. For example, a typical zoning restriction may set the minimum lot area on which a subdivider can build a single-family housing unit at 10,000 square feet. This means that the subdivider will be able to build four houses per acre. Many zoning authorities now establish special density zoning standards for certain subdivisions. **Density zoning** ordinances restrict the *average maximum number of houses per acre* that may be built within a particular subdivision. If the area is density zoned at an average maximum of four houses per acre, for example, by *clustering* building lots, the developer is free to achieve an open effect. Regardless of lot size or the number of units, the subdivider will be consistent with the ordinance as long as the average number of units in the development remains at or below the maximum density. This average is called *gross density.*

Street patterns. By varying street patterns and clustering housing units, a subdivider can dramatically increase the amount of open and/or recreational space in a development. Some of these patterns are illustrated in figure 20.1.

The **gridiron pattern** evolved out of the government rectangular survey system. Featuring large lots, wide streets and limited-use service alleys, the system works reasonably well up to a point. An overabundance of grid-patterned streets often results in monotonous neighborhoods, with all lots facing busy streets. In addition, sidewalks are usually located adjacent to the streets, and the system provides for little or no open, park or recreational space.

The **curvilinear system** integrates major arteries of travel with smaller secondary and cul-de-sac streets carrying minor traffic. In addition, small open parks are often provided at intersections.

Clustering for open space. By slightly reducing lot sizes and **clustering** them around varying street patterns, a developer can house as many people in the same area as could be done using traditional subdividing plans, but with substantially increased tracts of open space.

**Figure 20.1
Street Patterns**

Gridiron

Curvilinear

Figure 20.2
Clustered Subdivision
Plan

Conventional Plan
12,500-square-foot lots
368 housing units
1.6 acres of parkland
23,200 linear feet of street

Cluster Plan
7,500-square-foot lots
366 housing units
23.5 acres of parkland
17,700 linear feet of street

PUD Type

For example, compare the two illustrations in figure 20.2. The first is a plan for a conventionally designed subdivision containing 368 housing units. It uses 23,200 linear feet of street and leaves only 1.6 acres open for park areas. Contrast this with the second subdivision pictured. Both subdivisions are equal in size and terrain. But when lots are minimally reduced in size and clustered around limited-access, cul-de-sac streets, the number of housing units remains nearly the same (366), with less street area (17,000 linear feet) and drastically increased open space (23.5 acres). In addition, with modern building designs this clustered plan could be modified to accommodate 550 patio homes or 1,100 townhouses.

Interstate Land Sales Full Disclosure Act

To protect consumers from "overenthusiastic sales promotions" in interstate land sales, Congress passed the **Interstate Land Sales Full Disclosure Act**. The law requires those engaged in the interstate sale or leasing of 25 or more lots to file a *statement of record* and *register* the details of the land with HUD.

The seller is also required to furnish prospective buyers a **property report** containing all essential information about the property, such as distance over paved roads to nearby communities, number of homes currently occupied, soil conditions affecting foundations and septic systems, type of title a buyer will receive and existence of liens. The property report must be given to a prospective purchaser at least three business days before any sales contract is signed.

Any contract to purchase a lot covered by this act may be revoked at the purchaser's option until midnight of the seventh day following the signing of the contract. If a contract is signed for the purchase of a lot covered by the act and a property report is not given to the purchaser, an action to revoke the contract may be brought by the purchaser within two years.

If the seller misrepresents the property in any sales promotion, a buyer induced by such a promotion is entitled to sue the seller for civil damages under federal law. Failure to comply with the law may also subject a seller to criminal penalties of up to five years' imprisonment and a $10,000 fine for each violation.

State Subdivided Land Sales Laws

Many state legislatures have enacted their own subdivided land sales laws. Some affect only the sale of land located outside of the state to state residents, while others affect sales of land located both inside and outside the state. Generally, these state land sales laws tend to be stricter and more detailed than the federal law. As a real estate salesperson or broker, you must know the specifics of your state's law.

Summary

A *subdivider* buys undeveloped acreage, divides it into smaller parcels, and develops it or sells it. A *land developer* builds homes on the lots and sells them, through the developer's own sales organization or through local real estate brokerage firms. City planners and land developers, working together, plan whole communities that are later incorporated into cities, towns or villages.

Land development must comply with the master plans adopted by counties, cities, villages or towns. This may entail approval of land-use plans by local *planning committees* or *commissioners.*

The process of subdivision includes dividing the tract of land into *lots and blocks* and providing for *utility easements,* as well as laying out street patterns and widths. A subdivider must generally record a completed *plat of subdivision,* with all necessary approvals of public officials, in the county where the land is located. Subdividers usually place *restrictions* upon the use of all lots in a subdivision as a general plan for the benefit of all lot owners.

Subdivisions that are to be submitted for approval for FHA loan insurance must meet certain *FHA minimum standards.*

By *varying street patterns and housing density,* and *clustering housing units,* a subdivider can dramatically increase the amount of open and recreational space within a development.

Subdivided land sales are regulated on the federal level by the *Interstate Land Sales Full Disclosure Act.* This law requires developers engaged in interstate land sales or the leasing of 25 or more units to register the details of the land with HUD. At least three business days before any sales contract is signed, such developers must also provide prospective purchasers with a property report containing all essential information about the property. Subdivided land sales are also regulated by many states' laws.

Questions

1. To control and maintain the quality and character of a subdivision, a developer will establish which of the following?

   a. easements
   b. deed restrictions
   c. buffer zones
   d. b and c

2. An owner of a large tract of land who, after adequate study of all facts, legally divides the land into lots of suitable size and location for the construction of residences, is known as a:

   a. subdivider.
   b. land developer.
   c. land planning commissioner.
   d. all of the above

3. A map illustrating the sizes and locations of streets and lots in a subdivision is called a:

   a. gridiron pattern.
   b. survey.
   c. plat of subdivision.
   d. property report.

4. Which of the following is *not* included in the FHA minimum standards for subdivisions?

   a. provisions for shopping must be available
   b. lots must be of uniform size
   c. streets must be of approved width and be paved
   d. the area must be free from hazards

5. *Gross density* refers to which of the following?

   a. the maximum number of residents that may, by law, occupy a subdivision
   b. the average maximum number of houses per acre that may, by law, be built in a subdivision
   c. the maximum size lot that may, by law, be built in a subdivision
   d. the minimum number of houses that may, by law, be built in a subdivision

6. The type of street pattern that is based on the rectangular survey system is called the:

   a. block plan.
   b. gridiron system.
   c. rectangular streets plan.
   d. cul-de-sac system.

7. FHA minimum standards for land development:

   I. must be complied with by all subdividers.
   II. concern only the design and construction of buildings.

   a. I only   c. both I and II
   b. II only   d. neither I nor II

8. Legal restrictions established by a recorded deed or subdivision plat, if permitted by public policy and not in violation of constitutional or statutory rights, are enforceable through:

   a. zoning ordinances.
   b. court injunctions.
   c. covenants.
   d. all of the above

9. Soil absorption and drainage are measured by a:

   a. land survey.
   b. plat of subdivision.
   c. density test.
   d. percolation test.

10. Which of the following items are *not* usually designated on the plat for a new subdivision?

    a. easements for sewer and water mains
    b. land to be used for streets, schools and civic facilities
    c. numbered lots and blocks
    d. prices of residential and commercial lots

11. The possibility of pollution has led to:
    I. elimination of the general use of the septic system as a means of sewage disposal.
    II. strict compliance with local zoning laws in drawing up a plan for sewage disposal.
       a. I only   c. both I and II
       b. II only   d. neither I nor II

12. A street pattern featuring housing units grouped into large, cul-de-sac blocks is generally called a:
    a. cluster plan.
    b. curvilinear system.
    c. rectangular street system.
    d. gridiron system.

13. In compliance with the Interstate Land Sales Full Disclosure Act, which of the following kinds of information need *not* be included in a property report given to a land buyer?
    a. soil conditions affecting foundations
    b. financial conditions of the seller
    c. number of homes currently occupied
    d. existence of liens

14. Many real estate brokers serve as agents for developers in:
    I. instructing the developers in their legal responsibilities.
    II. finding property buyers.
       a. I only   c. both I and II
       b. II only   d. neither I nor II

15. To protect the public from fraudulent interstate land sales, a developer involved in interstate land sales of 25 or more lots must:
    I. provide each purchaser with a report of the details of the land, as registered with HUD.
    II. pay the prospective buyer's expenses to see the property involved.
       a. I only   c. both I and II
       b. II only   d. neither I nor II

16. A subdivider can increase the amount of open and/or recreational space in a development by:
    a. varying street patterns.
    b. meeting FHA standards.
    c. clustering housing units.
    d. a and c

21

Fair Housing Laws and Ethical Practices

Key Terms

Blockbusting
Civil Rights Act of 1866
Code for Equal Opportunity
Code of Ethics
Department of Housing and Urban Development
Equal Credit Opportunity Act
Federal Fair Housing Act of 1968
Office of Equal Opportunity
Redlining
Steering

Overview

In order to achieve and maintain a favorable reputation in the community, a real estate licensee must be able to demonstrate more than good business ability. It is crucial that the licensee's *ethics,* or business principles, be above reproach as well. The various state license laws require licensees to adhere to certain ethical practices, as do the codes of ethics subscribed to by members of professional real estate organizations. Further, the federal and state governments have enacted laws that require licensees to follow ethical practices when dealing with the public, in order to ensure equal opportunity in housing for everyone. This chapter will deal with such fair housing laws and will examine the codes of ethical practices to which most brokers and salespeople adhere.

Equal Opportunity in Housing

Brokers and salespeople who offer residential property for sale anywhere in the United States must be aware of the federal, state and local laws pertaining to human rights and nondiscrimination. These laws, under such titles as open housing, fair housing or equal opportunity housing, generally prohibit undesirable and discriminatory activities. Their provisions affect every phase of the real estate sales process from listing to closing, and *all brokers and salespeople must comply with them.*

The goal of legislators who have enacted fair housing laws and regulations is to create a single, unbiased housing market—one in which every homeseeker has the opportunity to buy any home in the area he or she chooses, provided the home is within the homeseeker's financial means. Since most of the housing in the United States is produced and marketed through the private real estate market, owners, real estate brokers, apartment management companies, real estate boards, lending agencies, builders and developers must all take a part in creating this single housing market.

As a potential licensee, the student of real estate must be aware of undesirable and illegal housing practices in order to recognize and avoid them. The licensee must realize that failure to comply with fair housing practices is not only a criminal act, but also grounds for license revocation.

In Practice...

State laws may be stricter than the federal requirements we will discuss in this chapter. It is imperative that the licensee learn all pertinent state regulations.

Federal Fair Housing Laws

The efforts of the federal government to guarantee equal housing opportunities to all U.S. citizens began over one hundred years ago with the passage of the **Civil Rights Act of 1866.** This law, an outgrowth of the Fourteenth Amendment, prohibits any type of discrimination based on race. "All citizens of the United States shall have the same right in every state and territory as is enjoyed by white citizens thereof to inherit, purchase, lease, sell, hold, and convey real and personal property." A summary of federal fair housing laws appears in table 21.1.

Aside from a few isolated court decisions, there was little effort to enforce the principles of fair housing until 1962, when President John Kennedy issued *Executive Order No. 11063.* This order guaranteed nondiscrimination in all housing financed by FHA and VA loans. Because of the relatively small percentage of housing affected by Executive Order No. 11063, however, it had limited impact.

The scope of the federal government's fair housing regulation was expanded by the *Civil Rights Act of 1964,* which prohibited discrimination in any housing program that receives whole or partial federal funding. However, as only a very small percentage of housing in the United States is government-funded, this law also had little impact on the housing industry.

Fair Housing Act of 1968. In 1968, two major events occurred that greatly encouraged the progress of fair housing. The first of these was the passage of the

	Law	Purpose
Table 21.1 **Summary of Federal** **Fair Housing Laws**	Civil Rights Act of 1866	Prohibits discrimination in housing based on race without exception
	Executive Order No. 11063	Prohibits discrimination in housing funded by FHA or VA loans
	Civil Rights Act of 1964	Prohibits discrimination in federally funded housing programs
	Title VIII of the Civil Rights Act of 1968 (Federal Fair Housing Act)	Prohibits discrimination in housing based on race, color, religion or national origin with certain exceptions
	Housing and Community Development Act of 1974	Extends prohibitions to discrimination in housing based on sex

Federal Fair Housing Act, which is contained in *Title VIII of the Civil Rights Act of 1968.* This law provides that it is unlawful to discriminate on the basis of race, color, religion or national origin when selling or leasing residential property. It covers dwellings and apartments, as well as vacant land acquired for the construction of residential buildings, and prohibits the following discriminatory acts:

1. refusing to sell, rent or negotiate with any person, or otherwise making a dwelling unavailable to any person.
2. changing terms, conditions or services for different individuals as a means of discrimination.
3. practicing discrimination through any statement or advertisement that restricts the sale or rental of residential property.
4. representing to any person, as a means of discrimination, that a dwelling is not available for sale or rental.
5. making a profit by inducing owners of housing to sell or rent because of the prospective entry into the neighborhood of persons of a particular race, color, religion or national origin.
6. altering the terms or conditions for a home loan to any person who wishes to purchase or repair a dwelling, or otherwise denying such a loan, as a means of discrimination.
7. denying people membership or limiting their participation in any multiple listing service, real estate brokers' organization or other facility related to the sale or rental of dwellings, as a means of discrimination.

The following exemptions to the Federal Fair Housing Act also are provided:

1. The sale or rental of a single-family home is exempted when the home is owned by an individual who does not own more than three such homes at one time and when the following conditions exist: (a) a broker, salesperson or agent is not used and (b) discriminatory advertising is not used. If the owner is not living in the dwelling at the time of the transaction or was not the most recent occupant, then only one such sale by an individual is exempt from the law within any 24-month period.

2. The rental of rooms or units is exempted in an owner-occupied one- to four-family dwelling.

3. Use of dwelling units owned by religious organizations may be restricted to people of the same religion if membership in the organization is not restricted on the basis of race, color or national origin.

4. A private club that is not in fact open to the public may restrict the rental or occupancy of lodgings that it owns to its members, as long as the lodgings are not operated commercially.

In addition to the general provisions of the Federal Fair Housing Law, the Department of Housing and Urban Development has issued numerous rules and regulations that establish guidelines for the real estate industry in such specific areas as advertising and marketing procedures.

Jones **v.** *Mayer.* The second significant fair housing development of 1968 was the Supreme Court decision in the case of *Jones* v. *Alfred H. Mayer Company,* 392, U.S. 409 (1968). In its ruling, the Court upheld the previously discussed Civil Rights Act of 1866, which "prohibits all racial discrimination, private or public, in the sale and rental of property."

The importance of this decision rests in the fact that while the 1968 federal law exempted individual homeowners and certain groups, the 1866 law *prohibits all racial discrimination without exception.* So despite any exemptions in the 1968 law, an aggrieved person may seek a remedy for racial discrimination under the 1866 law against *any* homeowner, regardless of whether or not the owner employed a real estate broker and/or advertised the property.

Amendments to Fair Housing Law. Subsequent amendments to the Federal Fair Housing Act of 1968, such as the Housing and Community Development Act of 1974, have extended the prohibitions to discrimination based on sex and instituted the use of an equal housing opportunity poster. This poster, which can be obtained from HUD (illustrated in figure 21.1), features the equal housing opportunity slogan, an equal housing statement pledging adherence to the fair housing act and support of affirmative marketing and advertising programs, and the equal housing opportunity logo shown in figure 21.2.

When HUD investigates a broker for discriminatory practices, it may consider failure to display the poster prima facie evidence of discrimination.

Equal Credit Opportunity Act. The federal **Equal Credit Opportunity Act** prohibits discrimination based on race, color, religion, national origin, sex, marital status or age (if the applicant has reached the age of contractual capacity) in the granting of credit. Credit applicants must be considered only by criteria based on income, net worth, job stability and satisfactory credit rating.

Blockbusting and Steering

Blockbusting and steering are undesirable housing practices frequently discussed in connection with fair housing. **Blockbusting** means *inducing homeowners to sell by making representations regarding the entry or prospective entry of minority persons into the neighborhood.* The blockbuster frightens homeowners into selling, and makes a profit by buying the homes cheaply and selling them at considerably higher prices to minority persons. The Federal Fair Housing Act specifically prohibits this practice.

Figure 21.1
Equal Housing
Opportunity Poster

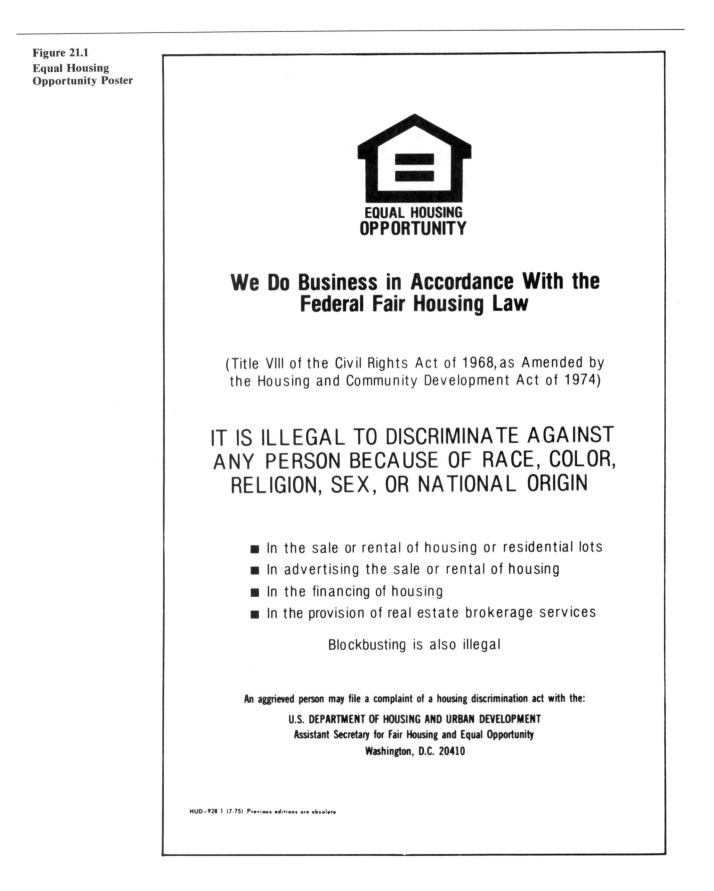

**Figure 21.2
Equal Housing
Opportunity Symbol**

**EQUAL HOUSING
OPPORTUNITY**

Steering is the channeling of homeseekers to particular areas either to maintain the homogeneity of an area or to change the character of an area in order to create a speculative situation. This practice makes certain homes unavailable to homeseekers on the basis of race or national origin; on these grounds it is prohibited by the provisions of the Federal Fair Housing Act. Steering is often difficult to detect, however, because the steering tactics can be so subtle that the home seeker may be unaware that his or her choice has been limited.

Redlining

The practice of refusing to make mortgage loans or issue insurance policies in specific areas without regard to the economic qualifications of the applicant is known as **redlining.** This practice, which often contributes to the deterioration of older, transitional neighborhoods, is frequently based on racial grounds rather than on any real objections to the applicant. It is important to note that a lending institution that refuses a loan solely on sound economic grounds cannot be accused of redlining.

In an effort to counteract redlining, the federal government passed the *Home Mortgage Disclosure Act* in 1975. This act requires all institutional mortgage lenders with assets in excess of $10 million and one or more offices in a given geographic area to make annual reports by census tracts of all mortgage loans the institution makes or purchases. This law enables the government to detect lending or insuring patterns that might constitute redlining.

Enforcement

The Federal Fair Housing Act is administered by the **Office of Equal Opportunity** (OEO) under the direction of the Secretary of the **Department of Housing and Urban Development** (HUD). Any aggrieved person may file a complaint with the secretary or the secretary's delegate within 180 days after a discriminatory action occurs. Complaints may be reported to: Fair Housing, Dept. of Housing and Urban Development, Washington, DC 20410, or to Fair Housing c/o the nearest HUD regional office.

After investigating a complaint, HUD will decide whether or not to attempt to resolve the dispute and will notify the complainant of the decision within 30 days after the complaint is filed. The secretary's efforts to resolve the dispute are limited to conference, conciliation and persuasion. If HUD decides to attempt conciliation, the complainant should wait to see if the matter can be settled out of court before filing suit; HUD will terminate all efforts at conciliation when the case actually comes to trial in court. An aggrieved person always has the option to take the alleged violator to court, whether or not a complaint has been filed with HUD. If the agency is investigating the incident, however, the courts generally wait until it has completed its efforts before going ahead with the case.

If HUD is unable to obtain voluntary compliance from the accused violator within 30 days after the complaint is filed, the complainant then has another 30 days in which to file suit in the appropriate court. In states with fair housing laws that are substantially equivalent to federal statutes, such suits must be brought in state court within the time period specified by state law. If no such law exists, the complaint may be taken to a U.S. district court if a suit is filed within 180 days after the discriminatory action occurs.

In addition, court actions may be brought by the attorney general in cases where accused violators of the Federal Fair Housing Act of 1968 are engaged in practices that show a pattern of discrimination.

Complaints brought under the Civil Rights Act of 1866 must be taken directly to a federal court.

Substantially Equivalent State Laws

Whenever a state or municipality has a fair housing law that has been ruled *substantially equivalent* to the federal law, all complaints in that state or locality, including those filed with HUD, are referred to and handled by the state enforcement agencies. To be considered substantially equivalent, the local law and its related regulations must contain prohibitions comparable to the federal law. In addition, the state or locality must show that its local enforcement agency is taking sufficient affirmative action in processing and investigating complaints and in finding remedies for discriminatory practices. Contact your nearest HUD regional office to find out if the law in your state or municipality has been ruled substantially equivalent to the federal law.

Threats or Acts of Violence

The Federal Fair Housing Act of 1968 contains criminal provisions protecting the rights of those who seek the benefits of the open housing law as well as owners, brokers or salespeople who aid or encourage the enjoyment of open housing rights. Unlawful actions involving threats, coercion and intimidation are punishable by appropriate civil action. In such cases, the victim should report the incident immediately to the local police and to the nearest office of the Federal Bureau of Investigation.

Implications for Brokers and Salespeople

To a large extent, the laws place the burden of responsibility for effecting and maintaining fair housing on real estate licensees—brokers and salespeople. And brokers and salespeople *must* comply with the laws; it's as simple as that. The laws are explicit and widely known. Anyone who violates them, whether intentionally or unintentionally, should be aware of the legal ramifications. In such cases, the complainant does not have to prove guilty knowledge or specific intent—only the fact that discrimination occurred.

How does a broker go about complying with the laws and making that policy known? As mentioned earlier, HUD regulations require that a public statement in the form of an approved fair housing poster must be displayed by a broker in any place of business where housing is offered for sale or rent (including model homes). HUD also offers guidelines for nondiscriminatory language and illustrations for use in real estate advertising. The agency further requires every broker to take affirmative marketing action in the choice of advertising media and in individual canvassing in order to assure that all interested individuals have the same range of housing options.

In addition, the NATIONAL ASSOCIATION OF REALTORS® suggests that a broker's position can be emphasized and problems can be avoided by the prominent display of a sign stating that it is against company policy as well as state and federal laws to offer any information on the racial, ethnic or religious composition of a neighborhood or to place restrictions on listing, showing or providing information on the availability of homes for any of these reasons. If a prospect still expresses a locational preference for housing based upon race, the association's guidelines suggest the following response: "I cannot give you that kind of advice. I will show you several homes that meet your specifications. You will have to decide which one you want."

There's more to fair housing practices than just following the letter of the law. Discrimination involves a sensitive area, human emotions—specifically, fear and self-preservation based on considerable prejudice and misconception. The broker or salesperson who complies with the law still has to deal, in many cases, with a general public whose attitudes cannot be altered by legislation alone. Therefore, a licensee who wishes to comply with the fair housing laws and also succeed in the real estate business must work to educate the public.

For every broker and salesperson, a sincere, positive attitude toward fair housing laws is a good start in dealing with this sensitive issue. It provides effective models for all who come in contact with the licensee. Active cooperation with local real estate board programs and community committees is also an excellent idea. This evidences the licensee's willingness to serve the community and observe the laws, and it helps to change public attitudes. Both factors can result in good public relations and, ultimately, more business for the licensee.

Standards of Professional Practice

Professional Organizations

Years ago, real estate brokers realized the need for an organization to assist them in improving their business abilities and educating the public about the value of qualified real estate brokers. The NATIONAL ASSOCIATION OF REALTORS® (NAR) was organized in 1908 (as the National Association of Real Estate Boards) to meet this need. This association has grown with the business and today is one of the leading trade organizations in the country. It is the parent organization of most local real estate boards throughout the United States, and the professional activities of all REALTORS®—brokers and salespeople who are active members of local boards affiliated with the national association—are governed by the association's Code of Ethics. (Note that a licensed broker or salesperson is not required to become a REALTOR®.)

There are also many independent real estate boards and other professional associations that were organized to set high standards for their members, promote their members' best interests and educate the public about the real estate profession. The National Association of Real Estate Brokers (Realtists) was founded in 1947. Its membership includes individual members, as well as brokers, who belong to state and local real estate boards affiliated with the organization. The members also subscribe to a code of ethics that sets professional standards for all Realtists.

Code of Ethics

The importance of adhering to a set of ethical business standards cannot be overemphasized. At least one state real estate commission has adopted a code of ethics as part of its real estate license law, and others may follow this example.

The NAR adopted its **Code of Ethics** in 1913. Through the years it has proved helpful to everyone in the real estate business because it contains practical applications of business ethics and statements of good practices that everyone in the business should know and carefully follow. A real estate business is only as good as its reputation, and reputations are built on sound business practices and fair dealings with clients, other real estate brokers and the general public. The NAR also publishes interpretations of the Code known as Standards of Practice that local boards may follow in hearings that involve violations of the Code. The REALTORS® Code of Ethics and Standards of Practice appear in figure 21.3.

Code for Equal Opportunity

In order to better support fair housing opportunities in its members' communities, the NAR has adopted a **Code for Equal Opportunity**. The Code basically sets forth suggested standards of conduct for REALTORS® so that they may comply with the letter as well as the spirit of the fair housing laws. The Code provides that:

1. In the sale, purchase, exchange, rental or lease of real property, REALTORS® and their REALTOR-Associates® have the responsibility to offer equal service to all clients and prospects without regard to race, color, religion, sex or national origin. This encompasses:
   a. standing ready to enter broker-client relationships or to show property equally to members of all races, creeds or ethnic groups.
   b. receiving all formal written offers and communicating them to the owner.
   c. exerting their best efforts to conclude all transactions.
   d. maintaining equal opportunity employment practices.
2. Members, individually and collectively, in performing their agency functions, have no right or responsibility to volunteer information regarding the racial, creedal or ethnic composition of any neighborhood or any part thereof.
3. Members shall not engage in any activity that has the purpose of inducing panic selling.
4. Members shall not print, display or circulate any statement or advertisement with respect to the sale or rental of a dwelling that indicates any preference, limitations or discrimination based on race, color, religion, sex or ethnic background.
5. Members who violate the spirit or any provision of this Code for Equal Opportunity shall be subject to disciplinary action.

The Code of Ethics and the Code for Equal Opportunity are two segments of the NAR's overall equal opportunity program, which is designed to ensure that no person is denied equal professional real estate services. The national association has also developed an Affirmative Marketing Agreement through which participating members inform the minority community of available real estate services and encourage the participation of minorities in the housing industry.

Summary

The federal regulations regarding equal opportunity in housing are principally contained in two laws. The *Civil Rights Act of 1866* prohibits all racial discrimination, and the *Federal Fair Housing Act* (Title VIII of the Civil Rights Act of 1968), as amended by the Housing and Community Development Act of 1974, prohibits discrimination on the basis of race, color, religion, sex or national origin in the sale or rental of residential property. Discriminatory actions include refusing to deal with an individual or a specific group, changing any terms of a real estate or loan transaction, changing the services offered for any individual or group, making statements or advertisements that indicate discriminatory restrictions or otherwise attempting to make a dwelling unavailable to any person or group because of race, color, religion, sex or national origin.

Complaints under the Federal Fair Housing Act may be reported to and investigated by the *Department of Housing and Urban Development*. Such complaints may also be taken directly to a U.S. district court. In states and localities that have enacted fair housing legislation that is "substantially equivalent to the federal law," complaints are handled by state and local agencies and state courts. Complaints under the Civil Rights Act of 1866 must be taken to a federal court.

A real estate business is only as good as its reputation. Real estate licensees can maintain good reputations by demonstrating good business ability and adhering to an ethical standard of business practices. Many licensees subscribe to a code of ethics as members of professional real estate organizations. The *Code of Ethics* of the NATIONAL ASSOCIATION OF REALTORS® is reprinted in this chapter. The provisions of this and the *Code for Equal Opportunity* suggest an excellent set of standards for all licensees to follow.

Figure 21.3
REALTORS® Code of
Ethics and Standards of
Practice

Code of Ethics and Standards of Practice

of the
NATIONAL ASSOCIATION OF REALTORS®

Where the word REALTOR® is used in this Code and Preamble,
it shall be deemed to include REALTOR-ASSOCIATE®. Pro-
nouns shall be considered to include REALTORS® and
REALTOR-ASSOCIATE®s of both genders.

Preamble...

Under all is the land. Upon its wise utilization and widely allocated ownership depend the survival and growth of free institutions and of our civilization. The REALTOR® should recognize that the interests of the nation and its citizens require the highest and best use of the land and the widest distribution of land ownership. They require the creation of adequate housing, the building of functioning cities, the development of productive industries and farms, and the preservation of a healthful environment.

Such interests impose obligations beyond those of ordinary commerce. They impose grave social responsibility and a patriotic duty to which the REALTOR® should dedicate himself, and for which he should be diligent in preparing himself. The REALTOR®, therefore, is zealous to maintain and improve the standards of his calling and shares with his fellow REALTORS® a common responsibility for its integrity and honor. The term REALTOR® has come to connote competency, fairness, and high integrity resulting from adherence to a lofty ideal of moral conduct in business relations. No inducement of profit and no instruction from clients ever can justify departure from this ideal.

In the interpretation of this obligation, a REALTOR® can take no safer guide than that which has been handed down through the centuries, embodied in the Golden Rule, "Whatsoever ye would that men should do to you, do ye even so to them."

Accepting this standard as his own, every REALTOR® pledges himself to observe its spirit in all of his activities and to conduct his business in accordance with the tenets set forth below.

ARTICLE 1

The REALTOR® should keep himself informed on matters affecting real estate in his community, the state, and nation so that he may be able to contribute responsibly to public thinking on such matters.

ARTICLE 2

In justice to those who place their interests in his care, the REALTOR® should endeavor always to be informed regarding laws, proposed legislation, governmental regulations, public policies, and current market conditions in order to be in a position to advise his clients properly.

ARTICLE 3

It is the duty of the REALTOR® to protect the public against fraud, misrepresentation, and unethical practices in real estate transactions. He should endeavor to eliminate in his community any practices which could be damaging to the public or bring discredit to the real estate profession. The REALTOR® should assist the governmental agency charged with regulating the practices of brokers and salesmen in his state.

- ### Standard of Practice 3-1

   "The REALTOR® shall only be obligated under Article 3 with respect to real estate related activities and transactions involving the REALTOR® as a principal, agent, or subagent."

ARTICLE 4

The REALTOR® should seek no unfair advantage over other REALTORS® and should conduct his business so as to avoid controversies with other REALTORS®.

- ### Standard of Practice 4-1

   "The REALTOR® shall not misrepresent the availability of access to show or inspect a listed property."

ARTICLE 5

In the best interests of society, of his associates, and his own business, the REALTOR® should willingly share with other REALTORS® the lessons of his experience and study for the benefit of the public, and should be loyal to the Board of REALTORS® of his community and active in its work.

ARTICLE 6

To prevent dissension and misunderstanding and to assure better service to the owner, the REALTOR® should urge the exclusive listing of property unless contrary to the best interest of the owner.

ARTICLE 7

In accepting employment as an agent, the REALTOR® pledges himself to protect and promote the interests of the client. This obligation of absolute fidelity to the client's interests is primary, but it does not relieve the REALTOR® of the obligation to treat fairly all parties to the transaction.

- ### Standard of Practice 7-1

   "Unless precluded by law, government rule or regulation, or agreed otherwise in writing, the REALTOR® shall submit to the seller all offers until closing. Unless the REALTOR® and the seller agree otherwise, the REALTOR® shall not be obligated to continue to market the property after an offer has been accepted. Unless the subsequent offer is contingent upon the termination of an existing contract, the REALTOR® shall recommend that the seller obtain the advice of legal counsel prior to acceptance. (Cross-reference Article 17.)"

- ### Standard of Practice 7-2

   "The REALTOR®, acting as listing broker, shall submit all offers to the seller as quickly as possible."

- ### Standard of Practice 7-3

   "The REALTOR®, in attempting to secure a listing, shall not deliberately mislead the owner as to market value."

- ### Standard of Practice 7-4

   (Refer to Standard of Practice 22-1, which also relates to Article 7, Code of Ethics.)

- ### Standard of Practice 7-5

   (Refer to Standard of Practice 22-2, which also relates to Article 7, Code of Ethics.)

- ### Standard of Practice 7-6

   "The REALTOR®, when acting as a principal in a real estate transaction, cannot avoid his responsibilities under the Code of Ethics."

ARTICLE 8

The REALTOR® shall not accept compensation from more than one party, even if permitted by law, without the full knowledge of all parties to the transaction.

ARTICLE 9

The REALTOR® shall avoid exaggeration, misrepresentation, or concealment of pertinent facts relating to the property or the transaction. The REALTOR® shall not, however, be obligated to discover latent defects in the property or to advise on matters outside the scope of his real estate license.

**Figure 21.3
(Cont.)**

- **Standard of Practice 9-1**

  "The REALTOR® shall not be a party to the naming of a false consideration in any document, unless it be the naming of an obviously nominal consideration."

- **Standard of Practice 9-2**

  (Refer to Standard of Practice 21-3, which also relates to Article 9, Code of Ethics.)

- **Standard of Practice 9-3**

  (Refer to Standard of Practice 7-3, which also relates to Article 9, Code of Ethics.)

- **Standard of Practice 9-4**

  "The REALTOR® shall not offer a service described as 'free of charge' when the rendering of a service is contingent on the obtaining of a benefit such as a listing or commission."

- **Standard of Practice 9-5**

  "The REALTOR® shall, with respect to the subagency of another REALTOR®, timely communicate any change of compensation for subagency services to the other REALTOR® prior to the time such REALTOR® produces a prospective buyer who has signed an offer to purchase the property for which the subagency has been offered through MLS or otherwise by the listing agency."

- **Standard of Practice 9-6**

  "REALTORS® shall disclose their REALTOR® status when seeking information from another REALTOR® concerning real property for which the other REALTOR® is an agent or subagent."

- **Standard of Practice 9-7**

  "The offering of premiums, prizes, merchandise discounts or other inducements to list or sell is not, in itself, unethical even if receipt of the benefit is contingent on listing or purchasing through the REALTOR® making the offer. However, the REALTOR® must exercise care and candor in any such advertising or other public or private representations so that any party interested in receiving or otherwise benefiting from the REALTOR®'s offer will have clear, thorough, advance understanding of all the terms and conditions of the offer. The offering of any inducements to do business is subject to the limitations and restrictions of state law and the ethical obligations established by Article 9, as interpreted by any applicable Standard of Practice."

- **Standard of Practice 9-8**

  "The REALTOR® shall be obligated to discover and disclose adverse factors reasonably apparent to someone with expertise in only those areas required by their real estate licensing authority. Article 9 does not impose upon the REALTOR® the obligation of expertise in other professional or technical disciplines. (Cross-reference Article 11.)"

ARTICLE 10

The REALTOR® shall not deny equal professional services to any person for reasons of race, creed, sex, or country of national origin. The REALTOR® shall not be party to any plan or agreement to discriminate against a person or persons on the basis of race, creed, sex, or country of national origin.

ARTICLE 11

A REALTOR® is expected to provide a level of competent service in keeping with the standards of practice in those fields in which the REALTOR® customarily engages.

The REALTOR® shall not undertake to provide specialized professional services concerning a type of property or service that is outside his field of competence unless he engages the assistance of one who is competent on such types of property or service, or unless the facts are fully disclosed to the client. Any person engaged to provide such assistance shall be so identified to the client and his contribution to the assignment should be set forth.

The REALTOR® shall refer to the Standards of Practice of the National Association as to the degree of competence that a client has a right to expect the REALTOR® to possess, taking into consideration the complexity of the problem, the availability of expert assistance, and the opportunities for experience available to the REALTOR®.

- **Standard of Practice 11-1**

  "Whenever a REALTOR® submits an oral or written opinion of the value of real property for a fee, his opinion shall be supported by a memorandum in his file or an appraisal report, either of which shall include as a minimum the following:

  1. Limiting conditions
  2. Any existing or contemplated interest
  3. Defined value
  4. Date applicable
  5. The estate appraised
  6. A description of the property
  7. The basis of the reasoning including applicable market data and/or capitalization computation

  "This report or memorandum shall be available to the Professional Standards Committee for a period of at least two years (beginning subsequent to final determination of the court if the appraisal is involved in litigation) to ensure compliance with Article 11 of the Code of Ethics of the NATIONAL ASSOCIATION OF REALTORS®."

- **Standard of Practice 11-2**

  "The REALTOR® shall not undertake to make an appraisal when his employment or fee is contingent upon the amount of appraisal."

- **Standard of Practice 11-3**

  "REALTORS® engaged in real estate securities and syndications transactions are engaged in an activity subject to regulations beyond those governing real estate transactions generally, and therefore have the affirmative obligation to be informed of applicable federal and state laws, and rules and regulations regarding these types of transactions."

ARTICLE 12

The REALTOR® shall not undertake to provide professional services concerning a property or its value where he has a present or contemplated interest unless such interest is specifically disclosed to all affected parties.

- **Standard of Practice 12-1**

  (Refer to Standards of Practice 9-4 ad 16-1, which also relate to Article 12, Code of Ethics.)

ARTICLE 13

The REALTOR® shall not acquire an interest in or buy for himself, any member of his immediate family, his firm or any member thereof, or any entity in which he has a substantial ownership interest, property listed with him, without making the true position known to the listing owner. In selling property owned by himself, or in which he has any interest, the REALTOR® shall reveal the facts of his ownership or interest to the purchaser.

- **Standard of Practice 13-1**

  "For the protection of all parties, the disclosures required by Article 13 shall be in writing and provided by the REALTOR® prior to the signing of any contract."

ARTICLE 14

In the event of a controversy between REALTORS® associated with different firms, arising out of their relationship as REALTORS®, the REALTORS® shall submit the dispute to arbitration in accordance with the regulations of their Board or Boards rather than litigate the matter.

Figure 21.3
(Cont.)

- **Standard of Practice 14-1**

  "The filing of litigation and refusal to withdraw from it by a REALTOR® in an arbitrable matter constitutes a refusal to arbitrate."

- **Standard of Practice 14-2**

  "The obligation to arbitrate mandated by Article 14 includes arbitration requests initiated by the REALTOR®'s client."

ARTICLE 15

If a REALTOR® is charged with unethical practice or is asked to present evidence in any disciplinary proceeding or investigation, he shall place all pertinent facts before the proper tribunal of the Member Board or affiliated institute, society, or council of which he is a member.

- **Standard of Practice 15-1**

  "The REALTOR® shall not be subject to disciplinary proceedings in more than one Board of REALTORS® with respect to alleged violations of the Code of Ethics relating to the same transaction."

- **Standard of Practice 15-2**

  "The REALTOR® shall not make any unauthorized disclosure or dissemination of the allegations, findings, or decision developed in connection with an ethics hearing or appeal."

ARTICLE 16

When acting as agent, the REALTOR® shall not accept any commission, rebate, or profit on expenditures made for his principal-owner, without the principal's knowledge and consent.

- **Standard of Practice 16-1**

  "The REALTOR® shall not recommend or suggest to a principal or a customer the use of services of another organization or business entity in which he has a direct interest without disclosing such interest at the time of the recommendation or suggestion."

ARTICLE 17

The REALTOR® shall not engage in activities that constitute the unauthorized practice of law and shall recommend that legal counsel be obtained when the interest of any party to the transaction requires it.

ARTICLE 18

The REALTOR® shall keep in a special account in an appropriate financial institution, separated from his own funds, monies coming into his possession in trust for other persons, such as escrows, trust funds, clients' monies, and other like items.

ARTICLE 19

The REALTOR® shall be careful at all times to present a true picture in his advertising and representations to the public. The REALTOR® shall also ensure that his status as a broker or a REALTOR® is clearly identifiable in any such advertising.

- **Standard of Practice 19-1**

  "The REALTOR® shall not submit or advertise property without authority, and in any offering, the price quoted shall not be other than that agreed upon with the owners."

- **Standard of Practice 19-2**

  (Refer to Standard of Practice 9-4, which also relates to Article 19, Code of Ethics.)

- **Standard of Practice 19-3**

  "The REALTOR®, when advertising unlisted real property for sale in which he has an ownership interest, shall disclose his status as both an owner and as a REALTOR® or real estate licensee."

- **Standard of Practice 19-4**

  "The REALTOR® shall not advertise nor permit any person employed by or affiliated with him to advertise listed property without disclosing the name of the firm."

- **Standard of Practice 19-5**

  "The REALTOR®, when acting as listing broker, retains the exclusive right to represent that he has 'sold' the property, even if the sale resulted through the cooperative efforts of another broker. However, after the transaction has been consummated, the listing broker may not prohibit a successful cooperating broker from advertising his 'participation' or 'assistance' in the transaction, or from making similar representations provided that any such representation does not create the impression that the cooperating broker had listed or sold the property. (Cross-reference Article 21.)"

ARTICLE 20

The REALTOR®, for the protection of all parties, shall see that financial obligations and commitments regarding real estate transactions are in writing, expressing the exact agreement of the parties. A copy of each agreement shall be furnished to each party upon his signing such agreement.

- **Standard of Practice 20-1**

  "At the time of signing or initialing, the REALTOR® shall furnish to the party a copy of any document signed or initialed."

- **Standard of Practice 20-2**

  "For the protection of all parties, the REALTOR® shall use reasonable care to ensure that documents pertaining to the purchase and sale of real estate are kept current through the use of written extensions or amendments."

ARTICLE 21

The REALTOR® shall not engage in any practice or take any action inconsistent with the agency of another REALTOR®.

- **Standard of Practice 21-1**

  "Signs giving notice of property for sale, rent, lease, or exchange shall not be placed on property without the consent of the owner."

- **Standard of Practice 21-2**

  "The REALTOR® obtaining information from a listing broker about a specific property shall not convey this information to, nor invite the cooperation of a third party broker without the consent of the listing broker."

- **Standard of Practice 21-3**

  "The REALTOR® shall not solicit a listing which is currently listed exclusively with another broker. However, if the listing broker, when asked by the REALTOR®, refuses to disclose the expiration date and nature of such listing; i.e., an exclusive right to sell, an exclusive agency, open listing, or other form of contractual agreement between the listing broker and his client, the REALTOR®, unless precluded by law, may contact the owner to secure such information and may discuss the terms upon which he might take a future listing or, alternatively, may take a listing to become effective upon expiration of any existing exclusive listing."

- **Standard of Practice 21-4**

  "The REALTOR® shall not use information obtained by him from the listing broker, through offers to cooperate received through Multiple Listing Services or other sources authorized by the listing broker, for the purpose of creating a referral prospect to a third broker, or for creating a buyer prospect unless such use is authorized by the listing broker."

- **Standard of Practice 21-5**

  "The fact that a property has been listed exclusively with a REALTOR® shall not preclude or inhibit any other REALTOR® from soliciting such listing after its expiration."

**Figure 21.3
(Cont.)**

• Standard of Practice 21-6

"The fact that a property owner has retained a REALTOR® as his exclusive agent in respect of one or more past transactions creates no interest or agency which precludes or inhibits other REALTORS® from seeking such owner's future business."

• Standard of Practice 21-7

"The REALTOR® shall be free to solicit a listing in respect to any property which is 'open listed' at any time."

• Standard of Practice 21-8

"When a REALTOR® is contacted by an owner regarding the sale of property that is exclusively listed with another broker, and the REALTOR® has not directly or indirectly initiated the discussion, unless precluded by law, the REALTOR® may discuss the terms upon which he might take a future listing or, alternatively, may take a listing to become effective upon expiration of any existing exclusive listing."

• Standard of Practice 21-9

"In cooperative transactions a REALTOR® shall compensate the co-operating REALTOR® (principal broker) and shall not compensate nor offer to compensate, directly or indirectly, any of the sales licensees employed by or affiliated with another REALTOR® without the prior express knowledge and consent of the cooperating broker."

• Standard of Practice 21-10

"Article 21 does not preclude REALTORS® from making general announcements to property owners describing their services and the terms of their availability even though some recipients may have exclusively listed their property for sale or lease with another REALTOR®. A general telephone canvass, general mailing or distribution addressed to all property owners in a given geographical area or in a given profession, business, club, or organization, or other classification or group is deemed 'general' for purposes of this standard.

Article 21 is intended to recognize as unethical two basic types of solicitation:

First, telephone or personal solicitations of property owners who have been identified by a real estate sign, multiple listing compilation, or other information service as having exclusively listed their property with another REALTOR®; and

Second, mail or other forms of written solicitations of property owners whose properties are exclusively listed with another REALTOR® when such solicitations are not part of a general mailing but are directed specifically to property owners identified through compilations of current listings, 'for sale' signs, or other sources of information required by Article 22 and Multiple Listing Service rules to be made available to other REALTORS® under offers of subagency or cooperation."

• Standard of Practice 21-11

"The REALTOR®, prior to accepting a listing, has an affirmative obligation to make reasonable efforts to determine whether the property is subject to a current, valid exclusive listing agreement."

ARTICLE 22

In the sale of property which is exclusively listed with a REALTOR®, the REALTOR® shall utilize the services of other brokers upon mutually agreed upon terms when it is in the best interests of the client.

Negotiations concerning property which is listed exclusively shall be carried on with the listing broker, not with the owner, except with the consent of the listing broker.

• Standard of Practice 22-1

"It is the obligation of the selling broker as subagent of the listing broker to disclose immediately all pertinent facts to the listing broker prior to as well as after the contract is executed."

• Standard of Practice 22-2

"The REALTOR®, when submitting offers to the seller, shall present each in an objective and unbiased manner."

• Standard of Practice 22-3

"The REALTOR® shall disclose the existence of an accepted offer to any broker seeking cooperation."

ARTICLE 23

The REALTOR® shall not publicly disparage the business practice of a competitor nor volunteer an opinion of a competitor's transaction. If his opinion is sought and if the REALTOR® deems it appropriate to respond, such opinion shall be rendered with strict professional integrity and courtesy.

The Code of Ethics was adopted in 1913. Amended at the Annual Convention in 1924, 1928, 1950, 1951, 1952, 1955, 1956, 1961, 1962, 1974, 1982, and 1986.

EXPLANATORY NOTE CONCERNING THE STANDARDS OF PRACTICE

The reader should be aware of the following policy which has been approved by the Board of Directors of the National Association:

"In filing a charge of an alleged violation of the Code of Ethics by a REALTOR®, the charge shall read as an alleged violation of one or more Articles of the Code. A Standard of Practice may only be cited in support of the charge."

The Standards of Practice are not an integral part of the Code but rather serve to clarify the ethical obligations imposed by the various Articles. The Standards of Practice supplement, and do not substitute for, the Case Interpretations in *Interpretations of the Code of Ethics*.

Modifications to existing Standards of Practice and additional new Standards of Practice are approved from time to time. The reader is cautioned to ensure that the most recent publications are utilized.

Questions

1. Which of the following acts is permitted under the Federal Fair Housing Act?

   a. advertising property for sale only to a special group
   b. altering the terms of a loan for a member of a minority group
   c. refusing to sell a home to an individual because of a poor credit history
   d. telling an individual that an apartment has been rented when in fact it has not

2. Complaints relating to the Civil Rights Act of 1866:

   a. must be taken directly to a federal court.
   b. are no longer reviewed in the courts.
   c. are handled by HUD.
   d. are handled by state enforcement agencies.

3. In business relations, a broker should:

   I. utilize the services of other brokers when it is in the clients' best interests.
   II. not publicly criticize the business practices of a competitor.

   a. I only   c. both I and II
   b. II only   d. neither I nor II

4. Under the Federal Fair Housing Act, complaints may be:

   a. filed with the Department of Housing and Urban Development.
   b. handled by the local U.S. district court.
   c. filed only if all court actions have been exhausted.
   d. a and b

5. Which of the following situations is (are) considered to be discriminatory under the Housing and Community Development Act of 1974?

   a. Residents of the Lovely Arms Apartments must meet income requirements.
   b. Merv Cane rejected a buyer for his home because the buyer wants Merv to carry the financing.
   c. The owner of a 20-unit apartment building refuses to rent apartments to women.
   d. All of the above are discriminatory.

6. Broker Beth Silverman informs homeowner James Albert of the prospective entry of a minority group into homeowner Albert's neighborhood. Broker Silverman, seeing that Albert is very upset, offers to buy Albert's house at a low price. Silverman is:

   I. guilty of steering.
   II. protecting the best interests of the homeowner.

   a. I only   c. both I and II
   b. II only   d. neither I nor II

7. After broker Harold Gorman takes a sale listing of a residence, the owner specifies that he will not sell his home to a black person. The broker should:

   I. say nothing and show the property to anyone who is interested, including blacks.
   II. explain to the owner that this violates federal law and he cannot do it.

   a. I only   c. both I and II
   b. II only   d. neither I nor II

8. The REALTORS® Code of Ethics suggests a set of standards for all brokers and salespeople to follow. Which of the following provisions is *not* contained in the Code?

   a. A REALTOR® should not engage in the unauthorized practice of law.
   b. A REALTOR® must protect the public against fraud and unethical practices in the real estate field.
   c. A REALTOR® should not accept compensation from more than one party without the full knowledge of all parties to the transaction.
   d. In the event of a REALTOR®'s controversy with another REALTOR®, the matter should be settled through litigation.

9. Under the Supreme Court decision in the case of *Jones* v. *Alfred H. Mayer Company:*
   a. racial discrimination is prohibited by any party in the sale or rental of real estate.
   b. sales by individual residential homeowners are exempted provided the owner does not employ a broker.
   c. laws against discrimination apply only to federally related transactions.
   d. a and b

10. The act of channeling homeseekers to a particular area either to maintain or to change the character of a neighborhood is:
    a. blockbusting.
    b. redlining.
    c. steering.
    d. permitted under the Fair Housing Act of 1968.

11. Joe Jones, a black real estate broker, offers a special discount to black customers. This practice is:
    a. satisfactory.
    b. illegal.
    c. legal, but ill-advised.
    d. not important.

12. The EZ-Go Mortgage Co. makes it a practice not to lend money to potential homeowners attempting to purchase property located in predominantly black neighborhoods. This practice is:
    a. blockbusting.
    b. redlining.
    c. illegal.
    d. b and c

13. A REALTOR® is prohibited from discriminating on the basis of race in his or her business practices by the:
    I. Fair Housing Act of 1968.
    II. REALTORS® Code of Ethics.
       a. I only
       b. II only
       c. both I and II
       d. neither I nor II

14. If a state or local law has been declared substantially equivalent to the federal Fair Housing Act, violations of the fair housing laws are referred to and handled by:
    a. federal courts.
    b. local boards of REALTORS®.
    c. state enforcement agencies.
    d. HUD.

15. Discrimination in housing is permitted on the basis of:
    a. sex.
    b. national origin.
    c. religion.
    d. none of the above

22

Real Estate Investment

Key Terms

Adjusted basis
Appreciation
Basis
Boot
Capital gain
Cash flow
Cost recovery
Depreciation
Exchange
General partnership

Installment sale
Leverage
Limited partnership
Pyramiding
Real estate investment syndicate
Real estate investment trust
Real estate mortgage investment conduit
Tax credits

Overview

The market for real estate investment is one of the most active in the country. Real estate can be used to generate income, build up equity and, to a limited extent, provide tax deductions that can be used to offset income from other sources. This chapter will present a basic introduction to real estate investment. Major emphasis is placed on investment opportunities open to small or beginning investors. Note that the examples and computations given in this chapter are symbolic and used for *illustrative purposes only*. Such examples are included in the discussion in order to explain a particular feature or concept of investment, *not to teach the reader how, when or what amount of money to invest.*

Investing in Real Estate

Often, customers expect a real estate broker or salesperson to act as an investment counselor. The broker or salesperson should always *refer a potential real estate investor to a competent tax accountant, attorney or investment specialist* who can give expert advice regarding the investor's specific interest.

Real estate practitioners should possess an essential knowledge of real estate investment so they can deal with customers on a basic level. Such knowledge begins with an examination of the traditional advantages and disadvantages of investing in real estate.

Advantages of Real Estate Investment

Traditionally, real estate investments have shown an overall *high rate of return*, generally higher than the prevailing interest rate charged by mortgage lenders. Theoretically, this means that an investor can use the *leverage* of borrowed money to finance a real estate purchase and feel relatively sure that, if held long enough, the asset will yield more money than it costs to finance the purchase.

Real estate values usually keep pace with the rate of inflation. Such an *inflation hedge* provides the real estate investor with relative assurance that if the purchasing power of the dollar decreases, the value of the investor's assets will increase to offset the inflationary effects. Inflation will be discussed in detail later in this chapter.

In addition, real estate entrepreneurs may enjoy various tax advantages that will also be discussed later in this chapter.

Disadvantages of Real Estate Investment

Unlike stocks and bonds, *real estate is not highly liquid* over a short period of time. This means that an investor cannot usually sell real estate quickly without taking some sort of loss. An investor in listed stocks need only call a stockbroker in order to liquidate a certain portion of such assets quickly when funds are needed. In contrast, even though a real estate investor may be able to raise a limited amount of cash by refinancing the property, that property is usually listed with a real estate broker and the investor may have to sell at a substantially lower price than full market value in order to facilitate a quick sale.

In addition, *it is difficult to invest in real estate without some degree of expert advice.* Investment decisions must be made based on a careful study of all the facts in a given situation, reinforced by a broad and thorough knowledge of real estate and the manner in which it affects and is affected by the marketplace—the human element. As mentioned earlier, *all investors should seek legal and tax counsel before making any real estate investments.*

Rarely can a real estate investor sit idly by and watch his or her money grow. *Management decisions must be made.* For example, can the investor effectively manage the property personally, or would it be preferable to hire a professional property manager? How much rent should be charged? How should repairs and tenant grievances be handled? "Sweat equity" (physical improvements accomplished by the investor personally) may be required to make the asset profitable.

Finally, and this is most important, *a high degree of risk* is often involved in real estate investment. There is always the possibility that an investor's property will decrease in value during the period it is held or that it will not generate an income sufficient to make it profitable.

The Investment

The most important form of real estate investment is *direct ownership*. Both individuals and corporations may own real estate directly and manage it for appreciation or cash flow (income). Property held for **appreciation** is generally expected to increase in value and to show a profit when sold at some future date. Income property is just that—property held for current income as well as a profit upon its sale.

Appreciation

Real estate is an avenue of investment open to those interested in holding property *primarily* for appreciation.

Two main factors affect appreciation: inflation and intrinsic value. **Inflation** is defined as the *increase in the amount of money in circulation, which results in a decline in its value coupled with a rise in wholesale and retail prices.* The **intrinsic value** of real estate is the result of a person's individual choices and preferences for a given geographical area, based on the features and amenities that the area has to offer. For example, property located in a well-kept suburb near business and shopping areas would have a greater intrinsic value to most people than similar property in a more isolated location. As a rule, the greater the intrinsic value, the more money a property can command upon its sale.

Quite often an investor speculates in purchases of either agricultural (farm) land or undeveloped (raw) land, located in what is expected to be a major path of growth. This type of investment carries with it many inherent risks. The investor must consider such questions as: How fast will the area develop? Will it grow sufficiently for the investor to make a good profit? Will the expected growth even occur? More important, will the profits eventually realized from the property be great enough to offset the costs (such as property taxes) of holding the land?

Despite these risks, land has historically been a good inflation hedge if held for a long term. It can also be a source of income to offset some of the holding costs. For example, agricultural land can be leased out for crops or timber production, or grazing. On the downside, the Internal Revenue Service does not allow the depreciation (cost recovery) of land. Also, such land may not be liquid (salable) at certain times under certain circumstances, because few people are willing to purchase raw or agricultural land on short notice.

Income

The wisest initial investment for a person who wishes to buy and personally manage real estate may be the purchase of rental income property.

Cash flow. The object of an investor's directing funds into income property is to generate spendable income, usually called cash flow. The **cash flow** is the total amount of money remaining after all expenditures have been paid, including taxes, operating costs and mortgage payments. The cash flow produced by any given parcel of real estate is determined by at least three factors: amount of rent received, operating expenses and method of debt repayment.

Generally, the amount of *rent* (income) that a property may command depends on a number of factors, including location, physical appearance and amenities. If the cash flow from rents is not enough to cover all expenses, a *negative cash flow* will result.

To keep cash flow high, an investor should *keep operating expenses low.* Such operating expenses include general maintenance of the building, repairs, utilities, taxes and tenant services (switchboard facilities, security systems and so forth). Poor or overly expensive management can also result in negative cash flow.

An investor often stands to make more money by investing borrowed money, usually obtained through a mortgage loan or deed of trust loan. *Low mortgage payments* spread over a long period of time result in a higher cash flow because they allow the investor to retain more income each month; conversely, higher mortgage payments would contribute to a lower cash flow.

Investment opportunities. Traditional income-producing property investments include apartment and office buildings, hotels, motels, shopping centers and industrial properties. Investors have historically found well-located single-family dwellings to be favorable investments.

Leverage

Leverage is the use of *borrowed money to finance the bulk of an investment.* As a rule, an investor can receive a maximum return from the initial investment (the down payment and closing and other costs) by:

1. making a small down payment;
2. paying a low interest rate; and
3. spreading mortgage payments over as long a period as possible.

As an example, the use of leveraging allows a person of modest income to buy a home valued at several times that amount, as the figure below illustrates.

The amount of the monthly payments will depend upon the interest rate charged and the loan term over which the principal (amount borrowed) must be repaid. When interest rates are comparatively low, borrowers frequently increase the amount of principal, by buying a more expensive home, taking a loan with a shorter term or making advance payments of principal. The 15-year mortgage loan, once a rarity, has now become commonplace thanks to the lowering of interest rates in the mid-1980s.

The effect of leveraging on an investor is to provide, on a sale of the asset, a return that is a reflection of the effect of market forces on the entire amount of the original purchase price, but is measured against only the actual cash invested. For example, if an investor spends $100,000 for rental property and makes a $20,000 down payment, then sells that property five years later for $125,000, the return over five years is $25,000. Disregarding ownership expenses, the return is not 25 percent ($25,000 compared to $100,000), but 125 percent of the original amount invested ($25,000 compared to $20,000).

Risks are generally proportionate to leverage. A high degree of leverage gives the investor and lender a high degree of risk; lower leverage results in a lower risk.

Equity buildup. Equity buildup is that portion of the payment directed toward the principal rather than the interest, *plus* any gain in property value due to appreciation. In a sense, equity buildup is like money in the bank to the investor. Although this accumulated equity is not realized as cash unless the property is sold or refinanced, the equity interest may be sold, exchanged or mortgaged (refinanced) to be used as leverage for other investments.

Pyramiding through refinancing. By holding and refinancing using equity and appreciation buildup, rather than selling or exchanging already-owned properties, an investor's holdings can be increased without investment of any additional capital. This practice is known as **pyramiding.** By reinvesting and doubling his or her holdings periodically, it is conceivable that an investor who started out with a small initial cash down payment could own (heavily mortgaged) properties worth hundreds of thousands or millions of dollars. With sufficient cash flow to cover all costs, if market values hold steady, the income derived from such assets could pay off the various mortgage debts and show a handsome profit.

Tax Benefits

One of the main reasons real estate investments were popular—and profitable—in the past was that federal law allowed investors to use losses generated by the investments to shelter income from other sources.

The Tax Reform Act of 1986 (TRA) has eliminated some tax advantages of owning investment real estate, but, with professional tax advice, the investor can still make a wise real estate purchase.

We have already discussed in Chapter 4 the change in the status of capital gains and the limitation on interest deductions brought about by TRA. We will now look at the consequences of the new law in other areas of importance to investors.

The discussions and examples used in this section are designed to introduce the reader to general tax concepts—a tax attorney or CPA should be consulted for further details on specific regulations. Internal Revenue Service regulations are subject to frequent change; again, consult a tax expert for up-to-date information.

Capital Gains

The tax law no longer favors long-term investments by reducing the taxable gain (profit) on their sale or exchange. What we term *capital gain* is still defined as the difference between the adjusted basis of property and its net selling price. The distinction between long-term and short-term capital gain has been eliminated. All such profit is now taxed as ordinary income. As pointed out earlier, the taxpayer who profits from a transaction involving property held for less than six months will actually benefit by the new, overall lower tax rates.

Basis. A property's cost basis will determine the amount of gain to be taxed. The basis of property is the investor's initial cost for the parcel of real estate. The in-

Original cost of buying the house

vestor adds to the basis the cost of any physical improvements subsequently made to the property, and subtracts from the basis the amount of any depreciation claimed as a tax deduction (explained later), to derive the property's **adjusted basis**. When the property is sold by the investor, the amount by which the sale price exceeds the property's adjusted basis is the capital gain taxable as income.

For example, an investor purchased a one-family dwelling for use as a rental property. The purchase price was $45,000, with the land value set at $10,000 and the value of the improvements at $35,000. The investor is now selling the property for $100,000. The land value is now $20,000. Shortly before the sale date, the investor made $3,000 worth of capital improvements to the home. Depreciation of $10,000 on the property improvements has been taken during the term of the investor's ownership. The investor will pay a broker's commission of 7 percent of the sale price and will also pay closing costs of $600. The investor's capital gain is computed as follows:

Selling price:		$100,000
Less:		
7% commission	$7,000	
closing costs	+ 600	
	$7,600	−7,600
Net sales price:		$ 92,400
Less value of land:		−20,000
		$ 72,400
Basis:		
building	$35,000	
improvements	+ 3,000	
	$38,000	
Less:		
depreciation	−10,000	
Adjusted basis:	$28,000	−28,000
Capital gain on improvements:		$ 44,400
Plus capital gain on land:		
value at sale	$20,000	
less original value	−10,000	
	$10,000	+ 10,000
Total capital gain:		$ 54,400
Amount taxable as		
ordinary income:		$ 54,400

Exchanges — amount of $ difference that you come ahead.

Real estate investors can defer taxation of capital gains by a property exchange. Even if property has appreciated greatly since its initial purchase, it may be exchanged for other property and the property owner will incur tax liability on the sale only if additional capital or property is also received. Note, however, that *the tax is deferred, not eliminated.* If the investor ever sells the property, the total capital gain will be taxed.

To qualify as a tax-deferred exchange, the properties involved must be of *like kind*—for example, real estate for real estate. Any additional capital or personal property included with the transaction to even out the exchange is considered

boot, and the party receiving it is taxed at the time of the exchange. The value of the boot is added to the basis of the property with which it is given.

For example, investor Brown owns an apartment building with an adjusted basis of $225,000 and a market value of $375,000. Brown exchanges the building plus $75,000 cash for another apartment building having a market value of $450,000. That building, owned by investor Grey, has an adjusted basis of $175,000. Brown's basis in the new building will be $300,000 (the $225,000 basis of the building exchanged plus the $75,000 cash boot paid) and Brown has no tax liability on the exchange. Grey must pay tax on the $75,000 boot received and has a basis of $175,000 (the same as the previous building) in the building now owned.

Depreciation (Cost Recovery)

Depreciation, or **cost recovery,** is an accounting concept. Depreciation allows an investor to recover the cost of an income-producing asset by way of tax deductions over the period of the asset's useful life.

While investors rarely purchase property without the expectation that it will appreciate over time, the view of the Internal Revenue Service is that all physical structures will deteriorate and hence lose value over time. Cost recovery deductions may be taken only on personal property and improvements to land, and only if they are used in a trade or business or for the production of income. Thus, a cost recovery deduction cannot be claimed on an individual's personal residence. *Land cannot be depreciated*—technically it never wears out or becomes obsolete.

If depreciation is taken in equal amounts over an asset's useful life, the method used is called *straight-line depreciation.* For certain property, it is also possible to use an *accelerated cost recovery system (ACRS)* to claim greater deductions in the early years of ownership, gradually reducing the amount deducted in each year of the useful life.

ACRS allows "recovery" (tax deduction) of a greater share of property value in the first years that the property is depreciated. In contrast, the *straight-line* method of depreciation allows for depreciation to be spread out evenly over the recovery period. The ability to take a larger deduction than that allowed under the straight-line method provides investors with a useful tool in developing an investment strategy.

Unfortunately, the treatment of real estate for depreciation purposes has undergone many changes over the last decade, and the new tax law has removed some of the advantageous provisions of the past.

For real property placed in service (acquired and producing income) before 1981, depreciation could be taken over the property's useful life (for example, 35 to 40 years in the case of a new building). The recovery period was reduced to 15 years for property placed in service as of January 1, 1981. The term was increased to 18 years for property placed in service after March 15, 1984, and 19 years for property placed in service after May 8, 1985. Either a straight-line or accelerated recovery system could be used. Those properties retain their former depreciation schedules.

For property placed in service as of January 1, 1987, however, the Tax Reform Act has increased the recovery period on residential rental property to 27.5 years and nonresidential property to 31.5 years. Just as important, only straight-line depreciation is allowed.

The impact on investors of the change in depreciation schedules will be to greatly decrease the allowable tax deductions in the early years of property ownership. The entire property value is still eventually recovered, but the investor must be prepared to have far less benefit from deductions in the early years of ownership.

Deductions and TRA '86

The Tax Reform Act of 1986 limits the deductibility of losses from rental property. The first $25,000 of loss can be used to offset income from any source provided that the investor *actively participates* in the management and operation of the property and has taxable income of no more than $100,000 before the deduction is made. The deduction is reduced by $.50 for every dollar of income over $100,000, and is thus eliminated completely when income reaches $150,000. Two examples will help to illustrate the impact of this law.

1. Harvey has adjusted gross income of $130,000 and losses of $20,000 from three apartment buildings that he owns and personally manages. Harvey is entitled to a deduction of only $10,000 (since the $25,000 maximum is reduced by $.50 for every dollar of the $30,000 Harvey earned over $100,000), reducing his taxable income to $120,000.
2. Helen has adjusted gross income of $100,000 and losses of $20,000 from rental property that she actively manages. Helen is entitled to a deduction of the full $20,000 (since her income doesn't exceed $100,000), reducing her taxable income to $80,000.

The deduction applies only when the taxpayer actively participates in managing the rental property. The involvement may be as great as personally managing the day-to-day operation of the rental property with no outside assistance, or as minimal as simply making management decisions, such as the approval of new tenants and lease terms, while hiring others to provide services.

The Tax Reform Act prevents an investor from using a loss from a passive activity (one in which the taxpayer is not an active participant) to shelter "active income" (such as wages) or "portfolio income" (such as stock dividends, bank interest and capital gains). An example of a passive investor is a limited partner, someone who contributes investment monies but has no voice in the operation of the investment.

While the deduction restrictions do not apply to people who invest in and *actively* run a trade or business, deduction of losses is restricted for those who invest in a business and then play only a passive role in its operation. Active involvement in the running of a trade or business must be "regular, continuous and substantial"—a greater degree of involvement than that required for rental real estate. The co-owner of a restaurant, for instance, would be required to take a participatory role in the day-to-day running of the business.

Generally, a passive investor can offset investment losses only against investment income. If the passive investor has no other current investment income, the loss may be carried over to offset investment income in future years. If the investment is sold before the loss is used, it may offset what would otherwise be taxable gain on the sale.

To ease the effect of the new law, investors can write off 65 percent of passive losses against noninvestment income in 1987, 40 percent in 1988, 20 percent in 1989, and 10 percent in 1990.

Tax credits. A **tax credit** is a direct reduction in tax due, rather than a deduction from income before tax is computed. A tax credit is therefore of far greater value.

Investors in older building renovations and low-income housing projects may use the designated tax credits (described below) to offset tax on up to $25,000 of other income. This is a major exception to the rule requiring active participation in the project. Even passive investors can take advantage of the tax credits. The maximum income level at which the credits can be taken is also higher. Investors with adjusted gross income of up to $200,000 are entitled to the full $25,000 off-set, which is reduced by $.50 for every additional dollar of income, and eliminated entirely for incomes above $250,000.

Since 1976, tax credits have been provided for taxpayers who renovate historic property. Historic property is property so designated by the Department of the Interior and listed in the *National Register of Historic Landmarks*, or property of historic significance that is located in an area certified by a state as a historic district.

The Tax Reform Act has reduced the allowable credit from 25 percent of the money spent on renovation of historic property to 20 percent of money so spent. The property can be depreciated, but the full amount of the tax credit must be subtracted from the basis derived by adding purchase cost and renovation expenses. (Formerly, only one-half of the amount of the tax credit had to be subtracted.)

The work must be accomplished in accordance with federal historic property guidelines and certified by the Department of the Interior. After renovation, the property must be used as a place of business or rented—it cannot be used as the personal residence of the person taking the tax credit.

Prior to the Tax Reform Act, a credit of 15% of renovation expenses was allowed for buildings at least 30 years old, even though not designated "historic." The credit was 20 percent for buildings at least 40 years old.

Under the new law, there is a credit of 10% of rehabilitation costs for nonhistoric buildings placed in service before 1936. Nonhistoric buildings must be nonresidential property.

Note: Special transition rules may make a rehabilitated property eligible for a 19-year recovery period.

The new law also provides tax credits ranging from 4 percent to 9 percent each year over a 10-year period for expenditures on new construction or renovation of low-income housing placed in service or acquired after 1986 and before 1990.

The new law is designed to eliminate the depreciation "losses" that shielded non-investment income from taxation and formed the basis for tax shelters in the past. Coupled with the significant changes in the deductibility of passive investment losses, the depreciation changes place new emphasis on sound economic analysis of potential investments.

Installment Sales

A taxpayer who sells real property valued at $150,000 or less and held for rental or for sale in the ordinary course of business, and receives payment on an installment basis, may report any profit on the transaction in the year actually received. Taxable income is based on the proportion of the profit to the total contract price received in the year reported. If the property value exceeds $150,000, all gain must be reported in the year of sale, no matter how little cash the seller actually receives at that time.

There are many complex provisions regarding installment sales. The details of any proposed transaction require consultation with an accountant and attorney.

Real Estate Investment Syndicates

A **real estate investment syndicate** is a form of business venture in which a group of people pool their resources to own and/or develop a particular piece of property. In this manner, people with only modest capital can invest in large-scale, high-profit operations, such as high-rise apartment buildings and shopping centers. A certain amount of profit is realized from rents collected on the investment, but the main return usually comes when the syndicate sells the property after sufficient appreciation.

Syndicate participation can take many different legal forms, from tenancy in common and joint tenancy to various kinds of partnerships, corporations and trusts. *Private syndication*, which generally involves a small group of closely associated and/or widely experienced investors, is distinguished from *public syndication,* which generally involves a much larger group of investors who may or may not be knowledgeable about real estate as an investment. The distinction between the two, however, is usually based on the nature of the arrangement between syndicator and investors, not on the type of syndicate. For this reason, any pooling of individuals' funds raises questions of registration of securities under federal securities laws and state securities laws, commonly referred to as *blue-sky laws.*

Securities laws include provisions to control and regulate the offering and sale of securities. This is to protect members of the public who are not sophisticated investors but may be solicited to participate. Real estate securities must be registered with state officials and/or with the federal Securities and Exchange Commission (SEC) when they meet the defined conditions of a public offering. The number of prospects solicited, the total number of investors or participants, the financial background and sophistication of the investors and the value or price per unit of investment are pertinent facts. *Salespeople of such real estate securities may be required to obtain special licenses.*

Forms of Syndicates

Real estate investment syndicates are usually organized as either general or limited partnerships.

A general partnership is organized so that *all members of the group share equally in the managerial decisions, profits and losses involved with the investment.* A certain member (or members) of the syndicate is designated to act as trustee for the group and holds title to the property and maintains it in the syndicate's name.

Under a **limited partnership** agreement, *one party* (or parties), usually a property developer or real estate broker, *organizes, operates and is responsible for the entire* *syndicate.* This person is called the *general partner.* The other members of the partnership are merely investors; they have no voice in the organization and direction of the operation. These *passive investors are called limited partners.* The limited partners share in the profits and compensate the general partner out of such profits. Unlike a general partnership, in which each member is responsible for the total losses (if any) of the syndicate, the limited partners stand to lose only as much as they invest—nothing more. The general partner(s) is totally responsible for any excess losses incurred by the investment. The sale of a limited partnership interest involves the sale of an *investment security,* as defined by the SEC. Therefore, such sales are subject to state and federal laws concerning the sale of securities. Unless exempt, the securities must be registered with the federal Securities and Exchange Commission and the appropriate state authorities.

Investors in investment syndicates must be particularly cautious in light of the new tax rules. Passive investors (such as limited partners) are now subject to the passive loss rules and must make investment decisions based on sound income and appreciation projections.

Real Estate Investment Trusts

By directing their funds into **real estate investment trusts (REITs),** real estate investors can take advantage of the same tax benefits as mutual fund investors. A real estate investment trust does not have to pay corporate income tax as long as 95 percent of its income is distributed to its shareholders and certain other conditions are met. There are three types of investment trusts: equity trusts, mortgage trusts and combination trusts. To qualify as a REIT, at least 75 percent of the trust's income must come from real estate.

Equity trusts. Much like mutual fund operations, equity REITs pool an assortment of large-scale income properties and sell shares to investors. This is in contrast to a real estate syndicate, through which several investors pool their funds in order to purchase *one* particular property. An equity trust also differs from a syndicate in that the trust realizes and directs its main profits through the *income* derived from the various properties it owns rather than from the sale of those properties.

Mortgage trusts. Mortgage trusts operate similarly to equity trusts, except that the mortgage trusts buy and sell real estate mortgages (usually short-term, junior instruments) rather than real property. A mortgage trust's major sources of income are mortgage interest and origination fees. Mortgage trusts may also make construction loans and finance land acquisitions.

Combination trusts. Combination trusts invest shareholders' funds in both real estate assets and mortgage loans. It has been predicted that these types of trusts will be best able to withstand economic slumps because they can balance their investments and liabilities more efficiently than can the other types of trusts.

Real Estate Mortgage Investment Conduits

The Tax Reform Act has created a new tax entity that may issue multiple classes of investor interests (securities) backed by a pool of mortgages.

The **real estate mortgage investment conduit (REMIC)** has complex qualification, transfer and liquidation rules. Qualifications include the "asset test" (substantially all assets after a startup period must consist of qualified mortgages and permitted investments) and the requirement that investors' interests consist of one or more classes of regular interests and a single class of residual interests. Holders of regular interests receive interest or similar payments based on either a fixed rate or variable rate, as allowed. Holders of residual interests receive distributions (if any) on a pro rata basis.

Summary

Traditionally, real estate investment has offered a *high rate of return*, while at the same time acting as an effective *inflation hedge*, and allowing an investor to make use of other people's money to make investments through *leverage*. There may also be tax advantages to owning rental real estate. On the other hand, real estate is *not a highly liquid investment* and often carries with it a *high degree of risk*. Also, it is difficult to invest in real estate without *expert advice,* and a certain amount of involvement is usually required to establish and maintain the investment.

Investment property held for *appreciation* purposes is generally expected to increase in value to a point where its selling price is enough to cover holding costs and show a profit as well. The two main factors affecting appreciation are *inflation* and the property's present and future *intrinsic value*. Real estate held for *income* purposes is generally expected to generate a steady flow of income, called *cash flow*, and to show a profit upon its sale.

An investor hoping to use maximum *leverage* in financing an investment should make a small down payment, pay low interest rates and spread mortgage payments over as long a period as possible. By holding and refinancing properties, known as *pyramiding,* an investor may substantially increase investment holdings without contributing additional capital.

By *exchanging* one property for another with an equal or greater selling value, an investor can *defer* paying tax on the gain realized until a sale is made. A total tax deferment is possible only if the investor receives no cash or other incentive to even out the exchange. If received, such cash or property is called *boot* and is taxed at the taxpayer's regular income-tax rate.

Depreciation (cost recovery) is a concept that allows an investor to recover in tax deductions the basis of an asset over the period of its useful life. Only costs of improvements to land may be recovered, not costs for the land itself.

The Tax Reform Act of 1986 has greatly limited the potential for investment losses to shelter other income, but *tax credits* are still allowed for projects involving low-income housing and older buildings.

An investor may defer federal income taxes on gain realized from the sale of an investment property through an *installment sale* of property valued at less than $150,000.

Individuals may also invest in real estate through an *investment syndicate;* these generally include *general and limited partnerships*. Other forms of real estate investment are the *real estate investment trust* (REIT) and the *real estate mortgage investment conduit* (REMIC).

The real estate broker and salesperson should be familiar with the rudimentary tax implications of real property ownership, but should refer clients to competent tax advisors for answers to questions on specific matters.

Questions

1. In 1988, the Smiths received capital gains of $22,000, which are:
   a. deductible only from passive income.
   b. taxed at their regular rate on 40 percent of value.
   c. included in their ordinary income.
   d. subject to the purchase price rule.

2. Harvey, a limited partner in a partnership that is renovating a historic waterfront property, is entitled to:
   a. offset no more than the amount he has at risk.
   b. offset his share of tax credits on income up to $100,000.
   c. offset his share of tax credits on income up to $200,000.
   d. offset his share of tax credits on income up to $250,000.

3. Helen has purchased a dilapidated town house that is 40 years old and of no particular historic value. Helen intends to renovate the townhouse and live in it. On her renovation expenditures, Helen will be entitled to tax credits of:
   a. $25,000.   c. $12,500.
   b. $0.   d. 25%.

4. Jim traded his office building purchased for $475,000 and valued at $650,000 for an office building valued at $750,000. Jim also paid $100,000 cash to the owner of the other building. Jim:
   a. received $100,000 "boot."
   b. must report $100,000 as income.
   c. must reduce his adjusted basis by $100,000.
   d. now has a property basis of $575,000.

5. An investor purchasing a parcel of real estate through the use of borrowed funds is taking advantage of:
   a. leverage.   c. capital gains.
   b. depreciation.   d. exchanging.

6. An investment syndicate in which all members share equally in the managerial decisions, profits and losses involved in the venture would be an example of which of the following?
   a. real estate investment trust
   b. limited partnership
   c. real estate mortgage trust
   d. general partnership

7. The increase of money in circulation coupled with a rise in prices, resulting in a decline in the value of money, is called:
   a. appreciation.   c. negative cash flow.
   b. inflation.   d. recapture.

8. To maintain a high degree of cash flow, an investor holding an income property should:
   I. keep operating expenses low.
   II. charge low rents so there will be few vacancies.
      a. I only   c. both I and II
      b. II only   d. neither I nor II

9. Investor Mary Clark is contemplating purchasing an apartment building for both income and appreciation purposes for $150,000. All else being equal, which of the following choices should yield Clark the largest percentage of return on her initial investment after the first year?
   a. Clark pays $150,000 cash for the property.
   b. Clark gives the seller a $75,000 down payment and the seller takes back a 15-year purchase-money mortgage for the balance at 10.5 percent interest.
   c. Clark gives the seller $15,000 down and obtains a 30-year mortgage for the balance at 11 percent interest.
   d. Clark gives the seller $20,000 down and agrees to pay the seller 10 percent of the unpaid balance each year for ten years, plus 10.5 percent interest.

10. For tax purposes, the initial cost of an investment property plus the cost of any subsequent improvements to the property, less recovery deductions, represents the investment's:
    a. adjusted basis.
    b. capital gains.
    c. basis.
    d. salvage value.

11. Julia Kinder is exchanging her apartment building for an apartment building of greater market value and must include a $10,000 boot to even out the exchange. Which of the following may she use as a boot?
    a. $10,000 cash
    b. common stock with a current market value of $10,000
    c. an auto with a current market value of $10,000
    d. any of the above if acceptable to the exchangers

12. Capital gains:
    I. may be realized only from the sale of improvements to real estate, not from the sale of land itself.
    II. are limited to 25 percent of an income property's gross income for the year of sale.
        a. I only
        b. II only
        c. both I and II
        d. neither I nor II

13. Toward which of the following might an investor direct his or her funds in order to hold real estate primarily for appreciation purposes?
    I. farmland
    II. shopping center
        a. I only
        b. II only
        c. both I and II
        d. neither I nor II

14. A property's equity represents its current value less which of the following?
    a. recovery deductions
    b. mortgage indebtedness
    c. physical improvements
    d. selling costs and recovery deductions

15. When an investor holds and refinances investment properties, using their equities as leverage, he or she is taking advantage of which of the following concepts?
    a. pyramiding
    b. negative cash flow
    c. recapture
    d. useful life

16. A new tax entity that issues securities backed by a pool of mortgages is a:
    a. REIT.
    b. REMIC.
    c. TRA.
    d. general partnership.

23

Closing the Real Estate Transaction

Key Terms

Accrued item
Closing agent
Closing statement
Credit
Debit
Doctrine of relation back
Escrow
Prepaid item
Proration
Real Estate Settlement Procedures Act (RESPA)
Uniform Settlement Statement

Overview

After securing and servicing a listing, advertising the property, finding and qualifying potential buyers and negotiating for and obtaining a signed sales contract on the seller's property, a real estate licensee is one step away from receiving a commission. That last step is the real estate closing, a procedure that includes both title and financial considerations. This chapter will discuss both aspects of real estate closing, focusing on the licensee's role in this concluding phase of a real estate transaction. Special emphasis will be placed on the computations necessary to settle all expenses between buyer and seller, and between seller and broker. The chapter also includes a detailed example of a real estate closing.

Closing the Transaction	The preceding chapters discuss the various elements involved in and leading up to the closing of a sale are just as necessary to real estate licensees. A real estate professional should be able to assist in preclosing arrangements and advise the parties in estimating their expenses and the approximate amounts the buyer will need and the seller will actually receive at the closing. The closing represents the culmination of the service the broker's firm provides. The sale, which the broker has negotiated, is completed, and the broker's commission (and thus the salesperson's commission) is generally paid out of the proceeds at the closing.
License Examination Closing Problems	In some states, a closing statement problem is part of the broker's licensing examination. Although the salesperson's examination does not usually include completion of a closing statement problem, most states require an applicant to compute prorations, and many include the completion of a sales contract and listing agreement from the description of a sample transaction.
At the Closing	Generally speaking, the closing of a real estate transaction involves a gathering of interested parties at which the promises made in the *real estate sales contract* are kept, or *executed;* that is, the seller's deed is delivered in exchange for the purchase price. In many sales transactions, two closings actually take place at this time: (1) the closing of the buyer's loan—the disbursal of mortgage funds by the lender—and (2) the closing of the sale. A closing involving all interested parties is often called a "round table close."

As discussed in Chapter 11, a sales contract is the blueprint for the completion of a real estate transaction. A contract should be complete and should provide for all possibilities in order to avoid misunderstandings that could delay or even prevent the closing of the sale. Before going ahead with the exchange, the parties should assure themselves that the various conditions and stipulations of their sales contract have been met.

The buyer will want to be sure that the seller is delivering good title and that the property is in the promised condition. This involves inspecting the title evidence, the deed the seller will give, any documents representing the removal of undesired liens and encumbrances, the survey, the termite report and any leases, if there are tenants on the premises. The seller will want to be sure that the buyer has obtained the stipulated financing and has sufficient funds to complete the sale. Both parties will wish to inspect the closing statement to make sure that all monies involved in the transaction have been properly accounted for. In doing this, the parties will most likely be represented by attorneys.

When the parties are satisfied that everything is in order, the exchange is made, and all pertinent documents are then recorded. The documents must be recorded in the correct order to avoid creating a defect in the title. For example, if the seller is paying off an existing loan and the buyer is obtaining a new loan, the seller's satisfaction of mortgage must be recorded before the seller's deed to the buyer. The buyer's new mortgage must then be recorded after the deed, since the lender cannot have a security interest in the buyer's property until it belongs to the buyer.

Where Closings Are Held and Who Attends

Closings may be held at a number of locations, including the offices of the title company, the lending institution, the office of one of the parties' attorneys, the offices of the broker, the county recorder (or other local recording official) or the escrow company. Those attending a closing may include any of the following interested parties:

1. buyer;
2. seller;
3. real estate agent (broker and/or salesperson);
4. attorney(s) for the seller and/or buyer;
5. representatives and/or attorneys for lending institutions involved with the buyer's new mortgage loan, the buyer's assumption of the seller's existing loan or the seller's payoff of an existing loan; and
6. representative of the title insurance company.

Closing agent. One person usually conducts the proceedings at a closing and calculates the official settlement, or division of charges and expenses between the parties. In some areas, real estate brokers preside; but more commonly, the **closing agent** is an escrow agent, the buyer's or seller's attorney, a representative of the lender or a representative of a title company. Some title companies and law firms employ paralegal assistants, called *closers,* who conduct all closings for their firms. The closer is the person in such offices who arranges the closing with the parties involved, prepares the closing statements, compares figures with lenders and orders title evidence, surveys and other miscellaneous items needed.

IRS reporting requirements. The Tax Reform Act of 1986 requires the reporting of real estate transactions to the Internal Revenue Service. The gross proceeds involved in the transaction, along with other information, must be reported by the person (including any attorney or title company) responsible for closing the transaction. If that person does not report, the responsibility then falls on (in the following order): the mortgage lender, the seller's broker, the buyer's broker or such other person as the regulations designate.

Broker's Role at Closing

Depending on the locality, the broker's role at a closing can vary from simply collecting the commission to conducting the proceedings. As discussed earlier in the text, a real estate broker is not authorized to give legal advice or otherwise engage in the practice of law. In some areas of the country, principally in some of the eastern states, this means that a broker's job is essentially over when the sales contract is signed; at that point, the attorneys take over. Even so, a broker's service generally continues after the contract is signed in that the broker advises the parties in practical matters and makes sure all the details are taken care of so that the closing can proceed smoothly. In this capacity the broker might make arrangements for such items as title evidence, surveys, appraisals, termite inspections and repairs, or might recommend sources of these services to the parties.

Lender's Interest in Closing

Whether a buyer is obtaining new financing or assuming the seller's existing loan, the lender wants to protect its security interest in the property—to make sure that the buyer is getting good, marketable title and that tax and insurance payments are maintained—so that there will be no liens with greater priority than the mortgage lien and the insurance will be paid up if the property is damaged or destroyed. For this reason, the lender will frequently require the following items: (1) a title insurance policy; (2) a fire and hazard insurance policy, with receipt for the premium; (3) additional information, such as a survey, a termite or other inspection report or a certificate of occupancy (for newly constructed buildings); (4) establishment of a reserve, or escrow, account for tax and insurance payments; and possibly (5) representation by its own attorney at the closing.

RESPA Requirements

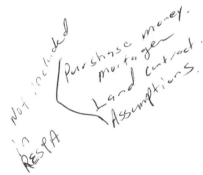

The federal **Real Estate Settlement Procedures Act (RESPA)**, enacted in 1974 and revised in 1975, was created to ensure that the buyer and seller in a residential real estate sale or transfer have knowledge of all settlement costs. In this context, residential real estate includes one- to four-family homes, cooperatives and condominiums. *RESPA requirements apply when the purchase is financed by a federally related mortgage loan.* Federally related loans include those (1) made by banks, savings and loan associations or other lenders whose deposits are insured by federal agencies (FDIC or FSLIC); (2) insured by the FHA or guaranteed by the VA; (3) administered by the U.S. Department of Housing and Urban Development; or (4) intended to be sold by the lender to Fannie Mae, Ginnie Mae or Freddie Mac.

RESPA regulations apply only to transactions involving new first mortgage loans. A transaction financed solely by a purchase-money mortgage taken back by the seller, an installment contract (land contract, contract for deed) or the buyer's assumption of the seller's existing loan would not be covered by RESPA, unless the terms of the assumed loan are modified or the lender imposes charges of over $50 for the assumption. As of June 20, 1976, when a transaction is covered by RESPA, the following requirements must be complied with:

1. *Special information booklet:* Lenders must give a copy of the HUD booklet *Settlement Costs and You* to every person from whom they receive or for whom they prepare a loan application. This booklet provides the borrower with general information about settlement (closing) costs and explains the various RESPA provisions, including a line-by-line discussion of the Uniform Settlement Statement (see item 3).

2. *Good faith estimate of settlement costs:* At the time of the loan application, or within three business days, the lender must provide the borrower with a good faith estimate of the settlement costs the borrower is likely to incur. This estimate may be a specific figure or a range of costs based upon comparable past transactions in the area. In addition, if the lender requires use of a particular attorney or title company to conduct the closing, the lender must state whether it has any business relationship with that firm and must estimate the charges for this service.

3. *Uniform Settlement Statement (HUD Form 1):* RESPA provides that loan closing information must be prepared on a special HUD form, the **Uniform Settlement Statement,** designed to detail all financial particulars of a transaction. A copy of this form is illustrated in figure 23.1. The completed statement must itemize all charges imposed by the lender. Charges incurred by the buyer and seller, contracted for separately and outside the closing, do not have to be disclosed. Items paid for prior to the closing must be clearly marked as such on the statement and are omitted from the totals. This statement must be made available for inspection by the borrower *at or before* the closing. Upon the borrower's request, the closing agent must permit the borrower to inspect the settlement statement, to the extent that the figures are available, one busi-

ness day before the closing. Lenders must retain these statements for two years after the date of closing unless the loan (and its servicing) is sold or otherwise disposed of. The Uniform Settlement Statement may be altered to allow for local custom, and certain lines may be deleted if they do not apply in the area.

4. *Prohibition against kickbacks:* RESPA explicitly prohibits the payment of kickbacks, or unearned fees, such as when an insurance agency pays a kickback to a lender for referring one of the lender's recent customers to the agency. This prohibition does *not* include fee splitting between cooperating brokers or members of multiple-listing services, brokerage referral arrangements or the division of a commission between a broker and his or her salespeople.

RESPA is administered by the U.S. Department of Housing and Urban Development (HUD).

The Title Procedure

As discussed earlier, the principle of caveat emptor requires the purchaser and the purchaser's lender to assure themselves that the seller's property and title comply with the contract requirements. The sales contract usually includes time limitations for the parties to obtain and present title evidence and remove any objections to the title. A contract that includes the provision "time is of the essence" expresses the agreement of the parties that all *time limitations are to be met exactly as stated.*

The seller is usually required to show proof of ownership by producing a current *abstract* or *title commitment* from the title insurance company. When an abstract of title is used, the purchaser's attorney examines it and issues an opinion of title. This opinion, like the title commitment, sets forth the status of the seller's title, showing liens, encumbrances, easements, conditions or restrictions that appear on the record and to which the seller's title is subject.

On the date when the sale is actually completed, that is, the date of delivery of the deed, the buyer has a title commitment or an abstract that was issued several days or weeks before the closing. For this reason, the title or abstract company is usually required to make two searches of the public records. The first, as discussed, shows the status of the seller's title on the date of the sales contract; the seller usually pays the charges for this report (depending on local custom). The second search is made after the closing and covers the date when the deed is recorded to the purchaser; the purchaser generally pays to "bring the title down" to the closing date.

In this later search, the seller is usually required to execute an *affidavit of title.* This is a sworn statement in which the seller assures the title company (and the buyer) that since the date of the title examination there have been no judgments, bankruptcies or divorces involving the seller, no unrecorded deeds or contracts made, no repairs or improvements that have not been paid for, and no defects in the title that the seller knows of and that he or she is in possession of the premises. This form is always required by the title insurance company before it will issue an owner's policy, particularly an extended-coverage policy, to the buyer. Through this affidavit, the title company obtains the right to sue the seller if his or her statements in the affidavit prove incorrect.

In some areas where real estate sales transactions are customarily closed through an escrow, the escrow instructions usually include provision for an extended-coverage policy to be issued to the buyer as of the date of closing. In such cases, there is no gap between the date of commitment and the closing, so there is no need for the seller to execute an affidavit of title.

In certain areas of the country, primarily in the eastern states, it is strictly the buyer's responsibility to make sure that the seller's title is good. In such cases, the *buyer* generally orders and pays for the title evidence.

Checking the Premises

In general, it is important for the buyer to inspect the property to determine the interests of any parties in possession or other interests that cannot be determined from inspecting the public record. A *survey* is frequently required so that the purchaser will know the location and size of the property. The contract will specify whether the seller is to pay for this. It is usual for the survey to "spot" the location of all buildings, driveways, fences and other improvements located primarily on the premises being purchased, as well as any such improvements located on adjoining property that may encroach upon the premises being bought. The survey also sets out, in full, any existing easements and encroachments. So that the survey will clearly identify the location of the property, the house number, if any, should be stated.

Shortly before the closing takes place, the buyer will usually make a *final inspection* of the property with the broker. The purposes of the final inspection are to make sure that necessary repairs have been made, that the property has been well maintained (both inside and outside), that all fixtures are in place and that there has been no unauthorized removal or alteration of any part of the improvements.

Releasing Existing Liens

When the purchaser is paying cash or is obtaining a new mortgage in order to purchase the property, the seller's existing mortgage usually is paid in full and released of record. In order to know the exact amount required to pay the existing mortgage, the seller secures a current *payoff statement* from the mortgagee. This payoff statement sets forth the unpaid amount of principal, interest due through the date of payment, the fee for issuing the release deed, credits, if any, for tax and insurance reserves and any penalties that may be due because the loan is being prepaid before its maturity. The same procedure would be followed for any other liens that must be released before the buyer takes title.

For transactions in which the buyer is assuming the seller's existing mortgage loan, the buyer will want to know the exact balance of the loan as of the closing date. In some areas it is customary for the buyer to obtain an *estoppel certificate* from the seller, stating the exact balance due and the last interest payment made.

Closing in Escrow

As discussed in Chapter 11, a real estate transaction may be closed through an escrow. Although there are a few states where transactions are never closed in escrow, escrow closings are used to some extent in most states. In the western section of the country, the majority of transactions are closed in escrow.

An **escrow** is a method of closing in which a disinterested third party is authorized to act as escrow agent and is given the responsibility to coordinate the closing activities. The escrow agent may also be called the *escrow holder*. The escrow agent may be an attorney, a title company, a trust company, an escrow company or the escrow department of a lending institution. While many brokerages do offer escrow services, a broker cannot be a disinterested party in a transaction from which he or she expects to collect a commission. Because the escrow agent is placed in a position of great trust, many states have laws regulating escrow agents and limiting who may serve in this capacity.

The Escrow Procedure

When a transaction will be closed in escrow, the buyer and seller choose an escrow agent and execute escrow instructions to the escrow agent after the sales contract is signed. Once the contract is signed, the broker turns over the earnest money to the escrow agent, who deposits it in a special trust, or escrow, account.

The escrow instructions require the buyer and seller to deposit all pertinent documents and other items with the escrow agent before the specified date of closing. The seller will usually deposit:

1. the *deed* conveying the property to the buyer;
2. title *evidence* (abstract, title insurance policy or Torrens certificate);
3. existing fire and hazard *insurance* policies;
4. letter from the mortgagee of the existing mortgage, setting forth the *amount* needed to pay the loan in full, or the exact amount the buyer will assume;
5. *affidavits of title* (if required);
6. *payoff letter* (estoppel certificate) if the seller's mortgage is to be paid off; and
7. other instruments or documents necessary to clear the title or to complete the transaction.

The buyer will deposit:

1. the balance of the *cash needed* to complete the purchase;
2. *mortgage papers*, if the buyer is securing a new mortgage; and
3. other documents needed to complete the transaction.

The escrow agent is given the authority to examine the title evidence. When clear title is shown in the name of the buyer and all other conditions of the escrow agreement have been met, the agent is authorized to disburse the purchase price—minus all charges and expenses—to the seller and record the deed and mortgage or trust deed (if a new mortgage has been executed by the purchaser) as provided by the escrow instructions.

If the escrow agent's examination of the title discloses liens against the seller or a lien for which the seller is responsible, the escrow instructions usually provide that a portion of the purchase price can be withheld from the seller and used to pay such liens as are necessary to clear the title so the transaction can be closed.

If the seller cannot clear the title, or if for any reason the sale cannot be consummated and the buyer will not accept the title as it is, then the escrow instructions usually provide that the parties be returned to their former status. To accomplish this, the purchaser reconveys title to the seller and the escrow agent restores all purchase money to the buyer. Because the escrow is dependent upon specific conditions being met before the transfer becomes binding on the parties, the courts have held that the parties can be reinstated to their former status.

Some advantages of closing a sale through an escrow are: (1) the buyer's money will not be paid to the seller until the seller's title is acceptable under the terms of the contract, (2) the seller knows that the buyer's money must actually be received (the check must clear) before title passes, so the seller is assured of getting the purchase price and (3) neither party need be present when title is passed. Because the escrow agent will run a final inspection of the title before the closing date, *the buyer is protected from the risk of judgments and other liens originating against the seller's title prior to the date of closing.*

In Practice...

Fees charged by the escrow agent are customarily split between buyer and seller. However, a purchaser under new VA financing is not allowed to pay any escrow fees, so all such costs are the sole responsibility of the seller. In addition, FHA regulations stipulate that the buyer may pay up to one-half of fees charged by the escrow agent.

Doctrine of Relation Back

If a seller deposits the deed with an escrow agent under the terms of a valid escrow agreement and then dies, but thereafter the conditions of the escrow are satisfied, the *deed passes title to the purchaser as of the date it was delivered to the escrow agent.* This is called the **doctrine of relation back**—the title relates back to the date on which the deed was deposited in escrow. When the conditions of the escrow have not been met, however, the deed is not considered as having been delivered and title does not pass to the purchaser.

Preparation of Closing Statements

A typical real estate sales transaction involves numerous expenses for both parties in addition to the purchase price. Furthermore, there are a number of property expenses that the seller will have already paid in advance for a set period of time or that the buyer will pay in the future. The financial responsibility for these items must be *prorated,* or divided, between the buyer and the seller. In closing a transaction, it is customary to account for all these items by preparing a written statement to determine how much money the buyer needs and how much the seller will net after the broker's commission and expenses. Although there are many different formats of closing statements, or settlement statements, all are designed to achieve the same results.

How the Closing Statement Works

The completion of a **closing statement** involves an accounting of the parties' debits and credits. A **debit** is a charge, an amount that the party being debited owes and must pay at the closing. A **credit** is an amount entered in a person's favor—either an amount that the party being credited has already paid, an amount that he or she must be reimbursed for or an amount the buyer promises to pay in the form of a loan.

To determine the amount the buyer needs at the closing, the buyer's debits are totaled—any expenses and prorated amounts for items prepaid by the seller are added to the purchase price. Then the buyer's credits are totaled. These would include the earnest money (already paid), the balance of the loan the buyer is obtaining or assuming and the seller's share of any prorated items that the buyer will pay in the future. Finally, the total of the buyer's credits is subtracted from the total amount the buyer owes (debits) to arrive at the actual amount of cash the buyer must bring to the closing. Usually the buyer brings a cashier's check or a certified personal check.

A similar procedure is followed to determine how much money the seller will actually receive. The seller's debits and credits are each totaled. The credits would include the purchase price, plus the buyer's share of any prorated items that the seller has prepaid.

The seller's debits would include expenses, the seller's share of prorated items to be paid later by the buyer and the balance of any mortgage loan or other lien that the seller is paying off. Finally, the total of the seller's charges is subtracted from the total credits to arrive at the amount the seller will receive.

Expenses

In addition to the payment of the sales price and the proration of taxes, interest and the like, a number of other expenses and charges may be involved in a real estate transaction. These include the following items.

Broker's commission. The broker's commission is usually paid by the seller, since the broker is usually the seller's agent. When the buyer has employed the broker, the buyer pays the commission. As discussed in Chapter 5, it is important that the rate of commission for each transaction be negotiated between the broker and the principal and specifically stated in the listing agreement.

Attorney's fees. If either of the parties' attorneys will be paid from the closing proceeds, that party will be charged with the expense in the closing statement.

Recording expenses. The charges for recording different types of documents vary widely among and within states. In one county, for example, the charge for recording a single-page deed may be $10, and a four-page mortgage might be about $15. These charges are established by law and are based upon the number of words and pages included in the instrument. You should verify recording charges in your area.

The *seller* usually pays for recording charges (filing fees), which are necessary in order to clear all defects and furnish the purchaser with a clear title in accordance with the terms of the contract. Items customarily charged to the seller would include the recording of release deeds or satisfaction of mortgages, quitclaim deeds, affidavits, and satisfaction of mechanic's lien claims. The *purchaser* pays for recording charges incident to the actual transfer of title. Usually items include recording the deed that conveys title to the purchaser and a mortgage or trust deed executed by the purchaser.

Transfer tax. As discussed in Chapter 12, most states and/or counties require some form of transfer tax, conveyance fee or tax stamps on real estate conveyances. This expense is most often borne by the seller, although customs may vary.

Title expenses. The responsibility for title expenses varies according to local custom. As discussed earlier, in most areas the seller is required to furnish evidence of good title and pay for the title search. If the buyer's attorney inspects the evidence or if the buyer purchases title insurance policies, the buyer is charged for these expenses. In some situations the title or abstract company is required to make two searches of the public records: the first showing the status of the seller's title on the date of the sales contract, and the second continuing after the closing and through the date on which the purchaser's deed is recorded. In such cases, the seller pays for the initial search and the purchaser pays for the "later date" charge.

A title or abstract company will normally furnish an estimate, usually without charge, of the customary costs for these services in your area.

Loan fees. When the purchaser is securing a mortgage to finance the purchase, the lender (mortgage company) will ordinarily charge a service fee, loan origination fee, or mortgage commission of from one to three percent or more of the loan. The fee is a flat charge and is usually paid by the purchaser at the time the transaction is closed. If calculated as a percentage of the loan principal, such fees are spoken of as *points;* for example, a two-percent fee is called *two points.* If the buyer is assuming the seller's existing financing, there may be an assumption fee.

The seller also may be charged fees by a lender, if provided for in the contract. If the buyer finances the purchase with a VA loan, the seller may be required to pay discount points as discussed in Chapter 15. Also, under the terms of some mortgage loans, the seller may be required to pay a prepayment charge or penalty for paying off the existing mortgage loan in advance of its due date.

Tax reserves and insurance reserves (escrows). A *reserve* is a sum of money set aside to be used later for a particular purpose. The mortgage lender usually requires the borrower to establish and maintain a reserve in order to have sufficient funds to pay general real estate taxes and renew insurance when these items become due.

To set up the reserve, the borrower is required to make a lump-sum payment to the lender when the mortgage money is paid out (usually at the time of closing). The amount first paid into this reserve account should equal at least the earned (used up) portion of both the general real estate taxes and insurance—the amount of taxes or insurance premium for the period *prior* to closing the sale, usually including the date on which the sale is closed. Thereafter, the borrower is required to pay into the reserve an amount equal to one month's portion of the *estimated* general real estate tax and insurance premium as part of the monthly payment made to the mortgage company.

Appraisal fees. Either the seller or the purchaser pays the appraisal fees, depending on who orders the appraisal. When the buyer obtains a mortgage, it is customary for the lender to require an appraisal, which the buyer pays for. A typical residential mortgage appraisal may cost from $150 to $300.

Survey fees. The purchaser who obtains new mortgage financing customarily pays the survey fees. In some cases the sales contract may require the seller to furnish a survey.

Prorations

Most closings involve the division of financial responsibility between the buyer and seller for such items as loan interest, taxes, rents, fuel and utility bills. These allowances are called **prorations.** Prorations are necessary to ensure that expenses are fairly divided between the seller and the buyer. For example, the seller usually owes current taxes that have not been billed; the buyer would want this settled at the closing. In states where taxes must be paid in advance, the seller would be entitled to a rebate at the closing. If the buyer assumes the seller's existing mortgage, the seller usually owes the buyer an allowance for accrued interest through the date of closing.

Accrued items are items to be prorated—such as taxes—that have been earned during the occupancy or ownership of the seller but have not been paid by the seller, and are credited to the purchaser. (*Earned,* as used here, means owed by the seller.) Each accrued item will be paid by the purchaser at some later time, so the seller must pay a share (the earned portion) at the closing by giving a credit to the purchaser.

Prepaid items are items to be prorated—such as insurance—that have been prepaid by the seller but not fully earned (not fully used up). They are therefore credits to the seller.

General rules for prorating. The rules or customs governing the computation of prorations for the closing of a real estate sale vary widely from state to state. In many states the real estate boards and the bar association have established closing rules and procedures. In some cases these rules and procedures control closings for the entire state; in others they merely affect closings within a given city, town or county.

Here are some general rules to guide you in studying the closing procedure and preparing the closing statement:

1. In most states, the seller owns the property on the day of closing, and prorations or apportionments are usually made *to and including the day of closing*. In a few states, however, it is specifically provided that the buyer owns the property on the closing date and that adjustments shall be made as of the day preceding the day on which title is closed.

2. Mortgage interest, general real estate taxes, water taxes, insurance premiums and similar expenses are usually computed by using *360 days in a year and 30 days in a month*. However, the rules in some areas provide for computing prorations on the basis of the actual number of days in the calendar month of closing. The sales contract may specify which method is to be used.

3. Accrued *general real estate* taxes that are not yet due are usually prorated at the closing. When the amount of the current real estate tax cannot be definitely determined, the proration is usually based on the last obtainable tax bill. *Special assessments* for such municipal improvements as sewers, water mains or streets are usually paid in annual installments over several years. As a general rule, the municipality charges the property owner annual interest on the outstanding balance of future installments. In a sales transaction, the seller pays the current installment and the buyer assumes all future installments. *The special assessment installment is generally not prorated at the closing;* some buyers, however, insist that the seller allow them a credit for the seller's share of the interest to the closing date.

4. *Rents* are usually adjusted on the basis of the *actual* number of days in the month of closing. It is customary for the seller to receive the rents for the day of closing and to pay all expenses for that day. If any rents for the current month are uncollected when the sale is closed, the buyer will often agree by a separate letter to collect the rents if possible and remit the pro rata share to the seller.

5. *Security deposits* made by tenants to cover the last month's rent of the lease or to cover the cost of repairing damage caused by the tenant are generally trans-

ferred by the seller to the buyer. Some leases may require the tenant's consent to such a transfer of the deposit.

6. Unpaid *wages of building employees* are prorated if the sale is closed between wage payment dates.

7. There is little uniformity in the rules covering *chattels and fixtures*. Each area has certain established customs. However, the following items normally are considered to be fixtures and are included in the conveyance free and clear of liens, unless there is an agreement otherwise: draperies, shades, blinds, screens, storm doors and windows, plumbing and heating equipment, built-in appliances and tools. In apartment buildings, the following also may be included: hall carpets, refrigerators, gas and electric stoves, and such garden tools as lawn mowers and hoses.

You should verify these proration rules with the customs in your area.

Accounting for Credits and Charges

The items that must be accounted for in the closing statement fall into two general categories: (1) prorations or other amounts due to either the buyer or seller (credit to) and paid for by the other party (debit to) and (2) expenses or items paid by the seller or buyer (debit only).

The following list shows which items are commonly credited to the buyer, and which to the seller. Other items may be included in such a list, depending upon the customs of your area.

Items Credited to Buyer (debited to seller)	**Items Credited to Seller** (debited to buyer)
1. buyer's earnest money*	1. sales price*
2. unpaid principal balance of outstanding mortgage being assumed by buyer*	2. prorated premium for unearned (prepaid) portion of fire insurance
3. earned interest on existing assumed mortgage not yet payable (accrued)	3. coal or fuel oil on hand, usually figured at current market price (prepaid)
4. earned portion of general real estate tax not yet due (accrued)	4. insurance and tax reserve (if any) when outstanding mortgage is being assumed by buyer (prepaid)
5. unearned portion of current rent collected in advance	5. refund of prepaid water charge and similar expenses
6. earned salary (and sometimes vacation allowance) of maintenance person	6. unearned portion of general real estate tax, if paid in advance
7. tenants' security deposits*	
8. purchase-money mortgage (see Chapter 15)	

*These items are not prorated; they are entered in full as listed.

Note that the *buyer's earnest money,* while credited to the buyer, *is not debited to the seller.* The buyer receives a credit because he or she has already paid that amount toward the purchase price; however, under the usual sales contract the money is held by the broker or escrow agent until the settlement, when it will be included as part of the total amount due the seller. Note also that if the seller is paying off an existing loan and the buyer is obtaining a new one, these two items are accounted for with a debit only to the seller for the amount of the payoff and a credit only to the buyer for the amount of the new loan.

Accounting for expenses. Expenses paid out of the closing proceeds are debited only to the party making the payment. Occasionally an expense item—such as an escrow fee, settlement fee, or, in a few areas, transfer tax—may be shared by the buyer and the seller, and each party will be debited for one-half the expense.

The Arithmetic of Prorating

Accurate prorating involves four considerations: (1) what the item being prorated is; (2) whether it is an accrued item that requires the determination of an earned amount; (3) whether it is a prepaid item that requires the unearned amount—a refund to the seller—to be determined; and (4) what arithmetic processes must be used. The information contained in the previous sections will assist in answering the first three questions.

The computation of a proration involves identifying a yearly charge for the item to be prorated, then dividing by 12 to determine a monthly charge for the item. It is usually also necessary to identify a daily charge for the item by dividing the monthly charge by the number of days in the month. These smaller portions are then multiplied by the number of months and/or days in the prorated time period to determine the accrued or unearned amount that will be figured in the settlement.

Using this general principle, there are three basic methods of calculating prorations:

1. The yearly charge is divided by a *360-day year,* or 12 months of 30 days each.
2. The monthly charge is divided by the *actual number of days in the month of closing* to determine the amount.
3. The *yearly charge is divided by 365* to determine the daily charge. Then the actual number of days in the proration period is determined, and this number is multiplied by the daily charge.

In some cases, when a sale is closed on the fifteenth of the month the one-half month's charge is computed by simply dividing the monthly charge by 2.

The final proration figure will vary slightly, depending on which computation method is used. The final figure will also vary according to the number of decimal places to which the division is carried. *All of the computations in this text are computed by carrying the division to three decimal places.* The third decimal place is rounded off to cents only after the final proration figure is determined.

Accrued Items

Consider unpaid real estate taxes, which are an accrued item. When the tax is levied for the calendar year and is payable during that year or in the following year, the accrued portion is for the period from January 1 to the date of closing (or to the day before the closing in states where the sale date is excluded). If the current tax bill has not yet been issued, the parties must agree on an estimated amount based on the previous year's bill and any known changes in assessment or tax levy for the current year.

For example, assume a sale is to be closed on September 17 and current real estate taxes of $1,200 are to be prorated accordingly. The accrued period, then, is 8 months and 17 days. First determine the prorated cost of the real estate tax per month and day:

$$\begin{array}{r} \$100 \text{ per month} \\ 12\overline{)\$1,200} \\ \text{months} \end{array} \qquad \begin{array}{r} 3.333 \text{ per day} \\ 30\overline{)\$100.000} \\ \text{days} \end{array}$$

Next, multiply these figures by the accrued period and add the totals to determine the prorated real estate tax:

$$\begin{array}{r} \$100 \\ \times \ 8 \text{ months} \\ \hline \$800 \end{array} \qquad \begin{array}{r} \$\ 3.333 \\ \times \ \ 17 \text{ days} \\ \hline \$56.661 \end{array} \qquad \begin{array}{r} \$800.000 \\ + \ 56.661 \\ \hline \$856.661 \end{array}$$

Thus, the accrued real estate tax for 8 months and 17 days is *$856.66* (rounded off to two decimal places after the final computation). This amount represents the seller's accrued *earned* tax; it will be *a credit to the buyer* and a *debit to the seller* on the closing statement.

To compute this proration according to the actual number of days in the accrued period, the following method would be used. The accrued period from January 1 to September 17 runs 260 days (January's 31 days plus February's 28 days, and so on). A tax bill of $1,200 ÷ 365 days = $3.288 per day. $3.288 × 260 days = $854.880, or *$854.88*.

In Practice...

On state brokers' examinations, tax prorations are usually based on a 30-day month (360-day year) unless specified otherwise in the problem. Note that this may differ with your local custom regarding tax prorations. Many title insurance companies provide proration charts that detail tax factors for each day in the year. To determine a tax proration using one of these charts, you would multiply the factor given for the closing date by the annual real estate tax.

Prepaid Items

Assume that the water is billed in advance by the city without using a meter. The six months' billing is $8 for the period ending October 31. The sale is to be closed on August 3. Since the water is paid to October 31, the prepaid time must be computed. Using a 30-day basis, the time period is the 27 days left in August plus two full months: $8 ÷ 6 = $1.333 per month. For one day, divide $1.333 by 30, which equals $.044 per day. The prepaid period is two months and 27 days, so:

$$\begin{array}{l} 27 \text{ days} \times \$.044 \quad = \$1.188 \\ 2 \text{ months} \times \$1.333 = \$2.666 \\ \hline \qquad\qquad\qquad \$3.854, \text{ or } \textit{\$3.85} \end{array}$$

This is a prepaid item and is *credited to the seller* and *debited to the buyer* on the closing statement.

To figure this on the basis of the actual days in the month of closing, the following process would be used:

$$\begin{array}{ll} \$1.333 \text{ per month} \div 31 \text{ days in August} & = \$.043 \text{ per day} \\ \text{August 4 through August 31} & = 28 \text{ days} \\ 28 \text{ days} \times \$.043 & = \$1.204 \\ 2 \text{ months} \times \$1.333 & = \$2.666 \\ \$1.204 + \$2.666 & = \$3.870, \text{ or } \textit{\$3.87} \end{array}$$

Prorating Prepaid Insurance Premiums

Insurance policies are written for periods of one, three and five years. The time period covered by an insurance policy includes the date the policy expires. Carefully check the period for which the premium has been paid when you figure insurance premium prorations. In figuring the proration of the insurance premium, you must ascertain the number of future days, months and years for which the premium has been paid. The formula commonly used for this purpose is as follows (the dates given are examples):

	Years	Months	Days
Premium paid to (April 19, 1986)	1985	15 ~~16~~	50
Date of closing (May 24, 1984)	~~1986~~	~~4~~	~~19~~
Number of future years, months,	1984	5	24
and days for which premium is paid	1	10	26

Start with the "days" column. When, as in this example, the days on the top line are less than those on the bottom line, borrow one month from the "months" column and increase the "days" by 30 or 31, *using the number of days in the month of closing.* In this case, May has 31 days, so you will borrow 31 to make 50 days. Then subtract 24 days from 50 days and enter 26 days.

Then move to the months. When the number of months on the top line is less than that on the bottom, borrow a year by reducing the "years" by one and adding 12 months to the "months" column. Subtract the months; then subtract the years.

The completed example with all adjustments made would be as follows:

	Years	Months	Days
Premium paid to (April 19, 1986)	1983	17	
Closing date (May 24, 1984)	~~1984~~	~~5~~	24
Unearned, or unexpired, period	1983	6	15
		11	9

A mortgage lender who wishes to determine the initial deposit for a borrower to establish an insurance reserve for future insurance renewals must compute the *earned* portion of the insurance premium. Use the same process, except that the closing date is on the top line and the beginning date of the insurance policy is on the bottom line. When borrowing a month and converting it to days in this procedure, use the number of days in the month the insurance began.

	Years	Months	Days
Date of closing	1984	5	24
Beginning date of insurance	1983	6	15
Earned, or expired, period		11	9

In Practice...

Three-year homeowner's insurance policies are no longer common, due to the high cost of such coverage. Where such policies do exist, many insurance companies will not allow them to be assumed. The seller will cancel his or her policy and the buyer will take out a new one, both on the closing date. However, most state brokers' exams still include problems dealing with three-year policies to be assumed by the purchaser.

The Closing Statement

As stated previously, there are many possible formats for settlement computations. The remaining portion of this chapter illustrates a sample transaction using the HUD Uniform Settlement Statement that appears in figure 23.1. The requirements of the Real Estate Settlement Procedures Act (RESPA) were discussed earlier.

Basic Information of Offer and Sale

John and Joanne Iuro listed their home at 3045 North Racine Avenue in Riverdale, Illinois, with the Open Door Real Estate Company. The listing price was $118,500, and possession could be given within two weeks after all parties had signed the contract. Under the terms of the listing agreement, the sellers agreed to pay the broker a commission of six percent of the sales price.

On May 18, the Open Door Real Estate Company submitted a contract offer to the Iuros from Brook Redemann, a bachelor, presently residing at 22 King Court, Riverdale. Redemann offered $115,000, with earnest money/down payment of $23,000, and the remaining $92,000 of the purchase price to be obtained through a new conventional loan. No private mortgage insurance will be necessary as the loan-to-value ratio will not exceed 80 percent. The Iuros signed the contract on May 29, 1988. Closing was set for June 15, 1988, at the office of the Open Door Real Estate Company, 720 Main Street, Riverdale.

The unpaid balance of the Iuros' mortgage as of June 1, 1988 will be $57,700. Payments are $680 per month with interest at 11 percent per annum on the unpaid balance.

The sellers submitted evidence of title in the form of a title insurance binder at a cost of $10. The title insurance policy paid by the seller at the time of closing cost an additional $540 including $395 for lender's coverage and $145 for homeowner's coverage. Recording charges of $20 were paid for the recording of two instruments to clear defects in the sellers' title, and state transfer tax in the amount of $115 ($.50 per $500 of sale price or fraction thereof) were affixed to the deed. In addition, the sellers must pay an attorney's fee of $400 for preparation of the deed and for legal representation; this amount will be paid from the closing proceeds.

The buyer must pay an attorney's fee of $300 for examination of the title evidence and legal representation, as well as $10 to record the deed. These amounts will also be paid from the closing proceeds.

County real estate taxes for the calendar year 1987, amounting to $1,725, have been paid, but taxes for the calendar year 1988 estimated to be in the same amount have not been paid. According to the contract, general real estate taxes, insurance premiums and mortgage interest are to be prorated on the basis of 30 days to a month.

Computing the Prorations and Charges

Following are illustrations of the various steps in computing the prorations and other amounts to be included in the settlement thus far.

1. *Closing date:* June 15, 1988
2. *Commission:* 6% × $115,000 (sales price) = *$6,900*

Figure 23.1
RESPA Uniform
Settlement Statement

A. SETTLEMENT STATEMENT U.S. DEPARTMENT OF HOUSING AND URBAN DEVELOPMENT
HUD-1 Rev. 3/86   OMB NO. 2502-0265 (Exp. 12-31-86)

B. TYPE OF LOAN				
1. ☐ FHA 2. ☐ FmHA 3. ☒ CONV. UNINS. 4. ☐ VA 5. ☐ CONV. INS.	6. File Number	7. Loan Number	8. Mortgage Insurance Claim Case Number	

C. NOTE: *This form is furnished to give you a statement of actual settlement costs. Amounts paid to and by the settlement agent are shown. Items marked "(p.o.c.)" were paid outside the closing; they are shown here for informational purposes and are not included in the totals.*

D. NAME AND ADDRESS OF BORROWER:	E. NAME AND ADDRESS OF SELLER:	F. NAME AND ADDRESS OF LENDER:
Brook Redemann 22 King Court Riverdale, Illinois	John and Joanne Iuro 3045 North Racine Avenue Riverdale, Illinois	Thrift Federal Savings 1100 Fountain Plaza Riverdale, Illinois

G. PROPERTY LOCATION: 3045 North Racine Avenue Riverdale, Illinois	H. SETTLEMENT AGENT: Open Door Real Estate Company PLACE OF SETTLEMENT: Open Door Real Estate Company 720 Main Street, Riverdale, Illinois	I. SETTLEMENT DATE: June 15, 1988

J. SUMMARY OF BORROWER'S TRANSACTION		K. SUMMARY OF SELLER'S TRANSACTION	
100. GROSS AMOUNT DUE FROM BORROWER:		**400. GROSS AMOUNT DUE TO SELLER:**	
101. Contract sales price	$115,000.00	401. Contract sales price	$115,000.00
102. Personal property		402. Personal property	
103. Settlement charges to borrower (line 1400)	5,075.84	403.	
104.		404.	
105.		405.	
Adjustments for items paid by seller in advance		*Adjustments for items paid by seller in advance*	
106. City/town taxes to		406. City/town taxes to	
107. County taxes to		407. County taxes to	
108. Assesments to		408. Assesments to	
109.		409.	
110.		410.	
111.		411.	
112.		412.	
120. GROSS AMOUNT DUE FROM BORROWER	$120,075.84	**420. GROSS AMOUNT DUE TO SELLER**	$115,000.00
200. AMOUNTS PAID BY OR IN BEHALF OF BORROWER:		**500. REDUCTIONS IN AMOUNT DUE TO SELLER:**	
201. Deposit or earnest money	23,000.00	501. Excess deposit (see instructions)	
202. Principal amount of new loan(s)	92,000.00	502. Settlement charges to seller (line 1400)	8,080.00
203. Existing loan(s) taken subject to		503. Existing loan(s) taken subject to	
204.		504. Payoff of first mortgage loan	57,964.47
205.		505. Payoff of second mortgage loan	
206.		506.	
207.		507.	
208.		508.	
209.		509.	
Adjustments for items unpaid by seller		*Adjustments for items unpaid by seller*	
210. City/town taxes to		510. City/town taxes to	
211. County taxes 1/1/88 to 6/15/88	790.63	511. County taxes 1/1/88 to 6/15/88	790.63
212. Assesments to		512. Assesments to	
213.		513.	
214.		514.	
215.		515.	
216.		516.	
217.		517.	
218.		518.	
219.		519.	
220. TOTAL PAID BY/FOR BORROWER	$115,790.63	**520. TOTAL REDUCTION AMOUNT DUE SELLER**	$ 66,835.10
300. CASH AT SETTLEMENT FROM/TO BORROWER		**600. CASH AT SETTLEMENT TO/FROM SELLER**	
301. Gross amount due from borrower (line 120)	120,075.84	601. Gross amount due to seller (line 420)	115,000.00
302. Less amounts paid by/for borrower (line 220)	(115,790.63)	602. Less reductions in amount due seller (line 520)	(66,835.10)
303. CASH (☐ FROM) (☐ TO) BORROWER	$ 4,285.21	**603. CASH (☐ TO) (☐ FROM) SELLER**	$ 48,164.90

I have carefully reviewed the HUD-1 Settlement Statement and to the best of my knowledge and belief, it is a true and accurate statement of all receipts and disbursements made on my account or by me in this transaction. I further certify that I have received a copy of the HUD-1 Settlement Statement.

_____   _____
Borrower   Seller

_____   _____
Borrower   Seller

The HUD-1 Settlement Statement which I have prepared is a true and accurate account of this transaction. I have caused or will cause the funds to be disbursed in accordance with this statement.

_____   _____
Settlement Agent   Date

Warning: It is a crime to knowingly make false statements to the United States on this or any other similar form. Penalties upon conviction can include a fine and imprisonment. For details see: Title 18 U.S. Code Section 1001 and Section 1010.

2128 (6-86) 41b

**Figure 23.1
(Cont.)**

— 2 —

L. SETTLEMENT CHARGES	PAID FROM BORROWER'S FUNDS AT SETTLEMENT	PAID FROM SELLER'S FUNDS AT SETTLEMENT
700. TOTAL SALES/BROKER'S COMMISSION based on price $ 115,000 @ 6 % =$6,900.00		
Division of Commission (line 700) as follows:		
701. $ to		
702. $ to		
703. Commission paid at Settlement		$6,900.00
704.		
800. ITEMS PAYABLE IN CONNECTION WITH LOAN		
801. Loan Origination Fee %	$ 920.00	
802. Loan Discount 2 %	$1,840.00	
803. Appraisal Fee $125.00 to Swift Appraisal	POC	
804. Credit Report $ 60.00 to ACME Credit Bureau	POC	
805. Lender's Inspection Fee		
806. Mortgage Insurance Application Fee to		
807. Assumption Fee		
808. Application Fee		
809. Wholesale Interest Differential Fee		
810. Underwriting Fee		
811. Buydown Fee		
812. Commitment Fee		
813.		
814. Messenger Service		
815. Shortfall		
816.		
817.		
818.		
819.		
900. ITEMS REQUIRED BY LENDER TO BE PAID IN ADVANCE		
901. Interest from 6/16/88 to 6/30/88 @ $ 25.556 /day	383.34	
902. Mortgage Insurance Premium for months to		
903. Hazard Insurance Premium for 1 years to Hite Insurance Co.	345.00	
904. One-Time FHA Insurance Premium		
905. VA Funding Fee		
906.		
907.		
1000. RESERVES DEPOSITED WITH LENDER		
1001. Hazard insurance 3 months @ $ 28.75 per month	86.25	
1002. Mortgage insurance months @ $ per month		
1003. City property taxes months @ $ per month		
1004. County property taxes 7 months @ $ 143.75 per month	1,006.25	
1005. Annual assessments months @ $ per month		
1006. months @ $ per month		
1007. months @ $ per month		
1008. months @ $ per month		
1100. TITLE CHARGES		
1101. Settlement or closing fee to		
1102. Abstract or title search to		
1103. Title examination to		
1104. Title insurance binder to		10.00
1105. Document preparation to		
1106. Notary fees to		
1107. Attorney's fees to	300.00	400.00
(includes above items numbers;)		
1108. Title insurance to		540.00
(includes above items numbers;)		
1109. Lender's coverage $ 395.00		
1110. Owner's coverage $ 145.00		
1111. Tax Service Contract Fee to		
1112. Amortization Schedule to		
1113.		
1114.		
1115.		
1116.		
1200. GOVERNMENT RECORDING AND TRANSFER CHARGES		
1201. Recording Fees: Deed $ 10.00 ; Mortgage $ 10.00 ; Releases $ 10.00	20.00	10.00
1202. City/county tax/stamps: Deed $; Mortgage $		
1203. State tax/Stamps: Deed $ 115.00 ; Mortgage $		115.00
1204. Record two documents to clear title		20.00
1205.		
1300. ADDITIONAL SETTLEMENT CHARGES		
1301. Survey to	175.00	
1302. Pest inspection to		85.00
1303.		
1304.		
1305.		
1400. TOTAL SETTLEMENT CHARGES (enter on lines 103, Section J and 502, Section K)	$5,075.84	$8,080.00

2128 (6-86) 41b Reverse   HUD-1 Rev. 5/76

3. *Seller's mortgage interest:*
   11% × $57,700 (principal due after June 1 payment) = $6,347 interest per year
   $6,347 ÷ 360 days = $17.631 interest per day
   15 days of accrued interest to be paid by the seller
   15 × $17.631 = $264.465, or $264.47 interest owed by the seller
   $57,700 + $264.465 = $57,964.47 payoff of seller's mortgage

4. *Real estate taxes* (estimated based on 1988 tax bill of $1,725):
   $1,725.00 ÷ 12 months = $143.75 per month
   $ 143.75 ÷ 30 days = $ 4.792 per day
   The earned period is from January 1, 1988, to and including June 15, 1988,
   and equals 5 months, 15 days:
   $143.75 × 5 months = $718.750
   $4.792 × 15 days   = $ 71.880
   $790.630, or *$790.63 seller owes buyer*

5. *Transfer tax* ($.50 per $500 of consideration or fraction thereof):
   $115,000 ÷ $500 = $230
   $230 × $.50 = *$115.00 transfer tax owed by seller*

The sellers' loan payoff is $57,964.47 and they must pay an additional $10 to record the mortgage release, as well as $85 for a pest inspection. The buyer's new
loan is from Thrift Federal Savings, 1100 Fountain Plaza, Riverdale, in the
amount of $92,000 at 10 percent interest. In connection with this loan, he will be
charged $125 to have the property appraised by Swift Appraisal and $60 for a
credit report from the Acme Credit Bureau. (Since appraisal and credit reports
are performed prior to loan approval, they are paid at the time of loan application, regardless of whether or not the transaction eventually closes. These items
will be noted as POC—paid outside closing—on the settlement statement.) In
addition, buyer Redemann will pay for interest on his loan for the remainder of
the month of closing—15 days at $25.556 per day, or $383.34. His first full payment (including July's interest) will be due August 1. He must deposit $1,006.25,
or 7/12 of the anticipated 1988 county real estate tax (of $1,725) into a tax reserve
account. A one-year hazard insurance premium at $3 per $1,000 of appraised
value ($115,000 ÷ 1,000 × 3 = 345) is paid in advance to Hite Insurance Company.
An insurance reserve to cover the premium for three months is deposited with the
lender. Redemann will have to pay an additional $10 to record the mortgage and
$175 for a survey. He will also pay a loan origination fee of $920, and two discount points.

The Uniform Settlement Statement is divided into twelve sections. The most important information is included in Sections J, K, and L. The borrower's and
seller's summaries (J and K) are very similar to one another and are used as are
the other formats of closing statements illustrated in this chapter. For example, in
Section J, the summary of the borrower's transaction, the buyer-borrower's debits
are listed in lines 100 through 112 and totaled on line 120 (gross amount due from
borrower). The total of the settlement costs itemized in Section L of the statement is entered on line 103 as one of the buyer's charges. The buyer's credits are
listed on lines 201 through 219 and totaled on line 220 (total paid by/for borrower). Then, as with the other statements, the buyer's credits are subtracted from
the charges to arrive at the cash due from the borrower to close (line 303).

In Section K, the summary of the seller's transaction, the sellers' credits are entered on lines 400 through 412 and totaled on line 420 (gross amount due to
seller). The sellers' debits are entered on lines 501 through 519 and totaled on line

520 (total reduction amount due seller). The total of the sellers' settlement charges is on line 502. Then the debits are subtracted from the credits to arrive at the cash due to the sellers in order to close (line 603).

Section L is a summary of all the settlement charges for the transaction; the buyer's expenses are listed in one column and the sellers' expenses are listed in the other. Note that if an attorney's fee is listed as a lump sum in line 1107, the settlement should list by line number the services that were included in that total fee.

Summary

Closing a sale involves both title procedures and financial matters. The broker, as agent of the seller, should be present at the closing to see that the sale is actually concluded and to account for the earnest money deposit.

The federal Real Estate Settlement Procedures Act (RESPA) requires disclosure of all settlement costs when a real estate purchase is financed by a federally related mortgage loan. RESPA requires lenders to use a Uniform Settlement Statement to detail the financial particulars of a transaction.

Usually the buyer's attorney examines the title evidence to ensure that the seller's title is acceptable. The gap in time between the date of the abstract or title commitment and the closing date is covered by the seller's *affidavit of title.*

The sale may be closed in *escrow* so that the buyer can be assured of receiving good title as described in the sales contract and the seller can be assured that all funds due him or her are held in cash by the escrow agent.

The actual amount to be paid by the buyer at the closing is computed by preparation of a *closing,* or *settlement, statement.* This lists the sales price, earnest money deposit and all adjustments and prorations due between buyer and seller. The purpose of this statement is to determine the net amount due the seller at closing. The form is signed by both parties to evidence their approval.

Questions

1. Which of the following is true of real estate closings in most states?
   a. Closings are generally conducted by real estate salespeople.
   b. The buyer usually receives the rents for the day of closing.
   c. The buyer must reimburse the seller for any title evidence provided by the seller.
   d. The seller usually pays the expenses for the day of closing.

2. When an item to be prorated has been earned (is owing) but has not been paid by the seller:
   a. the amount owed is a credit to the buyer.
   b. the amount owed is a debit to the seller.
   c. the amount owed is a debit to the buyer.
   d. a and b

3. When the item to be prorated has been paid by the seller but not fully earned (or used up):
   a. the unused portion is a credit to the seller.
   b. the unused portion is a credit to the buyer.
   c. the unused portion is prorated.
   d. the unused portion is a debit to the seller.

4. The final inspection is the time to make sure:
   a. all necessary repairs have been made.
   b. the property has been well maintained.
   c. there has been no unauthorized removal or alteration of any improvement.
   d. all of the above

5. All encumbrances and liens shown on the report of title, other than those waived or agreed to by the purchaser and listed in the contract, must be removed so that the title can be delivered free and clear. The removal of such encumbrances is the duty of the:
   a. buyer.   c. broker.
   b. seller.   d. title company.

6. Legal title always passes from the seller to the buyer:
   a. on the date of execution of the deed.
   b. when the closing statement has been signed.
   c. when the deed is placed in escrow.
   d. when the deed is delivered.

7. The advantages of closing a real estate sales transaction in escrow include the fact that:
   I. the seller is assured of receiving the buyer's payment for the property.
   II. the buyer is assured that payment will be made only when good title to the property is received.
      a. I only   c. both I and II
      b. II only   d. neither I nor II

8. The closing statement will disclose to the seller:
   I. the amount of money the seller will receive at the closing.
   II. the amount the buyer must bring to the closing.
      a. I only   c. both I and II
      b. II only   d. neither I nor II

9. Which one of the following items is *not* usually prorated between buyer and seller at the closing?
   a. recording charges
   b. general taxes
   c. rents
   d. mortgage interest

Questions 10 through 16 pertain to certain items as they would normally appear on a closing statement.

10. The sales price of the property is a:
    I. credit to the seller.
    II. debit to the buyer.
        a. I only   c. both I and II
        b. II only   d. neither I nor II

11. The earnest money left on deposit with the broker is a:
    a. credit to the seller.
    b. credit to the buyer.
    c. debit to the seller.
    d. debit to the buyer.

12. The principal amount of the purchaser's new mortgage loan is a:
    a. credit to the seller.
    b. credit to the buyer.
    c. debit to the seller.
    d. none of the above

13. Unpaid real estate taxes, water service, waste disposal service and so forth are a:
    I. credit to the buyer.
    II. debit to the seller.
        a. I only   c. both I and II
        b. II only   d. neither I nor II

14. The broker's commission is a:
    a. credit to the buyer.
    b. debit to the seller.
    c. debit to the buyer.
    d. a and b

15. Interest proration on an existing assumed mortgage is a:
    a. credit to the seller.
    b. debit to the buyer.
    c. debit to the seller.
    d. a and b

16. Fuel oil left in a holding tank on the property is a:
    I. credit to the buyer.
    II. debit to the seller.
        a. I only   c. both I and II
        b. II only   d. neither I nor II

17. The *doctrine of relation back* is most closely associated with which of the following?
        a. escrow   c. prorations
        b. RESPA   d. title evidence

18. The RESPA Uniform Settlement Statement must be used to illustrate all settlement charges:
    a. for every real estate transaction.
    b. for transactions financed by VA and FHA loans only.
    c. for transactions financed by federally related mortgage loans.
    d. for all transactions in which mortgage financing is involved.

19. Which of the following would a lender generally require to be produced at the closing?
    a. title insurance policy
    b. market value appraisal
    c. application
    d. credit report

20. When a transaction is to be closed in escrow, the seller generally deposits all but which of the following items with the escrow agent before the closing date?
    a. deed to the property
    b. title evidence
    c. estoppel certificate
    d. cash needed to complete the purchase

Real Estate Mathematics Review

Mathematics plays an important role in the real estate business. Math is involved in nearly every aspect of a typical transaction, from the moment a listing agreement is filled out until the final monies are paid out at the closing. Reflecting this, many states' real estate license examinations contain a substantial number of questions that involve math.

This review is designed to familiarize you with some of the basic mathematical formulas that are most frequently used in the computations required on state licensing examinations. These same computations are also important in day-to-day real estate transactions. Some of this material has been covered in detail in the text. In these cases, reference is made to the appropriate chapter. If you feel you need additional help in working these problems, you are referred to *Mastering Real Estate Mathematics*, Fourth Edition, by Ventolo, Allaway and Irby, published by Real Estate Education Company.

Percentages

Many real estate computations are based on the calculation of percentages. A percentage expresses a portion of a whole. For example, 50% means 50 parts of the possible 100 parts that comprise the whole. Percentages greater than 100% contain more than one whole unit. Thus, 163% is one whole and 63 parts of another whole. Remember that a whole is always expressed as 100%.

In problems involving percentages, *the percentages must be converted to either decimals or fractions*. To convert a percentage to a decimal, place a decimal two places to the left and drop the percent sign. Thus,

$$60\% = .6 \qquad 7\% = .07 \qquad 175\% = 1.75$$

To change a percentage to a fraction, place the percentage over 100. For example:

$$50\% = \frac{50}{100} \qquad 115\% = \frac{115}{100}$$

These fractions may then be *reduced* to make it easier to work the problem. To reduce a fraction, determine the lowest number by which both numerator and denominator can be evenly divided, and divide each of them by that number. For example:

$$25/100 = 1/4 \text{ (both numbers divided by 25)}$$
$$49/63 = 7/9 \text{ (both numbers divided by 7)}$$

Percentage problems contain three elements: *percentage, total* and *part*. To determine a specific percentage of a whole, multiply the total by the percentage. This is illustrated by the following formula:

$$\text{total} \times \text{percent} = \text{part}$$
$$200 \times 5\% = \mathbf{10}$$

This formula is used in calculating mortgage loan interests, brokers' commissions, loan origination fees, discount points, amount of earnest money deposits and income on capital investments.

For example: A broker is to receive a 7% commission on the sale of a $150,000 house. What will the broker's commission be?

$$.07 \times \$150{,}000 = \textbf{\$10,500 broker's commission}$$

A variation, or inversion, of the percentage formula is used to find the total amount when the part and percentage are known:

$$\text{total} = \frac{\text{part}}{\text{percent}}$$

For example: The Masterson Realty Company received a $4,500 commission for the sale of a house. The broker's commission was 6% of the total sales price. What was the total sales price of this house?

$$\frac{\$4{,}500}{.06} = \textbf{\$75,000 total sales price}$$

This formula is used to calculate the total sales price when the amount and percentage of commission or earnest money deposit are known. It also is used in computing the total mortgage loan principal still due if the monthly payment and interest rate are known, rent due if the monthly payment and interest rate are known and market value of property if the assessed value and the ratio (percentage) of assessed value to market value are known.

To determine the percentage when the amounts of the part and the total are known:

$$\text{percent} = \frac{\text{part}}{\text{total}}$$

This formula may be used to determine the tax rate when the taxes and assessed value are known, or the commission rate if the sales price and commission amount are known.

You can use the following diagram as an aid in remembering the three formulas just discussed:

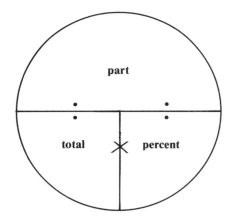

Rates

Property taxes, transfer taxes, and insurance premiums are usually expressed as rates. A *rate* is the cost, expressed as the amount of cost per unit. For example, tax might be computed at the rate of $5 per $100 of assessed value in a certain county. The formula for computing rates is:

$$\text{value} \times \text{rate} = \text{total}$$

For example: A house has been assessed at $90,000 and is taxed at an annual rate of $2.50 per $100 assessed valuation. What is the yearly tax?

$$\$90{,}000 \times \frac{\$2.50}{\$100} = \text{total annual tax}$$

$$\overset{900}{\$90{,}000} \times \frac{\$2.50}{\underset{1}{\$100}} = \text{total annual tax}$$

$$900 \times \$2.50 = \textbf{\$2,250 total annual tax}$$

See Chapter 10 for a further discussion of tax computations.

Areas and Volumes

People in the real estate profession must know how to compute the area of a parcel of land or figure the amount of living area in a house. To compute the area of a square or rectangular parcel, use the formula:

$$\text{length} \times \text{width} = \text{area}$$

Thus, the area of a rectangular lot that measures 200 feet long by 100 feet wide would be:

$$200' \times 100' = \textbf{20,000 square feet}$$

Area is always expressed in square units. Table MR-1 showing the relationship of different units of measurement is provided on the following page.

To compute the amount of surface in a triangular-shaped area, use the formula:

$$\text{area} = \tfrac{1}{2}(\text{base} \times \text{height})$$

The base of a triangle is the bottom, the side on which the triangle rests. The height is an imaginary straight line extending from the point of the uppermost angle straight down to the base:

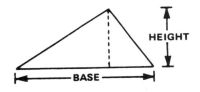

For example: A triangle has a base of 50 feet and a height of 30 feet. What is its area?

$$\tfrac{1}{2}(50' \times 30') = \text{area in square feet}$$
$$\tfrac{1}{2}(1{,}500 \text{ square feet}) = \textbf{750 square feet}$$

To compute the area of an irregular room or parcel of land, divide the shape into regular rectangles, squares, or triangles. Next, compute the area of each regular figure and add the areas together to obtain the total area.

Example: Compute the area of the hallway shown in the following example:

First make a rectangle and a triangle by drawing a single line through the figure as shown here:

Table MR-1   **Units of Measurement**

1 foot . . . . 12 inches
1 yard . . . . 3 feet or 36 inches
_____
1 square foot . . . . 144 square inches
1 square yard . . . . 9 square feet
_____
1 cubic foot . . . . 1,728 cubic inches
1 cubic yard . . . . 27 cubic feet

Compute the area of the rectangle:

$$\text{area} = \text{length} \times \text{width} \qquad 16' \times 6' = 96 \text{ sq. ft.}$$

Compute the area of the triangle:

$$\text{area} = \tfrac{1}{2}(\text{base} \times \text{height}) \qquad \tfrac{1}{2}(4' \times 6') = \tfrac{1}{2}(24 \text{ sq. ft.}) = 12 \text{ sq. ft.}$$

Total the two areas:

$$96 + 12 = \textbf{108 square feet in total area}$$

The cubic capacity of an enclosed space is expressed as volume. Volume is used to describe the amount of space in any three-dimensional area. It would be used, for example, in measuring the interior airspace of a room to determine what capacity heating unit is required. The formula for computing cubic or rectangular volume is:

$$\text{volume} = \text{length} \times \text{width} \times \text{height}$$

Volume is always expressed in cubic units.

For example: The bedroom of a house is 12 feet long, 8 feet wide, and has a ceiling height of 8 feet. How many cubic feet does the room enclose?

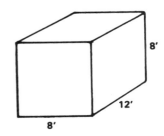

$8' \times 12' \times 8' = \textbf{768 cubic feet}$

To compute the volume of a triangular space, such as the airspace in an A-frame house, use the formula:

volume $= \frac{1}{2}$ (base $\times$ height $\times$ width)

For example: What is the volume of airspace in the house shown below?

First, divide the house into two shapes, rectangular and triangular, as shown:

Find the volume of T:

volume $= \frac{1}{2}$ (base $\times$ height $\times$ width)

$\frac{1}{2}$ ($25' \times 10' \times 40'$) $= \frac{1}{2}$ (10,000 cu. ft.) $= 5,000$ cu. ft.

Find the volume of R:

$25' \times 40' \times 12' = 12,000$ cubic feet

Total volumes T and R:

$5,000 + 12,000 = \textbf{17,000 cubic feet of airspace in the house}$

Cubic measurements of volume are used to compute the construction costs per cubic foot of a building, the amount of airspace being sold in a condominium unit or the heating and cooling requirements for a building.

Remember that when either area or volume is computed, *all dimensions used must be given in the same unit of measure.* For example, you may not multiply 2 feet by 6 inches to get the area; you have to multiply 2 feet by ½ foot.

Prorations

As discussed in Chapter 23, the proration of taxes, insurance premiums and other items is customary when a real estate transaction is closed. Questions concerning closing statements generally appear in real estate brokers' examinations. They appear less often in salespersons' exams. Knowledge of the arithmetic of prorations is valuable to all real estate licensees in the course of their business.

When an item is to be prorated, the charge must first be broken down into yearly, monthly, and daily amounts, depending on the type of charge. These smaller amounts are then multiplied by the number of years, months, and days in the prorated time period to determine the accrued or unearned amount to be credited or debited at the closing. Depending on local custom, prorations may be made on the basis of a standard 30-day month (360-day year), 365-day year, or the actual number of days in the month of closing.

For example, consider a three-year prepaid insurance policy with a premium of $450. The policy became effective on March 1, 1985; the date of the closing is August 9, 1986. The initial step in determining the unearned amount of the premium that will be credited to the seller at the closing is to figure out the number of years, months, and days not yet used up as of August 9, 1986 as follows:

$$
\begin{array}{c c c}
 & \overset{7}{} & \overset{15}{} \quad \overset{32}{} \\
1988 & 3 & 1 \\
1986 & 8 & 9 \\
\hline
1 & 7 & 23
\end{array}
$$
or 1 year, 7 months, and 23 days unearned.

Then the yearly, monthly, and daily breakdowns of the premium amount are determined. (Remember to carry all computations to three decimal places until a final figure is reached, then round off to the nearest penny.) First, divide the premium amount by three to determine the yearly charge:

$$
\frac{\$150.000}{3)\$450.00} \text{ yearly premium}
$$

Next, divide the yearly charge by 12 to determine the monthly premium:

$$
\frac{\$12.500}{12)\$150.000} \text{ monthly premium}
$$

Assuming your area computes such charges on the basis of a 30-day month, divide the monthly charge by 30 to arrive at the daily premium:

$$
\frac{\$.417}{30)\$12.500} \text{ daily premium}
$$

Finally, you must multiply the yearly, monthly, and daily premium amounts by the appropriate number of years, months, and days to determine the unearned amount to be prorated:

$150.000/1 year

$12.500
×   7
——————
$87.500/7 months

$ .417
×   23
——————
$ 9.591/23 days

$150.000
  87.500
+9.591
——————
$247.091, or *$247.09 unearned insurance premium*
        (a credit to the seller and a debit to the buyer)

Similar computations are used to prorate other items, such as real estate taxes and mortgage interest. For a more detailed discussion of closing statement computations, refer to Chapter 23.

Questions

1. Broker Sally Smith, of Happy Valley Realty, recently sold Jack and Jill Hawkins's home for $79,500. Smith charged the Hawkinses a 6½ percent commission and will pay 30 percent of that amount to the listing salesperson and 25 percent to the selling salesperson. What amount of commission will the listing salesperson receive from the Hawkins sale?

   a. $5,167.50   c. $3,617.25
   b. $1,550.25   d. $1,291.87

2. Susan Silber signed an agreement to purchase a condominium apartment from Perry and Marie Morris. The contract stipulated that the Morrises replace the damaged bedroom carpet. The carpet Silber has chosen costs $16.95 per square yard plus $2.50 per square yard for installation. If the bedroom dimensions are as illustrated, how much will the Morrises have to pay for the job?

   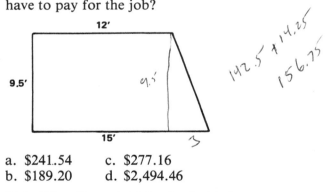

   a. $241.54   c. $277.16
   b. $189.20   d. $2,494.46

3. Hal, Olive, Ron and Marvin decided to pool their savings and purchase a small apartment building for $125,000. If Hal invested $30,000 and Olive and Ron each contributed $35,000, what percentage of ownership was left for Marvin?

   a. 20%   c. 28%
   b. 24%   d. 30%

4. Harold Barlow is curious to know how much money his son and daughter-in-law still owe on their mortgage loan. Barlow knows that the interest portion of their last monthly payment was $391.42. If the Barlows are paying interest at the rate of 11½ percent, what was the outstanding balance of their loan before that last payment was made?

   a. $43,713.00   c. $36,427.50
   b. $40,843.83   d. $34,284.70

5. Nick and Olga Stravinski bought their home on Sabre Lane a year ago for $98,500. Property in their neighborhood is said to be increasing in value at a rate of 5 percent annually. If this is true, what is the current market value of the Stravinskis' real estate?

   a. $103,425
   b. $93,575
   c. $104,410
   d. none of the above is within $50

6. The DeHavilands' home on Dove Street is valued at $95,000. Property in their area is assessed at 60 percent of its value, and the local tax rate is $2.85 per hundred. What is the amount of the DeHavilands' annual taxes?

   a. $2,451   c. $135.38
   b. $1,470.60   d. $1,624.50

7. The Fitzpatricks are planning to construct a patio in their backyard. An illustration of the surface area to be paved appears here. If the cement is to be poured as a 6″ slab, how many cubic feet of cement will be poured into this patio?

   a. 660 cubic feet   c. 330 cubic feet
   b. 450 cubic feet   d. 195 cubic feet

8. Happy Morgan receives a monthly salary of $1,000 plus 3 percent commission on all of his listings that sell and 2.5 percent on all his sales. None of the listings that Morgan took sold last month, but he received $4,175 in salary and commission. What was the value of the property Morgan sold?

   a. $147,000   c. $122,500
   b. $127,000   d. $105,833

9. The Salvatinis' residence has proved difficult to sell. Salesperson Martha Kelley suggests it might sell faster if they enclose a portion of the backyard with a privacy fence. If the area to be enclosed is as illustrated, how much would the fence cost at $6.95 per linear foot?

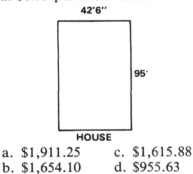

42'6"

95'

HOUSE

   a. $1,911.25   c. $1,615.88
   b. $1,654.10   d. $955.63

10. Andrew McTavish leases the 12 apartments in the Overton Arms for a total monthly rental of $4,500. If this figure represents an 8 percent annual return on McTavish's investment, what was the original cost of the property?

   a. $675,000   c. $54,000
   b. $450,000   d. $56,250

For the following questions regarding closing statement prorations, base your calculations on a 30-day month. Carry all computations to three decimal places until the final solution.

11. A sale is to be closed on March 15, 1986. Real estate taxes for the current year have not been paid; taxes for 1985 amounted to $1,340. What is the amount of the real estate tax proration to be credited to the buyer?

   a. $1,060.84   c. $223.33
   b. $279.16   d. $1,116.60

12. The buyers are assuming an outstanding mortgage, which had an unpaid balance of $58,200 after the last payment on August 1. Interest at 12 percent per annum is paid in advance each month; the sale is to be closed on August 11. What is the amount of mortgage interest proration to be credited to the seller at the closing?

   a. $698.40   c. $213.40
   b. $582.00   d. $368.60

13. The buyer is assuming the seller's three-year fire and hazard insurance policy, which is due to expire on May 31, 1989. The original cost of the premium was $680. What is the amount of insurance proration that will be charged to the buyer at the closing on September 20, 1988?

   a. $158.04   c. $144.80
   b. $540.87   d. $226.66

14. In a sale of residential property, real estate taxes for the current year amounted to $975 and have already been paid by the seller. The sale is to be closed on October 26; what is the amount of real estate tax proration to be credited the seller?

   a. $173.33   c. $798.96
   b. $162.50   d. $83.96

15. The buyer is assuming the seller's mortgage. The unpaid balance after the most recent payment (the first of the month) was $61,550. Interest is paid in arrears each month at 13 percent per annum. The sale is to be closed on September 22; what is the amount of mortgage interest proration to be credited to the buyer at the closing?

   a. $666.97   c. $177.82
   b. $488.97   d. $689.01

16. A 100-acre farm is divided into house lots. The streets require one-eighth of the whole farm, and there are 140 lots. How many square feet are there in each lot?

   a. 35,004   c. 27,225
   b. 31,114   d. 43,560

17. Riley's commission on a sale was $14,100, which was 6 percent of the sales price. What was the sales price?

   a. $235,000   c. $846,000
   b. $154,255.31   d. $234,500

Figure 1 (cont.)
Architectural Styles

DUTCH COLONIAL

2½ STORIES

GAMBREL ROOF

DORMERS

DUTCH DOOR

FRENCH PROVINCIAL

STEEP HIP ROOF

1½-2½ STORIES

CURVED WINDOW TRIM
THAT EXTENDS THROUGH
THE CORNICE

GEORGIAN

CHIMNEYS AT
EITHER END

HIP ROOF

COLONIAL

2-3 STORIES

COLUMN-SUPPORTED
COLONNADE

SYMMETRICAL

Figure 2
Roof Designs

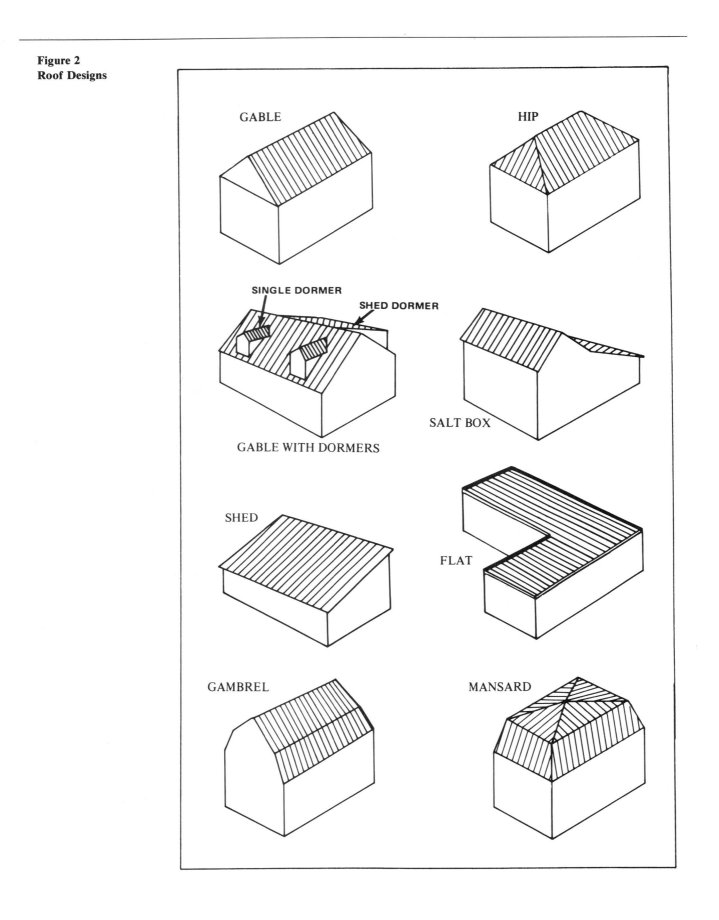

Figure 3
Roof Framing Systems

SLOPED ROOF JOISTS

LOAD BEARING WALL

LOAD BEARING WALL

NON-LOAD BEARING WALL

RIDGE BOARD

RAFTERS

JOIST AND RAFTER

CEILING JOISTS

CENTRAL LOAD BEARING WALL

LOAD BEARING WALL

LOAD BEARING WALL

ROOF TRUSSES

TRUSS

LOAD BEARING WALL

NON-LOAD BEARING WALL

LOAD BEARING WALL

UPPER CHORD

SPLIT RING AND BOLT

LOWER CHORD

GUSSET PLATE

In a truss roof the upper and lower chords are joined together by either a gusset plate or a split ring and bolt.

Figure 4
Exterior Structural Walls
and Framing

PLATFORM FRAME

BALLOON FRAME

RAFTER
JOIST
STUD
PLATE
1" x 4" LET-IN BRACE
STUD
PLATE
JOIST
STUD
BRIDGING
SHEATHING
JOIST
SILL
FOUNDATION WALL

RAFTER
JOIST
PLATE
STUD
1" x 4" LET-IN BRACE
JOIST
STUD
FIRESTOPPING
RIBBON
JOIST
SUBFLOORING
SHEATHING
SILL

POST AND BEAM FRAME

ROOF BEAMS
RIDGE BEAM
POST
PLANK FLOORING
(TONGUE AND GROOVE)
FLOOR BEAM
STUD WALL
STUD POST
SOLE PLATE
BLOCK
SILL PLATE
BAND

Figure 4 (cont.)
Exterior Structural Walls
and Framing

HOUSE DIAGRAM

1. FOOTING	22. MUNTIN	43. FIRESTOP
2. FOUNDATION DRAIN TILE	23. WINDOW SASH	44. DOWNSPOUT
3. FELT JOINT COVER	24. EAVE (ROOF PROJECTION)	45. LATHS
4. FOUNDATION WALL	25. WINDOW JAMB TRIM	46. PLASTER BOARD
5. DAMPPROOFING OR WEATHERPROOFING	26. DOUBLE WINDOW HEADER	47. PLASTER FINISH
	27. CEILING JOIST	48. MANTEL
6. BACKFILL	28. DOUBLE PLATE	49. ASH DUMP
7. ANCHOR BOLT	29. STUD	50. BASE TOP MOLDING
8. SILL	30. RAFTERS	51. BASEBOARD
9. TERMITE SHIELD	31. COLLAR BEAM	52. SHOE MOLDING
10. FLOOR JOIST	32. GABLE END OF ROOF	53. FINISH MOLDING
11. BAND OR BOX SILL	33. RIDGE BOARD	54. BRIDGING
12. PLATE	34. CHIMNEY POTS	55. PIER
13. SUBFLOORING	35. CHIMNEY CAP	56. GIRDER
14. BUILDING PAPER	36. CHIMNEY	57. FOOTING
15. WALL STUD	37. CHIMNEY FLASHING	58. RISER
16. DOUBLE CORNER STUD	38. ROOFING SHINGLES	59. TREAD
17. INSULATION	39. ROOFING FELTS	60. STRINGER
18. BUILDING PAPER	40. ROOF SHEATHING	61. CLEANOUT DOOR
19. WALL SHEATHING	41. EAVE TROUGH OR GUTTER	62. CONCRETE BASEMENT FLOOR
20. SIDING	42. FRIEZE BOARD	63. CINDER FILL
21. MULLION		

Glossary of Real Estate Terms

Abstract of title The condensed history of a title to a particular parcel of real estate, consisting of a summary of the original grant and all subsequent conveyances and encumbrances affecting the property and a certification by the abstractor that the history is complete and accurate.

Abstract of title with lawyer's opinion An abstract of title that a lawyer has examined and has certified to be, in his or her opinion, an accurate statement of fact.

Acceleration clause The clause in a mortgage or trust deed that can be enforced to make the entire debt due immediately if the mortgagor defaults on an installment payment or other covenant.

Accession Acquiring title to additions or improvements to real property as a result of the annexation of fixtures or the accretion of alluvial deposits along the banks of streams.

Accretion The increase or addition of land by the deposit of sand or soil washed up naturally from a river, lake or sea.

Accrued items On a closing statement, items of expense that are incurred but not yet payable, such as interest on a mortgage loan or taxes on real property.

Acknowledgment A formal declaration made before a duly authorized officer, usually a notary public, by a person who has signed a document.

Acre A measure of land equal to 43,560 square feet; 4,840 square yards; 4,047 square meters; 160 square rods; or 0.4047 hectare.

Actual notice Express information or fact; that which is known; direct knowledge.

Adjusted basis *See* Basis.

Ad valorem tax A tax levied according to value, generally used to refer to real estate tax. Also called the *general tax*.

Adverse possession The actual, open, notorious, hostile and continuous possession of another's land under a claim of title. Possession for a statutory period may be a means of acquiring title.

Affidavit of title A written statement, made under oath by a seller or grantor of real property and acknowledged by a notary public, in which the grantor: (1) identifies him- or herself and indicates marital status; (2) certifies that since the examination of the title on the date of the contracts no defects have occurred in the title; and (3) certifies that he or she is in possession of the property (if applicable).

Agency coupled with an interest An agency relationship in which the agent is given an estate or interest in the subject of the agency (the property).

Agent One who acts or has the power to act for another. A fiduciary relationship is created under the *law of agency* when a property owner, as the principal, executes a listing agreement or management contract authorizing a licensed real estate broker to be his or her agent.

Air lot A designated airspace over a piece of land. An air lot, like surface property, may be transferred.

Air rights The right to use the open space above a property, usually allowing the surface to be used for another purpose.

Alienation The act of transferring property to another. Alienation may be voluntary, such as by gift or sale, or involuntary, as through eminent domain or adverse possession.

Alienation clause The clause in a mortgage or trust deed that states that the balance of the secured debt becomes immediately due and payable at the mortgagee's option if the property is sold by the mortgagor. In effect, this clause prevents the mortgagor from assigning the debt without the mortgagee's approval.

Allodial system A system of land ownership in which land is held free and clear of any rent or service due to the government; commonly contrasted to the feudal system. Land is held under the allodial system in the United States.

Amortized loan A loan in which the principal as well as the interest is payable in monthly or other periodic installments over the term of the loan.

Antitrust laws Laws designed to preserve the free enterprise of the open marketplace by making illegal certain private conspiracies and combinations formed to minimize competition. Most violations of antitrust laws in the real estate business involve either *price fixing* (brokers conspiring to set fixed compensation rates) or *allocation of customers or markets* (brokers agreeing to limit their areas of trade or dealing to certain areas or properties).

Apportionment clause Clause in an insurance policy providing that, if the insured is covered by more than one policy, any payments will be apportioned according to the amount of coverage.

Appraisal An estimate of the quantity, quality or value of something. The process through which conclusions of property value are obtained; also refers to the report that sets forth the process of estimation and conclusion of value.

Appreciation An increase in the worth or value of a property due to economic or related causes, which may prove to be either temporary or permanent; opposite of depreciation.

Assemblage The combining of two or more adjoining lots into one larger tract in order to increase their total value.

Assessment The imposition of a tax, charge or levy, usually according to established rates.

Assignment The transfer in writing of interest in a bond, mortgage, lease or other instrument.

Assumption of mortgage Acquiring title to property on which there is an existing mortgage and agreeing to be personally liable for the terms and conditions of the mortgage, including payments.

Attachment The act of taking a person's property into legal custody by writ or other judicial order in order to hold it available for application to that person's debt to a creditor.

Automatic extension A clause in a listing agreement that states that the agreement will continue automatically for a certain period of time after its expiration date. In many states, use of this clause is discouraged or prohibited.

Avulsion The sudden tearing away of land, as by earthquake, flood, volcanic action or the sudden change in the course of a stream.

Balloon payment A final payment of a mortgage loan that is considerably larger than the required periodic payments because the loan amount was not fully amortized.

Bargain and sale deed A deed that carries with it no warranties against liens or other encumbrances but that does imply that the grantor has the right to convey title. The grantor may add warranties to the deed at his or her discretion.

Base line One of a set of imaginary lines running east and west and crossing a principal meridian at a definite point, used by surveyors for reference in locating and describing land under the rectangular (U.S. government) survey system of property description.

Basis The financial interest that the Internal Revenue Service attributes to an owner of an investment property for the purpose of determining annual depreciation and gain or loss on the sale of the asset. If a property was acquired by purchase, the owner's basis is the cost of the property plus the value of any capital expenditures for improvements to the property, minus any depreciation allowable or actually taken. This new basis is called the *adjusted basis.*

Benchmark A permanent reference mark or point established for use by surveyors in measuring differences in elevation.

Beneficiary 1. The person for whom a trust operates, or in whose behalf the income from a trust estate is drawn. 2. A lender who lends money on real estate and takes back a note and trust deed from the borrower.

Bilateral contract *See* Contract.

Binder An agreement that may accompany an earnest money deposit for the purchase of real property as evidence of the purchaser's good faith and intent to complete the transaction.

Blanket mortgage A mortgage covering more than one parcel of real estate, providing for each parcel's partial release from the mortgage lien upon repayment of a definite portion of the debt.

Blockbusting The illegal practice of inducing homeowners to sell their properties by making representations regarding the entry or prospective entry of persons of a particular race or national origin into the neighborhood.

Blue-sky laws Common name for those state and federal laws that regulate the registration and sale of investment securities.

Boot Money or property given to make up any difference in value or equity between two properties in an *exchange.*

Branch office A secondary place of business apart from the principal or main office from which real estate business is conducted. A branch office usually must be run by a licensed real estate broker working on behalf of the broker who operates the principal office.

Breach of contract Violation of any terms or conditions in a contract without legal excuse; for example, failure to make a payment when it is due.

Broker One who acts as an intermediary on behalf of others for a fee or commission.

Brokerage The bringing together of parties interested in making a real estate transaction.

Broker-salesperson A person who has passed the broker's licensing examination but is licensed to work only on behalf of a licensed broker.

Building code An ordinance that specifies minimum standards of construction for buildings in order to protect public safety and health.

Bulk transfer *See* Uniform Commercial Code.

Bundle of legal rights The concept of land ownership that includes *ownership of all legal rights to the land*—for example, possession, control within the law and enjoyment.

Capital gain Profit earned from the sale of an asset.

Capitalization A mathematical process for estimating the value of a property using a proper rate of return on the investment and the annual net income expected to be produced by the property. The formula is expressed:

$$\frac{\text{Income}}{\text{Rate}} = \text{Value}$$

Capitalization rate The rate of return a property will produce on the owner's investment.

Cash flow The net spendable income from an investment, determined by deducting all operating and fixed expenses from the gross income. If expenses exceed income, a *negative cash flow* is the result.

Caveat emptor A Latin phrase meaning "Let the buyer beware."

Certificate of sale The document generally given to the purchaser at a tax foreclosure sale. A certificate of sale does not convey title; normally it is an instrument certifying that the holder received title to the property after the redemption period passed and that the holder paid the property taxes for that interim period.

Certificate of title A statement of opinion on the status of the title to a parcel of real property based on an examination of specified public records.

Chain of title The succession of conveyances, from some accepted starting point, whereby the present holder of real property derives title.

Chattel *See* Personal property.

Closing statement A detailed cash accounting of a real estate transaction showing all cash received, all charges and credits made and all cash paid out in the transaction.

Cloud on the title Any document, claim, unreleased lien or encumbrance that may impair the title to real property or make the title doubtful; usually revealed by a title search and removed by either a quitclaim deed or suit to quiet title.

Clustering The grouping of homesites within a subdivision on smaller lots than normal, with the remaining land used as common areas.

Codicil A supplement or addition to a will, executed with the same formalities as a will, that normally does not revoke the entire will.

Cognovit *See* Confession of judgment clause.

Coinsurance clause A clause in insurance policies covering real property that requires the policyholder to maintain fire insurance coverage generally equal to at least 80 percent of the property's actual replacement cost.

Commingling The illegal act of a real estate broker who places client or customer funds with personal funds. By law, brokers are required to maintain a separate *trust account* for other parties' funds held temporarily by the broker.

Commission Payment to a broker for services rendered, such as in the sale or purchase of real property; usually a percentage of the selling price of the property.

Common elements Parts of a property that are necessary or convenient to the existence, maintenance and safety of a condominium, or are normally in common use by all of the condominium residents. Each condominium owner has an undivided ownership interest in the common elements.

Common law The body of law based on custom, usage and court decisions.

Community property A system of property ownership based on the theory that each spouse has an equal interest in the property acquired by the efforts of either spouse during marriage. A holdover of Spanish law, found predominantly in Western states; the system was unknown under English common law.

Comparables Properties used in an appraisal report that are substantially equivalent to the subject property.

Competent parties People who are recognized by law as being able to contract with others; those of legal age and sound mind.

Competitive market analysis A comparison of the prices of recently sold homes that are similar to a listing seller's home in terms of location, style and amenities.

Condemnation A judicial or administrative proceeding to exercise the power of eminent domain, through which a government agency takes private property for public use and compensates the owner.

Condition A contingency, qualification or occurrence upon which an estate or property right is gained or lost.

Condominium The absolute ownership of a unit in a multi-unit building based on a legal description of the airspace the unit actually occupies, plus an undivided interest in the ownership of the common elements, which are owned jointly with the other condominium unit owners.

Confession of judgment clause A provision that may be included in notes, leases and contracts by which the debtor, lessee or obligor authorizes any attorney to go into court to confess a judgment against him or her for a default in payment. Also called a *cognovit*.

Consideration 1. That which is received by the grantor in exchange for his or her deed. 2. Something of value that induces a person to enter into a contract.

Construction loan *See* Interim financing.

Constructive eviction 1. Actions of a landlord that so materially disturb or impair a tenant's enjoyment of the leased premises that the tenant is effectively forced to move out and terminate the lease without liability for any further rent. 2. A purchaser's inability to obtain clear title.

Constructive notice Notice given to the world by recorded documents. All people are charged with knowledge of such documents and their contents, whether or not they have actually examined them. Possession of property is also considered constructive notice that the person in possession has an interest in the property.

Contract A legally enforceable promise or set of promises that must be performed and for which, if a breach of the promise occurs, the law provides a remedy. A contract may be either *unilateral,* by which only one party is bound to act, or *bilateral,* by which all parties to the instrument are legally bound to act as prescribed.

Conventional loan A loan that is not insured or guaranteed by a government source.

Cooperative A residential multi-unit building whose title is held by a trust or corporation that is owned by and operated for the benefit of persons living within the building, who are the beneficial owners of the trust or stockholders of the corporation, each possessing a proprietary lease.

Corporation An entity or organization, created by operation of law, whose rights of doing business are essentially the same as those of an individual. The entity has continuous existence until it is dissolved according to legal procedures.

Correction lines Provisions in the rectangular survey (government survey) system made to compensate for the curvature of the earth's surface. Every fourth township line (at 24-mile intervals) is used as a correction line on which the intervals between the north and south range lines are remeasured and corrected to a full six miles.

Cost approach The process of estimating the value of a property by adding to the estimated land value the appraiser's estimate of the reproduction or replacement cost of the building, less depreciation.

Cost recovery An Internal Revenue Service term for *depreciation.*

Counseling The business of providing people with expert advice on a subject, based on the counselor's extensive, expert knowledge.

Counteroffer A new offer made as a reply to an offer received. It has the effect of rejecting the original offer, which cannot be accepted thereafter unless revived by the offeror.

Covenant A written agreement between two or more parties in which a party or parties pledge to perform or not perform specified acts with regard to property; usually found in such real estate documents as deeds, mortgages, leases and contracts for deed.

Covenant of quiet enjoyment The covenant implied by law by which a landlord guarantees that a tenant may take possession of leased premises, and that the landlord will not interfere in the tenant's possession or use of the property.

Credit On a closing statement, an amount entered in a person's favor—either an amount the party has paid or an amount for which the party must be reimbursed.

Curtesy A life estate, usually a fractional interest, given by some states to the surviving husband in real estate owned by his deceased wife.

Datum A horizontal plane from which heights and depths are measured.

Debit On a closing statement, an amount charged; that is, an amount that the debited party must pay.

Decedent A person who has died.

Dedication The voluntary transfer of private property by its owner to the public for some public use, such as for streets or schools.

Deed A written instrument that, when executed and delivered, conveys title to or an interest in real estate.

Deed in trust An instrument that grants a trustee under a land trust full power to sell, mortgage and subdivide a parcel of real estate. The beneficiary controls the trustee's use of these powers under the provisions of the trust agreement.

Deed of trust *See* Trust deed.

Deed restrictions Clauses in a deed limiting the future uses of the property. Deed restrictions may impose a vast variety of limitations and conditions—for example, they may limit the density of buildings, dictate the types of structures that can be erected or prevent buildings from being used for specific purposes or even from being used at all.

Default The nonperformance of a duty, whether arising under a contract or otherwise; failure to meet an obligation when due.

Defeasance clause A clause used in leases and mortgages that cancels a specified right upon the occurrence of a certain condition, such as cancellation of a mortgage upon repayment of the mortgage loan.

Defeasible fee estate An estate in which the holder has a fee simple title that may be divested upon the occurrence or nonoccurrence of a specified event. There are two categories of defeasible fee estates: fee simple determinable and fee simple subject to a condition subsequent.

Deficiency judgment A personal judgment levied against the mortgagor when a foreclosure sale does not produce sufficient funds to pay the mortgage debt in full.

Delinquent taxes Unpaid taxes that are past due.

Demand The amount of goods people are willing and able to buy at a given price; often coupled with *supply*.

Density zoning Zoning ordinances that restrict the maximum average number of houses per acre that may be built within a particular area, generally a subdivision.

Depreciation 1. In appraisal, a loss of value in property due to any cause, including physical deterioration, *functional obsolescence* and *environmental obsolescence*. 2. In real estate investment, an expense deduction for tax purposes taken over the period of ownership of income property.

Descent Acquisition of an estate by inheritance in which an heir succeeds to the property by operation of law.

Determinable fee estate A fee simple estate in which the property automatically reverts to the grantor upon the occurrence of a specified event or condition.

Devise A gift of real property by will. The donor is the devisor, and the recipient is the devisee.

Direct market comparison approach The process of estimating the value of a property by examining and comparing actual sales of comparable properties.

Dominant tenement A property that includes in its ownership the appurtenant right to use an easement over another person's property for a specific purpose.

Dower The legal right or interest, recognized in some states, that a wife acquires in the property her husband held or acquired during their marriage. During the husband's lifetime, the right is only a possibility of an interest; upon his death it can become an interest in land.

Dual agency Representing both parties to a transaction. This is unethical unless both parties agree to it, and it is illegal in many states.

Duress Unlawful constraint or action exercised upon a person whereby the person is forced to perform an act against his or her will. A contract entered into under duress is voidable.

Earnest money deposit Money deposited by a buyer under the terms of a contract, to be forfeited if the buyer defaults but applied on the purchase price if the sale is closed.

Easement A right to use the land of another for a specific purpose, such as for a right-of-way or utilities; an incorporeal interest in land. An *easement appurtenant* passes with the land when conveyed.

Easement by necessity An easement allowed by law as necessary for the full enjoyment of a parcel of real estate; for example, a right of ingress and egress over a grantor's land.

Easement by prescription An easement acquired by continuous, open and hostile use of the property for the period of time prescribed by state law.

Easement in gross An easement that is not created for the benefit of any *land* owned by the owner of the easement but that attaches *personally to the easement owner.* For example, a right granted by Eleanor Franks to Joe Fish to use a portion of her property for the rest of his life would be an easement in gross.

Economic obsolescence *See* Environmental obsolescence.

Emblements Growing crops, such as grapes and corn, that are produced annually through labor and industry; also called *fructus industriales.*

Eminent domain The right of a government or municipal quasi-public body to acquire property for public use through a court action called *condemnation,* in which the court decides that the use is a public use and determines the compensation to be paid to the owner.

Employee Someone who works as a direct employee of an employer and has employee status. The employer is obligated to withhold income taxes and social security taxes from the compensation of employees. *See also* Independent contractor.

Employment contract A document evidencing formal employment between employer and employee or between principal and agent. In the real estate business, this generally takes the form of a listing agreement or management agreement.

Enabling acts State legislation that confers zoning powers on municipal governments.

Encroachment A building or some portion of it—a wall or fence for instance—that extends beyond the land of the owner and illegally intrudes upon some land of an adjoining owner or a street or alley.

Encumbrance Anything—such as a mortgage, tax, or judgment lien, an easement, a restriction on the use of the land or an outstanding dower right—that may diminish the value of a property.

Environmental obsolescence Reduction in a property's value caused by outside factors; also called economic obsolescence.

Equalization The raising or lowering of assessed values for tax purposes in a particular county or taxing district to make them equal to assessments in other counties or districts.

Equalization factor A factor (number) by which the assessed value of a property is multiplied to arrive at a value for the property that is in line with state-wide tax assessments. The *ad valorem tax* would be based upon this adjusted value.

Equitable lien *See* Statutory lien.

Equitable title The interest held by a vendee under a contract for deed or an installment contract; the equitable right to obtain absolute ownership to property when legal title is held in another's name.

Equity The interest or value that an owner has in property over and above any mortgage indebtedness.

Erosion The gradual wearing away of land by water, wind and general weather conditions; the diminishing of property by the elements.

Escheat The reversion of property to the state or county, as provided by state law, in cases where a decedent dies intestate without heirs capable of inheriting, or when the property is abandoned.

Escrow The closing of a transaction through a third party called an *escrow agent,* or *escrowee,* who receives certain funds and documents to be delivered upon the performance of certain conditions outlined in the escrow instructions.

Escrow instructions A document that sets forth the duties of the escrow agent, as well as the requirements and obligations of the parties, when a transaction is closed through an escrow.

Estate at sufferance The tenancy of a lessee who lawfully comes into possession of a landlord's real estate but who continues to occupy the premises improperly after his or her lease rights have expired.

Estate at will An estate that gives the lessee the right to possession until the estate is terminated by either party; the term of this estate is indefinite.

Estate for years An interest for a certain, exact period of time in property leased for a specified consideration.

Estate from period to period *See* Periodic estate.

Estate in land The degree, quantity, nature and extent of interest that a person has in real property.

Estate taxes Federal taxes on a decedent's real and personal property.

Estoppel Method of creating an agency relationship in which someone states incorrectly that another person is his or her agent, and a third person relies on that representation.

Estoppel certificate A document in which a borrower certifies the amount owed on a mortgage loan and the rate of interest.

Eviction A legal process to oust a person from possession of real estate.

Evidence of title Proof of ownership of property; commonly a certificate of title, an abstract of title with lawyer's opinion or a Torrens registration certificate.

Exchange A transaction in which all or part of the consideration is the transfer of *like-kind* property (such as real estate for real estate).

Exclusive-agency listing A listing contract under which the owner appoints a real estate broker as his or her exclusive agent for a designated period of time to sell the property, on the owner's stated terms, for a commission. The owner reserves the right to sell without paying anyone a commission if he or she sells to a prospect who has not been introduced or claimed by the broker.

Exclusive right-to-sell A listing contract under which the owner appoints a real estate broker as his or her exclusive agent for a designated period of time, to sell the property on the owner's stated terms, and agrees to pay the broker a commission when the property is sold, whether by the broker, the owner or another broker.

Executed contract A contract in which all parties have fulfilled their promises and thus performed the contract.

Execution The signing and delivery of an instrument. Also, a legal order directing an official to enforce a judgment against the property of a debtor.

Executory contract A contract under which something remains to be done by one or more of the parties.

Expenses Short-term costs, such as minor repairs, regular maintenance and renting costs, that are deducted from an investment property's income.

Express agreement An oral or written contract in which the parties state the contract's terms and express their intentions in words.

Fee simple estate The maximum possible estate or right of ownership of real property, continuing forever. Sometimes called a *fee* or *fee simple absolute*.

Feudal system A system of ownership usually associated with precolonial England, in which the king or other sovereign is the source of all rights. The right to possess real property was granted by the sovereign to an individual as a life estate only. Upon the death of the individual, title passed back to the sovereign, not to the decedent's heirs.

FHA loan A loan insured by the Federal Housing Administration and made by an approved lender in accordance with the FHA's regulations.

Fiduciary relationship A relationship of trust and confidence, as between trustee and beneficiary, attorney and client, or principal and agent.

Financing statement *See* Uniform Commercial Code.

Fixture An item of personal property that has been converted to real property by being permanently affixed to the realty.

Foreclosure A legal procedure whereby property used as security for a debt is sold to satisfy the debt in the event of default in payment of the mortgage note or default of other terms in the mortgage document. The foreclosure procedure brings the rights of all parties to a conclusion and passes the title in the mortgaged property to either the holder of the mortgage or a third party who may purchase the realty at the foreclosure sale, free of all encumbrances affecting the property subsequent to the mortgage.

Fraud Deception intended to cause a person to give up property or a lawful right.

Freehold estate An estate in land in which ownership is for an indeterminate length of time, in contrast to a *leasehold estate*.

Functional obsolescence A loss of value to an improvement to real estate arising from functional problems, often caused by age or poor design.

Future interest A person's present right to an interest in real property that will not result in possession or enjoyment until some time in the future, such as a reversion or right of reentry.

Gap A defect in the chain of title of a particular parcel of real estate; a missing document or conveyance that raises doubt as to the present ownership of the land.

General agent One who is authorized by a principal to represent the principal in a specific range of matters.

General lien The right of a creditor to have all of a debtor's property—both real and personal—sold to satisfy a debt.

General partnership *See* Partnership.

General tax *See* Ad valorem tax.

General warranty deed A deed in which the grantor fully warrants good clear title to the premises. Used in most real estate deed transfers, a general warranty deed offers the greatest protection of any deed.

Government lot Fractional sections in the rectangular (U.S. government) survey system that are less than one quarter-section in area.

Government survey system *See* Rectangular survey system.

Grantee A person who receives a conveyance of real property from a grantor.

Granting clause Words in a deed of conveyance that state the grantor's intention to convey the property at the present time. This clause is generally worded as "convey and warrant," "grant," "grant, bargain and sell" or the like.

Grantor The person transferring title to or an interest in real property to a grantee.

Gross income multiplier A figure used as a multiplier of the gross rental income of a property to produce an estimate of the property's value.

Gross lease A lease of property according to which a landlord pays all property charges regularly incurred through ownership, such as repairs, taxes, insurance and operating expenses. Most residential leases are gross leases.

Ground lease A lease of land only, on which the tenant usually owns a building or is required to build as specified in the lease. Such leases are usually long-term net leases; the tenant's rights and obligations continue until the lease expires or is terminated through default.

Habendum clause That part of a deed beginning with the words, "to have and to hold," following the granting clause and defining the extent of ownership the grantor is conveying.

Heir One who might inherit or succeed to an interest in land under the state law of descent when the owner dies without leaving a valid will.

Highest and best use That possible use of land that would produce the greatest net income and thereby develop the highest land value.

Holdover tenancy A tenancy whereby a lessee retains possession of leased property after the lease has expired, and the landlord, by continuing to accept rent, agrees to the tenant's continued occupancy as defined by state law.

Holographic will A will that is written, dated and signed in the testator's handwriting.

Homeowner's insurance policy A standardized package insurance policy that covers a residential real estate owner against financial loss from fire, theft, public liability and other common risks.

Homestead Land that is owned and occupied as the family home. In many states, a portion of the area or value of this land is protected or exempt from judgments for debts.

Hypothecation The pledge of property as security for a loan.

Implied agreement A contract under which the agreement of the parties is demonstrated by their acts and conduct.

Improvement 1. Any structure, usually privately owned, erected on a site to enhance the value of the property—for example, building a fence or a driveway. 2. A publicly owned structure added to or benefiting land, such as a curb, sidewalk, street or sewer.

Income approach The process of estimating the value of an income-producing property by capitalization of the annual net income expected to be produced by the property during its remaining useful life.

Incorporeal right A nonpossessory right in real estate; for example, an easement or right-of-way.

Independent contractor Someone who is retained to perform a certain act but who is subject to the control and direction of another only as to the end result and not as to the way in which the act is performed. Unlike an employee, an independent contractor pays for all expenses and social security and income taxes and receives no employee benefits. Many real estate salespeople are independent contractors.

Inheritance taxes State-imposed taxes on a decedent's real and personal property.

Installment contract A contract for the sale of real estate whereby the purchase price is paid in periodic installments by the purchaser, who is in possession of the property even though title is retained by the seller until a future date, which may be not until final payment. Also called a *contract for deed* or *articles of agreement for warranty deed.*

Installment sale A transaction in which the sales price is paid in two or more installments over two or more years. If the sale meets certain requirements, a taxpayer can postpone reporting such income until future years by paying tax each year only on the proceeds received that year.

Interest A charge made by a lender for the use of money.

Interim financing A short-term loan usually made during the construction phase of a building project (in this case, often referred to as a *construction loan*).

Intestate The condition of a property owner who dies without leaving a valid will. Title to the property will pass to the decedent's heirs as provided in the state law of descent.

Investment Money directed toward the purchase, improvement and development of an asset in expectation of income or profits.

Involuntary alienation *See* Alienation.

Joint tenancy Ownership of real estate between two or more parties who have been named in one conveyance as joint tenants. Upon the death of a joint tenant, the decedent's interest passes to the surviving joint tenant or tenants by the *right of survivorship.*

Joint venture The joining of two or more people to conduct a specific business enterprise. A joint venture is similar to a partnership in that it must be created by agreement between the parties to share in the losses and profits of the venture. It is unlike a partnership in that the venture is for one specific project only, rather than for a continuing business relationship.

Judgment The formal decision of a court upon the respective rights and claims of the parties to an action or suit. After a judgment has been entered and recorded with the county recorder, it usually becomes a general lien on the property of the defendant.

Judicial precedent In law, the requirements established by prior court decisions.

Junior lien An obligation, such as a second mortgage, that is subordinate in right or lien priority to an existing lien on the same realty.

Laches An equitable doctrine used by courts to bar a legal claim or prevent the assertion of a right because of undue delay or failure to assert the claim or right.

Land The earth's surface, extending downward to the center of the earth and upward infinitely into space, including things permanently attached by nature, such as trees and water.

Land contract *See* Installment Contract.

Lease A written or oral contract between a landlord (the lessor) and a tenant (the lessee) that transfers the right to exclusive possession and use of the landlord's real property to the lessee for a specified period of time and for a stated consideration (rent). By state law, leases for longer than a certain period of time (generally one year) must be in writing to be enforceable.

Leasehold estate A tenant's right to occupy real estate during the term of a lease, generally considered to be a personal property interest.

Legacy A disposition of money or personal property by will.

Legal description A description of a specific parcel of real estate complete enough for an independent surveyor to locate and identify it.

Lessee *See* Lease.

Lessor *See* Lease.

Leverage The use of borrowed money to finance the bulk of an investment.

Levy To assess; to seize or collect. To levy a tax is to assess a property and set the rate of taxation. To levy an execution is to officially seize the property of a person in order to satisfy an obligation.

License 1. A privilege or right granted to a person by a state to operate as a real estate broker or salesperson. 2. The revocable permission for a temporary use of land—a personal right that cannot be sold.

Lien A right given by law to certain creditors to have their debts paid out of the property of a defaulting debtor, usually by means of a court sale.

Lien theory Some states interpret a mortgage as being purely a lien on real property. The mortgagee thus has no right of possession, but must foreclose the lien and sell the property, if the mortgagor defaults.

Life estate An interest in real or personal property that is limited in duration to the lifetime of its owner or some other designated person or persons.

Life tenant A person in possession of a life estate.

Limited partnership *See* Partnership.

Liquidity The ability to sell an asset and convert it into cash, at a price close to its true value, in a short period of time.

Lis pendens A recorded legal document giving constructive notice that an action affecting a particular property has been filed in either a state or a federal court.

Listing agreement A contract between a landowner (as principal) and a licensed real estate broker (as agent) by which the broker is employed as agent to sell real estate on the owner's terms within a given time, for which service the landowner agrees to pay a commission.

Listing broker The broker in a multiple-listing situation from whose office a listing agreement is initiated, as opposed to the *selling broker,* from whose office negotiations leading up to a sale are initiated. The listing broker and the selling broker may be the same person. *See also* Multiple listing.

Littoral rights 1. A landowner's claim to use water in large navigable lakes and oceans adjacent to his or her property. 2. The ownership rights to land bordering these bodies of water up to the high-water mark.

Lot-and-block system A method of describing real property that identifies a parcel of land by reference to lot and block numbers within a subdivision, as specified on a recorded subdivision plat.

Management agreement A contract between the owner of income property and a management firm or individual property manager that outlines the scope of the manager's authority.

Market A place where goods can be bought and sold, and a price established.

Marketable title Good or clear title, reasonably free from the risk of litigation over possible defects.

Market comparison approach *See* Direct market comparison approach.

Market value The most probable price property would bring in an arm's-length transaction under normal conditions on the open market.

Master plan A comprehensive plan to guide the long-term physical development of a particular area.

Mechanic's lien A statutory lien created in favor of contractors, laborers and materialmen who have performed work or furnished materials in the erection or repair of a building.

Meridian One of a set of imaginary lines running north and south and crossing a base line at a definite point, used in the rectangular (U.S. government) survey system of property description.

Metes-and-bounds description A legal description of a parcel of land that begins at a well-marked point and follows the boundaries, using directions and distances around the tract back to the place of beginning.

Mill One-tenth of one cent. Some states use a mill rate to compute real estate taxes; for example, a rate of 52 mills would be $0.052 tax for each dollar of assessed valuation of a property.

Minor Someone who has not reached the age of majority and therefore does not have legal capacity to transfer title to real property.

Money judgment A court judgment ordering payment of money rather than specific performance of a certain action. *See also* Judgment.

Month-to-month tenancy A periodic tenancy under which the tenant rents for one month at a time. In the absence of a rental agreement (oral or written), a tenancy is generally considered to be month to month.

Monument A fixed natural or artificial object used to establish real estate boundaries for a metes-and-bounds description.

Mortgage A conditional transfer or pledge of real estate as security for the payment of a debt. Also, the document creating a mortgage lien.

Mortgagee A lender in a mortgage loan transaction.

Mortgage lien A lien or charge on the property of a mortgagor that secures the underlying debt obligations.

Mortgagor A borrower who pledges (hypothecates) property as security for a loan.

Multiple listing clause A provision in an exclusive listing for the additional authority and obligation on the part of the listing broker to distribute the listing to other brokers in the multiple-listing organization.

Negotiable instrument A written promise or order to pay a specific sum of money that may be transferred by endorsement or delivery. The transferee then has the original payee's right to payment.

Net lease A lease requiring the tenant to pay not only rent but costs incurred in maintaining the property, including taxes, insurance, utilities and repairs.

Net listing A listing based on the net price the seller will receive if the property is sold. Under a net listing, the broker can offer the property for sale at the highest price obtainable in order to increase the commission. This type of listing is outlawed in many states.

Nonconforming use A use of property that is permitted to continue after a zoning ordinance prohibiting it has been established for the area.

Nonhomogeneity A lack of uniformity; dissimilarity. Since no two parcels of land are exactly alike, real estate is said to be nonhomogeneous.

Note *See* Promissory note.

Novation Substituting a new obligation for an old one, or substituting new parties to an existing obligation.

Nuncupative will An oral will declared by the testator in his or her final illness, made before witnesses and afterwards reduced to writing.

Offer and acceptance Two essential components of a valid contract; a "meeting of the minds."

Open-end mortgage A mortgage loan that is expandable by increments up to a maximum dollar amount, the full loan being secured by the same original mortgage.

Open listing A listing contract under which the broker's commission is contingent upon the broker's producing a ready, willing and able buyer before the property is sold by the seller or another broker.

Option An agreement to keep open for a set period an offer to sell or purchase property.

Option listing Listing with a provision that gives the listing broker the right to purchase the listed property.

Ostensible agency A form of implied agency relationship created by the actions of the parties involved rather than by written agreement or document.

Parcel A specific portion of a large tract of real estate; a lot.

Parol evidence rule A rule of evidence providing that a written agreement is the final expression of the agreement of the parties, not to be varied or contradicted by prior or contemporaneous oral or written negotiations.

Participation financing A mortgage in which the lender participates in the income of the mortgaged venture beyond a fixed return or receives a yield on the loan in addition to the straight interest rate.

Partition The division of cotenants' interests in real property when the parties do not all voluntarily agree to terminate the co-ownership; takes place through court procedures.

Partnership An association of two or more individuals who carry on a continuing business for profit as co-owners. Under the law, a partnership is regarded as a group of individuals rather than as a single entity. A *general partnership* is a typical form of joint venture, in which each general partner shares in the administration, profits and losses of the operation. A *limited partnership* is a business arrangement whereby the operation is administered by one or more general partners and funded, by and large, by limited or silent partners, who are by law responsible for losses only to the extent of their investments.

Party wall A wall that is located on or at a boundary line between two adjoining parcels of land and is used or is intended to be used by the owners of both properties.

Patent A grant or franchise of land from the United States government.

Percentage lease A lease, commonly used for commercial property, whose rental is based on the tenant's gross sales at the premises; it usually stipulates a base monthly rental plus a percentage of any gross sales above a certain amount.

Periodic estate An interest in leased property that continues from period to period—week to week, month to month, or year to year.

Personal property Items, called *chattels,* that do not fit into the definition of real property; movable objects.

Physical deterioration A reduction in a property's value resulting from a decline in physical condition; can be caused by action of the elements or by ordinary wear and tear.

Planned unit development A planned combination of diverse land uses, such as housing, recreation and shopping, in one contained development or subdivision.

Plat A map of a town, section or subdivision indicating the location and boundaries of individual properties.

Plottage The increase in value or utility resulting from the consolidation *(assemblage)* of two or more adjacent lots into one larger lot.

Point A unit of measurement used for various loan charges; one point equals one percent of the amount of the loan.

Point of beginning In a metes-and-bounds legal description, the starting point of the survey, situated in one corner of the parcel; all metes-and-bounds descriptions must follow the boundaries of the parcel back to the point of beginning.

Point of equilibrium The point on a graph at which supply (production) and demand (consumption) curves meet.

Police power The government's right to impose laws, statutes and ordinances, including zoning ordinances and building codes, to protect the public health, safety and welfare.

Power of attorney A written instrument authorizing a person, the *attorney-in-fact,* to act as agent on behalf of another person to the extent indicated in the instrument.

Prepayment penalty A charge imposed on a borrower who pays off the loan principal early. This penalty compensates the lender for interest and other charges that would otherwise be lost.

Price fixing *See* Antitrust laws.

Primary mortgage market *See* Secondary mortgage market.

Principal 1. A sum lent or employed as a fund or investment, as distinguished from its income or profits. 2. The original amount (as in a loan) of the total due and payable at a certain date. 3. A main party to a transaction—the person for whom the agent works.

Prior appropriation A concept of water ownership in which the landowner's right to use available water is based on a government-administered permit system.

Priority The order of position or time. The priority of liens is generally determined by the chronological order in which the lien documents are recorded; tax liens, however, have priority even over previously recorded liens.

Probate A legal process by which a court determines who will inherit a decedent's property and what the estate's assets are.

Procuring cause The effort that brings about the desired result. Under an open listing, the broker who is the procuring cause of the sale receives the commission.

Progression An appraisal principle that states that, between dissimilar properties, the value of the lesser-quality property is favorably affected by the presence of the better-quality property.

Promissory note A financing instrument that states the terms of the underlying obligation, is signed by its maker and is negotiable (transferable to a third party).

Property manager Someone who manages real estate for another person for compensation. Duties include collecting rents, maintaining the property and keeping up all accounting.

Prorations Expenses, either prepaid or paid in arrears, that are divided or distributed between buyer and seller at the closing.

Puffing Exaggerated or superlative comments or opinions.

Pur autre vie For the life of another. A life estate pur autre vie is a life estate that is measured by the life of a person other than the grantee.

Purchase-money mortgage A note secured by a mortgage or trust deed given by a buyer, as mortgagor, to a seller, as mortgagee, as part of the purchase price of the real estate.

Quiet title suit *See* Suit to quiet title.

Quitclaim deed A conveyance by which the grantor transfers whatever interest he or she has in the real estate, without warranties or obligations.

Range A strip of land six miles wide, extending north and south and numbered east and west according to its distance from the principal meridian in the rectangular survey (government survey) system of land description.

Ratification Method of creating an agency relationship in which the principal accepts the conduct of someone who acted without prior authorization as the principal's agent.

Ready, willing and able buyer One who is prepared to buy property on the seller's terms and is ready to take positive steps to consummate the transaction.

Real estate Land; a portion of the earth's surface extending downward to the center of the earth and upward infinitely into space, including all things permanently attached to it, whether naturally or artificially; any and every interest in land.

Real estate broker Any person, partnership, association or corporation who sells (or offers to sell), buys (or offers to buy) or negotiates the purchase, sale or exchange of real estate, or who leases (or offers to lease) or rents (or offers to rent) any real estate or the improvements thereon for others for a compensation or valuable consideration. A real estate broker may not conduct business without a real estate broker's license.

Real estate investment syndicate *See* Syndicate.

Real estate investment trust (REIT) Trust ownership of real estate by a group of individuals who purchase certificates of ownership in the trust, which in turn invests the money in real property and distributes the profits back to the investors free of corporate income tax.

Real estate license law State law enacted to protect the public from fraud, dishonesty and incompetence in the purchase and sale of real estate.

Real estate mortgage investment conduit (REMIC) A tax entity that issues multiple classes of investor interests (securities) backed by a pool of mortgages.

Real property The interests, benefits, and rights inherent in real estate ownership.

REALTOR® A registered trademark term reserved for the sole use of active members of local REALTOR® boards affiliated with the NATIONAL ASSOCIATION OF REALTORS®.

Reconciliation The final step in the appraisal process, in which the appraiser reconciles the estimates of value received from the market data, cost and income approaches to arrive at a final estimate of market value for the subject property.

Reconveyance deed A deed used by a trustee under a deed of trust to return title to the trustor.

Recording The act of entering or recording documents affecting or conveying interests in real estate in the recorder's office established in each county. Until it is recorded, a deed or mortgage ordinarily is not effective against subsequent purchasers or mortgagees.

Recovery fund A fund established in some states from real estate license revenues to cover claims of aggrieved parties who have suffered monetary damage through the actions of a real estate licensee.

Rectangular survey system A system established in 1785 by the federal government, providing for surveying and describing land by reference to principal meridians and base lines.

Redemption The buying back of real estate sold in a tax sale. The defaulted owner is said to have the right of redemption.

Redemption period A period of time established by state law during which a property owner has the right to redeem his or her real estate from a foreclosure or tax sale by paying the sales price, interest and costs. Many states do not have mortgage redemption laws.

Redlining The illegal practice of a lending institution denying loans or restricting their number for certain areas of a community.

Regression An appraisal principle that states that, between dissimilar properties, the value of the better property is adversely affected by the presence of the lesser-quality property.

Regulation Z Implements the Truth-in-Lending Act requiring credit institutions to inform borrowers of the true cost of obtaining credit.

Release deed A document, also known as a *deed of reconveyance,* that transfers all rights given a trustee under a trust deed loan back to the grantor after the loan has been fully repaid.

Remainder The remnant of an estate that has been conveyed to take effect and be enjoyed after the termination of a prior estate, such as when an owner conveys a life estate to one party and the remainder to another.

Renegotiable rate mortgage A mortgage loan in which the interest rate may increase or decrease at specified intervals, within certain limits based upon an economic indicator.

Rent A fixed, periodic payment made by a tenant of a property to the owner for possession and use, usually by prior agreement of the parties.

Rent schedule A statement of proposed rental rates, determined by the owner or the property manager or both, based on a building's estimated expenses, market supply and demand and the owner's long-range goals for the property.

Replacement cost The construction cost at current prices of a property that is not necessarily an exact duplicate of the subject property but serves the same purpose or function as the original.

Reproduction cost The construction cost at current prices of an exact duplicate of the subject property.

Restriction A limitation on the use of real property, usually originated in a deed by the owner or subdivider.

Reversion The remnant of an estate that the grantor holds after granting a life estate to another person.

Right of survivorship *See* Joint tenancy.

Riparian rights An owner's rights in land that borders on or includes a stream, river or lake. These rights include access to and use of the water.

Risk management Evaluation and selection of appropriate property and other insurance.

Sale and leaseback A transaction in which an owner sells his or her improved property and, as part of the same transaction, signs a long-term lease to remain in possession of the premises.

Sales contract A contract containing the complete terms of the agreement between buyer and seller for the sale of a particular parcel or parcels of real estate.

Salesperson A person who performs real estate activities while employed by or associated with a licensed real estate broker.

Satisfaction A document acknowledging the payment of a debt.

Secondary mortgage market A market for the purchase and sale of existing mortgages, designed to provide greater liquidity for mortgages; also called the *secondary money market*. Mortgages are first originated in the *primary mortgage market*.

Section A portion of a township under the rectangular survey (government survey) system. A township is divided into 36 sections, numbered 1 to 36. A section is a square with mile-long sides and an area of one square mile, or 640 acres.

Security deposit A payment by a tenant, held by the landlord during the lease term and kept (wholly or partially) on default or destruction of the premises by the tenant.

Selling broker *See* Listing broker.

Separate property Under community property law, property owned solely by either spouse before the marriage, acquired by gift or inheritance after the marriage or purchased with separate funds after the marriage.

Servient tenement Land on which an easement exists in favor of an adjacent property (called a dominant estate); also called a *servient estate*.

Setback The amount of space local zoning regulations require between a lot line and a building line.

Severalty Ownership of real property by one person only, also called *sole ownership*.

Severance Changing an item of real estate to personal property by detaching it from the land; for example, cutting down a tree.

Shared appreciation mortgage A mortgage loan in which the lender, in exchange for a loan with a favorable interest rate, participates in the profits (if any) the mortgagor receives when the property is eventually sold.

Situs The personal preference of people for one area over another, not necessarily based on objective facts and knowledge.

Sole ownership *See* Severalty.

Special agent One who is authorized by a principal to perform a single act or transaction; a real estate broker is usually a special agent authorized to find a ready, willing and able buyer for a particular property.

Special assessment A tax or levy customarily imposed against only those specific parcels of real estate that will benefit from a proposed public improvement like a street or sewer.

Special warranty deed A deed in which the grantor warrants, or guarantees, the title only against defects arising during the period of his or her tenure and ownership of the property and not against defects existing before that time, generally using the language, "by, through or under the grantor but not otherwise."

Specific lien A lien affecting or attaching only to a certain, specific parcel of land or piece of property.

Specific performance suit A legal action to compel a party to carry out the terms of a contract.

Spot zoning A change in a local zoning ordinance to permit a particular use that is inconsistent with the area's zoning classification. Spot zoning is not favored in the law.

Statute of frauds That part of a state law that requires certain instruments, such as deeds, real estate sales contracts and certain leases, to be in writing in order to be legally enforceable.

Statute of limitations That law pertaining to the period of time within which certain actions must be brought to court.

Statutory lien A lien imposed on property by statute—a tax lien, for example—in contrast to an *equitable lien,* which arises out of common law.

Steering The illegal practice of channeling home seekers to particular areas, either to maintain the homogeneity of an area or to change the character of an area in order to create a speculative situation.

Straight-line method A method of calculating depreciation for tax purposes, computed by dividing the adjusted basis of a property by the estimated number of years of remaining useful life.

Subdivider One who buys undeveloped land, divides it into smaller, usable lots and sells the lots to potential users.

Subdivision A tract of land divided by the owner, known as the *subdivider,* into blocks, building lots and streets according to a recorded subdivision plat, which must comply with local ordinances and regulations.

"Subject to" clause A clause in a deed specifying exceptions and reservations affecting the title.

Subletting The leasing of premises by a lessee to a third party for part of the lessee's remaining term. *See also* Assignment.

Subordination Relegation to a lesser position, usually in respect to a right or security.

Subordination agreement A written agreement between holders of liens on a property that changes the priority of mortgage, judgment and other liens under certain circumstances.

Subrogation The substitution of one creditor for another, with the substituted person succeeding to the legal rights and claims of the original claimant. Subrogation is used by title insurers to acquire from the injured party rights to sue in order to recover any claims they have paid.

Substitution An appraisal principle that states that the maximum value of a property tends to be set by the cost of purchasing an equally desirable and valuable substitute property, assuming that no costly delay is encountered in making the substitution.

Subsurface rights Ownership rights in a parcel of real estate to the water, minerals, gas, oil and so forth that lie beneath the surface of the property.

Suit for possession A court suit initiated by a landlord to evict a tenant from leased premises after the tenant has breached one of the terms of the lease or has held possession of the property after the lease's expiration.

Suit to quiet title A court action intended to establish or settle the title to a particular property, especially when there is a cloud on the title.

Supply The amount of goods available in the market to be sold at a given price. The term is often coupled with *demand.*

Surety bond An agreement by an insurance or bonding company to be responsible for certain possible defaults, debts or obligations contracted for by an insured party; in essence, a policy insuring one's personal and/or financial integrity. In the real estate business, a surety bond is generally used to ensure that a particular project will be completed at a certain date or that a contract will be performed as stated.

Surface rights Ownership rights in a parcel of real estate that are limited to the surface of the property and do not include the air above it (*air rights*) or the minerals below the surface (*subsurface rights*).

Survey The process by which boundaries are measured and land areas are determined; the on-site measurement of lot lines, dimensions and position of a house on a lot, including the determination of any existing encroachments or easements.

Syndicate A combination of people or firms formed to accomplish a business venture of mutual interest by pooling resources. In a *real estate investment syndicate,* the parties own and/or develop property, with the main profit generally arising from the sale of the property.

Tacking Adding or combining successive periods of continuous occupation of real property by adverse possessors. This concept enables someone who has not been in possession for the entire statutory period to establish a claim of adverse possession.

Taxation The process by which a government or municipal quasi-public body raises monies to fund its operation.

Tax credit An amount by which tax owed is reduced directly.

Tax deed An instrument, similar to a certificate of sale, given to a purchaser at a tax sale. *See also* Certificate of sale.

Tax levy *See* Levy.

Tax lien A charge against property, created by operation of law. Tax liens and assessments take priority over all other liens.

Tax rate The rate at which real property is taxed in a tax district or county. For example, in a certain county, real property may be taxed at a rate of .056 cents per dollar of assessed valuation.

Tax sale A court-ordered sale of real property to raise money to cover delinquent taxes.

Tenancy by the entirety The joint ownership, recognized in some states, of property acquired by husband and wife during marriage. Upon the death of one spouse, the survivor becomes the owner of the property.

Tenancy in common A form of co-ownership by which each owner holds an undivided interest in real property as if he or she were sole owner. Each individual owner has the right to partition. Unlike joint tenants, tenants in common have right of inheritance.

Tenant One who holds or possesses lands or tenements by any kind of right or title.

Tenant improvements Alterations to the interior of a building to meet the functional demands of the tenant.

Testate Having made and left a valid will.

Time is of the essence A phrase in a contract that requires the performance of a certain act within a stated period of time.

Time-share Ownership interest that may include an estate interest in property and which allows use of the property for a fixed or variable time period.

Title 1. The right to or ownership of land. 2. The evidence of ownership of land.

Title insurance A policy insuring the owner or mortgagee against loss by reason of defects in the title to a parcel of real estate, other than encumbrances, defects and matters specifically excluded by the policy.

Title theory Some states interpret a mortgage to mean that the lender is the owner of mortgaged land. Upon full payment of the mortgage debt, the borrower becomes the landowner.

Torrens system A method of evidencing title by registration with the proper public authority, generally called the registrar, named for its founder, Sir Robert Torrens.

Township The principal unit of the rectangular survey (government survey) system. A township is a square with six-mile sides and an area of 36 square miles.

Township line Lines running at six-mile intervals parallel to the base lines in the rectangular survey (government survey) system.

Trade fixtures Articles installed by a tenant under the terms of a lease and removable by the tenant before the lease expires. These remain personal property and are not true fixtures.

Transfer tax Tax stamps required to be affixed to a deed by state and/or local law.

Trust A fiduciary arrangement whereby property is conveyed to a person or institution, called a *trustee,* to be held and administered on behalf of another person, called a *beneficiary.* The one who conveys the trust is called the *trustor.*

Trust account *See* Commingling.

Trust deed An instrument used to create a mortgage lien by which the mortgagor conveys title to a trustee, who holds it as security for the benefit of the note holder (the lender); also called a *deed of trust.*

Trustee *See* Trust.

Trustee's deed A deed executed by a trustee conveying land held in a trust.

Undivided interest *See* Tenancy in common.

Unenforceable contract A contract that has all the elements of a valid contract, yet neither party can sue the other to force performance of it. For example, an unsigned contract is generally unenforceable.

Uniform Commercial Code A codification of commercial law, adopted in most states, that attempts to make uniform all laws relating to commercial transactions, including chattel mortgages and bulk transfers. Security interests in chattels are created by an instrument known as a *security agreement.* To give notice of the security interest, a *financing statement* must be recorded. Article 6 of the code regulates *bulk transfers*—the sale of a business as a whole, including all fixtures, chattels and merchandise.

Unilateral contract A one-sided contract wherein one party makes a promise in order to induce a second party to do something. The second party is not legally bound to perform; however, if the second party does comply, the first party is obligated to keep the promise.

Unity of ownership The four unities that are traditionally needed to create a joint tenancy—unity of title, time, interest and possession.

Urban renewal The acquisition of run-down city areas for purposes of redevelopment.

Useful life In real estate investment, the number of years a property will be useful to the investors.

Usury Charging interest at a higher rate than the maximum rate established by state law.

Valid contract A contract that complies with all the essentials of a contract and is binding and enforceable on all parties to it.

VA loan A mortgage loan on approved property made to a qualified veteran by an authorized lender and guaranteed by the Veterans Administration in order to limit the lender's possible loss.

Value The power of a good or service to command other goods in exchange for the present worth of future rights to its income or amenities.

Variable rate mortgage A mortgage loan in which the interest rate may increase or decrease at specified intervals within certain limits, based upon an economic indicator.

Variance Permission obtained from zoning authorities to build a structure or conduct a use that is expressly prohibited by the current zoning laws; an exception from the zoning ordinances.

Vendee A buyer.

Vendor A seller.

Voidable contract A contract that seems to be valid on the surface, but may be rejected or disaffirmed by one or both of the parties.

Void contract A contract that has no legal force or effect because it does not meet the essential elements of a contract.

Voluntary transfer *See* Alienation.

Waste An improper use or an abuse of a property by a possessor who holds less than fee ownership, such as a tenant, life tenant, mortgagor or vendee. Such waste ordinarily impairs the value of the land or the interest of the person holding the title or the reversionary rights.

Will A written document, properly witnessed, providing for the transfer of title to property owned by the deceased, called the *testator*.

Wraparound mortgage A method of refinancing in which the new mortgage is placed in a secondary, or subordinate, position; the new mortgage includes both the unpaid principal balance of the first mortgage and whatever additional sums are advanced by the lender. In essence, it is an additional mortgage in which another lender refinances a borrower by lending an amount over the existing first mortgage amount without disturbing the existence of the first mortgage.

Zoning ordinance An exercise of police power by a municipality to regulate and control the character and use of property.

Answer Key

Answer Key

Following are the correct answers to the review questions included in each chapter of the text (except Chapter 14, which has no questions). In parentheses following the correct answers are references to the pages where the question topics are discussed or explained. If you have answered a question incorrectly, be sure to go back to the page or pages noted and restudy the material until you understand the correct answer.

Chapter 1

1. c (4–5)
2. d (9)
3. c (4)
4. d (4)
5. d (5)
6. d (6)
7. a (5)
8. c (4)
9. b (3)
10. c (3)
11. b (3)
12. c (6)
13. b (5)
14. c (9)
15. d (9)
16. b (4–5)
17. c (6)

Chapter 2

1. b (22)
2. d (17)
3. b (22)
4. c (17)
5. a (19)
6. c (15–16)
7. b (18)
8. b (15–16)
9. c (19)
10. d (15)
11. a (17–18)
12. b (17–18)
13. c (16)
14. d (16)
15. c (21)

16. a (18)
17. c (19)
18. d (22)
19. d (23)
20. c (19)

Chapter 3

1. b (28)
2. a (31)
3. a (28)
4. c (32)
5. d (30–31)
6. d (29–30)
7. c (29)
8. b (29)
9. d (32)
10. d (29)
11. d (31–32)

Chapter 4

1. d (39–40)
2. d (41–42)
3. b (41)
4. d (40)
5. d (43)
6. a (38)
7. c (39)
8. c (40–41)
9. b (44)
10. a (45)
11. c (41–42)
12. d (43)
13. b (37)
14. a (40)
15. b (41)

16. d (41–42)
17. c (367)
18. a (41–42)
19. b (42)
20. d (42)

Chapter 5

1. d (53)
2. a (51)
3. d (52)
4. d (56–57)
5. b (56)
6. b (51)
7. b (59)
8. c (56–57)
9. a (57)
10. a (57)
11. a (52)
12. c (51)
13. a (52)
14. c (52–53)
15. b (59–60)
16. d (59–60)
17. d (51)
18. c (58)
19. a (55
20. d (52)

Chapter 6

1. b (67)
2. c (67–68)
3. b (70)
4. a (67)
5. d (68)
6. c (69)

7. c (367)
8. c (69)
9. d (69)
10. d (70–71)
11. d (74)
12. d (69–71)
13. c (70)
14. b (68)
15. d (367)

Chapter 7

1. c (83)
2. b (79)
3. d (86 and 90)
4. a (85)
5. a (80)
6. b (87)
7. a (83)
8. c (82)
9. d (88–89)
10. b (83)
11. d (89)
12. a (82)
13. a (86)
14. c (82)
15. c (89)
16. a (80)
17. c (91)
18. d (85–86)
19. c (79)
20. c (80)

Chapter 8

1. d (101)
2. d (97)
3. c (99)
4. d (99)
5. b (106–107)
6. b (97)
7. d (99)
8. a (105)
9. a (103)
10. b (102)
11. b (99)
12. d (105–106)
13. c (106)
14. d (107)
15. d (103)
16. b (107)
17. a (103)
18. b (99)

19. c (99)
20. a (102)
21. b (107)
22. a (108)
23. a (106–107)
24. b (109)

Chapter 9

1. b (115)
2. b (119)
3. d (117)
4. d (119)
5. a (117)
6. b (115)
7. a (120)
8. c (119)
9. b (119–120)
10. b (118–120)
11. d (118–120)
12. c (118–120)
13. b (125)
14. d (115–117)
15. d (122)
16. a (124)
17. a (119)
18. c (118–120)
19. d (119)
20. b (125)

Chapter 10

1. d (131–132)
2. d (132)
3. c (136)
4. b (132)
5. b (137)
6. c (134)
7. d (138)
8. c (135)
9. c (133)
10. c (138)
11. b (131)
12. a (138–139)
13. c (131–132)
14. b (132)
15. a (137)
16. a (137–138)
17. b (135)
18. c (138)
19. d (140)
20. d (139)

Chapter 11

1. d (145)
2. b (155)
3. c (146)
4. a (155)
5. d (145–146)
6. d (150)
7. b (148)
8. b (149)
9. c (147 and 150)
10. b (146)
11. b (147)
12. c (148–149)
13. a (155)
14. d (157)
15. b (157–158)
16. c (150)
17. d (149)
18. c (151)
19. b (154)
20. d (154–155)
21. a (155)
22. b (155)
23. c (156)
24. d (157)
25. b (150)

Chapter 12

1. d (165 and 174)
2. a (165)
3. b (166)
4. b (169)
5. d (176)
6. c (167)
7. b (174)
8. a (167–168)
9. b (169)
10. a (176)
11. a (172)
12. d (173)
13. c (170)
14. a (165)
15. c (178)
16. d (170)
17. b (173)
18. c (173)
19. b (173)
20. d (174)
21. b (175)
22. b (165)

23. d (170)
24. d (173)
25. a (168)

Chapter 13

1. d (190)
2. c (189)
3. b (186)
4. a (186)
5. d (187)
6. c (190)
7. c (187)
8. b (189)
9. d (188)
10. a (188)
11. b (185–186)
12. a (185)
13. d (190)
14. a (188)
15. c (191)
16. d (185)
17. c (189)
18. b (192)
19. d (197)
20. a (185)

Chapter 15

1. b (227)
2. c (206)
3. a (211)
4. b (234)
5. d (210)
6. c (228)
7. d (227)
8. d (229)
9. c (233)
10. b (233)
11. c (224–225)
12. d (233)
13. a (205)
14. b (223)
15. a (213)
16. a (207)
17. b (223)
18. c (367)
19. b (234)
20. d (235)
21. b (223)
22. d (213–214)
23. b (205)

24. d (221)
25. c (214)

Chapter 16

1. d (252)
2. d (243)
3. c (255)
4. c (254)
5. d (253)
6. a (244)
7. c (249)
8. c (254 and 367)
9. a (244)
10. c (252)
11. c (245)
12. d (245)
13. d (245 and 249)
14. b (253)
15. b (254)
16. a (250)
17. d (253)
18. d (253)
19. b (251)
20. b (250)

Chapter 17

1. b (271)
2. d (261 and 269)
3. d (268)
4. c (271)
5. c (261)
6. c (268–269)
7. d (270)
8. b (269)
9. d (267–268)
10. a (267)
11. d (268)
12. c (271)
13. d (268)
14. c (271)
15. c (269)

Chapter 18

1. c (284)
2. d (277)
3. b (279)
4. a (278)
5. d (279)
6. a (283)
7. d (286)

8. c (283)
9. b (284)
10. d (284)
11. c (282)
12. b (281–283)
13. c (284)
14. a (277)
15. b (284)
16. c (282)
17. b (280)
18. d (280)
19. b (284)
20. a (281)
21. b (283)
22. d (283)

Chapter 19

1. a (298)
2. a (296)
3. c (297)
4. d (296–297)
5. b (298–299)
6. d (295)
7. d (297)
8. c (298)
9. c (299)
10. d (295)
11. b (299)
12. d (296)
13. a (299)
14. b (297)
15. b (297)

Chapter 20

1. b (307)
2. a (305)
3. c (307)
4. b (307)
5. b. (308)
6. b (308)
7. d (307)
8. b (307)
9. d (305)
10. d (306–307)
11. c (305)
12. a (308)
13. b (309)
14. b (305)
15. a (309)
16. d (307 and 309)

Chapter 21

1. c (316)
2. a (315)
3. c (321–322)
4. d (316)
5. c (317)
6. d (317)
7. b (320)
8. d (322)
9. a (316)
10. c (317)
11. b (316)
12. d (317
13. c (316 and 321)
14. c (320)
15. d (315)

Chapter 22

1. c (334)
2. d (338)

3. b (338)
4. d (335–336)
5. a (333)
6. d (339)
7. b (332)
8. a (332)
9. c (332–334)
10. a (335)
11. d (335–336)
12. d (334)
13. a (332)
14. b (334)
15. a (334)
16. b (340)

Chapter 23

1. d (352)
2. d (355)
3. a (355)
4. d (349)

5. b (349)
6. d (345)
7. c (351)
8. c (351)
9. a (354)
10. c (355)
11. b (355)
12. b (355)
13. c (355)
14. b (352)
15. c (355)
16. d (355)
17. a (351)
18. c (347)
19. a (348–349)
20. d (350)

Mathematics Review Answer Key

1. $79,500 sale price $\times$ 6½% commission =
   $79,500 $\times$ .065 = $5,167.50, Happy Valley's commission
   $5,167.50 $\times$ 30% or $5,167.50 $\times$ .30 = $1,550.25, listing
   salesperson's commission

b. $1,550.25

2.

12' $\times$ 9.5' = 114 square feet, area of rectangle
½ (3' $\times$ 9.5') = ½ (28.5) = 14.25 square feet, area of triangle
114 + 14.25 = 128.25 square feet
To convert square feet to square yards divide by 9:
128.25 $\div$ 9 = 14.25 square yards
$16.95 carpet + $2.50 installation = $19.45 cost per square yard
$19.45 $\times$ 14.25 square yards = $277.1625 rounded to $277.16

c. $277.16

3. $30,000 Peters + $35,000 Gamble + $35,000 Clooney = $100,000
   $125,000–$100,000 = $25,000, Considine's contribution

a. 20%

$$\frac{\text{part}}{\text{total}} = \text{percent}$$
$25,000 \div \$125,000 = .20 \text{ or } 20\%$

4. $391.42 × 12 = \$4,697.04$, annual interest
$$\frac{\text{part}}{\text{percent}} = \text{total}$$
$4,697.04 \div 11\frac{1}{2}\%$ or $\$4,697.04 \div .115 = \$40,843.826$
rounded to $40,843.83

b. $40,843.83

5. $98,500 × 5\% = \$98,500 × .05 = \$4,925$, annual increase in value
$98,500 + \$4,925 = \$103,425$, current market value

a. $103,425

6. $95,000 × 60\% = \$95,000 × .60 = \$57,000$, assessed value
Divide by 100 because tax rate is stated per hundred dollars:
$57,000 \div 100 = \$570$
$570 × \$2.85 = \$1,624.50$, annual taxes

d. $1,624.50

7.

$22' × 15' = 330$ square feet, area of rectangle
$\frac{1}{2} (4' × 15') = \frac{1}{2} (60) = 30$ square feet, area of each triangle
$30 × 2 = 60$ square feet, area of two triangles
$330 + 60 = 390$ square feet, surface area to be paved
$6''$ deep $= \frac{1}{2}$ foot
$390 × \frac{1}{2} = 195$ cubic feet, cement needed for patio

d. 195 cubic feet

8. $4,175–\$1,000$ salary $= \$3,175$ commission on sales
$3,175 \div 2.5\% = \$3,175 \div .025 = \$127,000$, value of property sold

b. $127,000

9. two sides of $95'$ plus one side of $42'6''$
$95' × 2 = 190$ feet
$42'6'' = 42.5$ feet
$190 + 42.5 = 232.5$ linear feet
$232.5 × \$6.95 = \$1,615.875$ rounded to $1,615.88

c. $1,615.88

10. $4,500 × 12 = $54,000 annual rental
    $54,000 ÷ 8% = $54,000 ÷ .08 = $675,000, original cost of property

a. $675,000

11. $1,340 ÷ 12 months = $111.667/month
    $111.667 ÷ 30 days = $3.722/day
    $111.667 × 2 months = $223.334
    $3.722 × 15 days = $55.83
    $223.334 + $55.83 = $279.164 rounded to $279.16

b. $279.16

12. $58,200 × 12% = $58,200 × .12 = $6,984
    $6,984 ÷ 12 months = $582/month
    $582 ÷ 30 days = $19.40/day
    30-day month–11 days = 19 days
    $19.40 × 19 days = $368.60

d. $368.60

13.   1988   17
       1989   5   31   policy expiration date
     –1988   9   20   closing date
    ─────────────────────
               8   11 = 8 months, 11 days
    $680 ÷ 3 years = $226.667/year
    $226.667 ÷ 12 months = $18.889/month
    $18.889 ÷ 30 days = $.630/day
    $18.889 × 8 months = $151.112
    $.630 × 11 days = $6.926
    $151.112 + $6.926 = $158.038 rounded to $158.04

a. $158.04

14. $975 ÷ 12 months = $81.25/month
    $81.25 ÷ 30 days = $2.708
    $81.25 × 2 months = $162.500
    $2.708 × 4 days = $10.832
    $162.500 + $10.832 = $173.332 rounded to $173.33

a. $173.33

15. $61,550 × 13% = $61,550 × .13 = $8,001.500
    $8,001.500 ÷ 12 months = $666.792/month
    $666.792 ÷ 30 days = $22.226/day
    $22.226 × 22 days = $488.972 rounded to $488.97

b. $488.97

16. 43,560 sq. ft./acre × 100 acres = 4,356,000 sq. ft.
    4,356,000 total sq. ft. × 1/8 = 544,500 sq. ft. for streets
    4,356,000–544,500 = 3,811,500 sq. ft. for lots
    3,811,500 sq. ft. ÷ 140 lots = 27,225 sq. ft./lot

c. 27,225

17. $14,100 commission ÷ 6% commission rate =
    $14,100 ÷ .06 = $235,000 sales price

a. $235,000

Index

More Real Estate Books That Help You Get Ahead...

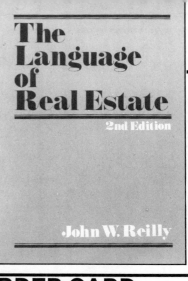

THE LANGUAGE OF REAL ESTATE, 2nd Edition
by John W. Reilly

An excellent reference manual that can serve as a supplement or as a main text if terminology is stressed. This text contains definitions, explanations and applications for a variety of real estate terms—everything from *AAA tenant* to *zoning estoppel*.

The second edition features:
• definitions for 2,200-plus terms—over 500 are new!
• a subject classification of terms
• three special appendices—a list of common real estate abbreviations; the REALTOR'S® Code of Ethics; and a sample closing problem

Check box #16 on the order card. $24.95 Order Number 1961-01 copyright 1982

15-DAY FREE EXAMINATION ORDER CARD

Please send me the books I have indicated. I'll receive a refund with no further obligation for any books I return within the 15-day period.

Detach, Sign, and Mail in the Postage-Paid envelope today!

NAME _____

ADDRESS _____

CITY/STATE/ZIP _____

TELEPHONE( ) _____

TEXTBOOKS

		Order #		Price	Total Amount
☐	1.	1970-04	Questions & Answers to Help You Pass the Real Estate Exam, 2nd ed.	$19.95	_____
☐	2.	1970-02	Guide To Passing the Real Estate Exam (ACT), 2nd ed.	$19.95	_____
☐	3.	1970-01	The Real Estate Education Company Exam Manual, 4th ed. (ETS)	$19.95	_____
☐	4.	1970-06	Real Estate Exam Guide (ASI)	$19.95	_____
☐	5.	1970-03	How To Prepare for the Texas Real Estate Exam, 3rd ed.	$19.95	_____
☐	6.	1556-10	Fundamentals of Real Estate Appraisal, 4th ed.	$34.95	_____
☐	7.	1557-10	Essentials of Real Estate Finance, 4th ed.	$34.95	_____
☐	8.	1559-01	Essentials of Real Estate Investment, 3rd ed.	$34.95	_____
☐	9.	1513-01	Real Estate Fundamentals	$22.95	_____
☐	10.	1551-10	Property Management, 3rd ed.	$31.95	_____
☐	11.	1560-01	Real Estate Law, 2nd ed.	$38.95	_____
☐	12.	1965-01	Real Estate Brokerage: A Success Guide, 2nd ed.	$31.95	_____
☐	13.	1510-01	Modern Real Estate Practice, 11th ed.	$32.95	_____
☐	14.	1510-	Supplements for Modern Real Estate Practice are available for many states. Indicate the state you're interested in _____	$10.95	_____
☐	15.	1510-02	Modern Real Estate Practice Study Guide, 11th ed.	$13.95	_____
☐	16.	1961-01	The Language of Real Estate, 2nd ed.	$24.95	_____
☐	17.	1512-10	Mastering Real Estate Mathematics, 4th ed.	$22.95	_____
☐	18.	1512-16	How To Use the HP-18C in Real Estate	$21.95	_____
☐	19.	1560-08	Agency Relationships in Real Estate	$22.95	_____

PROFESSIONAL BOOKS

		Order #		Price	Total Amount
☐	20.	1913-01	List for Success	$18.95	_____
☐	21.	1913-04	Close for Success	$18.95	_____
☐	22.	1913-03	How to Avoid the 10 Biggest Home-Buying Traps, Revised Ed.	$10.95	_____
☐	23.	1913-02	The Complete Guide to Factory-Made Houses, Revised Ed.	$10.95	_____
☐	24.	1926-01	Classified Secrets	$29.95	_____
☐	25.	1907-01	Power Real Estate Listing	$14.95	_____
☐	26.	1907-02	Power Real Estate Selling	$14.95	_____
☐	27.	5606-24	The Mortgage Kit	$13.95	_____
☐	28.	4105-07	How To Profit from Real Estate	$19.95	_____
☐	29.	4105-06	How To Sell Apartment Buildings	$17.95	_____

PRICES SUBJECT TO CHANGE WITHOUT NOTICE

PAYMENT MUST ACCOMPANY ALL ORDERS: (check one)
☐ Check or money order payable to Real Estate Education Company
☐ Charge to my credit card (circle one) **VISA** or **MasterCard** or **AMEX**

Account No. _____ Exp. date _____

Signature _____

Book Total _____

Orders shipped to AZ, CA, CO, CT, FL, IL, MI, MN, NJ, NY, TX, VA, and WI must include applicable sales tax. _____

Postage/Handling $4.00 + .50 postage for each additional book _____

TOTAL _____

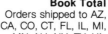

Or call toll-free 1-800-428-3846; In Illinois, 1-800-654-8596 (charge orders only).

710180

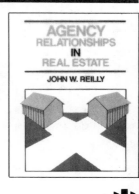